WOMEN IN THE TREES

Women in the Trees

U.S. WOMEN'S SHORT STORIES ABOUT

BATTERING AND RESISTANCE,

1839–1994

EDITED BY

SUSAN KOPPELMAN

BEACON PRESS

BOSTON

Beacon Press
25 Beacon Street
Boston, Massachusetts 02108-2892

Beacon Press books are published under the auspices of
The Unitarian Universalist Association of Congregations.

02 01 00 99 98 97 96   8 7 6 5 4 3 2 1

Sources for the epigraphs in this book follow the text.

Text design by Richard E. Rosenbaum

A portion of the editor's proceeds from this book
will be donated to battered women's shelters.

Library of Congress Cataloging-in-Publication Data
Women in the trees : U.S. women's short stories about battering and
resistance, 1839–1994 / edited by Susan Koppelman.
    p. cm.
    ''Published under the auspices of the Unitarian Universalist
Association of Congregations''—T.p. verso.
    Includes bibliographical references.
    ISBN 0-8070-6777-6
    1. Abused women—United States—Fiction.   2. Man-woman
relationships—United States—Fiction.   3. Short stories, American
—Women authors.   I. Koppelman, Susan.   II. Unitarian Universalist
Association of Congregations.
PS648.A32W66   1996
813'.0108353—dc20
                                                    95-45624

To every woman who has apologized to her husband for flinching
when he reached toward her, because he said he'd
hit her if she didn't
To every woman who so much wanted her children to have
"normal" lives that she hid the bruises — until she found the
bruises on their bodies and threw him out
To every woman who ever wondered, even if for just a
minute, if maybe it *was* her fault — It's Not Your Fault!
To every woman who has survived
To every woman who has escaped
To every woman who has died
To everyone who has ever helped a woman escape
To everyone who has ever confronted a batterer

The December 18, 1752 issue of the *New York Gazette* reported that an "odd Sect of People" had appeared in New Jersey calling themselves Regulars. They dressed in women's clothes, painted their faces and then went to the homes of reported wife-beaters where they would strip the abusing husband and flog him with rods chanting, "Woe to the men that beat their wives." The article concluded, "It seems that several Persons in the Borough (an 'tis said some very deservedly) have undergone the Discipline, to the no small Terror of others, who are in any Way conscious of deserving the same Punishment."

A later letter by a "Prudence Goodwife," whose husband had been beaten, referred to the vigilantes as "regulators," meaning those who tried to regulate the moral balance of the community. She was pleased with their effectiveness. . . . "They have regulated my dear husband, and the rest of the Bad Ones hereabouts, that they are afraid of using such Barbarity; and I must with Pleasure acknowledge, that since my Husband has felt what whipping was, he has entirely left off whipping me, and promises faithfully he will never begin again."

—William E. Burroughs, *Vigilante!*

The first time a man hits a woman, she should get out of the relationship. Stop believing a man when he says, "I'm sorry, baby, I'll never do it again." Every study I have seen says he WILL do it again. Wife beaters almost never stop.

—Ann Landers

Annually, an estimated four million women are battered (assaulted, raped and/or murdered) by male partners. This figure is based on police reports, injury rates, hospital records and emergency shelter admissions (US Senate Judiciary Committee, 1992).

Some authors estimate the scope of female-to-male partner battering at about four to six percent of all battering cases. Yet claims about battered men . . . are generally used to attack social remedies for battered women. Any attempt to suggest male-female victimization rate parity with respect to intimate violence falls in the political, not scientific realm.

There simply is no sexual equality in intimate violence; physical aggression is highly gender-specific and asymmetrical. It is perpetuated by males against female intimates in 85 to 95 percent of heterosexual cases.

—Marcia Petchers

Amnesty International, an organization whose aim is to protect the rights of political prisoners world-wide, defines torture as . . . "the systematic and deliberate infliction of acute pain in any form by one person on another, or on a third person, in order to accomplish the purpose of the former against the will of the latter. . . . It can be safely said that under all circumstances, regardless of the context in which it is used, torture is outlawed under the common law of mankind. This being so, its use may properly be considered to be a crime against humanity."

Amnesty International distinguishes between physical and mental torture. They maintain: "In general the effect of physical torture such as beating, electroshock, near-drowning, sleep deprivation and drugs will be the same on any human system." On the other hand, mental or psychological torture "usually depends on the value system of the victim for its effect." Both kinds of torture occur in some marriages.

—Diana E. H. Russell, *Rape in Marriage*

We have a word for it now. Battering. But when I was a child . . . there weren't any words for it then, just women with bruised, purplish cheeks and eyelids that forced everyone to turn away, embarrassed for the women, belittled by their own fear of or inability to scream at her man, Shame! Shame!

There were no words for it then, just a belief everybody, even women, paid homage to, that, If he beat her that bad, she must've done something to deserve it. There were no words then, but the silence around us said, She's HIS woman, and besides a man's got a right. We have a word for it now. But men still feel they've got the right.

—Marita Golden, "Prefatory Note"

As you read the stories of these battered women I have known, you must remember that what happened to each of them could have happened to you or to someone you love. There is nothing special about these women's personalities, no great single event in any of their lives that made them choose to love an abusive partner. Their histories are similar to those of other women, except for the terrible secret of abuse they tried to hide as they did their best to cope with the men in their lives, men who sometimes loved them and sometimes beat them.

—Lenore E. Walker, "When Loves Turns to Terror"

It would seem inaccurate to speak of all the stories collected here as revenge narratives, but it does seem that each one unmasks patriarchy— lays it bare—in a way that avenges at least some of the wrongs done to

viii

women in its name. . . . For even when the story ends merely in a contradiction or a question, the text provides the reader with enough material to construct for herself a pleasure-giving ending wherein the heroine "gets even." Or, failing that, the writing process may itself be a vengeful act, as when the author depicts the ups and downs of being female . . . in such a way—say through irony or humor—that "masculinity" is stripped of its pretensions—a keen, though non-violent, form of revenge.

—Diana Velez, introduction to *Reclaiming Medusa*

every day in this country a woman gets raped every minute. 3 women get beaten every minute. these are

. . . average counts.

what am i counting if not casualties of battle?

why then don't we admit we are at war?

to stop violence against women we have to change schools, laws, a system where a few white men make a profit off our labor; almost all films, records, record jackets, tv, toys, advertising, the junk we get sold in paper cartons at the supermarket, isolated living situations and overcrowded living situations: every difficult edge of this culture contributes directly or indirectly to violence against women.

meanwhile there's another simpler fact:

men rape women because they can.

men beat women because they can.

our task then is to make abuse of women more and more risky, something men *can't* get away with.

—Melanie Kaye, "Scrambled Eggs 3"

"When there is no vision, the people perish." Proverbs 29:18. But when together we can dream a world of collective survival, we all flourish. That is the urgent challenge that is before us as feminist educators, workers, activists, mothers, artists, community organizers, dreamers, doers, survivors and sisters: bridging our differences and finding our power. That is the task we must turn to quickly, with all our collective energies.

—Caryn McTighe Musil, foreword to *Bridges of Power*

CONTENTS

ACKNOWLEDGMENTS

I have more people to thank for encouragement, emotional and material support, and good advice than there are pages in this book. Many of them are survivors of battering who need to continue to protect themselves and their children by remaining anonymous. To all of those who shared their stories with me, listened to mine, and read these stories—you are in here. Thank you.

I can, however, name others to whom I am grateful:

My son, Edward Nathan Koppelman Cornillon—who suggested that I make this book instead of just talking about the stories and shared with me the important personal issues we had to wrestle with then and now.

My daughter-in-law, Ellen Reid Cornillon, who came up with the working title "Sorry Doesn't Cut It Anymore" which helped define my attitude toward the material.

Nathan and Ellen, for helping me remain strong and determined to do the right thing with this material.

My husband, Dennis Mills, for reading and responding to at least forty-two of the seventy-six revisions of the introduction, for seeing me through this difficult part of my work, and for understanding how hard it is, still, sometimes, for me to feel safe.

Emily Toth, aka Ms. Mentor, who immediately recommended Kate Chopin's "In Sabine" and offered more of the encouragement she has given me for the last twenty-four years along with sage advice that in this case I didn't take all of.

Betty Burnett, as always, for discussing the ideas, for encouraging me when despair threatened, and for being the best writing doctor I've ever known.

Barbara Harman, for introducing me to the writing of Pearl Cleage, for helping in the struggle to think about this material, for many other kind and loving acts, and for creating the art that covers my walls and inspires me.

Martha Baker, a good neighbor and friend, for endless favors ranging from reading and commenting on the writing to letting me use her printer to emergency faxing to listening while I grieved and raged (and sometimes exulted) over various issues relating to getting this book done.

Martin Daniel Richardson, from Roxbury, Massachusetts, videographer and community activist, who spent hours talking with me about the stories and the subject of this book.

Frances B. Koppelman, my mother, who has always held out for me a vision of a better life.

Marya Van't Hul, my editor at Beacon, for going far beyond what an editor is usually expected to do these days. She has been thorough, thoughtful, patient, and imaginative in her involvement with this book.

Marilyn Heins, M.D., Tucson pediatrician and parent educator, who spent a lot of time discussing the demographics of the body and soul as they relate to the subject of this book, and for introducing me to

Marcia Niemann, director of advocacy for The Brewster Center, which provides shelter, counseling, and prevention in an ongoing commitment to Breaking the Cycle of Domestic Violence in Tucson, who talked with me, read a draft of the introduction, and responded with incredible generosity, some very good suggestions, important personal advice, and provocative questions.

Joanna Russ, who discussed the stories and the ideas with me and made wise suggestions, as she has for twenty-four years.

Annette Kolodny, who expressed her enthusiasm for the project as she has for all my work during the last eighteen years, and helped me locate

Sandra A. Zagarell, who helped me relocate the story in Caroline Kirkland's *A New Home, Who'll Follow?* I remembered but couldn't find.

Merrill Joan Gerber, who supported the idea from very early on and promptly gave me permission to use her story, "I Don't Believe This," the basis for her prize-winning novel, *King of the World*.

Pat Murphy, who electrified me by reading from "Women in the Trees" and made me a photocopy at the Imagination Conference at Cleveland State University's annual writers' conference, summer of 1994, as soon as I said I'd like to consider it for this collection, saying, "It would be good to have this story back in print."

Ann Allen Shockley, for helping me locate Jean Wheeler Smith Young and providing encouragement for this work.

Alix Kates Shulman, who located a copy of Pat Staten's story "The Day My Father Tried to Kill Us" from *Aphra* because my copy was already packed for the move to Tucson and who sent it to me posthaste along with several other suggestions.

Jane Curry, who believed me when I said it was all right to call as late as 3 A.M. because not only was I working that late, but I couldn't sleep anyway until I found the story I remembered Samantha telling but couldn't relocate. She told me right off where it was and mailed me a copy because my copy was packed in a box on its way to Tucson.

Melody Annaed, who heard about the project from our mutual friend Joanna Russ and suggested that I look again at the stories of Marjorie Kinnan Rawlings and Willa Cather.

Jane Bakerman, who thought about and discussed with me women's detective stories with her usual generosity and wide-ranging familiarity with the field.

Glynis Carr, who suggested and sent me a copy of "That She Would Dance No More" by Jean Wheeler Smith Young and discussed "Slavery's Pleasant Homes" with me at length, confirming my decision to use it.

Neal Chandler, who lent me his signed copy of Jane Bradley's *Power Lines* and who accepted a fax copy from Glynis Carr of "Slavery's Pleasant Homes" because my copy was already packed for the move to Tucson.

Terry Keegan of the Washington University's Olin Library, who provided me with a usable copy of Mary Heaton Vorse's "The Quiet Woman."

Annette Van Dyke, for directing my attention to and providing me with a copy of Beth Brant's story "Wild Turkeys."

Beverly Guy-Sheftall, for asking some important questions about the material and for helping with the searches for copyright owners of several stories I was determined to include but had reached a dead-end in my search for.

Jerome Nadelhaft, for sending me a copy of his article "Wife Torture: A Known Phenomenon in Nineteenth Century America" from *Journal of American Culture* 10, no. 3 (fall 1987).

Amy Ling, who introduced me to *Arranged Marriages* by Chitra Banerjee Divakaruni and discussed the subject of this book in relationship to her broad knowledge of Asian American women's literature.

The women of Antigone Books, the feminist bookstore in Tucson, who helped me find books and addresses.

Noreen Koppelman Goldstein, Esq., for good counsel.

Boris Cahan, for technical assistance at a critical juncture.

Hugh Foster, my computer consultant, for getting me out of a terrible jam when Anti C Mos virus invaded my computer.

The staff of the Cleveland Heights/University Heights Main Library on Lee and Dellwood, for helping me track down Pat Staten, for making a printer available to me, and for helping in many other ways, as they have helped me as a patron since 1945.

Patricia Harasume Leebove, for consulting with me on the poetry.

Meg Schoerke, for introducing me to the work of Karen Fiser and Linda McCarriston.

Mary Weems, for discussing the subject of this book and for sharing her poetry and short fiction with me.

Mayor and novelist Janet Majerus, Deputy City Manager Kimberley Trombly, Police Captain Samuel Wilcox, and Records Clerk Andrea Graham, all of University City, Missouri, my home for twenty-one years, for going beyond and above their jobs. Sisterhood and sometimes brotherhood is powerful. They, too, are outraged by the ways some men go unpunished for their abuse of women and in some cases are enabled by the law to retain the power to continue to threaten, exert control over, and thereby continue to abuse women years after the women think they have escaped, recovered, and survived.

Jane Dieckmann, copyeditor, for a splendidly sensitive and professional job of improving every detail of this book.

Denise Stinson, literary agent, whose immediate enthusiasm about this collection reignited my fading confidence.

The cats: Riff-Raff, who has lived in St. Louis, Cleveland, and now Tucson where he has met his first and only true love, One Note, our first Maine Coon; Sheila for whom seven lives were one too few, and all the kittens and all their kittens (thanks to Animal Crusaders there will be no more kittens from Sheila's line). In some short stories cats intervene when women are beaten by their domestic partners. I didn't have any of those stories in here because they weren't available. I didn't have cats during the worst of those awful years, but it's fun reading about how sometimes they commit murder on behalf of the women who love them. I have cats now. I wonder if they would have made a difference?

INTRODUCTION

Stories about women who are battered by their husbands have clustered in my memory, separating themselves from the thousands of others I have read as an historian of U.S. women's short stories. I wanted to choose the best from among them and put together a book that would show how important this subject has been in women's writing in this genre, in this country. I hoped the stories would help other women, as they had helped me, realize that they are not alone in their struggles to survive. I thought I could make this book and that it would be useful, but at the same time, I thought I could keep myself, my personal, real, private, historical self, out of this book.

But I can't.

I was a battered wife for eight and a half years, from my son's second birthday until, when he was ten and a half, I sent him to his grandmother's house so he wouldn't be there if all hell broke loose. I packed his father's clothes, put the suitcases out on the front porch, and locked my husband, the father of our child, out of our home, out of my life, and out of our son's life. I had been living in terror and despair. I wanted to get free, but I was afraid of what he might do, afraid it might be very bad . . .

I was afraid that my husband might break into the house, might beat me again, might come after me with a knife, and I didn't know how to protect myself when he did.

The term "domestic violence" wasn't in the vocabulary of the local police yet. In those days they recorded episodes of "assault" and they kept records of weapons used to assault a victim—all without noting that the assailant was a domestic partner. Previous experience had led me to believe that the police might not help. Neighbors and friends who saw and heard what was going on didn't intervene because they thought it was wrong to intervene in a marriage. Although I asked people for help, they turned away. Some say now that they were too afraid of him to try to help me. I had to figure out how to survive by myself and I was lucky. I survived.

Even though I had been an active feminist for twelve years, it still took me eight and a half years to end the relationship with this man. This man—with whom I had shared a life of eighteen years committed to peace, social justice, and the arts. This poet. This man who almost killed me.

People tell me now they knew what was happening back then. They say they didn't know what to do, how to help. I wonder if they know now what to do when it happens to other women they know. I wonder if they have learned to intervene.

If these stories had been available to me then, I might have recognized what was happening in our relationship earlier. Reading the voices of generations of women who knew what was happening, I might have felt less isolated. I might have gotten us out sooner.

These stories are one kind of intervention.

It doesn't seem real at first, even when there are bruises. How can someone who loves you treat you this way? You may believe—that is, you may make the same absurd leap of faith that most of us do the first time—that it was some sort of bizarre accident. He seems as shocked by his behavior as you are. He may cry, apologize, insist he didn't mean it, beg forgiveness, promise it will never happen again, protest his shame at what he has done, act out aggressively against himself in some dramatic way to prove that he'd rather cut off his right arm than ever hurt you again. We see "first blows" in many of the stories in this collection, and the batterers do all these things, as in "Jack the Fisherman," "Women in the Trees," and "Happy Ending," for example.

When he swears he will never hit us again, we believe him, as the women in the stories do. His grief and shame seem as great as our pain and shock. Sometimes we end up comforting him—although we may do so just to protect ourselves from further violence (we learn to become frightened of "provoking" him by not forgiving him).

When it *does* happen again, when his eyes change or his fists or his jaws clench in a way that has yet to become familiar—but will—we think that this man we love who swears he loves us has become insane. We believe that when he hits us, he is crazy. That is, he is not himself—because "himself" loves us and would never hurt us.

Physical violence is not the only or, perhaps, some might argue, even the worst kind of domestic violence. Emotional violence, spiritual assault, psychological damage, sexual violation, verbal abuse, intellectual battering—all of these forms of violence occur in marriage, wounding, terrifying, and diminishing the women who are the victims. One of the best stories of the several hundred I have read about wife abuse which does not include physical violence is "The Quiet Woman" by Mary Heaton Vorse. But underneath all nonphysical forms of violence is the ever-present threat of physical violence, of fists on flesh, and, even, the threat of murder.

The women who wrote these stories were certainly not insensitive to the pressures under which men struggle, flounder, and suffer. Many women writers describe the horrors of men's lives with compassion and sympathy. In probing the reasons for male descents into violence, the writers explore alcoholism and war, poverty and racism, hopelessness and drug addiction. In fact, many of the stories in this collection begin with a careful detailing of the ordeals of the couple, the family, or just the husband, who is often portrayed with particular sympathy. We meet Jean W. Smith Young's Ossie Lee in "That She Would Dance No More" before he meets Minnie Pearl and we quickly know him to be a man with an unbearable history of pain. If we are capable of caring for a fictional character, we cannot fail to care about Ossie Lee. We burn with rage at the arrogant patronizing cruelty of the racist white boss who misuses and exploits Ossie Lee's time and strength and we shudder with grief over his forlorn childhood. Elizabeth Stuart Phelps's story is *called* "Jack the Fisherman." It is *his* story. His life—ah! what a struggle! How predestined he seems to grief. But when he meets and loves Teen, our hearts rise with hope that their love, in the authenticity of which we believe despite Phelps's ironies, might save them from empty and despairing lives. The bodies of those who have known the trials of poverty tense along with those of the Hattori family as they brace for the hard times ahead when the price for strawberries falls so low it isn't worth harvesting a second best crop.

Something is wrong when men hurt the women who love them, the women they have promised to cherish. The stories in this collection look at this wrongness from many angles. Yet important as what "makes" the men become violent toward their wives is the way the women respond to the brutality.

Despite being in appalling danger, some of the women in the stories go to great lengths to preserve their marriages and to understand and forgive the batterer. The narrator's mother in Pat Staten's story "The Day My Father Tried to Kill Us," like many other highly creative women who are battered, is an improvisor.[1] In marriages characterized by abuse, the creative energies of the improvisor are often expended on basic survival, on coping with the abuser and the marriage. To borrow Alice Walker's phrase, when we go "in search of our mothers' gardens," the starkest evidence of expended creativity we often find is sometimes "just" that bare record of survival. In Dorothy Canfield's story

[1] I thank Louise Spizizen—musician, music critic, impresario, and biographer—for the term "improvisors" to describe the way some battered women survive. See her articles on musician and composer Johana Harris, "Johana and Roy Harris: Marrying a *Real* Composer," *The Musical Quarterly* 77, no. 4 (winter 1993), and "Why Are You Writing about Her? An Essay," *Belles Lettres* 10, no. 1 (fall 1994): 23.

"Pre-Freudian," Lucina shocks her family and her community when she leaves her husband close to the beginning of an escalating pattern of abuse. When his behavior begins to be directed toward others than his wife and he is actually judged insane by male medical experts, she returns to him immediately. She has promised herself to him in sickness and in health, and now it is clear that his abusive behavior is, indeed, a symptom of madness, and he is "in sickness." But she doesn't return to be a victim; she returns to be his caretaker. She gains the upper hand by improvising a treatment program that involves treating him always as if he were crazy. "Pre-Freudian" is, in a beautifully twisted way, a revenge story, for the husband will always be an invalid, that is, an *invalid* person—a person without validity.

But in his (anti-) social treatment of his wife, how different is he from the antiheroic Bohemian/beatnik husband of the late 1950s and 1960s portrayed in Andrea Dworkin's "bertha schneiders existential edge?" Is bertha's husband crazy as well? bertha schneider's response to her husband's abuse gives evidence of how paralyzing a woman's uncertainty about the source of her husband's brutality can be. Women's responses are most direct when they are the least ambivalent or the most indifferent to the meaning and motivation for his behavior. Once again, turning to "Pre-Freudian," Lucina is exemplary in both sets of responses to her abusive husband: in neither case will she tolerate it, but when her understanding of why he is violent changes, *how* she acts out her intolerance of his abuse changes.

María Cristina Mena shows us the batterer in "The Gold Vanity Set" as a man enacting conventions he can be turned away from with the right influence or intervention. In Chapter 1, the first letter in *A New Home, Who'll Follow?*, "Jack the Fisherman," and "After Saturday Nite Comes Sunday," the husband's brutality is blamed on addiction to alcohol or drugs and on environments that encourage both. Both Ann Allen Shockley in "To Be a Man" and Jean Wheeler Smith in "That She Would Dance No More" show us violence as a poisoned offspring of the soul-wearying demon we call racism—although they also show us that the woman who shares her batterer's oppression is neither an appropriate target for his frustration nor less frustrated and damaged than he by oppression.

But these stories are not value-free analyses of why men batter and, therefore, in some sense, an excuse or a justification for such behavior; these are profound examinations of character, of solipsism, of power that has corrupted, of moral laziness, of imaginations too impoverished to find ways of being that spring from the heart, from love, hope, and a sense of responsibility instead of from convention and an unearned sense of entitlement.

And there is no failure in being clear about one thing: Wife-beating is never all right; the "something wrong" is never wrong with the woman; she never deserves it. *It is not her fault.*

Despite his promises and despite her love, compassion, and understanding the batterer does it again. And again. Now he begins to blame his wife, to warn her that she "asks for it." He may beg her not to "make" him do it. We sigh with grief, exhaustion, fear, and frustration as we watch the women in these stories try to placate their brutal husbands. It's her fault in "Sweat" because she's too skinny; it's her fault in "Wild Turkeys" because she's a "dumb squaw"; it's her fault in "Women in the Trees" because she was too pleasant to a stranger. Barbara Harman's list of contradictory "rules" in "Happy Ending" makes evident all the ways in which the battered woman might behave to ward off punishment; as clear as the rules are, it is equally clear that they can't be followed, and that beatings will continue.

Some people ask, "Why does a woman stay in an abusive relationship?" Women never "stay" in battering marriages; the word "stay" inappropriately implies a static condition; in fact, the women in abusive marriages are never static: they are always in flux, always coping, hoping, and looking for an end to the abuse. Women struggle to survive in marriages in which their husbands continue to beat them, and they are often unable to leave those marriages for reasons that other people claim they cannot imagine. People usually announce this failure of their imaginations in a way that means "You wouldn't catch me staying with a guy who hit me" and "I'm not such a fool that I would choose a man who would hit me." Not only is their inability to imagine being an abused wife a "learned" dysfunction, but this inability to imagine changing places doesn't serve women's interests. The divisions among and between us, usually based on notions of difference which we haven't chosen and aren't responsible for and which are not salient to our common humanity, keep us isolated from each other.

Those closer to battering situations ask the more appropriate question: "What prevents her from leaving?" One reason is often that she is isolated. One of the first steps in the cycle of abuse is isolation from others who might help her, might intervene, might encourage her to leave. The husband isolates his wife in the stories by Kirkland, Child, Murphy, and Harman. The dilemma of the wife in "Happy Ending" ("he has never liked her family. Although she had few she could call friends, he has never liked them either") is shared by many of the women in these stories. There is nowhere to go and no one to help her get there, anyway.

The popular wisdom is: women who live in relationships with men who hit them are different from other women. But in fact they are no different from other women. "How" a woman "is" has no bearing on whether or not "her" man will abuse her. Compare the women in these stories: Amanda Powers Jones in Shirley Ann Taggart's "Ghosts Like Them" is college educated and a politically sophisticated civil rights activist while Aunt Marcelina in Rosalie Otero's "Las Dos Hermanas" is uneducated and compliant; 'Tite Reine, the little queen of Kate Chopin's "In Sabine," comes from people who would protect her if they knew what was happening, while both Mary in Alice Dunbar-Nelson's "Tony's Wife" and Petra in María Cristina Mena's "The Gold Vanity Set" are beaten in front of relatives, neighbors, and customers, and no one thinks intervention is called for; the young wife in Jane Bradley's "Noises" has seen her mother beaten and the young wife in Merrill Joan Gerber's "I Don't Believe This" comes from a family where such behavior was unknown; the women range from the newly wed in "Women in the Trees" to the long-married woman in "Chapter 1" to the very long married woman in Susan Glaspell's "A Jury of Her Peers." What commonalities do they have other than the random fact that they love men who have turned out to be batterers? Other than being battered, nothing. These authors know we cannot look to the victims to understand the choices of the abuser.

A man I have known for a very long time said to me recently, "A man who sleeps with a woman he has beaten is a fool. His life is in danger." [2]

And so, it would seem from some of these stories, it is.

Some people mistakenly believe that when a woman kills her batterer, it is an act of revenge. But killing a batterer is not revenge: it is self-defense. When nothing stops him and when nowhere is safe, killing him is the only way to save her own life. Some of the women in these stories survive by killing the men who have battered them. Perhaps the most satisfying of them is Fannie Hurst's "Hattie Turner versus Hattie Turner" because Hattie, who "was almost constantly rehearsing some plan for killing him," doesn't face punishment nor is anything risked when her fondest wish comes true. Or Estela Portillo Trambley's surrogate mother/daughter story, "If It Weren't for the Honeysuckle," in which women collaborate to end a reign of terror. Their alliance transforms them into powerful, purposeful, inventive strategists, brave, calm, and secure in the knowledge that they are doing what is necessary. Then, again, maybe the best one is the famous story by Susan Glaspell, "A Jury of Her Peers."

Zora Neale Hurston's "Sweat" and Trambley's "Honeysuckle" share the plot that feminist science fiction writer and literary critic Joanna Russ summarizes as "the biter bit." [3] The tables are turned; the bad guy gets it in the end; the heroic woman emerges triumphant—or emerges relatively unscathed, or emerges in a condition from which she can recover, or just plain emerges. The villain does not emerge.

American literature is not riddled with criminals who get away with crime, but it is rich with heroes who kill the beast, outwit the enemy, escape the victimizer, and steal the power of the oppressor. The plentitude of these stories in which women kill their abusers and get away with it—not even guilt pun-

---

[2] Dan Richardson, telephone conversation, summer 1995.
[3] Personal conversation, October 1994.

ishes them—reinforces the idea not of criminals but of cultural heroes. Even the stories in which the woman dies, such as Janet LaPierre's "The Man Who Loved His Wife," represent women's successful rebellions and acts of revenge against men who batter women. Besides the finality of death and the humiliation of exposure, men are punished in other ways.

Someone has said that men and women are afraid of each other in different ways: men are afraid women will laugh at them, and women are afraid men will kill them. Women do not laugh at men who commit violence against women. No woman whose stories I have read, including the great nineteenth-century humorist Marietta Holley, has been able to make humor out of this kind of brutality. Yet as brutal and terrifying as battering men can be, it is clear in these stories that they are also ridiculous. In the Holley "A Dorlesky-Burpy Family Story," Drusilla Burpy's husband is rendered ridiculous, a slap-stick figure, a puny small-minded Mutt. In Mena's story the abusive husband is tricked by a kind of magic that may cause him to restrain his brutality for the rest of his life. The biter is bit—fatally—in Hurston's "Sweat," and in Canfield's "Pre-Freudian" the abusive husband is sentenced to lifelong "treatment." These stories expose abusers for what they are: cowardly bullies, animated clichés, buffoons choosing to indulge in tantrums. These writers expose the men's mean secrets, their dishonor, and their pathetic excuses at self-justification. Even while men like these continue to kill some of us, those of us who have gotten safe (at least temporarily) are laughing at them. That laughter is healing and is our finest form of revenge.

One part of American folklore often represented in the movies, but almost never in life, is the avenging behavior of fathers and brothers against the man who hurts their daughters and sisters. Where are those avengers in women's short stories? Where are they in real life? One thing that makes women feel shame when they are battered is that no one notices or intervenes; it doesn't seem to matter to anyone. When there is no intervention, battered women feel abandoned and, in some cases, worthless, sometimes hopeless and suicidal, and sometimes filled with a lasting contempt for and/or distrust of people. They are lost to the social community.

Most of the women in this collection are bereft of intervention. Some help does come, however, to women who are being abused in three stories: "In Sabine" by Kate Chopin, "Las Dos Hermanas" by Rosalie Otero, and "That She Would Dance No More" by Jean Wheeler Smith. In the first a black man has done his best to protect the white woman, but cannot directly intervene without either becoming a murderer or inviting the murder of himself and the woman he is trying to protect. A white man can safely intervene however and does, and the woman is, presumably, safe thereafter. In "Las Dos Hermanas," only after decades of abuse, during which her sister Teresina has tried unsuccessfully to intervene, does Marcellina finally feel free to leave her batterer.

Her sister has encouraged her to leave and finally has been able to enlist the help of their clergyman. The intervention of the priest is successful. Padre O'Shaw is a man whose title lets us know he is more educated than the others in the story, and whose surname leads us to believe he belongs to an ethnic community and perhaps a race not her own—or her husband's. In both of these stories, the men who successfully intervene have more social power than the abusers.

In the third story both Minnie Pearl's sister and Miss Lula intervene when Ossie Lee beats Minnie Pearl at Miss Lula's place. Miss Lula with her rifle and her don't-trifle-with-me attitude establishes a space where Minnie Pearl can be safe. Although she goes home with Ossie Lee, she clearly has a safe place waiting for her when and if she ever changes her mind.

But what are the consequences of these interventions? The abusive husband of the girl Minnie Pearl changes, but only in his tactics; his twisted purpose and his access to Minnie Pearl remain the same. The battered woman of "In Sabine" begins to be transformed when offered a sympathetic ear and hope by the stranger who wanders into her private hell—the story is closest to a fairy tale that we have. She is enabled to escape to a safe environment where her batterer will not dare follow. And yet, the man who tells the story and invented the plan for her escape repeatedly protests that he intervened *because he didn't like the man*. While it is clear that he likes the woman and recognizes her class and racial claim on him as a protector, the implication is that if he had also liked her husband, found him genial, "civilized," and "in other ways" all right, he might not have intervened. After Aunt Marcellina leaves Uncle Flavio in "Las Dos Hermanas," Flavio disappears completely from the world in which our narrator lived—the world into which Marcellina has moved. The Church has sanctioned the separation and Flavio is stripped of the protection his wife's shame guaranteed him of social toleration for his behavior. But what did it take to "earn" this sanctioned separation? How much torture must Marcellina bear before there is a sanctioned intervention? How many years? Why?

None of these interventions is totally successful.

The interventions that work are those in Merrill Joan Gerber's "I Can't Believe This" and Beth Brant's "Wild Turkeys." In both stories the abused wives decide they want out and in these last decades of the twentieth century, there is finally a place to go, a social institution whose purpose is to facilitate intervention in wife battering. We witness history happening in this sequence of stories, the arrival of the battered women's shelter.

The absence of intervention has not gone unnoticed by our writers. Constance Pierce's story "Woman Waiting for Train at Dusk" invokes the complicity of all of us who know or suspect that a woman is being abused and don't intervene. It challenges us to notice what is happening to other women, even women we don't know. It reminds us of how often we look away from women who are in distress or danger. *The battering and murdering of women by people with whom they are in intimate relationships happens only because the society in which we all live lets them get away with everything else that leads up to it.*[4] In Pierce's story we are forced into the role of nonintervening observer of violence which then leads us back to all the earlier stories we have already read in this collection. We look for "neighboring" behavior that lets the batterer know that what he does with and to the woman he lives with is being observed. If he doesn't treat her well, we, the community, can intervene. The problem is that usually the community hasn't intervened.

Now, although the abuse rate may be rising, so is the rate of women intervening, fighting back, sharing strategies, and rallying around others who are escaping domestic terrorism, as we see in "Wild Turkeys." Beth Brant's story recognizes the alliance that exists among survivors or escapees of a batterer, battered women's shelter workers—who are equally cultural workers in the feminist revolution as our artists, our auto mechanics, our senators, and others —and friends of battered women on behalf of women they all care about. Brant's story also illustrates something about the statistics on battered women —no woman is untouched by the problem.

The historical range of these stories—1839 to 1994—shows up the disingenuousness of claims that we "didn't know" about the problem of battering, or weren't aware of it, until recent years. There is no question that in the short stories women have been writing in this country, at least since 1839, women have been telling the world that it is wrong, unacceptable, evil, ugly, and shameful for men to abuse women and/or children. And, furthermore, women writers show that it is never a woman's fault that she was beaten; she did not deserve to be beaten; and she could not have stopped the beating if she "tried harder" or somehow changed her behavior.

The earliest story I have yet discovered written by a woman in the United States about a husband assaulting his wife was told in 1839 by Caroline Kirkland in her persona as Mary Clavers, in just a single sentence in a single paragraph toward the end of her first fictionalized letter. The short story was still a new literary genre in the United States then. Stories were being published in newspapers and in a new kind of anthology known as the literary gift book or annual. Women had been active participants in the development of this literary form beginning in the early 1820s, and by the 1840s "important subjects" were still being introduced. Any story written before the middle 1840s is especially important, because it reveals an experience or theme crucial enough that it provoked a woman writer to break silence in a brand-new way

---

[4] This idea is based on Gordon Allport's book, *The Nature of Prejudice* (Cambridge, Mass: Addison-Wesley, 1954). He writes: "Violence is always an outgrowth of milder states of mind. Although most barking ... does not lead to biting, yet there is never a bite without previous barking" (p. 58).

(the short story) in order to tell it. But the story of the abusive drunken husband was already a story of such cultural familiarity in 1839 that it could be told with just an inference, a single sentence. In *A New Home, Who'll Follow?* a collection of stories written as letters to those "back home," Kirkland lets her readers know that the pioneer life in the Michigan wilderness is dangerous for women in a different way from the ways they have ever heard. There are four things a woman going into the wilderness must be wary of because any one of them can kill her. Three of them are well known: the unknown environment; wild animals; and strange men whose intentions cannot be assumed to be friendly. The fourth danger of the pioneer life was a woman's own husband. Away from all that you have both known all your lives, away from the people who have been family and neighbors to you since you were born, away from the protection all those familiars provide a woman, you can't trust your husband not to start beating you even if he never has before.

By 1887 the story of a drunken husband's brutality was so well known that in order to tell it yet again as the story of "Jack the Fisherman," Elizabeth Stuart Phelps's narrator affects boredom, saying in a nineteenth-century way, "You know how it is," over and over. Her story-telling rhythms and cadences remind the reader of an ancient story of mythic dimensions, a story immediately familiar.

Other stories of this period also seem to be written out of a sense that this is tried and true literary territory that needs to be reimagined by the writer, because the representations might have become clichéd. Indeed, how could they not? Phelps seems to ask, when the subject itself is so clichéd, as common as love stories. These stories are only some of the many literary expressions of shock, horror, and outrage aroused by what the English activist Frances Power Cobbe named in her 1878 essay "Wife-Torture in England." Wife battery and murder were deplored in any number of sociological tracts in the nineteenth century and a strong and organized anti-wife-abuse faction was found in the women's suffrage movement. Perhaps the strongest voice condemning wife torture, however, came from the temperance movement. Entire literary careers were founded on the writing of temperance novels, which emphasized a link between drunkenness and wife abuse.

The chronology of women's short stories about abused wives reveals peculiar gaps and bunchings. Literary work in this genre on this theme proceeded in fits and starts. Several gaps in the chronology of the stories in this collection reflect gaps in the literature at large as I have been able to recover it. A number of interesting and provocative stories were published between 1839 and 1859, while I have discovered none published in the 1860s or 1870s. Many appeared in the 1880s and early 1890s, the number dwindled between 1895 and early 1914, and again none were published between late 1914 and early 1917. The numbers increase beginning in late 1917 through the late 1930s, then none in the 1940s, and a small number between 1950 to 1965. Starting in the late 1960s, the stories appear in greater and greater numbers.

I assume these gaps can be correlated with many historical phenomena—among them wars (hot and cold) and their aftermaths, economic depressions, and ascendant social justice movements. Fewer stories about battering were published when the nation has been at war, when there wasn't a military or political need to honor and reward male violence and make it attractive to young men. Hence a virtual ban on stories that portray male violence as shameful, ugly, dishonorable, weak, brutal, uncivilized, or bullying is seen during the long periods surrounding the buildup to and aftermath of the Civil War, World War II, and the Korean "conflict," and the briefer period of World War I. And the periods of the great depressions of the 1890s and the 1930s and the lesser economic crisis of the late 1950s are also bereft of women's stories about wife abuse.

How are we to explain the synchronicity of the gaps in the availability of these stories with wars and economic depressions? Were women not writing stories about brutal men during wartime and during depressions? Were publishers not willing to publish stories about domestically brutal men when male violence was being equated with heroism and patriotism? Are we seeing women's self-silencing or men's silencing of women? Did women share in the demands for patriotism by backing off from exposing men's brutality in marriage? Or did enough men go off to kill each other that they stopped beating up women for those few years? (I doubt that explanation most of all.) Another question is: *Are there stories I have missed?* I hope readers of this collection will let me know about them.

The story of a husband battering the woman who loves him, or at least used to, is among the earliest told in short stories by women. As women from the diverse groups that make up the population of this country come from other languages, including oral traditions and silence, to the writing of their stories in English, they tell this story. In most of the earliest stories from a particular ethnic or racial group the writer distances herself and her own community from the subject of wife abuse by writing about other kinds of people. African American Dunbar-Nelson's story is about an ethnic white couple. This cross-racial portrayal has much in common with the Jewish Fannie Hurst's story about an ethnically undifferentiated but clearly Christian white couple. Northerner Lydia Maria Child's abuse story is about a southern white man beating a black woman. The earliest Hispanic woman (yet rediscovered) writing short stories in English for primarily Anglo audiences was María Cristina Mena, whose 1913 story "The Gold Vanity Set" resembles "Tony's Wife," "Hattie Turner versus Hattie Turner," and "Slavery's Pleasant Homes": each writer turns attention away from her own community while at the same time insisting on focusing attention on wife abuse. In "The Brown House" Japanese American Hisaye Yamamoto situates the battering in her own ethnic community—although distancing it a generation in the past.

The 1843 story by Lydia Maria Child, "Slavery's Pleasant Homes," is a germinal short story because it portrays a white man beating a black woman as an example of partner abuse. Working in the U.S. abolition movement, white women who spent their lives arguing against the evil of enslaving sister and brother human beings were learning to abhor their own less blatant slavery as white women without legal identity, without the right to own their own bodies after marriage,[5] their own earnings, their own time, or the products of their own labor. Black men and women of all colors were subject to physical "chastisement" by the white men who, by virtue of their "husbandness" or "ownerness," had the right of life and death over them.

White "ladies" could not speak of marital rape at all and could write about battering only in the contexts of the antislavery and temperance movements. Yet in their abolition stories they exposed not only the horrors to which Africans in this country were subjected but also their own suffering—although often in a displaced manner. Because the "good" or "superior" slaves were always represented in the abolition stories as fair-skinned and as having the sensibilities and morality associated with "good" or "civilized" white people, the indignities and worse visited upon "good" black women were "as if" they were being inflicted on white women. These stories gave white women a means of writing about their own agonies—thereby invoking not only the sisterhood they shared with each other, but their sisterhood with black women. They enabled them to begin an attempt to escape the silencing trap of their ethnically undifferentiated "whiteness." Additionally, although there are usually a number of other black people close by, the interracial violence in the stories by abolitionist women is characterized by isolation from other white people, the same isolation that figures so heavily in the portrayals of white-on-white battering. In stories where a white man abuses a white woman, whatever his other cruelties might be, the couple is always socially isolated. In the stories by ethnically undifferentiated white women about wife abuse, there's almost no sense of community; the action between the couple occurs in a social vacuum, often in rural or otherwise physically remote circumstances, as in "The Day My Father Tried to Kill Us" and "Women in the Trees." The community doesn't know, doesn't care, or doesn't exist.

---

[5] In 1978 educational campaigns were launched on college campuses and through professional associations at a time when there were forty-seven states where marital rape was *not* a crime. By the summer of 1993, twenty-five years later, North Carolina remained the only state where marital rape was not a crime (if force is used). In 1995, 185 UN delegations meeting in Beijing voted unanimously to repeal the marital privilege to rape. (This material is taken from a fund-raising letter sent in January 1996 by the National Clearinghouse on Marital and Date Rape, 2325 Oak St., Berkeley, California 94708.)

In stories by African American and Hispanic American women, on the other hand, the community does exist and often cares; the men almost never batter women in isolation. Only in these stories does the abuse take place in the context of a community that knows it's happening and comments on it, usually with negative judgments, as in "That She Would Dance No More," "Sweat," and "Las Dos Hermanas."

In the stories by Jewish women—Hurst, Dworkin, and Gerber—the abused woman is portrayed as more paralyzed by ambivalence about her abuse and her abuser than in the stories by other women. Hurst hasn't created a Jewish couple in Hattie and Herold Turner, but Hattie exhibits the ambivalence that characterizes the battered wives in "bertha schneiders existential edge" and "I Don't Believe This." Hattie Turner thinks something is wrong with her because she still responds sexually to her husband; Dworkin's bertha compares her abuse to the suffering in concentration camps and isn't certain she has a right to complain; and Gerber's Carol and her sister can't believe it's all happening and half the time don't know whether to laugh or cry. No one intervenes in these stories either: in Hurst's account the husband is too wealthy and powerful for those who know—his employees—to dare protest or intervene; Dworkin's story takes place in an era of "do your own thing," and people didn't interfere for philosophical reasons; and in Gerber's story no one could figure out at what point or how to intervene until Carol finally leaves for a battered women's shelter.

And what about the children? In fourteen of the twenty-nine stories in this collection children suffer the violence along with their mothers. What is the impact of the abuse of their mothers by their fathers on these children? It ranges from the reproduction by a daughter of her mother's response to battering in "Noises" to the reproduction by a son of the father's behavior toward his mother in "The Quiet Woman." When we read in "Happy Ending" that the "daughter is timid, already a target for school yard bullies; when he begins to yell, the child huddles against the wall, weeping and trembling," we might be reading about Mandy in "Ghosts Like Them" or Amy, whose father hit her mother only one time in "The Man Who Loved His Wife." And the abuse spills over onto the children, too, from the murder of a child in one story and the threat of child murder in "The Day My Father Tried To Kill Us" to Mandy's broken wrist and to the bite on the scalp of the younger son in "I Don't Believe This."

Quite apart from their subject matter, all these stories are wonderful examples of the short story genre in general and various short story subgenres in particular. Writers exposing wife abuse have used the conventions and forms of epistolary stories (Caroline Kirkland), abolition stories (Lydia Maria Child), temperance stories (Elizabeth Stuart Phelps), fantasy (Pat Murphy and Barbara

Harman), regionalism (Kate Chopin and Susan Glaspell), mother/daughter stories (Estella Portillo Trambley and Jane Bradley), detective stories (Fannie
Hurst, Janet LaPierre, and, again, Glaspell), women's friendship stories (Mary
Heaton Vorse and María Cristina Mena), sister stories (Rosalie Otero), mother/
son stories (again, Mary Heaton Vorse), blues fiction (Sonia Sanchez), short
short stories (Cisneros), magical realism (Pierce), and so forth. Almost every
style, literary school, and subgenre of the short story is represented in this
collection.

Some writers have given us literal (or as near literal as the artist can get)
portrayals of situations in which women are brutalized. These realistic or natu-
ralistic writing styles are deliberately as clear as clean panes of glass. The
authors consciously choose "invisible" literary styles, avoiding codes or subtleties that disguise the subject. It is impossible to think that these stories are
about something else, or about nothing at all. In these realistic stories—and
they make up the majority in this collection—the reader steps directly into the
writer's world. That doesn't mean the stories have no subtleties, no hidden
messages, no double entendres, or any of those treasures literary critics cherish.
But those hidden treasures usually are not those of the aesthete, but rather of
the political revolutionary who plants ideas like bombs waiting for detonation.
And they can detonate for each reader and for each generation of readers anew.
(Or not, if the time is not safe.)

Some stories approach wife battering from oblique angles, however, using
suggestion and indirection. Until a reader is so familiar with the multisided
profile of a situation, she cannot be sure she detects it when the angle of vision
is distant, partial, and allusive. In Constance Pierce's "Woman Waiting for
Train at Dusk," for instance, the reader can't be certain she's seeing what she
thinks she's seeing. The story poses the question: How does it affect me when
I recognize that some woman I don't know seems to be struggling with or
fleeing from an abusive situation? This story forces the reader to go through
the process of half-knowing, suspecting, hesitating to understand, and finally
recognizing what it is about. Hisaye Yamamoto approaches and retreats from
the episode of wife beating in "The Brown House" subtly and indirectly. We
hear the recitation of the woes of the Hattori family whose lives become a life
of waiting, a sort of suspension in discomfort. We are almost able to feel sorry
for Mr. Hattori who sacrifices the happiness of his wife and five sons to his
addiction. And then Yamamoto slips in the details of his brutality and we are
completely unprepared for it—and so the sideways glance at this knowledge
hits us full in the face—like his fist against her face.

Written stories, like narrated ones, are intended for an audience. In the
nineteenth century many writers addressed their audiences, writing directly to
the "dear reader." The closer a story is to its roots in an oral tradition, the

clearer it is that the author had a specific audience (and sometimes more than one) in mind and the easier it is to determine it.

One way to guess at a writer's intended audience is to examine the publication where her story first appeared. If the writer earns a living from her craft and if the publication is a profit-making one, we can be certain that the material was written for a specific, magazine-buying audience. More often than not, the editorial content of the publication enables us to figure out precisely who the intended audience was—middle-class white women, for instance, or middle-class black women, abolitionists, temperance reformers, feminists, political liberals, literary types.

In the case of these stories each writer must have believed that audiences existed who could understand and handle reading about men hurting women. And clearly the publishers shared that belief, because they bought the stories. We can also conclude that the intended audiences would not applaud or approve of men hurting women because in all these stories, women are the central characters, the perceiving consciousnesses, and the deliverers of moral judgments—and they think it is wrong for men to hurt women. Whatever else these women may be—and they may be almost *anything* else—it is their sense of right and wrong that dominates the moral atmosphere of the stories. No man is ever "justified" in hurting a woman. There is never any suggestion that the woman's pain isn't real or doesn't matter or is less important than whatever demon it was that motivated the man to hurt the woman.

We women have never kept silent about men's brutality, despite being enjoined to in order to be considered "proper," both by society and by the men who beat us. Many forms of intimidation have been used to silence us, from "Don't wash your dirty linen in public" to "Women control the relationships, so if it happens, it's your fault" to "You're always asking for it" to "Women are naturally masochistic" to "It's your fault for staying" to "If you tell anyone I'll kill you (or myself or our children)." These stories, heretofore unnoticed as supplying an important theme in our literature, are important threads in the weave of women's literary tradition; they constitute an equally important part of women's tradition of breaking silence in any way available in the struggle for justice and safety.

Women have never suffered passively. While the statistics about the number of women beaten and murdered continue to climb (in the United States a woman is beaten every nine seconds and four women are killed each day by husbands or lovers), the number of women who fight back increases and the alliances and institutions we are creating to support our struggle to survive multiply. Eventually our whole society will reach an understanding of just how much this violence costs and will develop a commitment to stopping it.

The condemnation of wife-beating and child-beating had . . . made substantial progress by the late nineteenth century. Contrary to some common misconceptions, wife-beating was not generally accepted as a head-of-household's right . . . but was considered a disreputable, seamy practice, and was effectively illegal in most states of the United States by 1870.
—Linda Gordon, *Heroes of Their Own Lives*

Chapter 1,
From *A New Home, Who'll Follow?*

CAROLINE KIRKLAND

Here are seen
No traces of man's pomp and pride; no silks
Rustle, nor jewels shine, nor envious eyes
Encounter ***
            Oh, there is not lost
One of earth's charms; upon her bosom yet
After the flight of untold centuries
The freshness of her far beginning lies.
                        —Bryant

Our friends in the "settlements" have expressed so much interest in such of our letters to them, as happened to convey any account of the peculiar features of western life, and have asked so many questions, touching particulars which we had not thought worthy of mention, that I have been for some time past contemplating the possibility of something like a detailed account of our experiences. And I have determined to give them to the world, in a form not very different from that in which they were originally recorded for our private delectation; nothing doubting, that a veracious history of actual occurrences, an unvarnished transcript of real characters, and an impartial record of every-day forms of speech (taken down in many cases from the lips of the speaker) will be pronounced "graphic," by at least a fair proportion of the journalists of the day.

'Tis true there are but meagre materials for anything which might be called a story. I have never seen a cougar—nor been bitten by a rattlesnake. The reader who has patience to go with me to the close of my desultory sketches,

I

must expect nothing beyond a meandering recital of common-place occurrences —mere gossip about every-day people, little enhanced in value by any fancy or ingenuity of the writer; in short, a very ordinary pen-drawing; which, deriving no interest from colouring, can be valuable only for its truth.

A home on the outskirts of civilization—habits of society which allow the maid and her mistress to do the honours in complete equality, and to make the social tea visit in loving conjunction—such a distribution of the duties of life as compels all, without distinction, to rise with the sun or before him—to breakfast with the chickens—then,

"Count the slow clock and dine exact at noon"—

to be ready for tea at four, and for bed at eight—may certainly be expected to furnish some curious particulars for the consideration of those whose daily course almost reverses this primitive arrangement—who "call night day and day night," and who are apt occasionally to forget, when speaking of a particular class, that "those creatures" are partakers with themselves of a common nature.

I can only wish, like other modest chroniclers, my respected prototypes, that so fertile a theme had fallen into worthier hands. If Miss Mitford, who has given us such charming glimpses of Aberleigh, Hilton Cross and the Loddon, had by some happy chance been translated to Michigan, what would she not have made of such materials as Tinkerville, Montacute, and the Turnip?

When my husband purchased two hundred acres of wild land on the banks of this to-be-celebrated stream, and drew with a piece of chalk on the bar-room table at Danforth's the plan of a village, I little thought I was destined to make myself famous by handing down to posterity a faithful record of the advancing fortunes of that favoured spot.

"The madness of the people" in those days of golden dreams took more commonly the form of city-building; but there were a few who contented themselves with planning villages, on the banks of streams which certainly never could be expected to bear navies, but which might yet be turned to account in the more homely way of grinding or sawing—operations which must necessarily be performed somewhere for the well-being of those very cities. It is of one of these humble attempts that it is my lot to speak, and I make my confession at the outset, warning any fashionable reader who may have taken up my book, that I intend to be "decidedly low."

Whether the purchaser of *our* village would have been moderate under all possible circumstances, I am not prepared to say, since, never having enjoyed a situation under government, his resources have not been unlimited;—and for this reason any remark which may be hazarded in the course of these my lucubrations touching the more magnificent plans of wealthier aspirants, must be received with some grains of allowance. "Il est plus aisé d'être sage pour les autres, que de l'être pour soi-même."

When I made my first visit to these remote and lonely regions, the scattered woods through which we rode for many miles were gay in their first gosling-green suit of half-opened leaves, and the forest odours which exhaled with the dews of morning and evening, were beyond measure delicious to one "long in populous cities pent." I desired much to be a little sentimental at the time, and feel tempted to indulge to some small extent even here—but I forbear; and shall adhere closely to matters more in keeping with my subject.

I think, to be precise, the time was the last, the very last of April, and I recollect well that even at that early season, by availing myself with sedulous application, of those times when I was fain to quit the vehicle through fear of the perilous mud-holes, or still more perilous half-bridged marshes, I picked upwards of twenty varieties of wild-flowers—some of them of rare and delicate beauty;—and sure I am, that if I had succeeded in inspiring my companion with one spark of my own floral enthusiasm, one hundred miles of travel would have occupied a week's time.

The wild flowers of Michigan deserve a poet of their own. Shelley, who sang so quaintly of "the pied wind-flowers and the tulip tall," would have found many a fanciful comparison and deep-drawn meaning for the thousand gems of the road-side. Charles Lamb could have written charming volumes about the humblest among them. Bulwer would find means to associate the common three-leaved white lily so closely with the Past, the Present, and the Future—the Wind, the stars, and the tripod of Delphos, that all future botanists, and eke all future philosophers, might fail to unravel the "linked sweetness." We must have a poet of our own.

Since I have casually alluded to a Michigan mud-hole, I may as well enter into a detailed memoir on the subject, for the benefit of future travellers, who, flying over the soil on rail-roads, may look slightingly back upon the achievements of their predecessors. In the "settlements," a mud-hole is considered as apt to occasion an unpleasant jolt—a breaking of the thread of one's reverie—or in extreme cases, a temporary stand-still or even an overturn of the rash or the unwary. Here, on approaching one of these characteristic features of the "West"—(How much does that expression mean to include? I never have been able to discover its limits)—the driver stops—alights—walks up to the dark gulf—and around it if he can get round it. He then seeks a long pole and sounds it, measures it across to ascertain how its width compares with the length of his wagon—tries whether its sides are perpendicular, as is usually the case if the road is much used. If he find it not more than three feet deep, he remounts cheerily, encourages his team, and in they go, with a plunge and a shock rather apt to damp the courage of the inexperienced. If the hole be narrow the hinder wheels will be quite lifted off the ground by the depression of their precedents, and so remain until by unwearied chirruping and some judicious touches of "the string" the horses are induced to struggle as for their lives; and if the fates are propitious they generally emerge on the opposite side, dragging the vehicle, or at least the fore wheels after them. When I first "penetrated the interior" (to use an indigenous phrase) all I knew of the wilds was from Hoffman's tour or Captain Hall's "graphic" delineations: I had some floating idea of "driving a barouche-and-four anywhere through the oak-openings"— and seeing "the murdered Banquos of the forest" haunting the scenes of their departed strength and beauty. But I confess, these pictures, touched by the glowing pencil of fancy, gave me but incorrect notions of a real journey through Michigan.

Our vehicle was not perhaps very judiciously chosen;—at least we have since thought so. It was a light high-hung carriage—of the description commonly known as a buggy or shandrydan—names of which I would be glad to learn the etymology. I seriously advise any of my friends who are about flitting to Wisconsin or Oregon, to prefer a heavy lumber-waggon, even for the use of the ladies of the family; very little aid or consolation being derived from making a "genteel" appearance in such cases.

At the first encounter of such a mud-hole as I have attempted to describe, we stopped in utter despair. My companion indeed would fain have persuaded me that the many wheel tracks which passed through the formidable gulf were proof positive that it might be forded. I insisted with all a woman's obstinacy that I could not and would not make the attempt, and alighted accordingly, and tried to find a path on one side or the other. But in vain, even putting out of the question my paper-soled shoes—sensible things for the woods. The ditch on each side was filled with water and quite too wide to jump over; and we were actually contemplating a return, when a man in an immense bear-skin cap and a suit of deer's hide, sprang from behind a stump just within the edge of the forest. He "poled" himself over the ditch in a moment, and stood beside us, rifle in hand, as wild and rough a specimen of humanity as one would wish to encounter in a strange and lonely road, just at the shadowy dusk of the evening. I did *not* scream, though I own I was prodigiously frightened. But our stranger said immediately, in a gentle tone and a with a French accent, "Me watch deer —you want to cross?" On receiving an answer in the affirmative, he ran in search of a rail which he threw over the terrific mud-hole—aided me to walk across by the help of his pole—showed my husband where to plunge—waited till he had gone safely through and "slow circles dimpled o'er the quaking mud"—then took himself off by the way he came, declining any compensation with a most polite "rien, rien!" This instance of true and genuine and generous politeness I record for the benefit of all bearskin caps, leathern jerkins and cowhide boots, which ladies from the eastward world may hereafter encounter in Michigan.

Our journey was marked by no incident more alarming than the one I have related, though one night passed in a wretched inn, deep in the "timbered land" —as all woods are called in Michigan—was not without its terrors, owing to the horrible drunkenness of the master of the house, whose wife and children were in constant fear of their lives, from his insane fury. I can never forget the countenance of that desolate woman, sitting trembling and with white, compressed lips in the midst of her children. The father raving all night, and coming through our sleeping apartment with the earliest ray of morning, in search of more of the poison already boiling in his veins. The poor wife could not forbear telling me her story—her change of lot—from a well-stored and comfortable home in Connecticut to this wretched den in the wilderness— herself and children worn almost to shadows with the ague, and her husband such as I have described him. I may mention here that not very long after I heard of this man in prison in Detroit, for stabbing a neighbour in a drunken brawl, and ere the year was out he died of delirium tremens, leaving his family destitute. So much for turning our fields of golden grain into "fire water"—a branch of business in which Michigan is fast improving.

Our ride being a deliberate one, I felt, after the third day, a little wearied, and began to complain of the sameness of the oak-openings and to wish we were fairly at our journey's end. We were crossing a broad expanse of what seemed at a little distance a smooth shaven lawn of the most brilliant green, but which proved on trial little better than a quaking bog—embracing within its ridgy circumference all possible varieties of

"Muirs, and mosses, slaps and styles"—

I had just indulged in something like a yawn, and wished that I could see our hotel. At the word, my companion's face assumed rather a comical expression, and I was so preparing to inquire somewhat testily what there was so laughable —I was getting tired and cross, reader—when down came our good horse to the very chin in a bog-hole, green as Erin on the top, but giving way on a touch, and seeming deep enough to have engulfed us entirely if its width had been proportionate. Down came the horse—and this was not al—down came the driver; and I could not do less than follow, though at a little distance—our good steed kicking and floundering—covering us with hieroglyphics, which would be readily deciphered by any Wolverine we should meet, though per- chance strange to the eyes of our friends at home. This mishap was soon amended. Tufts of long marsh grass served to assoilize our habiliments a little, and a clear stream which rippled through the marsh aided in removing the eclipse from our faces. We journeyed on cheerily, watching the splendid changes in the west, but keeping a bright look-out for bog-holes.

It *is* true that some men hate women even in their desire for them. And some men oppress the very women they love. But unlike the racist, they allow the object of their contempt to share the table with them. The hatred they feel for women does not translate into separatism. It is more insidiously intra-cultural, like class antagonism. But different, because it lives and breathes in the flesh and blood of our families, even in the name of love.

... What would a movement bent on the freedom of women of color look like?

—Cherrie Moraga, *"From a Long Line of Vendidas"*

Slavery's Pleasant Homes

A Faithful Sketch

LYDIA MARIA CHILD

'Thy treasures of gold
Are dim with the blood of the hearts thou hast sold;
Thy home may be lovely, but round it I hear
The crack of the whip, and the footsteps of fear.'

When Frederic Dalcho brought his young bride from New-Orleans to her Georgian home, there were great demonstrations of joy among the slaves of the establishment,—dancing, shouting, clapping of hands, and eager invocations of blessing on the heads of 'massa and missis'; for well they knew that he who manifested most zeal was likely to get the largest coin, or the brightest handkerchief.

The bride had been nurtured in seclusion, almost as deep as that of the oriental harem. She was a pretty little waxen plaything, as fragile and as delicate as the white Petunia blossom. She brought with her two slaves. Mars, a stalwart mulatto, of good figure, but a cunning and disagreeable expression of countenance. Rosa, a young girl, elegantly formed, and beautiful as a dark velvet carnation. The blush, so easily excited, shone through the transparent brown of her smooth cheek, like claret through a bottle in the sunshine. It was a beautiful contrast to see her beside her mistress, like a glittering star in attendance upon the pale and almost vanishing moonsickle. They had grown up from infancy together; for the mother of Rosa was foster-mother of Marion; and soon as the

6

little white lady could speak, she learned to call Rosa *her* slave. As they grew older, the wealthy planter's daughter took pride in her servant's beauty, and loved to decorate her with jewels. 'You shall wear my golden ornaments whenever you ask for them,' said she; 'they contrast so well with the soft, brown satin of your neck and arms. I will wear pearls and amethysts; but gold needs the dark complexion to show its richness. Besides, you are a handsome creature, Rosa, and gold is none too good for you.'

Her coachman, Mars, was of the same opinion: but the little petted coquette tossed her graceful head at him, and paid small heed to his flattering words. Not so with George, the handsome quadroon brother of Frederic Dalcho, and his favorite slave; but the master and mistress were too much absorbed with their own honey-moon, to observe them. Low talks among the rose-bushes, and stolen meetings by moonlight, passed unnoticed, save by the evil eyes of Mars. Thus it passed on for months. The young slaves had uttered the marriage vow to each other, in the silent presence of the stars.

It chanced, one day, that Rosa was summoned to the parlor to attend her mistress, while George stood respectfully, hat in hand, waiting for a note, which his master was writing. She wore about her neck a small heart and cross of gold, which her lover had given her the night before. He smiled archly, as he glanced at it, and the answer from her large, dark eyes was full of joyful tenderness. Unfortunately, the master looked up at that moment, and at once comprehended the significance of that beaming expression. He saw that it spoke whole volumes of mutual, happy love; and it kindled in him an unholy fire. He had never before realized that the girl was so very handsome. He watched her, as she pursued her work, until she felt uneasy beneath his look. From time to time, he glanced at his young wife. She, too, was certainly very lovely; but the rich, mantling beauty of the slave had the charm of novelty. The next day, he gave her a gay dress; and when he met her among the garden shrubbery, he turned her glossy ringlets over his finger, and called her a pretty darling. Poor Rosa hastened away, filled with terror. She wanted to tell her mistress all this, and claim her protection; but she dared not. As for George, he was of a proud and fiery nature, and she dreaded the storm it would raise in his breast. Her sleeping apartment adjoined that of her mistress, and she was now called to bring water to her master at a much later hour than had been usual with him. One night, no answer was given to the summons. Rosa was not in her room. When questioned in the morning, she stammered out an incoherent excuse, and burst into tears. She was ordered, somewhat sternly, to be very careful not to be again absent when called for.

Marion took an early opportunity to plead her favorite's cause. 'I have suspected, for some time,' said she, 'that George and Rosa are courting; and for my part, I should like very well to have them married.' Her husband made no reply, but abruptly left the room. His conduct toward George became singularly capricious and severe. Rosa wept much in secret, and became shy as a startled fawn. Her mistress supposed it was because Mr. Dalcho objected to her marriage, and suspected nothing more. She tried to remonstrate with him, and learn the nature of his objections; but he answered sharply, and left her in tears.

One night, Marion was awakened by the closing of the door, and found that Frederic was absent. She heard voices in Rosa's apartment, and the painful truth flashed upon her. Poor young wife, what a bitter hour was that!

In the morning, Rosa came to dress her, as usual, but she avoided looking in her face, and kept her eyes fixed on the ground. As she knelt to tie the satin shoe, Marion spoke angrily of her awkwardness, and gave her a blow. It was the first time she had ever struck her; for they really loved each other. The beautiful slave looked up with an expression of surprise, which was answered by a strange, wild stare. Rosa fell at her feet, and sobbed out, 'Oh, mistress, I am not to blame. Indeed, indeed, I am very wretched.' Marion's fierce glance melted into tears. 'Poor child,' said she, 'I ought not to have struck you; but, oh, Rosa, I am wretched, too.' The foster-sisters embraced each other, and wept long and bitterly; but neither sought any further to learn the other's secrets.

At breakfast, George was in attendance, but he would not look at Rosa, though she watched for a glance with anxious love. When she found an opportunity to see him alone, he was sullen, and rejected her proffered kiss. 'Rosa, where were you last night?' said he, hastily. The poor girl blushed deeply, and strove to take his hand; but he flung her from him, with so much force that she reeled against the wall. 'Oh, George,' said she, with bitter anguish, 'what *can* I do? I am his *slave.*' The justice of her plea, and the pathos of her tones, softened his heart. He placed her head on his shoulder, and said more kindly, 'Keep out of his way, dear Rosa; keep out of his way.'

Rosa made strong efforts to follow this injunction; and dearly did she rue it. George was sent away from the house, to work on the plantation, and they were forbidden to see each other, under penalty of severe punishment. His rival, Mars, watched them, and gave information of every attempt to transgress this cruel edict. But love was more omnipotent than fear of punishment, and the lovers did sometimes catch a stolen interview. The recurrence of this disobedience exasperated their master beyond endurance. He swore he would overcome her obstinacy, or kill her; and one severe flogging succeeded another, till the tenderly-nurtured slave fainted under the cruel infliction, which was rendered doubly dangerous by the delicate state of her health. Maternal pains came on prematurely, and she died a few hours after.

George wandered into the woods, and avoided the sight of his reckless master, who, on his part, seemed willing to avoid an interview. Four days had passed since Rosa's death, and the bereaved one had scarcely tasted food enough to sustain his wretched life. He stood beside the new-made grave, which he himself had dug. 'Oh, Father in Heaven!' he exclaimed, 'what would I give, if I had not flung her from me! Poor girl, *she* was not to blame.' He leaned his head against a tree, and looked mournfully up to the moon struggling through clouds. Cypresses reared their black forms against the sky, and the moss hung from bough to bough, in thick, funereal festoons. But a few months ago, how beautiful and bright was Nature—and now, how inexpressibly gloomy. The injustice of the past, and the hopelessness of the future, came before him with dreary distinctness. 'He is my brother,' thought he, 'we grew up side by side, children of the same father; but I am his slave. Handsomer, stronger, and more intelligent than he; yet I am his *slave*. And now he will sell me, because the murdered one will forever come up between us.'

He thought of Rosa as he first saw her, so happy, and so beautiful; of all her gushing tenderness; of her agonized farewell, when they last met; of her graceful form bleeding under the lash, and now lying cold and dead beneath his feet.

He looked toward his master's house. 'Shall I escape now and forever?' said he; 'or shall I first'—he paused, threw his arms widely upward, gnashed his teeth, and groaned aloud, 'God, pity me! He murdered my poor Rosa.'

On that night, Marion's sleep was disturbed and fitful. The memory of her foster-sister mingled darkly with all her dreams. Was that a shriek she heard? It was fearfully shrill in the night-silence! Half sleeping and half waking, she called wildly, 'Rosa! Rosa!' But a moment after, she remembered that Rosa's light step would never again come at her call. At last a drowsy slave answered the loud summons of her bell. 'I left your master reading in the room below,' said she; 'go and see if he is ill.' The girl came back, pallid and frightened. 'Oh, mistress, he is dead!' she exclaimed; 'there is a dagger through his heart.'

Neighbors were hastily summoned, and the slaves secured. Among them was George, who, with a fierce and haggard look, still lingered around Rosa's grave.

The dagger found in Frederic Dalcho's heart was the one he had himself been accustomed to wear. He lay upon the sofa, with an open book beside him, as if he had fallen asleep reading. A desk in the room was broken open, and a sum of money gone. Near it, was dropped a ragged handkerchief, known to belong to Mars. Suspicion hovered between him and George. Both denied the deed. Mars tried hard to fix the guilt on his hated rival, and swore to many falsehoods. But as some of these falsehoods were detected, and the stolen money was found hidden in his bed, the balance turned against him. After the brief, stern trial awarded to slaves, with slaveholders for judges and jurors, Mars was condemned to be hung. George thought of his relentless persecutions, and for a moment triumphed over the cunning enemy, who had so often dogged poor Rosa's steps; but his soul was too generous to retain this feeling.

The fatal hour came. Planters rode miles to witness the execution, and stood glaring at their trembling victim, with the fierceness of tigers. The slaves from miles around were assembled, to take warning by his awful punishment. The rope was adjusted on the strong bough of a tree. Mars shook like a leaf in the wind. The countenance of George was very pale and haggard, and his breast was heaving with tumultuous thoughts. 'He is my enemy,' said he to himself; ''tis an awful thing to die thus. The *theft* I did not commit; but if I take all the blame, they can do no more than hang me.'

They led the shivering wretch toward the tree, and were about to fasten the fatal noose. But George rushed forward with a countenance ghastly pale, and exclaimed, 'Mars is innocent. I murdered him—for he killed my wife, and hell was in my bosom.'

No voice praised him for the generous confession. They kicked and cursed him; and hung up, like a dog or a wolf, a man of nobler soul than any of them all.

The Georgian papers thus announced the deed: *'Fiend-like Murder.* Frederic Dalcho, one of our most wealthy and respected citizens, was robbed and murdered last week, by one of his slaves. The black demon was caught and hung; and hanging was too good for him.'

The Northern papers copied this version; merely adding, 'These are the black-hearted monsters, which abolition philanthropy would let loose upon our brethren of the South.'

Not one was found to tell how the slave's young wife had been torn from him by his own brother, and murdered with slow tortures. Not one recorded the heroism that would not purchase life by another's death, though the victim was his enemy. His very *name* was left unmentioned; he was only Mr. Dalcho's *slave!*

Not Comedy, Not Farce

The best we could do was laugh,
and we did, sheer slapstick
in his absence till the tears
we never shed for rage or grief
came down, crumbling our masks
in the pure theater of kitchen:

underpants on heads, costumes
of skillets or silverware, up
on the table or under it, we did
what they must have done out back
of their shanties, in firelight,
far from the Big House—

we danced, we mocked, we cast
our selves to the walls
as shadows big enough to face
a man made of too many lies.
In a morsel of safety you can
make of even the most brutal
tyrant a fool. In the presence
of even one other, a heart-stopping,

lawful terror makes a common
wound of all wounds, makes of all
cringings a shared wordless shame
as sure to bind as love. Music
on the radio, pillows stuffed under
our shirts to trump up the bullying

belly, we swagger-strutted, stumbled
over colors in the linoleum, un-zipped
our flies and watered them
wet, let his broken glasses dangle
like a monkey, off one ear, till our
sides hurt and we held them as we

never dared hold each other.
Long before he set foot on
the boot-camp-scoured front stairs,
sounding like a one-man barroom brawl
hauled up in a wooden wagon, we'd
finished our tea, pulled the plug

on the radio, put the dried cups
back in the closet, the pillows
under our heads, the knives and skillets
under our pillows—everything about us
gone back into dark and quiet, as if
none of it, or us, had eyes or ears.

—Linda McCarriston

A Dorlesky-Burpy Family Story

MARIETTA HOLLEY

Drusilla Burpy, she married a industrius, hard-workin' man,—one that never drinked a drop, and was sound on the doctrines, and give good measure to his customers: he was a grocer-man. And a master hand for wantin' to foller the laws of his country, as tight as laws could be follered. And so, knowin' that the law approved of "moderate correction" for wimmen, and that "a man might whip his wife, but not enough to endanger her life," he bein' such a master hand for wantin' to do every thing faithful, and do his very best for his customers, it was s'posed that he wanted to do his best for the law; and so, when he got to whippin' Drusilla, he would whip her *too* severe—he would be *too* faithful to it.

You see, the way ont was, what made him whip her at all wuz, she was cross to him. They had nine little children. She always thought that two or three children would be about all one woman could bring up well "by hand," when that one hand wuz so awful full of work, as will be told more ensuin'ly. But he felt that big families wuz a protection to the Government; and "he wanted fourteen boys," he said, so they could all foller their father's footsteps, and be noble, law-making, law-abiding citizens, jest as he was.

But she had to do every mite of the housework, and milk cows, and make butter and cheese, and cook and wash and scour, and take all the care of the children, day and night, in sickness and in health, and spin and weave the cloth for their clothes (as wimmen did in them days), and then make 'em, and keep 'em clean. And when there wuz so many of 'em, and only about a year's difference in their ages, some of 'em—why, I s'pose she sometimes thought more of her own achin' back than she did of the good of the Government; and she would get kinder discouraged sometimes, and be cross to him.

And knowin' his own motives was so high and loyal, he felt that he ought to whip her. So he did.

And what shows that Drusilla wuzn't so bad as he s'posed she wuz, what shows that she did have her good streaks, and a deep reverence for the law, is, that she stood his whippin's first-rate, and never whipped him.

Now, she wuz fur bigger than he wuz, weighed 80 pounds the most, and might have whipped him if the law had been such.

But they was both law-abidin', and wanted to keep every preamble; so she stood it to be whipped, and never once whipped him in all the seventeen years they lived together.

She died when her twelfth child was born: there wus jest 13 months differ-ence in the age of that and the one next older. And they said she often spoke out in her last sickness, and said,—

"Thank fortune, I have always kept the law."

And they said the same thought wus a great comfort to him in his last moments.

He died about a year after she did, leaving his 2nd wife with twins and a good property.

Perhaps the most common way that batterers attempt to excuse their violent behavior is by an appeal to loss of control. . . . To what extent does alcohol cause loss of control over one's behavior? [A 1974] study of family violence . . . establishes drunken behavior as learned (rather than purely chemically induced) behavior [which] varies widely from culture to culture. . . . Because it is believed to lead to loss of control, people behave as though it actually has the property, and use this "loss of control" to disavow or neutralize deviant behavior such as wife beating.

—James Ptacek, *"Why Do Men Batter Their Wives?"*

Jack the Fisherman

ELIZABETH STUART PHELPS

I

Jack was a Fairharbor boy. This might be to say any of several things; but it is at least sure to say one,—he was a fisherman, and the son of a fisherman.

When people of another sort than Jack's have told their earthly story through, the biography, the memorial, the obituary remains. Our poet, preacher, healer, politician, and the rest pass on to this polite sequel which society has ordained for human existence. When Jack dies, he stops. We find the fisherman squeezed into some corner of the accident column: "Washed overboard," or "Lost in the fog," and that is the whole of it. He ends just there. There is no more Jack. No fellow-members in the Society for Something-or-Nothing pass resolutions to his credit and the consolation of his family. No funeral discourse is preached over him and privately printed at the request of the parishioners. The columns of the religious weekly to which he did not subscribe contain no obituary sketches signed by the initials of friends not thought to be too afflicted to speak a good word for a dead man. From the press of the neighboring city no thin memorial volume sacred to his virtues and stone-blind to his defects shall ever issue. Jack needs a biographer. Such the writer of this sketch would fain aspire to be.

Jack was born at sea. His father was bringing his mother home from a visit at a half-sister's in Nova Scotia, for Jack's mother was one of those homesick, clannish people who pine without their relations as much as some of us pine with ours; and even a half-sister was worth more to her in her fanciful and feeble condition than a whole one is sure to be to bolder souls.

She had made her visit at her half-sister's, and they had talked over receipts, and compared yeast, and cut out baby-things, and turned dresses, and dyed flannel, and gone to prayer-meetings together; and Jack's mother was coming home, partly because Jack's father came for her, and partly because he happened to come sober, which was a great point, and partly because the schooner had to sail, which was another,—she was coming home, at all events, when a gale struck them. It was an ugly blow. The little two-masted vessel swamped, in short, at midnight of a moonlit night, off the coast, just the other side of seeing Cape Ann light. The crew were picked up by a three-master, and taken home. Aboard the three-master, in fright and chill and storm, the little boy was born. They always said that he was born in Fairharbor. In fact, he was born rounding Eastern Point. "The toughest place to be borned in, this side o' Torment," Jack's father said. But Jack's mother said nothing at all.

Jack's father kept sober till he got the mother and the child safely into the little crumbling, gray cottage in half of whose meagre dimensions the family kept up the illusion which they called home. Then, for truth compels me, I must state that Jack's father went straightway out upon what, in even less obscure circles than his, it is customary to call "a tear." There seems to be something in the savage, incisive fitness of this word which has over-ridden all mere distinctions of class or culture, and must ultimately make it a classic in the language. "I've stood it long as I ken stand, and I'm goin' on a tear,—I'm a-goin' on a *netarnal* tear," said Jack's father to his oldest dory-mate, a fellow he had a feeling for, much as you would for an oar you had handled a good many years; or perhaps a sail that you were used to, and had patched and watched, and knew the cracks in it, and the color of it, and when it was likely to give way, and whereabouts it would hold.

In fact, that proved to be, in deed and truth, an eternal tear for Jack's father. Drunk as a fisherman could be,—and that is saying a good deal,—he reshipped that night, knowing not whither nor why, nor indeed knowing that the deed was done; and when he came to himself he was twelve hours out, on his way to the Banks of Newfoundland; and the young mother, with her baby on her arm, looked out of the frosty window over the foot of her old bedstead, and watched for him to come, and did not like to tell the neighbors that she was short of fuel.

She was used to waiting—women are; Fairharbor women always are. But she had never waited so long before. And when, at the end of her waiting, the old dory-mate came in one night and told her that it happened falling from the mast because he was not sober enough to be up there, Jack's mother said she had always expected it. But she had not expected it, all the same. We never expect trouble, we only fear it. And she had put the baby on the edge of the bed and got upon her knees upon the floor, and laid her face on the baby, and tried to say her prayers,—for she was a pious little woman, not knowing any better,—but found she could not pray, she cried so. And the old dory-mate told her not to try, but to cry as hard as she could. And she told him he was very kind; and so she did. For she was fond of her husband although he got drunk, —because he got drunk, one is tempted to say. Her heart had gone the way of the hearts of drunkards' wives: she loved in proportion to her misery, and gave on equation with what she lost. All the woman in her mothered her husband when she could no longer wifely worship him. When he died she felt as if she had lost her eldest child. So, as I say, she kneeled with her face on the baby, and cried as if she had been the blessedest of wives. Afterward she thought of this with self-reproach. She said one day to the old dory-mate:—

"When my trouble came, I did not pray to God. I'd ought to have. But I only cried at Him."

Jack had come into the world in a storm, and he began it stormily. He was a big, roaring baby, and he became a restless boy. His mother's gentle and unmodified femininity was helpless before the problem of this wholly mascu-line little being. She said Jack needed a man to manage him. He smoked at six; he lived in the stables and on the wharves at eight; he came when he got ready, and went when he pleased; he obeyed when he felt like it, and when he was punished, he kicked. Once, in an imaginative moment, he bit her.

She sent him to pack mackerel, for they were put to it to keep soul and body together, and he brought home such habits of speech as even the Fairharbor woman had never heard. From her little boy, her baby,—not yet old enough to be out of short trousers, and scarcely out of little sacks, had he been *yours,* my Lady, at the pretty age when one still fastens lace collars round their necks, and has them under shelter by dark, and hears their prayers, and challenges the breath of heaven lest it blow too rudely on some delicate forming fibre of soul or body,—from her little boy, at eight years old, the mother first learned the abysses of vulgarity in a seaport town.

It must be admitted that her education in this respect had been defective. She had always been one of the women in whose presence her neighbors did not speak too carelessly.

But Jack's mother had the kind of eyes which do not see mire,—the meek, religious, deep-blue eye which even growing sons respect while they strike the tears from it. At his worst Jack regarded her as a species of sacred fact, much like heaven or a hymn. Sometimes on Sunday nights he stayed at home with her; he liked to hear her sing. She sang "Rock of Ages" in her best black alpaca, with her work-worn hands crossed upon the gingham apron which she put on to save the dress.

But ah, she said, Jack needed a man to manage him. And one day when she said this, in spite of her gentle unconsciousness, or because of it, the old dory-mate to whom she said it said he thought so too, and that if she had no objections he would like to be that man.

And the Fairharbor widow, who had never thought of such a thing, said she didn't know as she had; for nobody knew, she said, how near to starving they had come; and it was something to have a sober man. So, on this reasonable basis, Jack acquired a step-father, and his step-father sent him straightway to the Grand Banks.

He meant it well enough, and perhaps it made no difference in the end. But Jack was a little fellow to go fishing,—only ten. His first voyage was hard: it was a March voyage; he got badly frostbitten, and the skipper was rough. He was knocked about a good deal, and had the measles by himself in his berth; and the men said they didn't know they had brought a baby to the Banks, for they were very busy; and Jack lay and cried a little, and thought about his mother, and wished he hadn't kicked her, but forgot it when he got well. So he swaggered about among the men, as a boy does when he is the only one in a crew, and aped their talk, and shared their grog, and did their hard work, and learned their songs, and came home with the early stages of moral ossification as well set in upon his little heart as a ten-year-old heart allows.

The next voyage did not mend the matter; nor the next. And though the old dory-mate was an honest fellow, he had been more successful as a dory-mate than he was as a step-father. He and Jack did not "get on." Sometimes Jack's mother wondered if he *had* needed a man to manage him; but she never said so. She was a good wife, and she had fuel enough, now; she only kissed Jack and said she meant it for the best, and then she went away and sang "Rock of Ages" to the tune of Martyn, very slowly and quite on the wrong key. It seemed to make her feel better, poor thing. Jack sometimes wondered why.

When he was twelve years old he came home from a winter voyage one night, and got his pay for his share,—boy's pay, yet, for a boy's share; but bigger than it used to be,—and did not go home first, but went rollicking off with a crowd of Portuguese. It was a Sunday night, and his mother was expecting him, for she knew the boat was in. His step-father expected him too,—and his money; and Jack knew that. His mother had been sick, but Jack did not know that; she had been very sick, and had asked for him a great deal. There had been a baby,—born dead while its father was off-shore after cod,—and it had been very cold weather; and something had gone wrong.

At midnight of that night some one knocked at the door of the crumbling cottage. The step-father opened it; he looked pale and agitated. Some boys were there in a confused group; they bore what seemed to be a lifeless body on a drag, or bob-sled; it was Jack, dead drunk.

It was the first time,—he was only twelve,—and one of the Fairharbor boys took the pipe from his mouth to explain.

"He was trapped by an *I*-talian, and they've stole every cent off him, 'n' kicked him out, 'n' lef' him, stranded like a monk-fish, so me and the other fellers we borryed a sled and brung him home, for we thought his mother'd rather. He ain't dead, but he's just as drunk as if he was sixty!"

The Fairharbor boy mentioned this circumstance with a kind of abnormal pride, as if such superior maturity were a point for a comrade to make note of. But Jack's step-father went out softly, and shut the door, and said:—

"Look here, boys,—help me in with him, will you? Not *that* way. His mother's in there. She died an hour ago."

II

And so the curse of his heredity came upon him. She never knew, thank Heaven. Her knowledge would have been a kind of terrible fore-omniscience, if she had. She would have had no hope for him from that hour. Her experience would have left her no illusions. The drunkard's wife would have educated the drunkard's mother too "liberally" for that. She would have taken in the whole scope and detail of the future in one midnight moment's breadth, as a problem in the higher mathematics may rest upon the width of a geometrical point. But she did not know. We say—I mean, it is our fashion of saying—that she did not know. God was merciful. She had asked for Jack, it seemed, over and over, but did not complain of him for not coming; she never complained of Jack. She said the poor boy must have stayed somewhere to have a pleasant time; and she said they were to give her love to him, if he came in while she was asleep. And then she asked her husband to sing "Rock of Ages" for her, because she did not feel very strong. He couldn't sing,—more than a halibut, poor fellow; but he did not like to disappoint her, for he thought she looked what he called "miser'ble"; so he sat down by the bed, and raised his hoarse, weather-beaten voice to the tune of Martyn, as best he could, and mixed up two verses inextricably with a line from "Billy's on the bright blue sea," which he added because he saw he must have something to fill out, and it was all he could think of,— but she thanked him very gently, and said he sang quite well; and said once more that he was to give her love to Jack; and went to sleep afterward; and by and by, they could not wake her to see her boy of twelve brought to her drunk.

The curse of his heredity was upon him. We may blame, we may loathe, we may wonder, we may despair; but we must not forget. There were enough to blame without remembering. Jack, like all drunkards, soon learned this. In fact, he did not remember it very well himself,—not having been acquainted with his father; and never sentimentalized over himself nor whined for his bad luck, but owned up to his sins, with the bluntness of an honest, bad fellow. He was rather an honest fellow, in spite of it all. He never lied when he was sober.

If the curse of his ancestry had come upon him, its compensatory temperament came too. Jack had the merry heart of the easy drinker.

Born with his father's alcoholized brain-cells, poor baby, endowed with the narcotined conscience which this species of parentage bequeathes, he fell heir to the kind of attractiveness that goes with the legacy.

He was a happy-go-lucky fellow. Life sat airily on him. He had his mother's handsome eyes dashed with his father's fun (for she couldn't take a joke, to save her); he told a good story; he did a kind deed; he was generous with his money, when he had any, and never in the least disturbed when he hadn't. He was popular to the dangerous extent that makes one's vices seem a kind of social introduction, and not in Jack's circle alone, be it said. Every crew wanted him. Drunk or sober, as a shipmate he was at par. It was usually easy for him to borrow. The fellows made up his fines for him; there was always somebody to go bail for him when he got before the police-court. Arrested perhaps a half dozen times a year, in his maddest years, he never was sent to the House in his life. There were always people enough who thought it a pity to let such a good fellow go to prison. He had—I was going to say as a matter of course he had —curly hair. One should not omit to notice that he was splendidly tattooed. He was proud, as seamen are, of his brawny arms, dashed from wrist to shoulder with the decorative ingenuity of his class. Jack had aesthetic views of his own, indeed, about his personal allowance of indigo. He had objected to the custom-ary medley of anchors, stars, and crescents, and exhibited a certain reserve of taste, which was rather interesting. On his left arm he bore a very crooked lighthouse rising from a heavy sea; he was, in fact, quite flooded along the bicipital muscle with waves and billows, but nothing else interfered with the massive proportions of the effect. This was considered a masterly design, and Jack was often called upon to push up his sleeve and explain how he came by the inspiration.

Upon the other arm he wore a crucifix, ten inches long; this was touched with blood-red ink; the dead Christ hung upon it, lean and pitiful. Jack said he took the crucifix against his drowning. It was an uncommonly large and ornate crucifix.

Jack was a steady drinker at nineteen. At twenty-five he was what either an inexperienced or a deeply experienced temperance missionary would have called incurable. The intermediate grades would have confidently expected to save him.

Of course he reformed. He would not have been interesting if he had not. The unmitigated sot has few attractions even for seafaring society. It is the foil and flash, the by-play and side-light of character, that "lead us on." Jack was always reforming. After that night when he was brought home on the bob-sled, the little boy was as steady and as miserable as he knew how to be for a long time; he drew the unfortunate inference that the one involved the other. By the time his mother's grave was green with the scanty Fairharbor church-yard grass,—for even the sea-wind seems to have a grudge against the very dead for choosing dry graves in Fairharbor, and scants them in their natural covering, —by that time rank weeds had overgrown the sorrow of the homeless boy. He and his step-father "got on" less than ever now, as was to be expected; and when one day Jack announced with characteristic candor that he was going to get drunk if he went to Torment for it, the two parted company; and the crumbling cottage knew Jack no more. By and by, when his step-father was drowned at Georges', Jack borrowed the money for some black gloves and a hat-band. He had the reputation of being a polite fellow; the fishermen spelled it t-o-n-y. Truth to tell, the old dory-mate had wondered sometimes on Sunday afternoons if he *had* been the man to manage Jack; and felt that the main object of his marriage had been defeated.

Jack, as I say, was always reforming. Every temperance society in the city had a hand at him. They were of the old-fashioned, easy type which took their responsibilities comfortably. They held him out on a pair of moral tongs, and tried to toast his misdemeanors out of him, before a quick fire of pledges and badges; and when he tumbled out of the tongs, and asked the president and treasurer why they didn't bow to him in the street when he was drunk, or why, if he was good enough for them in the lodge-room, he wasn't good enough to shake hands with before folks on the post-office steps, or propounded any of those ingenious posers with which his kind are in the habit of disturbing the benevolent spirit, they snapped the tongs too, and turned him over to the churches.

These touched him gingerly. They invited him into the free pews,—a dismal little row in the gallery,—sent him a tract or two, and asked him a few well-meant and very confusing religious questions, to which Jack's replies were far from satisfactory. One ardent person, a recent convert, coaxed him into a weekly prayer-meeting. It was a very good, honest, uninteresting prayer-meeting, and there were people sitting there beside him with clean lives and clear faces whose motives Jack was not worthy to understand, and he knew enough to know it. But it happened to be a foreign mission prayer-meeting, devoted to the Burmese field; which was, therefore, be it said, not so much an argument against foreign missions, as a deficient means of grace to the fisher-man. Jack was terribly bored. He ran his hands through his curls, and felt for his tobacco, and whispered to the young convert to know if there weren't any waits in the play so a man could get out without hurting anybody's feelings. But just then the young convert struck up a hymn, and Jack stayed.

He liked the singing. His restless, handsome face took on a change such as a windy day takes on toward dusk, when the breeze dies down. When he found that they were singing "Rock of Ages," he tried to sing it too,—for he was a famous tenor on deck. But when he had sung a line or two,—flash! down in one of the empty pews in front, he saw a thin old lady with blue eyes, sitting in a black alpaca dress, with her hands clasped on her gingham apron.

"That's my mother. Have I got the jim-jams?" asked this unaccustomed worshiper of himself. But then he remembered that he was sober. He could sing no longer after this, but bowed his head and looked into his old felt hat, and wondered if he were going to cry, or get religion. In point of fact, he did neither of these things, because a very old church-member arose just then, and said he saw a poor cast-away in our midst to-night, and he besought the prayers of the meeting for his soul. Jack stopped crying. He looked hard at the old church member. He knew him; had always known him. The fisherman waited till that prayer was through,—it was rather a long prayer,—and then he too sprang to his feet. He looked all around the decorous place; his face was white with the swift passion of the drinking man.

"I never spoke in meetin' in my life," said Jack in an unsteady voice. "I ain't religious. I drink. But I'm sober to-night, and I've got something to say to you. I heard what that man said. I know him. He's old Jim Crownoby. I've always knowed Jim Crownoby. He owns a sight of property in this town. He's a rich man. He owns that block on Black Street. You know he does. You can't deny it. Nor he can't neither. All I want to say is, I've got drunk in one of them places of his time and again; and if there ain't anybody but *him* to pray for my soul, I'd rather go to the devil."

Jack stopped short, jammed on his hat, and left the meeting. In the shocked rustle that followed, some one had the tact to start "Rescue the perishing," as the fisherman strode down the broad aisle. He did not go again. The poor young convert followed him up for a week or two, and gave him an expensive Testament, bought out of an almost invisible personal income, in vain.

"I've no objections to you," said Jack candidly; "I'm much obliged to ye for yer politeness, sir. But them churches that sub-leases to a rumseller, I don't think they onderstand a drinkin' man. Hey? Well, ain't he their biggest rooster, now? Don't he do the heft of the payin', and the tallest of their crowin', consequent? Thought so. Better leave me go, sir. I ain't a pious man; I'm a fisherman."

"Fishes," said Jack, "is no fools."

He gave voice to this remark one day in Boston, when he was twenty-five years old. He was trying to entertain a Boston girl; she was not familiar with Fairharbor or with the scenery of his calling; he wanted to interest her; he liked the girl. He had liked a good many girls, it need not be said; but this one had laid upon the fisherman—she knew not how, he knew not why, and what man or woman of us could have told him?—the power that comes not of reason, or of time, or of trying, or of wisdom, or of fitness, but of the mystery to which, when we are not speaking of Jack, we give the name of love. It seems a sacrilege, admit, to write it here, and of these two. But there, again, it would be easy to be wrong. The study of the relativity of human feeling is a delicate science; it calls for a fine moral equipment. If this were the high-water mark of nature for Jack—and who shall say?—the tide shall have its sacred due, even down among those weeds and in that mud. He liked that girl, among them all, and her he thought of gently. He had known her a long time; as much as three months. When the vessel came into Boston to sell halibut, he had a few days there, drifting about as seamen do, homeless and reckless; dashing out the wages just paid off, in ways that sometimes he remembered and sometimes he forgot, and that usually left him without a dollar toward his next fine when he should be welcomed by the police court of his native city on returning home.

Jack thought, I say, gravely of this girl. He never once took her name in vain among the fellows; and she had not been a very good girl, either. But Jack reflected that he was not very good himself, if you came to that. His downright, honest nature stood him in stead in this moral distinction; there was always a broad streak of generosity in him at his worst; it goes with the temperament, we say, and perhaps we say it too often to give him half the credit of it.

She was a pretty girl, and she was very young. She had told Jack her story, as they strolled about the bright Boston streets on comfortable winter evenings; when he took her to the variety show, or to the oyster-shop, and they talked together. Jack pitied her. Perhaps she deserved it; it was a sad little story—and she was so very young! She had a gentle way with Jack; for some reason, God knows why, she had trusted him from the first, and he had never once been known to disturb her trust. That was the pleasant part of it.

On this evening that we speak of, Jack was sober. He was often sober when he had an evening to spend with the Boston girl; not always—no; truth must be told. She looked as pretty as was in her, that night; she had black eyes and a kind of yellow hair that Jack had never seen crinkled low on the forehead above black eyes before; he thought her as fine to look at as any actress he ever saw; for the stage was Jack's standard of the magnificent, as it is to so many of his sort. The girl's name was Teen. Probably she had been called Christine once, in her country home; she even told Jack that she had been baptized.

"I wasn't, myself," said Jack; "I roared so, they darsen't do it. My mother got me to church, for she was a pious woman, and I pummeled the parson in the face with both fists, and she said she come away, for she was ashamed of me. She always said that christenin' wasn't never legal. It disappointed her, too. I was an awful baby."

"I should think likely," said Teen with candor. "Do you set much by your mother?"

"She's dead," said Jack in a subdued voice. Teen looked at him; she had never heard him speak like that.

"I 'most wished mine was," said the girl; "she'd 'a' ben better off—along of me."

"That's so," said Jack.

The two took a turn in silence up and down the brightly lighted street; their thoughts looked out strangely from their marred young faces; they felt as if they were in a foreign country. Jack had meant to ask her to take a drink, but he gave it up; he couldn't, somehow.

"Was you always a fisherman?" asked Teen, feeling, with a woman's tact, that somebody must change the current of the subject.

"I was a fisherman three generations back," Jack answered her; "borned a fisherman, you bet! I couldn't 'a' ben nothin' else if I'd drownded for it. It's a smart business. You hev to keep your wits about you. Fishes is no fools."

"Ain't they?" asked the girl listlessly. She was conscious of failing in conversational brilliancy; but the truth was, she couldn't get over what they had been saying: it was always unfortunate when she remembered her mother. Jack began to talk to her about his business again, but Teen did not reply; and when he looked down at her to see what ailed her, there were real tears rolling over her pretty cheeks.

"Why, Teen!" said Jack.

"Leave go of me, Jack!" said Teen, "and let me get off; I ain't good company to-night. I've got the dumps. I can't entertain ye, Jack. And, Jack— don't let's talk about mothers next time, will we? It spoils the evenin'. Leave go of me, and I'll go home by my own self. I'd rather."

"I won't leave go of you!" cried Jack, with a sudden blazing purpose lighting up all the corners of his soul. It was a white light, not unholy; it seemed to shine through and through him with a soft glow like a candle on an altar. "I'll never leave go of you, Teen, if you'll say so. I'd rather marry you."

"Marry *me?*" said Teen.

"Yes, marry you. I'd a sight rather. There, now! It's out with it. What do you say to that, Teen?"

With one slow finger-tip Teen wiped away the tears that fell for her mother. A ring on her finger glistened in the light as she did this. She saw the sparkle, tore off the ring and dashed it away; it fell into the mud, and was trodden out of sight instantly. Jack sprang gallantly to pick it up.

"Don't you touch it!" cried the girl. She put her bared hand back upon his arm. The ring had left a little mark upon her finger; she glanced at this, and looked up into Jack's handsome face; he looked very kind.

"Jack, dear," said Teen softly, "I ain't fit to marry ye."

"You're fitter 'n I be," answered Jack manfully.

Teen sighed; she did not speak at once; other tears came now, but these were tears for herself and for Jack. Jack felt this, after his fashion; they gave him singular confusion of mind.

"I wouldn't cry about it, Teen. You needn't have me if you don't want to."

"But I *do* want to, Jack."

"Honest?"

"Honest it is, Jack."

"Will ye make a good wife, Teen?" asked Jack, after some unprecedented thought.

"I'll try, Jack."

"You'll never go back on me, nohow?"

"I ain't that sort!" cried the girl, drawing herself up a little. A new dignity sat upon her with a certain grace which was beautiful to see.

"Will you swear it, Teen?"

"If you'd rather, Jack."

"What'll you swear by, now?" asked Jack. "You must swear by all you hold holy."

"What *do* I hold holy?" mused Teen.

"Will you swear," continued Jack seriously, "will you swear to me by the Rock of Ages?"

"What's that?" asked the girl.

"It's a hymn-tune. I want you to swear me by the Rock of Ages that you'll be that you say you will to me. Will you do it, Teen?"

"Oh, yes," said Teen, "I'll do it. Where shall we come across one?"

"I guess I can find it," Jack replied. "I can find 'most anything I set out to."

So they started out at random, in their reckless fashion, in the great city, to find the Rock of Ages for the asking.

Jack led his companion hither and yon, peering into churches and vestries and missions, and wherever he saw signs of sacred things. Singing they heard abundantly in the gay town; songs merry, mad, and sad, but not the song for a girl to swear by that she would be true wife to a man who trusted her.

Wandering thus, on the strange errand whose pathos was so far above their own dream or knowledge, they chanced at last upon the place and the little group of people known in that part of Boston as Mother Mary's meeting.

The girl said she had been there once, but that Mother Mary was too good for her; she was one of the real kind. Everybody knew Mother Mary and her husband; he was a parson. They were poor folks themselves, Teen said, and understood poor folks, and did for them all the year round, not clearing out, like rich ones, when it came hot weather, but stood by 'em, Teen said. They kept the little room open, and if you wanted a prayer you went in and got it, just as you'd call for a drink or a supper; it was always on hand for you, and a kind word sure to come with it, and you always knew where to go for 'em; and Mother Mary treated you like folks. She liked her, Teen said. If she'd been a different girl, she'd have gone there of a cold night all winter. But Teen said she felt ashamed.

"I guess she'll have what I'm after," said Jack. "She sounds like she would. Let's go in and see."

So they went into the quiet place among the praying people, and stood staring, for they felt embarrassed. Mother Mary looked very white and peaceful; she was a tall, fair woman; she wore a black dress with white about the bosom; it was a plain, old dress, much mended. Mother Mary did not look rich, as Teen had said. The room was filled with poor creatures gathered about her like her children, while she talked with them and taught them as she could. She crossed the room immediately to where the young man stood, with the girl beside him.

"We've come," said Jack, "to find the Rock of Ages." He drew Teen's hand through his arm, and held it for a moment; then, moved by some fine instinct mysterious to himself, he lifted and laid it in Mother Mary's own.

"Explain it to her, ma'am," he said; "tell her, won't you? I'm going to marry her, if she'll have me. I want her to swear by somethin' holy she'll be a true wife to me. She hadn't anything particularly holy herself, and the holiest thing I know of is the Rock of Ages. I've heard my mother sing it. She's dead. We've been huntin' Boston over to-night after the Rock of Ages."

Mother Mary was used to the pathos of her sober work, but the tears sprang now to her large and gentle eyes. She did not speak to Jack,—could not possibly, just then; but, delaying only for the moment till she could command herself, she flung her rich, maternal voice out upon the words of the old hymn. Her husband joined her, and all the people present swelled the chorus.

> "Rock of Ages, cleft for me!
> Let me hide myself in thee;
>
> . . .
>
> Be of sin the perfect cure,
> Cleanse me from its guilt and power."

They sang it all through,—the three verses that everybody knows,—and Jack and Teen stood listening. Jack tried to sing himself; but Teen hid her face, and cried upon his arm.

"Thou must save," sang the praying people; *"Thou must save, and thou alone!"*

The strain died solemnly; the room was quiet; the minister yonder began to pray, and all the people bowed their heads. But Mother Mary stood quite still, with the girl's hand trembling in her own.

"Swear it, Teen!" Jack bent down his curly head and whispered; he would not shame his promised wife before these people. "Swear by *that* you'll be true wife to me!"

"I swear it, Jack," sobbed Teen. "If *that's* the Rock of Ages, I swear by it, though I was to die for it, I'll be an honest wife to you."

"Come back when you've got your license," said Mother Mary, smiling through her tears, "and my husband will marry you if you want him to."

"We'll come to-morrow," Jack answered gravely.

"Jack," said Teen in her pretty way,—for she had a very pretty way,— 'if I'm an honest wife to you, will you be *kind* to me?" She did not ask him to swear it by the Rock of Ages. She took his word for it, poor thing! Women do.

III

Mother Mary's husband married them next day at the Mission meeting; and Mother Mary sat down at the melodeon in the corner of the pleasant place, and played and sang Toplady's great hymn for them, as Jack had asked her. It was his wedding march. He was very sober and gentle,—almost like a better man. Teen thought him the handsomest man she had ever seen.

"Oh, I say, Teen," he nodded to her, as they walked away, "one thing I forgot to tell you,—I'm reformed."

"Are you, Jack?"

"If I ever drink a drop again, so help me"—But he stopped.

"So help you, Rock of Ages?" asked the new-made wife. But Jack winced; he was honest enough to hesitate at this.

"I don't know's I'd darst—*that,*" he added ruefully. "But I'm reformed. I have lost all hanker for liquor. I shall never drink again. You'll see, Teen."

Teen did see, as was to be expected. She saw a great deal, poor thing! Jack did not drink—for a long time; it was nearly five months, for they kept close count. He took her to Fairharbor, and rented the old half of the crumbling cottage where his mother used to sit and watch for him on long, late evenings. The young wife did the watching now. They planted some cinnamon rosebushes by the doorsteps of the cottage, and fostered them affectionately. Jack was as happy and sober as possible, to begin with. He picked the cinnamon roses and brought them in for his wife to wear. He was proud to have a home of his own; he had not expected to; in fact, he had never had one since that night when his mother said they were to give her love to him, if he came home while she was asleep. He had beaten about, sleeping for the most part in his berth, and sailing again directly; he had never had any place, he said, to hang his winter clothes in; closets and bureaus seemed treasure-houses to him, and the kitchen fire a luxury greater than a less good-looking man would have deserved. When he came home, drenched and chilly, from a winter voyage, and Teen took the covers off, and the fiery heart of the coals leaped out to greet him, and she stood in the rich color, with her yellow hair, young and fair and sweet as any man's wife could look, and said she had missed him, and called him her dear husband, Jack even went so far as to feel that Teen was the luxury. He treated her accordingly; that was at first. He came straight home to her; he kept her in flour and fuel; she had the little things and the gentle words that women need. Teen was very fond of him. This was the first of it,—I was going to say this was the worst of it. All there was of Teen seemed to have gone into her love for Jack. A part of Jack had gone into his love for Teen. Teen was very happy, to begin with. The respectable neighbors came to see her, and said, "We're happy to make your acquaintance." Nobody knew that it had not always been so that Teen's acquaintance would have been a source of social happiness. And she wrote to her mother that she was married; and her mother came on to make her a little visit; and Teen cried her soul out for joy. She was very modest and home-keeping and loving; no wife in the land was truer than this girl he had chosen was to the fisherman who chose her. Jack knew that. He believed in her. She made him happy; and therefore she kept him right.

All this was at first. It did not last. Why should we expect that, when we see how little there is in the relation of man and woman which lasts? If happy birth and gentle rearing, and the forces of what we call education, and the silken webs of spun refinements, are so strained in the tie which requires two who cannot get away from each other to make each other happy, how should we ask, of the law of chances, the miracle for Teen and Jack?

There was no miracle. No transubstantiation of the common bread to holy flesh was wrought upon that poor altar. Their lot went the way of other lots, with the facts of their history dead against them. Trouble came, and poverty, and children, and care, and distaste. Jack took to his old ways, and his wife to the tears that they bring. The children died; they were poor sickly babies, who wailed a little while in her arms, and slipped out because there wasn't enough to them to stay. And the gray house was damp. Some said it was diphtheria; but their mother said it was the will of God. She added: Might his will be done! On the whole she was not sorry. Their father struck her when he was in liquor. She thought if the babies lived they might get hurt. A month before the last one was born she showed to Jack's biographer a bruise across her shoulder, long and livid. She buttoned her dress over it with hasty repentance.

"Maybe I'd oughtn't to have told," she said. "But he said he'd be *kind* to me."

Jack was very sorry about this when he was sober. He kissed his wife, and bought a pair of pink kid shoes for the baby, which it never grew large enough to wear.

I am not writing a temperance story, only the biography of a fisherman, and a few words will say better than many how it was. Alcoholized brain-cells being one of the few bequests left to society which the heirs do not dispute, Jack went back to his habits with the ferocity that follows abstinence. Hard luck came. Teen was never much of a housekeeper; she had left her mother too early; had never been taught. Things were soggy, and not always clean; and she was so busy in being struck and scolded, and in bearing and burying babies, that it grew comfortless beside the kitchen fire. The last of the illusions which had taken the name of home within the walls of the crumbling half-cottage withered out of it, just as the cinnamon roses did the summer Jack watered them with whiskey by a little emotional mistake.

A worse thing had happened, too. Some shipmate had "told" in the course of time; and Teen's prematrimonial story got set adrift upon the current—one of the cruelest currents of its kind—of Fairharbor gossip. The respectable neighbors made her feel it, as only respectable neighbors do such things. Jack, raging, overhead her name upon the wharves. Teen had been "that she said she would" to him. He knew it. No matron in the town had kept her life or heart more true. In all her sickness and trouble and slackness, and in going cold or hungry, and in her vivid beauty that none of all these things could quench, Teen had carried a sweet dignity of her own as the racer in the old Promethean festival carried the torch while he ran against the wind. Jack knew,—oh yes, he knew. But he grew sullen, suspicious. When he was drunk he was always jealous; it began to take that form. When he was sober he still admired his wife; sometimes he went so far as to remember that he loved her. When this happened, Teen dried her eyes, and brushed her yellow hair, and washed up the kitchen floor, and made the coffee, and said to the grocer when she paid for the sugar, "My husband has reformed."

One night Jack came home unexpectedly; a strange mood sat upon him, which his wife did not find herself able to classify by any of the instant and exquisite perceptions which grow, like new faculties, in wives. He had been drinking heavily when he left her, and she had not looked for him for days; if he sailed as he was, it would be a matter of weeks. Teen went straight to him; she thought he might be hurt; she held out her arms as she would to one of her children; but he met her with a gesture of indifference, and she shrank back.

"She's here," said Jack. "Mother Mary's in this d—town. I see her."

"I wish she'd talk to you," said Teen, saying precisely the wrong thing by the fatal instinct which so often possesses drunkards' wives.

"You do, do you?" quoth Jack. "Well, I don't. I haven't give her the chance." He crushed on his hat and stole out of the house again.

But his mood was on him yet; the difference being that his wife was out of it. He sulked and skulked about the streets alone for a while; he did not go back to the boys just then, but wandered with the apparent aimlessness in which the most tenacious aims are hidden. Mother Mary and her husband were holding sailors' meetings in the roughest quarter of the town. There was need enough of Mother Mary in Fairharbor. A crowd had gathered to hear the novelty. Fairharbor seamen were none too used to being objects of consideration; it was a matter of mark that a parson and a lady should hire a room from a rich fish-firm, pay for it out of their own scanty pockets, and invite one in from deck or wharf, in one's oil-clothes or jumper, to hear what a messmate of Jack's called a "high-toned prayer." He meant perhaps to convey the idea that the petition treated the audience politely.

Jack followed the crowd in the dark, shrinking in its wake, for he was now sober enough not to feel like himself. He waited till the last of the fellows he knew had gone into the place, and then crept up on tiptoe, and put his face against the window of the salt-cod warehouse where the little congregation was gathered, and looked in. The room was full and bright. It wore that same look of peace and shelter which he remembered. Mother Mary stood, as she had stood before, tall and pale in her black dress, with the white covering on her bosom. Her husband had been speaking to the fishermen, and she, as Jack put his gnarled hand to his excited eyes and his eyes to the window-glass, turned her face full about, to start the singing. She seemed to Jack to look at him. Her look was sad. He felt ashamed, and cowered down below the window-sill. But he wanted to hear her sing,—he had never heard anybody sing like Mother Mary,—and so he stayed there for a little while, curled against the fish-house. It began to rain, and he was pretty wet; but Jack was in his jumper, and a ragged old jumper at that; he knew he was not so handsome as he used to be; he felt that he cut a poor figure even for a drunken fisherman; all the self-respect that life had left him shrank from letting Mother Mary see him. Jack would not go in. A confused notion came to him, as he crouched against the warehouse, in the showers, that it was just as well it should rain on him; it might wash him. He pushed up his sleeves and let the rain fall on his arms. He found an old Cape Ann turkey box there was lying about, turned it edgewise so that one ragged knee might rest upon it, and thus bring his eye to a level with the window-sill, while yet he could not be seen from within. So he crouched listening. The glimmer from the prayer-room came across the fisherman's bared right arm, and struck the crucifix. Jack had the unconscious attitude of one sinking, who had thrown up his arms to be saved. The Christ on the crucifix looked starved and sickly. Jack did not notice the crucifix.

At this moment Mother Mary's yearning voice rang out above the hoarse chorus of the fishermen, whose weather-ragged and reverent faces lifted themselves mistily before her, as if they had been the countenance of one helpless man:—

"Rock of Ages, cleft for me!"

"Oh, my God!" cried Jack.

IV

It was the next day that some one told Mother Mary, at the poor boarding-house where she stayed, that a woman wanted a few words with her. The visitor was Teen. She was worn and wan and sobbing with excitement. Her baby was soon to be born. She did not look as if she had enough to eat. She had come, she said, just to see Mother Mary, just to tell her, for Jack never would tell himself, but she was sure her husband had reformed; he would never drink again; he meant to be a sober man; and Mother Mary ought to know she did it, for she did, God bless her!

"I've walked all this way to bless you for myself," said Teen. "I ain't very fit for walkin', nor I can't afford a ferry-ticket, for he didn't leave me nothin' on this trip, but I've come to bless you. My husband come to your meetin', Mother Mary, by himself, Jack did. He never goes to no meetin's,—nobody couldn't drove him; but he come to yours because he says you treat a man like folks, and he wouldn't go inside, for he'd ben drinkin' and he felt ashamed. So he set outside, up on a box behind the winder and he peeked in. And he said it rained on him while he set peekin', for he wanted to get a look at you. And he come home and told me, for we'd had some words beforehand, and I was glad to see him. I was settin' there and cryin' when he come. 'I wouldn't, Teen,' says he, 'for I've seen Mother Mary, and I'm reformed,' says he. So he told me how he set up on the box and peeked. He says you looked straight at him. He says you stood up very tall and kind of white. He says you read something out of a book, and then you sang to him. He says the song you sang was Rock of Ages, and it made him feel so bad I had to cry to see him. He come in, and he got down on the lounge against our window, and he put his hand acrost his eyes and groaned like he was hurted in an accident. And he says, 'Teen, I wish't I was a better man.' And I says, 'Jack, I wish't you was.' And he says, 'I lost the hanker when I heard her sing the Rock of Ages, and if I lost the hanker I could swear off.' So I didn't answer him, for if I says, 'Do swear off,' he'd just swear on,—they won't, you know, for wives. But I made him a cup of coffee, for I didn't know what else to do, and I brought it to him on the lounge, and he thanked me. 'Teen,' he says, 'I'll never drink a drop again, so help me Mother Mary!' And then he kissed me,—for they don't, you know, after you've been married. And he's gone out haddockin', but we parted very kind. And so I come to tell you, for it mayn't be many days that I could walk it, and I've ben that to him as I said I should, and I thought you'd better know."

"You've had no breakfast," answered Mother Mary, "and you've walked too far. Here, stop at the Holly Tree as you go home; get a bowl of soup; and take the ferry back. There, there! don't cry quite so hard. I'll try to stay a little longer. I won't leave town till Jack comes in. It *takes* the Rock of Ages to cure the hanker, Teen. But I've seen older men than he is stop as if they had been stopped by a lasso thrown from heaven. If there's any save in him," added Mother Mary below her breath, "he shall have his chance, this time."

He went aboard sober, and sober he stayed. He kept a good deal by himself and thought of many things. His face paled out and refined, as their faces do, from abstinence; the ghost of his good looks hovered about him; he mended up his clothes; he did a kind turn to a messmate now and then; he told some excellent clean stories, and raised the spirits of the crew; he lent a dollar to a fellow with the rheumatism who had an indebtedness to liquidate for St. Galen's Oil. When he had done this, he remembered that he had left his wife without money, and said aloud: "That's a d—mean trick to play on a woman."

He had bad luck, however, that trip; his share was small; he made seven dollars and twenty-seven cents in three weeks. This was conceded by the crew of the fishing-schooner (her name was the Destiny) to be because Jack had "sworn off." It is a superstition among them. One unfamiliar with the lives of these men will hammer cold iron if he thinks to persuade them that rum and luck do not go together; or that to "reform" does not imply a reduction of personal income. You might as well try to put the fisherman's fist into a Honiton lace jumper, as the fisherman's mind into proportion upon this point.

Therefore Jack took his poor trip carelessly; it was to be expected; he would explain it to Mother Mary when he got in. He drank nothing at all; and they weighed for home.

When Jack stepped off the Destiny, at Zephaniah Salt & Co.'s wharf at Fairharbor, after that voyage, clean, pale, good-natured, and sober, thinking that he would get shaved before he hurried home to Teen, and wishing he could pay the grocer's bill upon the way, and thinking that, in default of this, he would start an account at the market, and carry her a chop or a sausage, in fact, thinking about her with an absorption which resembled consideration, if not affection,—suddenly he caught her name upon the wharves.

It may have been said of accident, or of the devil,—God knew; they may have been too drunk to notice Jack at first, or they may have seen and scented from afar the bad blood they stirred, like the hounds they were. It will never be told. The scandal of such places is incredibly barbarous, but it is less than the barbarity of drinking men to a man who strikes out from among themselves, and fights for his respectability.

The words were few,—they are not for us,—but they were enough to do the deed. Jack was quite sober. He understood. They assailed the honor of his home, the truth of his wife; they hurled her past at her and at himself; they derided the trust which he had in her in his absence; they sneered at the "reformed man" whose domestic prospects were—as they were; they exulted over him with the exultation in the sight of the havoc wrought, which is the most inexplicable impulse of evil.

Everybody knew how hot-blooded Jack was; and when the fury rushed red over his face painted gray by abstinence, there was a smart scattering upon the wharves.

His hand clapped to his pockets; but his was an old, cheap, rusty pistol (he had swapped a Bible and his trawls for it once, upon a spree, and got cheated); it held but one cartridge, and his wrist shook. The shot went sputtering into the water, and no harm came of it. Jack jammed the pistol back into his pocket; he glared about him madly, but had his glare for his pains; the men were afraid of him; he was alone upon the wharf.

It can hardly be said that he hesitated. Would that it could. Raving to himself,—head down, hands clenched, feet stumbling like a blind man's,—the fisherman sank into the first open door he staggered by, as a seiner, pierced by an invisible swordfish, sinks into the sea. He had fifteen such places to pass before he reached his house. His chances were—as such chances go—at best.

He drank for half an hour—an hour—a half more—came out, and went straight home.

It was now night of a February day. It had not been a very cold day; a light, clean snow had fallen, which was thawing gently. Jack, looking dimly on through his craze, saw the light of his half of the gray cottage shining ahead; he perceived that the frost was melted from the windows. The warm color came quietly down to greet him across the fresh snow; it had to him in his delirium the look of a woman's eyes when they are true, and lean out of her love to greet a man. He did not put this to himself in these words, but only said:—

"Them lamps look like she used to,—curse her!" and so went hurtling on.

He dashed up against the house, as a bowsprit dashes on the rocks, took one mad look through the unfrosted window, below the half-drawn curtain, and flung himself against the door, and in.

His wife sat there in the great rocking-chair, leaning back; she had a pillow behind her, and her feet on the salt-fish box which he had covered once to make a cricket for her, when they were first married. She looked pale and pretty— very pretty. She was talking to a visitor who sat upon the lounge beside her. It was a man. Now, Jack knew this man well; it was an old messmate; he had sworn off, a year ago, and they had gone different ways; he used to be a rough fellow; but people said now you wouldn't know him.

"I ain't so drunk but I see who you be, Jim," began the husband darkly; "I'll settle with *you* another day. I've got that to say to my wife I'd say better if we missed your company. Leave us by ourselves!"

"Look here, Jack," Jim flashed good-humoredly, "you're drunk, you know. She'll tell you what I come for. You ask her. Seein' she wasn't right smart,— and there's them as says she lacked for victuals,—my wife sent me over with a bowl of cranberry sass, so help me Heaven!"

"I'll kill *you* some other evenin'. Leave us be!" cried Jack.

"We was settin' and talkin' about the Reform Club when you come in," objected Jim, with the patience of an old friend. "We was wonderin' if we couldn't get you to sign, Jack. Ask her if we wasn't. Come, now! I wouldn't make a fool of myself if I was you, Jack. See there. You've set her to cryin' already. And she ain't right smart."

"Clear out of my house!" [1] thundered Jack. "Leave us be by ourselves!"

"I don't know's I'd oughter," hesitated Jim.

"Leave us be! or I won't leave you be a d—minute longer! Ain't it my house? Get out of it!"

"It is, that's a fact," admitted the visitor, looking perplexed; "but I declare to Jupiter I don't know's I'd oughter leave it, the way things look. Have your senses, Jack, my boy! *Have* your senses! She ain't right smart."

But with this Jack sprang upon him, and the wife cried out between them, for the love of mercy, that murder would be done.

"Leave us be!" she pleaded, sobbing. "Nothin' else won't pacify him. Go, Jim, go, and shut the door, and thank her, for the cranberry sarse was very kind of her, and for my husband's sake don't tell nobody he wasn't kind to me. There. That's right. There."

She sank back into the rocking-chair, for she was feeble still, and looked gently up into her husband's face. All the tones of her agitated voice had changed.

She spoke very low and calmly, as if she gathered her breath for the first stage of a struggle whose nature she solemnly understood. She had grown exceedingly pale.

"Jack, dear?" softly.

"I'll give ye time," he answered with an ominous quiet. "Tell yer story first. Out with it!"

"I haven't got nothin' to tell, Jack. He brought the cranberry sarse, for his wife took care of me, and she was very kind. And he set a little, and we was talkin' about the club, just as he says we was. It's Mother Mary's club, Jack. She's made Jim secretary, and she wanted you to join, for I told her you'd reformed. Oh, Jack, I told her you'd reformed!—Jack, Jack! Oh, Jack! What are you goin' to do to me! What makes you look like that?—Jack, Jack, *Jack!*"

"Stand up here!" he raved. He was past reason, and she saw it; he tore off his coat and pushed up his sleeves from his tattooed arms.

"You've played me false, I say! I trusted ye, and you've tricked me. I'll teach ye to be the talk upon the wharves another time when I get in from Georges'!"

She stood as he bade her, tottered and sank back; crawled up again, holding

---

[1] Such peculiarities of Jack's pronunciation as were attributable to his condition will not be reproduced here.

by the wooden arm of the rocking-chair, and stretched one hand out to him, feebly. She did not dare to touch him; if she had clung to him, he would have throttled her. When she saw him rolling up his sleeves, her heart stood still. But Teen thought: "I will not show him I'm afraid of him. It's the only chance I've got."

The poor girl looked up once into his face, and thought she smiled.

"Jack? *Dear* Jack!"

"I'll teach ye! I'll teach ye!"

"Oh, wait a moment, Jack. For the love of Heaven,—stop a minute! I've been that I said I'd be to you, since we was married. I've been an honest wife to you, my boy, and there's none on earth nor heaven as can look me in the eye and darst to say I haven't. I swore to you upon the Rock of Ages, Mother Mary witnessin',—why, Jack!" her voice sank to infinite sweetness, "have you forgotten? You ain't yourself, poor boy. You'll be so sorry. I ain't very strong, yet,—you'd feel bad if you should hit me—again. I'd hate to have you feel so bad. Jack, dear, don't. Go look in the other room, before you strike again. Ye ain't seen it yet. Jack, for the love of mercy!—Jack! Jack!"

"Say you've played me false, and I'll stop. Own up, and I'll quit. Own up to me, I say!"

"I can't own up to you, for I swore you by the Rock of Ages; I swore you I would be an honest wife. You may pummel me to death, but I'll not lie away them words I swore to you . . . by that, . . . Jack, for the love of Heaven, don't you, Jack! For the way you used to feel to me, dear, dear Jack! For the sake of the babies we had, . . . and you walked beside of me, to bury 'em! Oh, for God's sake . . . *Jack!* . . . Oh, you said you'd be *kind* to me . . . Oh, you'll be so sorry! For the love of pity! For the love of God! Not the *pistol!* Oh, for the Rock of"—

But there he struck her down. The butt end of the weapon was heavy enough to do the deed. He struck, and then flung it away.

Upon his bared arm, as it came crashing, the crucifix was spattered red.

V

He stood up stupidly and looked about the room. The covers were off the kitchen stove, and the heart of the coals blazed out. Her yellow hair had loosened as she fell, and shone upon the floor.

He remembered that she spoke about the other room, and said of something yonder, that he hadn't seen it yet. Confusedly he wondered what it was. He stumbled in and stared about the bedroom. It was not very light there, and it was some moments before he perceived the cradle, standing straight across his way. The child waked as he hit the cradle, and began to cry, stretching out its hands.

He had forgotten all about the baby. There had been so many.

"You'd better get up, Teen," he said as he went out; "it's cryin' after you."

He shut the door and staggered down the steps. He hesitated once, and thought he would go back and say to her:—

"What's the use of layin' there?"

But he thought better, or worse, of it, and went his way. He went out and reshipped at once, lingering only long enough to drink madly on the way, at a place he knew, where he was sure to be let alone. The men were afraid of Jack, when he was so far gone under as this. Nobody spoke to him. He went down to Salt Brothers' wharf, opposite Salt & Co.'s, and found the Daredevil, just about to weigh. She was short by one hand, and took him as he was.

He was surprised to find himself aboard when the next sun went down; he had turned in his bunk and was overheard to call for Teen, ordering her to do some service for him, testily enough.

"Oh," he muttered, "she ain't here, is she? Be blasted if I ain't on the Daredevil."

He was good for nothing, for a matter of days, and silent or sullen for the trip. It had been a heavy spree. He fell to, when he came to himself, and fished desperately; his luck turned, and he made money; he made seventy-five dollars. They were gone three weeks. They had a bitter voyage, for it was March.

They struck a gale at Georges', and another coming home. It snowed a great deal, and the rigging froze. The crew were uncommonly cold. They kept the steward cooking briskly, and four or five hot meals a day were not enough to keep one's courage up. They were particular about their cooking, as fishermen are, and the steward of the Daredevil was famous in his calling. But it was conceded to be unusually cold, even for March, at Georges'. One must keep the blood racing, somehow, for life's sake.

Whiskey flowed fast between meals. Jack was observed not to limit himself. "It was for luck," he said. Take it through, it was a hard trip. The sober men —there were some—looked grim and pinched; the drinkers, ugly.

"It's a hound's life," said a dory-mate of Jack's one day. His name was Rowe—Rowe Salt; he was a half-brother of Jim's. But Jim was at home. And Teen, of course, was at home. Jack had not spoken of her; he had thought of her,—he had thought of nothing else. God knows what those thoughts had been. When Rowe spoke to him in this fashion, Jack looked hard at him.

"I've ben thinkin' ef it disobligated a feller," he said.

"Hey?" asked Rowe.

"If you was treated like folks; but you ain't. You're froze. You're soaked. You're wrecked. Your nets is stole. You're drove off in the fog. You're drownded, and you lose your trawls. If you swear off, you miss your luck. It's dirty aboard. Folks don't like the looks of you. There's alwers a hanker in the pit o' your stomick. When you get upon a tear you don't know what you—do to—folks."

Jack stopped himself abruptly, and leaned upon his oar; they were trawling, and the weather grew thick.

"Rowe," he said, staring off into the fog, "did ye ever think we was like fishes, us fishin' folks?"

"I don't know's I hev," said the dory-mate, staring too.

"Well, we be, I think. We live in it and we're drownded in it, and we can't get out on't—we can't *get* out. We look like 'em, too. I've thought about that. Some of us look like haddock. You've got the halibut look, yourself. Skipper, he's got the jib of a monk-fish,—you ken see it for yourself. There's a man I messed with, once, reminded me of a sculpin. I guess I'd pass for a lobster, myself,—for color, anyhow. We take it out someways, each on us. Don't ye know the look the women folks have when they get old and have gone hungry? You can tell by the build of a boy which way he'll turn out,—halibut way, or hake, or mebbe mackerel if he's sleek and little. It's a kind of a birth-mark, I shouldn't wonder. There's no gettin' out on't, no more'n it out of you. Sometimes I used to think—

"Good Lord!" cried Jack. He laid down his oar again, and the dory wheeled to starboard sharply.

"Rowe Salt, you look there! You tell me if you see a woman yonder, on the water!"

"You've got the jim-jams, Jack. Women folks don't walk at Georges'. I can't see nothin' nowhere, but it's thick as"—

"It's thick as hell," interrupted Jack, "and there's a woman walkin' on the water,—Lord! don't you see her? Lord! her hair is yeller hair, and it's streamin' over her,—don't *you* see her? She's walkin' on this devilish fog to-wards the dory,—Teen? Teen! There! Lord save me, Rowe, if I didn't see my wife come walkin' towards us, us settin' in this dory! Hi-i-igh! I'll swear off when I get home. I'll tell her so. I hate to see such things."

"You see, Rowe," Jack added presently,—for he had not spoken after that, but had fallen grimly to work; it was ten below, and the wind was taking the backward spring for a bitter blow; both men, tugging at their trawls through the high and icy sea, were suffering too much to talk,—"ye see we had some words before I come aboard, and she warn't right smart. The baby can't be very old. I don' know how old it is. I was oncommon drunk; I don't remember what I did to her. I'm afraid I hit her,—for I had some words with her. I wish't I was at home. She won't tell nobody. She never does. But I'm set to be at home and tell her I've sworn off. I've got money for her this trip, too; I'm afraid she's in a hurry for it."

After this outburst of confidence, Jack seemed to cling to his dory-mate; he followed him about deck, and looked wistfully at him. Jack had begun to take on the haggard look of the abstainer once again. The crew thought he did not seem like himself. He had stopped drinking, abruptly, after that day in the fog, and suffered heavily from the weather and from exposure.

"I say, Rowe," he asked one day, "if anything was to happen, would you jest step in and tell my wife I didn't believe that yarn about her? She'll know."

Now it befell, that when they were rounding Eastern Point, and not till then, they bespoke the Destiny, which was outward bound, and signaled them. She drew to speaking distance, and her skipper had a word with the master of the Daredevil, but he spoke none too loud, and made his errand quickly, and veered to his own course, and the two boats parted company, and the Daredevil came bustling in. They were almost home.

It was remembered afterward that Jack was badly frostbitten upon that voyage; he looked badly; he had strange ways; the men did not know exactly how to take him. He was overheard to say:—

"*I* ain't a-goin' to go to Georges' again."

Rowe Salt overheard this, after the skipper of the Destiny had signaled and tacked. Jack was sitting aft alone, when he said it, looking seaward. He had paid little or no attention to the incident of the Destiny, but sat staring, plunged in some mood of his own which seemed as solitary, as removed from his kind and from their comprehension, as the moods of mental disorder are from the sane.

So then, with such dexterity as the ignorant man could muster, Salt got his friend down below, on some pretext, and stood looking at him helplessly.

"You don't look well, Rowe," Jack suggested pleasantly.

"Jack," said his dory-mate, turning white enough, "I'll make no bones of it, nor mince nothin', for somebody's got to tell ye, and they said it must be me. There's a warrant after ye. The sheriff's on the tug betwixt us and the wharf. She's layin' off the island, him aboard of her."

"I never was in prison," faltered Jack. "The boys have always bailed me."

"'T ain't a bailin' matter, Jack, this time."

"What did you say?"

"I said it wasn't a bailin' business. Somebody's got to tell you."

Jack gazed confidingly up into his friend's face.

"What was it that I done, old boy? Can't ye tell me?"

"Let the sheriff tell you. Ask the sheriff. I'd rather it was the sheriff told you, Jack."

"Tell me what it is I done, Rowe Salt; I'd tell *you.*"

He looked puzzled.

"The sheriff knows more about it nor I do," begged the fisherman; "don't make an old messmate tell you."

"All right," said Jack, turning away. He had now grown very quiet. He pleaded no more, only to mutter once:—

"I'd rather heard it from a messmate."

Rowe Salt took a step or two, turned, stopped, stirred, and turned again.

"You killed somebody, then, if you will know."

"*Killed* somebody?"

"Yes."

"I was drunk and killed somebody?"

"Lord help you, yes."

"I hope,"—hoarsely—"look here, Salt,—*I hope Teen won't know.*

"I say, Rowe," after a long pause, "who was it that I killed?"

"Ask the sheriff."

"Who was it that I killed?"

"The skipper'll tell you, mebby. I won't. No, I vow I won't. Let me go. I've done my share of this. Let me up on deck! I want the air!"

"I won't let you up on deck—so help me!—till you tell!"

"Let me off, Jack, let me off!"

"Tell me who it was, I say!"

"Lord in heaven, the poor devil don't *know*,—he really don't."

"I thought you would ha' told me, Rowe," said Jack with a smile,—his old winning smile, that had captivated his messmates all his life.

"I *will* tell you!" cried Rowe Salt with an oath of agony. "You killed your wife! You murdered her. She's dead. Teen ain't to home. She's dead."

VI

They made way for him at this side and at that, for he sprang up the gangway, and dashed among them. When he saw them all together, and how they looked at him, he stopped. A change seemed to strike his purpose, be it what it might.

"Boys," said Jack, looking all about, "ye won't have to go no bail for me. I'll bide my account, this time."

He parted from them, for they let him do the thing he would, and got himself alone into the bows, and there he sank down, crouching, and no one spoke to him.

The Daredevil rounded Eastern Point, and down the shining harbor, all sails set, came gayly in. They were almost home.

Straightway there started out upon the winter sea a strong, sweet tenor, like a cry. It was Jack's voice,—everybody knew it. He stood by himself in the bows, back to them, singing like an angel or a madman,—some said this, some said the other,—

"Rock of Ages, cleft for me!
Let me hide myself in thee; . . .

Thou must save, and thou alone . . .

When I soar to worlds unknown,
See thee on thy judgment throne," —

sang Jack.

With the ceasing of his voice, they divined how it was, by one instinct, and every man sprang to him. But he had leaped and gained on them.

The waters of Fairharbor seemed themselves to leap to greet him as he went down. These that had borne him and ruined him buried him as if they loved him. He had pushed up his sleeves for the spring, hard to the shoulder, like a man who would wrestle at odds.

As he sank, one bared arm, thrust above the crest of the long wave, lifted itself toward the sky. It was his right arm, on which the crucifix was stamped.

VII

White and gold as the lips and heart of a lily, the day blossomed at Fairharbor one June Sunday, when these things were as a tale that is told. It was a warm day, sweet and still. There was no wind, no fog. The harbor wore her innocent face. She has one; who can help believing in it, to see it? The waves stretched themselves upon the beach as if they had been hands laid out in benediction; and the colors of the sky were like the expression of a strong and solemn countenance.

So thought Mother Mary, standing by her husband's side that day, and looking off from the little creature in her arms to the faces of the fishermen gathered there about her for the service. It was an open-air service, held upon the beach, where the people she had served and loved could freely come to her —and would. They had sought the scene in large numbers. The summer people, too, strolled down, distant and different, and hung upon the edges of the group. They had a civil welcome, but no more. This was a fisherman's affair; nobody needed them; Mother Mary did not belong to them.

"The meetin 's ours," said Rowe Salt. "It's us she's after. The boarders ain't of no account to her."

His brother Jim was there with Rowe, and Jim's wife, and some of the respectable women neighbors. The skipper of the Daredevil was there, and so were many of Jack's old messmates. When it was understood that Mother Mary had adopted Jack's baby, the news had run like rising tide, from wharf to wharf, from deck to deck,—everybody knew it, by this time. Almost everybody was there, to see the baptism. The Fairharbor fishermen were alert to the honor of their guild. They turned out in force to explain matters, sensitive to show their best. They would have it understood that one may have one's faults, but one does not, therefore, murder one's wife.

The scene in the annals and the legends of Fairharbor was memorable, and will be long. It was as strange to the seamen as a leaf thrown over from the pages of the Book of Life, inscribed in an unknown tongue of which they only knew that it was the tongue of love. Whether it spoke as of men or of angels, they would have been perplexed to say.

Into her childless life, its poverty, its struggles, its sacrifices, and its blessed hope, Mother Mary's great heart took the baby as she took a man's own better nature for him; that which lay so puny and so orphaned in those wild lives of theirs, an infant in her hands.

Jack's baby—*Jack's* baby and Teen's, as if it had been anybody else's baby, was to be baptized "like folks." Jack's baby, poor little devil, was to have his chance.

The men talked it over gravely; it affected them with a respect one would not anticipate, who did not know them. They had their Sunday clothes on. They were all clean. They had a quiet look. One fellow who had taken a little too much ventured down upon the beach; but he was hustled away from the christening, and ducked in the cove, and hung upon the rocks to dry. One must be sober who helped to baptize that baby.

This was quite understood.

They sang the hymn, Jack's hymn and Teen's: of course they sang the Rock of Ages; and Mother Mary's husband read "the chapter" to them, as he was used, and spoke to them; and it was so still among them that they could hear each wave of the placid sea beat evenly as if they listened to the beating of a near and mighty peaceful heart. Mother Mary spoke with them herself a little. She told them how she took the child, in despair of the past, in hope of the future; in pain and in pity, and in love; yearning over him, and his, and those who were of their inheritance, and fate, their chances, and their sorrows, and their sins. She told them of the child's pure heart within us all, which needs only to be mothered to be saved; which needs only that we foster it, to form it; which needs that we treat it as we do other weak and helpless things, whether in ourselves or in another. What was noble in them all, she said, was to them like this little thing to her. It was a trust. She gave it to them, so she said, as she took the baby, here before their witnessing, to spare him from their miseries, if she might.

They were touched by this, or they seemed to be; for they listened from their souls.

"We'd oughter take off our hats," somebody whispered. So they stood uncovered before the minister, and Mother Mary, and Jack's poor baby. The sacred drops flashed in the white air. Dreamily the fishermen heard the sacred words:—

"In the name of the Father: And of the Son: And of the Holy Ghost. Amen."

But no one heard the other words, said by Mother Mary close and low, when she received the child into her arms again, and bowed her face above it:—

"My son, I take thee for the sake and for the love of thy father, and of thy mother. Be thou their holy ghost."

But the fishermen, used not to understand her, but only to her understanding them, perceiving that she was at prayer, they knew not why, asking of Heaven they knew not what,—the fishermen said:—

"Amen, *Amen."*

Some abusive people are adept at picking out a trait that a woman is most pleased about and using it against her. . . . Treasuring her independence of spirit. . . , for instance, can be made to seem like a flaw. Independence becomes rejection or selfishness. . . . When the woman begins to believe that her virtues are her flaws, her ability to make other judgments becomes impaired as well. . . . When an abused woman begins to doubt that she has that one special trait she has always felt secure about, the rest of her self-concept is quickly called into question.

—Ginny NiCarthy, *Getting Free*

In Sabine

KATE CHOPIN

The sight of a human habitation, even if it was a rude log cabin with a mud chimney at one end, was a very gratifying one to Grégoire.

He had come out of Natchitoches parish, and had been riding a great part of the day through the big lonesome parish of Sabine. He was not following the regular Texas road, but, led by his erratic fancy, was pushing toward the Sabine River by circuitous paths through the rolling pine forests.

As he approached the cabin in the clearing, he discerned behind a palisade of pine saplings an old negro man chopping wood.

"Howdy, Uncle," called out the young fellow, reining his horse. The negro looked up in blank amazement at so unexpected an apparition, but he only answered: "How you do, suh," accompanying his speech by a series of polite nods.

"Who lives yere?"

"Hit's Mas' Bud Aiken w'at live' heah, suh."

"Well, if Mr. Bud Aiken c'n affo'd to hire a man to chop his wood, I reckon he won't grudge me a bite o' suppa an' a couple hours' res' on his gall'ry. W'at you say, ole man?"

"I say dit Mas' Bud Aiken don't hires me to chop 'ood. Ef I don't chop dis heah, his wife got it to do. Dat w'y I chops 'ood, suh. Go right 'long in, suh; you g'ine fine Mas' Bud some'eres roun', ef he ain't drunk an' gone to bed."

Grégoire, glad to stretch his legs, dismounted, and led his horse into the small inclosure which surrounded the cabin. An unkempt, vicious-looking little Texas pony stopped nibbling the stubble there to look maliciously at him and his fine sleek horse, as they passed by. Back of the hut, and running plumb up against the pine wood, was a small, ragged specimen of a cotton-field.

Grégoire was rather undersized, with a square, well-knit figure, upon which his clothes sat well and easily. His corduroy trousers were thrust into the legs of his boots; he wore a blue flannel shirt; his coat was thrown across the saddle. In his keen black eyes had come a puzzled expression, and he tugged thoughtfully at the brown moustache that lightly shaded his upper lip.

He was trying to recall when and under what circumstances he had before heard the name of Bud Aiken. But Bud Aiken himself saved Grégoire the trouble of further speculation on the subject. He appeared suddenly in the small doorway, which his big body quite filled; and then Grégoire remembered. This was the disreputable so-called "Texan" who a year ago had run away with and married Baptiste Choupic's pretty daughter, 'Tite Reine, yonder on Bayou Pierre, in Natchitoches parish. A vivid picture of the girl as he remembered her appeared to him: her trim rounded figure; her piquant face with its saucy black coquettish eyes; her little exacting, imperious ways that had obtained for her the nickname of 'Tite Reine, little queen. Grégoire had known her at the 'Cadian balls that he sometimes had the hardihood to attend.

These pleasing recollections of 'Tite Reine lent a warmth that might otherwise have been lacking to Grégoire's manner, when he greeted her husband.

"I hope I fine you well, Mr. Aiken," he exclaimed cordially, as he approached and extended his hand.

"You find me damn' porely, suh; but you've got the better o' me, ef I may so say." He was a big good-looking brute, with a straw-colored "horse-shoe" moustache quite concealing his mouth, and a several days' growth of stubble on his rugged face. He was fond of reiterating that women's admiration had wrecked his life, quite forgetting to mention the early and sustained influence of "Pike's Magnolia" and other brands, and wholly ignoring certain inborn propensities capable of wrecking unaided any ordinary existence. He had been lying down, and looked frouzy and half asleep.

"Ef I may so say, you've got the better o' me, Mr.—er"—

"Santien, Grégoire Santien. I have the pleasure o' knowin' the lady you married, suh; an' I think I met you befo',—somew'ere o' 'nother," Grégoire added vaguely.

"Oh," drawled Aiken, waking up, "one o' them Red River Sanchuns!" and his face brightened at the prospect before him of enjoying the society of one of the Santien boys. "Mortimer!" he called in ringing chest tones worthy a commander at the head of his troop. The negro had rested his axe and appeared to be listening to their talk, though he was too far to hear what they said.

"Mortimer, come along here an' take my frien' Mr. Sanchun's hoss. Git a move thar, git a move!" Then turning toward the entrance of the cabin he called back through the open door: "Rain!" it was his way of pronouncing

'Tite Reine's name. "Rain!" he cried again peremptorily; and turning to Grégoire: "she's 'tendin' to some or other housekeepin' truck." 'Tite Reine was
back in the yard feeding the solitary pig which they owned, and which Aiken
had mysteriously driven up a few days before, saying he had bought it at Many.

Grégoire could hear her calling out as she approached: "I'm comin', Bud.
Yere I come. W'at you want, Bud?" breathlessly, as she appeared in the door
frame and looked out upon the narrow sloping gallery where stood the two
men. She seemed to Grégoire to have changed a good deal. She was thinner,
and her eyes were larger, with an alert, uneasy look in them; he fancied the
startled expression came from seeing him there unexpectedly. She wore cleanly
homespun garments, the same she had brought with her from Bayou Pierre; but
her shoes were in shreds. She uttered only a low, smothered exclamation when
she saw Grégoire.

"Well, is that all you got to say to my frien' Mr. Sanchun? That's the way
with them Cajuns," Aiken offered apologetically to his guest; "ain't got sense
enough to know a white man when they see one." Grégoire took her hand.

"I'm mighty glad to see you, 'Tite Reine," he said from his heart. She
had for some reason been unable to speak; now she panted somewhat hysterically:—

"You mus' escuse me, Mista Grégoire. It's the truth I did n' know you firs',
stan'in' up there." A deep flush had supplanted the former pallor of her face,
and her eyes shone with tears and ill-concealed excitement.

"I thought you all lived yonda in Grant," remarked Grégoire carelessly,
making talk for the purpose of diverting Aiken's attention away from his wife's
evident embarrassment, which he himself was at a loss to understand.

"Why, we did live a right smart while in Grant; but Grant ain't no parish to
make a livin' in. Then I tried Winn and Caddo a spell; they was n't no better.
But I tell you, suh, Sabine's a damn' sight worse than any of 'em. Why, a man
can't git a drink o' whiskey here without going out of the parish fer it, or across
into Texas. I'm fixin' to sell out an' try Vernon."

Bud Aiken's household belongings surely would not count for much in
the contemplated "selling out." The one room that constituted his home was
extremely bare of furnishing,—a cheap bed, a pine table, and a few chairs, that
was all. On a rough shelf were some paper parcels representing the larder. The
mud daubing had fallen out here and there from between the logs of the cabin;
and into the largest of these apertures had been thrust pieces of ragged bagging
and wisps of cotton. A tin basin outside on the gallery offered the only bathing
facilities to be seen. Notwithstanding these drawbacks, Grégoire announced his
intention of passing the night with Aiken.

"I'm jus' goin' to ask the privilege o' layin' down yere on yo' gall'ry
to-night, Mr. Aiken. My hoss ain't in firs'-class trim; an' a night's res' ain't
goin' to hurt him o' me either." He had begun by declaring his intention of

pushing on across the Sabine, but an imploring look from 'Tite Reine's eyes had stayed the words upon his lips. Never had he seen in a woman's eyes a look of such heartbroken entreaty. He resolved on the instant to know the meaning of it before setting foot on Texas soil. Grégoire had never learned to steel his heart against a woman's eyes, no matter what language they spoke.

An old patchwork quilt folded double and a moss pillow which 'Tite Reine gave him out on the gallery made a bed that was, after all, not too uncomfortable for a young fellow of rugged habits.

Grégoire slept quite soundly after he laid down upon his improvised bed at nine o'clock. He was awakened toward the middle of the night by some one gently shaking him. It was 'Tite Reine stooping over him; he could see her plainly, for the moon was shining. She had not removed the clothing she had worn during the day; but her feet were bare and looked wonderfully small and white. He arose on his elbow, wide awake at once. "W'y, 'Tite Reine! w'at the devil you mean? w'ere 's yo' husban'?"

"The house kin fall on 'im, 't en goin' wake up Bud w'en he's sleepin'; he drink' too much." Now that she had aroused Grégoire, she stood up, and sinking her face in her bended arm like a child, began to cry softly. In an instant he was on his feet.

"My God, 'Tite Reine! w'at's the matta? you got to tell me w'at's the matta." He could no longer recognize the imperious 'Tite Reine, whose will had been the law in her father's household. He led her to the edge of the low gallery and there they sat down.

Grégoire loved women. He liked their nearness, their atmosphere; the tones of their voices and the things they said; their ways of moving and turning about; the brushing of their garments when they passed him by pleased him. He was fleeing now from the pain that a woman had inflicted upon him. When any overpowering sorrow came to Grégoire he felt a singular longing to cross the Sabine River and lose himself in Texas. He had done this once before when his home, the old Santien place, had gone into the hands of creditors. The sight of 'Tite Reine's distress now moved him painfully.

"W'at is it, 'Tite Reine? tell me w'at it is," he kept asking her. She was attempting to dry her eyes on her coarse sleeve. He drew a handkerchief from his back pocket and dried them for her.

"They all well, yonda?" she asked, haltingly, "my popa? my moma? the chil'en?" Grégoire knew no more of the Baptiste Choupic family than the post beside him. Nevertheless he answered: "They all right well, 'Tite Reine, but they mighty lonesome of you."

"My popa, he got a putty good crop this yea'?"

"He made right smart o' cotton fo' Bayou Pierre."

"He done haul it to the relroad?"

"No, he ain't quite finish pickin'."

"I hope they all ent sole 'Putty Girl'?" she inquired solicitously.

"Well, I should say not! Yo' pa says they ain't anotha piece o' hossflesh in the pa'ish he'd want to swap fo' 'Putty Girl.' " She turned to him with vague but fleeting amazement,—"Putty Girl" was a cow!

The autumn night was heavy about them. The black forest seemed to have drawn nearer; its shadowy depths were filled with the gruesome noises that inhabit a southern forest at night time.

"Ain't you 'fraid sometimes yere, 'Tite Reine?" Grégoire asked, as he felt a light shiver run through him at the weirdness of the scene.

"No," she answered promptly, "I ent 'fred o' nothin' 'cep' Bud."

"Then he treats you mean? I thought so!"

"Mista Grégoire," drawing close to him and whispering in his face, "Bud's killin' me." He clasped her arm, holding her near him, while an expression of profound pity escaped him. "Nobody don' know, 'cep' Unc' Mort'mer," she went on. "I tell you, he beats me; my back an' arms—you ought to see—it's all blue. He would 'a' choke' me to death one day w'en he was drunk, if Unc' Mort'mer had n' make 'im lef go—with his axe ov' his head." Grégoire glanced back over his shoulder toward the room where the man lay sleeping. He was wondering if it would really be a criminal act to go then and there and shoot the top of Bud Aiken's head off. He himself would hardly have considered it a crime, but he was not sure of how others might regard the act.

"That's w'y I wake you up, to tell you," she continued. "Then sometime' he plague me mos' crazy; he tell me 't ent no preacher, it's a Texas drummer w'at marry him an' me; an' w'en I don' know w'at way to turn no mo', he say no, it's a Meth'dis' archbishop, an' keep on laughin' 'bout me, an' I don' know w'at the truth!"

Then again, she told how Bud had induced her to mount the vicious little mustang "Buckeye," knowing that the little brute would n't carry a woman; and how it had amused him to witness her distress and terror when she was thrown to the ground.

"If I would know how to read an' write, an' had some pencil an' paper, it's long 'go I would wrote to my popa. But it's no pos'office, it's no relroad,— nothin' in Sabine. An' you know, Mista Grégoire, Bud say he's goin' carry me yonda to Vernon, an' fu'ther off yet,—'way yonda, an' he's goin' turn me loose. Oh, don' leave me yere, Mista Grégoire! don' leave me behine you!" she entreated, breaking once more into sobs.

"'Tite Reine," he answered, "do you think I'm such a low-down scound'el as to leave you yere with that"—He finished the sentence mentally, not wishing to offend the ears of 'Tite Reine.

They talked on a good while after that. She would not return to the room where her husband lay; the nearness of a friend had already emboldened her to inward revolt. Grégoire induced her to lie down and rest upon the quilt that she had given to him for a bed. She did so, and broken down by fatigue was soon fast asleep.

He stayed seated on the edge of the gallery and began to smoke cigarettes which he rolled himself of périque tobacco. He might have gone in and shared Bud Aiken's bed, but preferred to stay there near 'Tite Reine. He watched the two horses, tramping slowly about the lot, cropping the dewy wet tufts of grass.

Grégoire smoked on. He only stopped when the moon sank down behind the pine-trees, and the long deep shadow reached out and enveloped him. Then he could no longer see and follow the filmy smoke from his cigarette, and he threw it away. Sleep was pressing heavily upon him. He stretched himself full length upon the rough bare boards of the gallery and slept until day-break.

Bud Aiken's satisfaction was very genuine when he learned that Grégoire proposed spending the day and another night with him. He had already recognized in the young creole a spirit not altogether uncongenial to his own.

'Tite Reine cooked breakfast for them. She made coffee; of course there was no milk to add to it, but there was sugar. From a meal bag that stood in the corner of the room she took a measure of meal, and with it made a pone of corn bread. She fried slices of salt pork. Then Bud sent her into the field to pick cotton with old Uncle Mortimer. The negro's cabin was the counterpart of their own, but stood quite a distance away hidden in the woods. He and Aiken worked the crop on shares.

Early in the day Bud produced a grimy pack of cards from behind a parcel of sugar on the shelf. Grégoire threw the cards into the fire and replaced them with a spic and span new "deck" that he took from his saddlebags. He also brought forth from the same receptacle a bottle of whiskey, which he presented to his host, saying that he himself had no further use for it, as he had "sworn off" since day before yesterday, when he had made a fool of himself in Cloutierville.

They sat at the pine table smoking and playing cards all the morning, only desisting when 'Tite Reine came to serve them with the gumbo-filé that she had come out of the field to cook at noon. She could afford to treat a guest to chicken gumbo, for she owned a half dozen chickens that Uncle Mortimer had presented to her at various times. There were only two spoons, and 'Tite Reine had to wait till the men had finished before eating her soup. She waited for Grégoire's spoon, though her husband was the first to get through. It was a very childish whim.

In the afternoon she picked cotton again; and the men played cards, smoked, and Bud drank.

It was a very long time since Bud Aiken had enjoyed himself so well, and since he had encountered so sympathetic and appreciative a listener to the story of his eventful career. The story of 'Tite Reine's fall from the horse he told with much spirit, mimicking quite skillfully the way in which she had complained of never being permitted "to teck a li'le pleasure," whereupon he had kindly suggested horseback riding. Grégoire enjoyed the story amazingly, which encouraged Aiken to relate many more of a similar character. As the afternoon wore on, all formality of address between the two had disappeared: they were "Bud" and "Grégoire" to each other, and Grégoire had delighted Aiken's soul by promising to spend a week with him. 'Tite Reine was also touched by the spirit of recklessness in the air; it moved her to fry two chickens for supper. She fried them deliciously in bacon fat. After supper she again arranged Grégoire's bed out on the gallery.

The night fell calm and beautiful, with the delicious odor of the pines floating upon the air. But the three did not sit up to enjoy it. Before the stroke of nine, Aiken had already fallen upon his bed unconscious of everything about him in the heavy drunken sleep that would hold him fast through the night. It even clutched him more relentlessly than usual, thanks to Grégoire's free gift of whiskey.

The sun was high when he awoke. He lifted his voice and called imperiously for 'Tite Reine, wondering that the coffee-pot was not on the hearth, and marveling still more that he did not hear her voice in quick response with its, "I'm comin', Bud. Yere I come." He called again and again. Then he arose and looked out through the back door to see if she were picking cotton in the field, but she was not there. He dragged himself to the front entrance. Grégoire's bed was still on the gallery, but the young fellow was nowhere to be seen.

Uncle Mortimer had come into the yard, not to cut wood this time, but to pick up the axe which was his own property, and lift it to his shoulder.

"Mortimer," called out Aiken, "whur's my wife?" at the same time advancing toward the negro. Mortimer stood still, waiting for him. "Whur's my wife an' that Frenchman? Speak out, I say, before I send you to h—l."

Uncle Mortimer never had feared Bud Aiken; and with the trusty axe upon his shoulder, he felt a double hardihood in the man's presence. The old fellow passed the back of his black, knotty hand unctuously over his lips, as though he relished in advance the words that were about to pass them. He spoke carefully and deliberately:

"Miss Reine," he said, "I reckon she mus' of done struck Natchitoches pa'ish sometime to'ard de middle o' de night, on dat 'ar swif' hoss o' Mr. Sanchun's."

Aiken uttered a terrific oath. "Saddle up Buckeye," he yelled, "before I count twenty, or I'll rip the black hide off yer. Quick, thar! Thur ain't nothin' fourfooted top o' this earth that Buckeye can't run down." Uncle Mortimer scratched his head dubiously, as he answered:—

"Yas, Mas' Bud, but you see, Mr. Sanchun, he done cross de Sabine befo' sun-up on Buckeye."

Despite the immense achievements of the battered women's movement in the past fifteen years, those who work to stop violence against women —those who staff the hotlines and the shelters and the legal service centers, those who press to make law for legislative reform—know that the next time a woman is battered in the United States (which is to say within the next twelve seconds) few people will ask: What's wrong with that man? What makes him think he can get away with that? Is he crazy? Did the cops arrest him? Is he in jail? When will he be prosecuted? Is he likely to get a serious sentence? Is she getting adequate police protection? Are the children provided for? Did the court evict him from her house? Does she need any other help? Medical help maybe, or legal aid? New housing? Temporary financial aid? Child support?

No, the first question, and often the only question, that leaps to mind is: *Why doesn't she leave?*

— Ann Jones, *Next Time, She'll Be Dead*

Tony's Wife

ALICE DUNBAR-NELSON

"Gimme fi' cents worth o' candy, please." It was the little Jew girl who spoke, and Tony's wife roused herself from her knitting to rise and count out the multihued candy which should go in exchange for the dingy nickel grasped in warm, damp fingers. Three long sticks, carefully wrapped in crispest brown paper, and a half dozen or more of pink candy fish for lagniappe, and the little Jew girl sped away in blissful contentment. Tony's wife resumed her knitting with a stifled sigh until the next customer should come.

A low growl caused her to look up apprehensively. Tony himself stood beetle-browned and huge in the small doorway.

"Get up from there," he muttered, "and open two dozen oysters right away; the Eliots want 'em." His English was unaccented. It was long since he had seen Italy.

She moved meekly behind the counter, and began work on the thick shells. Tony stretched his long neck up the street.

"Mr. Tony, mama wants some charcoal." The very small voice at his feet must have pleased him, for his black brows relaxed into a smile, and he poked the little one's chin with a hard, dirty finger, as he emptied the ridiculously small bucket of charcoal into the child's bucket, and gave a banana for lagniappe.

49

The crackling of shells went on behind, and a stifled sob arose as a bit of sharp edge cut into the thin, worn fingers that clasped the knife.

"Hurry up there, will you?" growled the black brows; "the Eliots are sending for the oysters."

She deftly strained and counted them, and, after wiping her fingers, resumed her seat, and took up the endless crochet work, with her usual stifled sigh.

Tony and his wife had always been in this same little queer old shop on Prytania Street, at least to the memory of the oldest inhabitant in the neighbourhood. When or how they came, or how they stayed, no one knew; it was enough that they were there, like a sort of ancestral fixture to the street. The neighbourhood was fine enough to look down upon these two tumble-down shops at the corner, kept by Tony and Mrs. Murphy, the grocer. It was a semi-fashionable locality, far up-town, away from the old-time French quarter. It was the sort of neighbourhood where millionaires live before their fortunes are made and fashionable, high-priced private schools flourish, where the small cottages are occupied by aspiring school-teachers and choir-singers. Such was this locality, and you must admit that it was indeed a condescension to tolerate Tony and Mrs. Murphy.

He was a great, black-bearded, hoarse-voiced, six-foot specimen of Italian humanity, who looked in his little shop and on the prosaic pavement of Prytania Street somewhat as Hercules might seem in a modern drawing-room. You instinctively thought of wild mountain-passes, and the gleaming dirks of bandit contadini in looking at him. What his last name was, no one knew. Someone had maintained once that he had been christened Antonio Malatesta, but that was unauthentic, and as little to be believed as that other wild theory that her name was Mary.

She was meek, pale, little, ugly, and German. Altogether part of his arms and legs would have very decently made another larger than she. Her hair was pale and drawn in sleek, thin tightness away from a pinched, pitiful face, whose dull cold eyes hurt you, because you knew they were trying to mirror sorrow, and could not because of their expressionless quality. No matter what the weather or what her other toilet, she always wore a thin little shawl of dingy brick-dust hue about her shoulders. No matter what the occasion or what the day, she always carried her knitting with her, and seldom ceased the incessant twist, twist of the shining steel among the white cotton meshes. She might put down the needles and lace into the spool-box long enough to open oysters, or wrap up fruit and candy, or count out wood and coal into infinitesimal portions, or do her housework; but the knitting was snatched with avidity at the first spare moment, and the worn, white, blue-marked fingers, half enclosed in kid-glove stalls for protection, would writhe and twist in and out again. Little girls just learning to crochet borrowed their patterns from Tony's wife, and it was considered quite a mark of advancement to have her inspect a bit of lace done by eager, chubby fingers. The ladies in larger houses, whose husbands would be millionaires some day, bought her lace, and gave it to their servants for Christmas presents.

As for Tony, when she was slow in opening his oysters or in cooking his red beans and spaghetti, he roared at her, and prefixed picturesque adjectives to her lace, which made her hide it under her apron with a fearsome look in her dull eyes.

He hated her in a lusty, roaring fashion, as a healthy beefy boy hates a sick cat and torments it to madness. When she displeased him, he beat her, and knocked her frail form on the floor. The children could tell when this had happened. Her eyes would be red, and there would be blue marks on her face and neck. "Poor Mrs. Tony," they would say, and nestle close to her. Tony did not roar at her for petting them, perhaps, because they spent money on the multi-hued candy in glass jars on the shelves.

Her mother appeared upon the scene once, and stayed a short time; but Tony got drunk one day and beat her because she ate too much, and she disappeared soon after. Whence she came and where she departed, no one could tell, not even Mrs. Murphy, the Pauline Pry and Gazette of the block.

Tony had gout, and suffered for many days in roaring helplessness, the while his foot, bound and swathed in many folds of red flannel, lay on the chair before him. In proportion as his gout increased and he bawled from pure physical discomfort, she became light-hearted, and moved about the shop with real, brisk cheeriness. He could not hit her then without such pain that after one or two trials he gave up in disgust.

So the dull years had passed, and life had gone on pretty much the same for Tony and the German wife and the shop. The children came on Sunday evenings to buy the stick candy, and on week-days for coal and wood. The servants came to buy oysters for the larger houses, and to gossip over the counter about their employers. The little dry woman knitted, and the big man moved lazily in and out in his red flannel shirt, exchanged politics with the tailor next door through the window, or lounged into Mrs. Murphy's bar and drank fiercely. Some of the children grew up and moved away, and other little girls came to buy candy and eat pink lagniappe fishes, and the shop still thrived.

One day Tony was ill, more than the mummied foot of gout, or the wheeze of asthma; he must keep his bed and send for the doctor.

She clutched his arm when he came, and pulled him into the tiny room.

"Is it—is it anything much, doctor?" she gasped.

Æsculapius shook his head as wisely as the occasion would permit. She followed him out of the room into the shop.

"Do you—will he get well, doctor?"

Æsculapius buttoned up his frock coat, smoothed his shining hat, cleared his throat, then replied oracularly,

"Madam, he is completely burned out inside. Empty as a shell, madam, empty as a shell. He cannot live, for he has nothing to live on."

As the cobblestones rattled under the doctor's equipage rolling leisurely up Prytania Street, Tony's wife sat in her chair and laughed,—laughed with a hearty joyousness that lifted the film from the dull eyes and disclosed a sparkle beneath.

The drear days went by, and Tony lay like a veritable Samson shorn of his strength, for his voice was sunken to a hoarse, sibilant whisper, and his black eyes gazed fiercely from the shock of hair and beard about a white face. Life went on pretty much as before in the shop; the children paused to ask how Mr. Tony was, and even hushed the jingles on their bell hoops as they passed the door. Red-headed Jimmie, Mrs. Murphy's nephew, did the hard jobs, such as splitting wood and lifting coal from the bin; and in the intervals between tending the fallen giant and waiting on the customers, Tony's wife sat in her accustomed chair, knitting fiercely, with an inscrutable smile about her purple compressed mouth.

Then John came, introducing himself, serpent-wise, into the Eden of her bosom.

John was Tony's brother, huge and bluff too, but fair and blond, with the beauty of Northern Italy. With the same lack of race pride which Tony had displayed in selecting his German spouse, John had taken unto himself Betty, a daughter of Erin, aggressive, powerful, and cross-eyed. He turned up now, having heard of this illness, and assumed an air of remarkable authority at once.

A hunted look stole into the dull eyes, and after John had departed with blustering directions as to Tony's welfare, she crept to his bedside timidly.

"Tony," she said,—"Tony, you are very sick."

An inarticulate growl was the only response.

"Tony, you ought to see the priest; you mustn't go any longer without taking the sacrament."

The growl deepened into words.

"Don't want any priest; you're always after some snivelling old woman's fuss. You and Mrs. Murphy go on with your church; it won't make *you* any better."

She shivered under this parting shot, and crept back into the shop. Still the priest came the next day.

She followed him in to the bedside and knelt timidly.

"Tony," she whispered, "here's Father Leblanc."

Tony was too languid to curse out loud; he only expressed his hate in a toss of the black beard and shaggy mane.

"Tony," she said nervously, "won't you do it now? It won't take long, and it will be better for you when you go—Oh, Tony, don't—don't laugh. Please, Tony, here's the priest."

But the Titan roared aloud: "No; get out. Think I'm a-going to give you a chance to grab my money now? Let me die and go to hell in peace."

Father Leblanc knelt meekly and prayed, and the woman's weak pleadings continued,—

"Tony, I've been true and good and faithful to you. Don't die and leave me no better than before. Tony, I do want to be a good woman once, a real-for-true married woman. Tony, here's the priest; say yes." And she wrung her ringless hands.

"You want my money," said Tony, slowly, "and you sha'n't have it, not a cent; John shall have it."

Father Leblanc shrank away like a fading spectre. He came next day and next day, only to see re-enacted the same piteous scene,—the woman pleading to be made a wife ere death hushed Tony's blasphemies, the man chuckling in pain-racked glee at the prospect of her bereaved misery. Not all the prayers of Father Leblanc nor the wailings of Mrs. Murphy could alter the determination of the will beneath the shock of hair; he gloated in his physical weakness at the tenacious grasp on his mentality.

"Tony," she wailed on the last day, her voice rising to a shriek in its eagerness, "tell them I'm your wife; it'll be the same. Only say it, Tony, before you die!"

He raised his head, and turned stiff eyes and gibbering mouth on her; then, with one chill finger pointing at John, fell back dully and heavily.

They buried him with many honours by the Society of Italia's Sons. John took possession of the shop when they returned home, and found the money hidden in the chimney corner.

As for Tony's wife, since she was not his wife after all, they sent her forth in the world penniless, her worn fingers clutching her bundle of clothes in nervous agitation, as though they regretted the time lost from knitting.

When David came to The Women's Safe House with his mother and four siblings, he was sullen and withdrawn. He often acted out the abusive behavior of his father that he had witnessed at home. He cursed and threatened the staff, children, and other residents. He was disrespectful to his mother; he berated her and made threatening moves toward her several times.

He was only 8.

—Margaret Craven, fund-raising letter

The Quiet Woman

MARY HEATON VORSE

The dusk was wiping out the colors of the world, spreading over the tender greens and pale pinks an indefinite nameless color more beautiful than any we know. The apple-trees loomed up, great masses of bloom, and their sweetness drifted to Katherine mingled with the smell of young leaves' and spring,—it was as if all the souls of the myriad growing things had breathed themselves forth into the night.

The dusk deepened and then grew blonder; the moon was coming up. One could see again that the trees were green, one could see the small flowers in the lawn. The white trees cast deep shadows on the young grass. Everything was very still; Katherine thought that the beating of her own heart was too loud for the miracle of the night. Everything—the trees and sky and hills—gave her the sense that something wonderful was about to happen; surely they were only the setting for some greater miracle. Then there came over her an appalling sense of desolation. It was terrible that on this most lovely night she must be so alone; that there should be no kind hand anywhere to meet hers. Katherine's need of companionship grew more poignant; the beauty of the night weighed on her as too great a burden to be borne alone; but she listened in vain for the sound of a human voice mingled with the voices of the night. The neighboring houses turned blank, unlighted faces to her; Katherine was as solitary as if she had been adrift on some unknown sea.

Then, in the garden on the slope of the hill below a white shadow moved; it flitted about, unsubstantial, unreal, now stopping as if to look at the night, now moving on slowly, then lost to sight among the flower-laden shrubs. At last it stood out in a little open space, attentive, even reverent, in its attitude. Without realizing what she did, Katherine trailed through the wet grass toward the

54

motionless figure, her shawl hanging loose around her; it was as if one white spirit went forth to meet another like itself. She made her way through the loosely planted shrubbery which divided one garden from the other, and was near the other woman before she turned her head toward Katherine. She greeted Katherine quietly as if she had been waiting for her. They stood a moment in silence, then the woman said:

"I could not have stayed out here alone—" she stopped shyly and turned toward Katherine to see if she were understood, and Katherine wondered if here was some one as terribly alone as herself, as in need as she of sympathy. They looked at the night together, as silent as old friends who do not need to talk to one another; they did not know each other's names, and yet already they had ceased to be strangers; the fellowship of spring had brought them together.

A voice called from somewhere beyond a screen of white apple-trees, a man's voice, gay, mocking, jovial:

"Mother! mother! Where are you? Mother, you'll be *moonstruck.*"

The woman turned gravely to Katherine.

"My son is calling me," she told her. "Good-night, I am glad you came." Then she added wistfully, "This is the first time in many years that I have had a friend by me as I looked at the night."

With the sound of the man's voice and his gay, chaffing "Mother, you'll be *moonstruck,*" the mirage of the night had vanished; the frail, subtle tie that a moment before seemed to bind the two women into friendship had snapped. They hurried their several ways a little ashamed of themselves,—for what, they didn't know exactly.

Next morning, when Katherine came out, there was a woman working in the garden below. Katherine made no doubt that it was her friend of the moonlight and made her way towards her.

"I am your new neighbor, Katherine Paine," she said.

The older woman smiled at her, greeting her in silence; but it was a silence with a more enfolding welcome than any words Katherine had ever heard, and she knew that they had gone on with their friendship begun so oddly the night before, for all they ignored their first meeting as something too apart from the ordinary events of life to be discussed in broad daylight.

They walked several paces through the lovely garden before the older woman said, "I don't know whether you know my name or not—it's Eunice Gaunt." Her voice had none of the New England aggressiveness; it was indeed singularly sweet; it had a shy little note of hesitation very charming to listen to; and she chatted away about her garden as if to an old friend.

From the house there came the same jovial voice of the night before: "Mother, mother! Oh, there you are!" and a man swung down the path. He stared at Katherine in a way that was just short of disconcerting. It was almost as if he had said, "Yes, on the whole, I think you're a very pretty girl." He looked bold, stubborn, domineering; but one forgave him all that,—there was a large gayety about him that went to one's heart. As he put his hand on his mother's shoulder with an air of assured ownership, it flashed over Katherine that all the same this dark bold man was an odd sort of son for the delicate, sweet little lady to have mothered.

She was saying, "This is our new neighbor, Miss Paine—"

"Mr. Gaunt?" Katherine murmured in acknowledgment of his formal greeting.

"His name is Wetherill," Eunice Gaunt corrected tranquilly.

"Why in the world did you think my name was Gaunt?" he demanded. The stand-and-deliver tone of his question and the little lurking amusement in his voice embarrassed Katherine; before she could answer, his mother explained:

"I told her my name was Eunice Gaunt—and so of course—"

He burst out into loud, gay laughter. "Couldn't you," he asked, "for respectability's sake, add a 'Wetherill'?"

Mrs. Wetherill smiled gently at him. She seemed to have abstracted herself from the scene; it was as if she had actually walked away from them and left them together alone, as she replied,—

"I think of myself, I suppose, as 'Eunice Gaunt.' "

"She's only had forty years to get used to 'Wetherill,' Miss Paine." He turned a humorous eye on his mother, who kneeled down to examine a plant; she had ceased to have any connection with them.

"Well," said Wetherill, "I must go. I'm delighted to have met you, Miss Paine; it's nice you're our near neighbor,—I'm especially glad that you and my mother have made friends so soon. Good-by. Good-by 'Eunice Gaunt.' Please don't work too hard." He bent over her and drew her toward him. *"Promise* me you won't work too hard.—She does a man's work in this garden every day, Miss Paine.—You'll go in and lie down like a good girl.—Yes? and you'll call Ezra if you've anything heavy to lift.—Yes?" He kissed his mother, and with a pleasant nod to Katherine, was off.

"Come," Mrs. Wetherill said, "I want you to see my daffodil border under the hedge;" she took up the conversation where her son had broken it, quite as if he had not been there at all. "Do you mind my asking you," she continued, "what wind blew you here?"

"I always took care of my mother," Katherine answered; "she had been ailing for years. She died not long ago,—and I wanted a quiet place to rest."

Katherine had told the whole story of her uneventful life. It had left her at twenty-six with the eyes of a young girl.

For a moment Mrs. Wetherill looked at Katherine kindly; sweetly, as a sister might. Then, as if brooding over what she read in the girl's face, "How we eat up one another's lives!" she said.

Katherine had gone out that morning with an empty heart, and she came back with it filled. "Eunice Gaunt" had some way taken her in, opened the door of her heart to her; and Katherine wondered how she had passed by all the boundaries of reserve. She wondered again, as she had the night before, if her friend was perhaps as lonely as she; if, like herself, she needed so greatly the touch of a friendly hand; then she put that from her as absurd; there was a spiritual quality about the older woman, a sweet content that made the idea of her needing anything impossible, and companionship least of all.

Katherine had rented the house for the summer from an old friend of her mother's; so during the first few weeks of her stay a procession of ladies came to call, as they had evidently been asked to do by the owner of the house.

Mrs. Carling was the first to put the inevitable question, "How do you like Thornton?"

"Very much," Katherine answered, and added that she found her neighbor charming.

"Your neighbor?" Mrs. Carling wondered.

"Mrs. Wetherill," Katherine explained.

"Why, has *she* been up here?" asked the other.

"She 'runs in,' " said Katherine; "I think I 'ran in' first;" and Mrs. Carling gave forth an astonished.

"Well, well!" To Katherine's look of inquiry, she explained, "She's a very quiet woman and rarely goes anywhere, and when she does,—never a word out of her! Not a bit like her son. Henry's sociable enough."

She went away, leaving Katherine with the impression that Mrs. Wetherill's "running in" on her, which she had so taken as a matter of course, was for Mrs. Wetherill something very much out of the common. The other ladies of the village, as they called one after another, made this certain. The news of Mrs. Wetherill's neighborliness had gone forth,—had been discussed, it was evident; and Katherine became very well acquainted with two people whom she amused herself by calling Mrs. Wetherill and Eunice Gaunt. One she knew only by hearsay. She was a silent woman, but so kindly that in the hard little New England village she was well beloved. Though she was no recluse and attended club meeting, doing her share of work in the village, she seldom opened her lips; and as for strangers,—why, Mrs. Wetherill never went to see *them.* Of Mrs. Wetherill, Katherine was sure that she had never had so much as a glimpse; she couldn't in the least identify her with Eunice Gaunt. Eunice Gaunt for all her shy, hesitating manner had plenty to say—to Katherine any-way; companionship with her had a significance far beyond any companionship Katherine ever had. There was a certain freshness to all her words, as if her very silence had kept her mind young. Her thoughts came out clear and shining, minted quite fresh. How different the two, the Mrs. Wetherill of Thornton and her friend Eunice Gaunt were, Katherine could gauge by the curiosity their friendship excited. How alone Eunice Gaunt had been, she saw only too plainly by the subdued, almost tremulous eagerness with which she gave Katherine her friendship.

She couldn't help wondering why her friend was shut so closely in the house of herself,—Eunice Gaunt couldn't indeed have been more separated from the world around her had there been question of locks and keys.

"The house of herself," was Eunice Gaunt's own word.

"We all of us keep the real 'me' locked up in the house of ourself," she had said once to Katherine. "Sometimes it is self-consciousness that turns the key, and sometimes shyness, and more often circumstances." Then she added wistfully, "Some happy people come in and out at will." They walked side by side toward the little wood. Then Eunice Gaunt put her hand on the younger woman's with an indescribable gesture of tenderness. "You open the door for me, my dear," she said.

They stood face to face, silent in the contentment of perfect understanding, and Katherine went home, to wonder again why this loving, lovable woman should live so aloof from her fellows. How aloof this was, she found out the first time they went out together; it was a party at Mrs. Carling's, and not only, as Mrs. Carling said, was there "not a word out of Mrs. Wetherill," but no promise of words or anything else. A diffident, smiling little old lady was all she seemed, who, as Mrs. Carling had put it, "wouldn't say 'Boh' to a goose;" one would as soon have expected treasures of companionship and understanding from the tufted chair on which she was sitting. As they left the house Henry Wetherill joined them.

"Well, mother," he chaffed, "did you tell them how to raise strawberries as good as yours?"—and without waiting for an answer, "Mother, you know," he explained, "is forever telling people how to raise things like hers; but *I* always have thought she was like the housekeepers who leave out the important thing when they give away their receipts."

There was a little edge of patronizing sarcasm in his tone, a mere suggestion only, so imperceptible that Katherine thought she must be mistaken. Mrs. Wetherill hadn't noticed it. She smiled absently at her son, and absently she left on Katherine the burden of keeping up a conversation,—which she did not unwillingly. She liked Henry Wetherill, even if his abrupt way of asking questions disconcerted her to dumbness.

Mrs. Wetherill turned in at her own gate, saying good-by to Katherine with the same gentle formality she had shown in taking leave of the other ladies.

"I'll walk over with Miss Paine," Henry announced; and Mrs. Wetherill replied with a smiling, aloof, "Very well, dear," and "Good-by, Katherine."

Once at Katherine's gate, "I think I'll come up and sit on your piazza," he said,—"if you'll let me, I mean." He might have been asking permission smilingly of a child of twelve. He arranged himself comfortably in a big piazza chair, and from his attitude a passer-by would have gathered that he was a daily visitor, so much at home he seemed.

He stared at Katherine in his embarrassing way; and when she felt herself flushing and caught a twinkle of a smile in his eyes, she had an unreasoning impulse to run away and lock the door in the face of this man, who stared one into self-consciousness and then smiled tolerantly over one's confusion.

There was, however, no hint of the smile in his voice as he said, "You don't know how glad I am that you and mother are such friends. I'm like my father, —I hate a gadding, gossiping woman; but I think mother goes too far the other way."

Katherine warmed to him over his concern for his mother, and for a while they chatted together. To Katherine's shy invitation to come again,—"As often as you like," he answered warmly.

When he left, Katherine felt that her house was empty, his large radiant personality had so filled it. This was not to be the last she saw of him that day. Later, as she made her way through the shrubbery in search of his mother, she heard Wetherill's voice saying, "Why don't you put them where Mrs. Wetherill told you to?"

His voice was not raised beyond his usual tone, but it cut like a knife. One couldn't call it bullying; it was a finer and more wounding way of getting what one wanted. "Why"—he continued in exactly the same pitch—"don't you answer me?"

Katherine knew he could continue indefinitely on the same insulting key. Through the bushes she could see the old gardener grubbing away at a flower-bed, Wetherill standing over him. While the old man did not answer or pause in his work, every outline of his old, bent figure expressed indignant protest. Mrs. Wetherill stood a few paces distant, trowel in hand; she was gazing off at the distant horizon, calm-browed, apparently unconscious of everything around her.

"*Why* didn't you put them where you were told? You think you know everything about a garden,—but you're here, aren't you, to do what Mrs. Wetherill says?"

Katherine had gained the open lawn and was only a few steps away from her friends.

"Why—" Henry began again.

The old man jumped to his feet, his brown face red under the tan.

"I *be* doin' what she told me," he cried angrily. Then, appealing to Mrs. Wetherill, "Ain't I settin' them plants where you said?"

It seemed to Katherine that Mrs. Wetherill brought herself back as from a distance, and that it was an effort for her to realize what was going on.

"Why of course you are, Ezra," she answered, "why not?" She looked with surprise at the angry faces of the two men; then she saw Katherine. "Why, my dear child," she cried joyously, and stopped herself abruptly.

"Do you mind telling me," Henry asked his mother politely, "why in the world you let me sail into Ezra as I've been doing on your behalf, when after all he was doing what you said?"

She looked at him mildly. "I didn't hear what you were saying, Henry," she replied. Henry threw out his hands despairingly.

"Did you ever see such a pair, Miss Paine? I was perfectly sure Ezra was planting those roses where I heard mother tell him not to. I go for him loud enough to be heard across the street, and there she stands and, perfectly unruffled, lets me maul him. Actually she hasn't heard a word!"

He turned to his mother. "Where were you anyway? I never saw such an absent-minded woman! I talk and talk to her and I might as well be at the other side of a plate-glass window. Ezra, you old fool, why didn't you tell me sooner?"

Henry was entirely restored to good-humor now, and his question to Ezra was almost an apology; but the old man did not answer or take any notice of him beyond hunching an offish shoulder.

"Look at them, Miss Paine," Henry exclaimed. "They never speak! Sometimes I think I'll buy a parrot for company!" He had put a large arm around his mother's neck and lifted her face up toward him like a child's. "Why don't you listen when I talk to you?" he demanded with savage affection.

"You're so like your father, dear," she replied irrelevantly.

Henry Wetherill hastened to fulfill his promise of coming often to see Katherine. Indeed he formed a pleasant habit of "dropping in" for a few moments' chat, and while he was there he would not take his eyes from her. She resented this at first; in the end she liked it, in much the fearsome way she liked Henry Wetherill. She was filled with a sense of excitement when she was with him. Conversation with him was an adventure. She could never tell when he would swoop down on her and extinguish her. What he did to give her this impression she could not for the life of her have told; but with him she felt she had to fight for her life or cease to be; the irritating part of it was that he was largely and serenely unaware of the effect he produced, and it is a humiliating thing to be fighting for life with a force which doesn't even realize that there is a fight.

So, between her companionship with the mother and her friendship with the son,—for that, in spite of everything, was what it was coming to be,—Katherine found her life very full. She turned her face resolutely from that blank time when she would have to go away,—after her tenancy had finished there was really no good excuse to keep her in a snowbound New England village,—and when one day Henry Wetherill abruptly asked her what her plans for the winter were, she told him promptly,—

"Oh, I'll go South, I suppose."

At that moment Mrs. Carling came in, and when, in a few minutes, Henry Wetherill left. Mrs. Carling hardly waited for his broad shoulders to be turned before she raised significant eyebrows at Katherine, and followed it up with a surprised, "Well, you *have* done it—to be sure!"

"Done it!" Katherine wondered.

"Mother and son both! Well I declare," her visitor pursued with relish.

Evenly, but with inward annoyance, Katherine turned the subject. Mrs. Carling, however, had given her a clue to something that had mystified her. For the past few weeks Henry's mother, in some indescribable fashion, had seemed to slip away from her. There had been nothing one could put one's finger on; one could only say in the good old phrase that "things were different." There had been a mute appeal in her friend's eyes that Katherine now thought she understood.

"I must stop his coming here so much," Katherine decided; but in the bottom of her heart she knew how powerless she was to stop Henry Wetherill in anything that he wanted to do.

As he came up the path next day Katherine noticed that his brows were drawn in a sombre line. But as he saw her on the piazza waiting for him, he smiled at her brilliantly, and Katherine felt as if the sun had come out in the midst of a thunderstorm.

"Do you know," he began without preamble, his eyes looking directly into hers, "what I was thinking about when I came up the walk? I was wondering what would become of us all when you went. You don't know, I suppose, what you mean to me—I'm as lonely in a way as mother. Until you came I didn't know there was any other way to be—" He faltered a moment; and there was something very appealing in his hesitation: after all, he needed companionship and affection as do the weaker people of the world, and this touched Katherine to the quick. They stood facing each other, troubled and embarrassed, Katherine's heart beating fast. Now she knew: yesterday's absurdity had become the reality of to-day.

"You see how it is,—you can't go away; you mustn't. I've *got* to have you." Then, as Katherine would have spoken,—for it seemed to her that for all his tone of eager pleading she was being swept down the swift-flowing stream of his desire, and she wanted very much to tell him the truth, which was that she didn't love him in the very least,—he stopped her.

"I know what you want to say. You want to tell me you don't care for me. I know that. But you don't hate me—you like me even, and after we're married I'd be a poor sort of a fellow if I couldn't make you care."

He cared; that was the principal thing after all, his manner seemed to say.

"It's all so right, don't you see," he pleaded eagerly. "You so belong to us."

The "It's all so right" was what won her. What if she didn't love him? It *was* all so right. The "us" touched her too. His constant thought for his mother was one of the things that drew her most to him.

"How would your mother feel about it?" Katherine asked shyly.

His mother's attitude in the matter had evidently never occurred to him. He looked at her blankly. "Why shouldn't she like it?" he demanded with a touch of anger. It was as if he had said, "Let her not like it and she'll see what she'll get;" and the little vague terror that he had given her from the first came over her; but it vanished as he laughed his loud boyish laugh.

"What an idea!" he shouted; "why, I can't remember mother's not liking anything I've done since I was grown up. She likes *everything* I do," he repeated with serene assurance. "What made you think she wouldn't like it,— my marrying you?" he persisted.

"Why, it's seemed to me that the more I saw of you the less I saw of her; the better I got to know you the more she withdrew herself," Katherine faltered.

He looked at her, a tender glow in his eyes. "Don't worry about that," he assured her lightly. "Mother's only part there most of the time; she's the most absent-minded woman in the world—always in the clouds."

And Katherine forbore telling him how much "Eunice Gaunt" was "there" when her son wasn't. He evidently was not aware of her curious smiling aloofness. Katherine longed to ask him if he never got behind it, never saw the other side; but she only insisted, "I don't think she'll like it."

"What a funny girl you are," he said, smiling. "We'll find mother and ask her, and then—"

"And then," Katherine interrupted, "if she doesn't like it—I love her so dearly I couldn't for the world—"

"You'll see," Henry Wetherill repeated. There was not a shadow of doubt in him; if there was anything he was sure of, it was his mother.

They found Mrs. Wetherill in the garden. "Mother," he called to her joy-ously, "this foolish girl thinks you wouldn't like me to marry her." His tone was gay, happy, assured. There was a certain finality in it also, as if she already belonged to him, as he added, "Tell her you think she'll be a good wife to me."

For a fraction of a second, Mrs. Wetherill stared at them wide-eyed. Then, "She would make the best wife in the world for any one," she cried warmly, and kissed Katherine.

"You see," Henry triumphed, and Katherine wondered if he actually had not noticed that his mother had turned white at his words; if he could not see how her hands trembled as she smiled her little vague smile at him.

"I'll leave you to talk things over," he told them. Mrs. Wetherill stood watching him until he disappeared beyond the tawny lilies into the house.

"Now tell me the truth," Katherine said gently, taking both her friend's hands in her own.

Mrs. Wetherill raised her troubled, sombre face to hers; her mouth quivered pitifully; slow tears gathered in her eyes.

"You don't need to say anything," Katherine went on still more tenderly, "I can understand. He's your only son—"

But as Henry Wetherill's mother whispered under her breath, "Oh, I can't live it all over again," Katherine understood that here was more than a mother who finds it hard to give up her dear son.

"You're so near me," Mrs. Wetherill went on, so low that it was as if she were afraid to hear her own words, "that I can't let you suffer what you would have to. You're so near me that you seem to me like my own child—"

In this moment they passed beyond the door of friendship. They stood for the moment closer than it is often possible for one human being to come to another. They were at the very threshold of Eunice Gaunt's hidden life. For Katherine's sake she had opened a door that such women keep closed even against themselves.

"I hoped," she went on, "that you would see for yourself,—you see so many things other people don't—"

"You don't think I'd be happy with Henry," Katherine suggested gently. She was beginning to read the riddle of her friend's life,—her curious relation with her son; her attitude toward the world began to have a new meaning.

"Men like Henry don't know how they hurt women like us," Henry's mother said gently. It was an apology, not an accusation. "Henry's like his father," she went on in the same gentle tone. "All the Wetherill men are alike. They crush the weaker people around them out of existence; they don't mean to,—they don't even know they do it." While she told what her son was, she had to cry out in the same breath, "It's not his fault." With a gesture of unfathomable motherliness, as if Katherine were really her daughter, she put her hand on the girl's head and gazed long into her eyes.

"My dear," she asked, "do you *love* Henry? Your face is the face of a little girl, as it was when I first saw you"—

"He said," Katherine faltered, "that it didn't matter,—that he would make me like him."

"Poor Henry," said his mother; "if you had loved him—there wouldn't have been anything to say. I should have lived over through you all that has been hard in my life. It would have been like having my own at war with my own. I should have had to know that no day of yours went by without its humiliation, without its bruise. I should have known that it was my son's fault.

He couldn't help doing it,—and you couldn't help him. You would try and try, and then you would see that neither patience nor submission nor love could change him."

All the things Katherine had failed to understand fitted in together like parts of a puzzle. Now she knew why her friend was as she was. Henry's father and Henry had shut her into the "house of herself" with their noisy wounding anger, with their wounding laughter. She had a sharp vision of Henry's bullying tenderness, of his mocking laugh, of the glimpse she had had of his insatiable irritation; and a fear of him came over her, the fear of the weaker animal for the stronger. She meditated over what she saw, and Eunice brooded over her own past; at last she cried out,—it was her only moment of bitterness,—

"They are the men with no woman in them. They are the ones who first created our meannesses and weaknesses and then laughed and scolded and sneered at us for being as they make us." Her voice softened. "They can't help themselves for their unconscious abuse of power," she said.

This was her final judgment of the two men who had made up her life—her husband and her son. It was her only revolt, her only outward sign of discontent. Now she stood upright, as immovable as a figure of justice, and in her Katherine saw more than a woman telling the long tragedy of her life. It was as if through the voice of her friend she heard the immemorial cry of all the weaker creatures who have suffered through the strong. Without passion or anger she put in words woman's world-old quarrel with man. Bits of it would come to Katherine long afterwards.

"They are the sort of men who make cowards and liars of women," was one.

"I understood the meannesses of women when I had been married a few years."

"Often I have seen on a woman's face a look of anger or fear or cunning, and I knew that here was another of me. There are more of us than you think, and we use in self-defense guile, or flattery, or affection, or submission, according to our natures."

"There are few women who haven't been sneered at and reproached for being women."

She told her story, a few sentences at a time; and unconsciously she showed Katherine her final victory, her acceptance of life as it was, the conquest of her own inward peace. She told how she had borne their unconscious brutality, first with tears, then with smiling aloofness; her road to escape had been a withdrawal from them and from every one, for she had left no point where they could hurt her.

"How did you bear it all?" Katherine asked at last.

Her friend looked at her in gentle surprise. "I loved both of them dearly always," she said. "And I knew they loved me even more dearly. Love goes deeper than understanding. We've lived our lives, Henry and Henry's father and I, talking different languages; but I have always been upheld by their love for me and, curiously enough, by their dependence on me. If you—had cared—" she did not finish, but smiled at Katherine, all tenderness in her eyes. Then Katherine knew that the secret of her inner content was more than self-mastery; she had always had them, whatever else had been lacking; mysteriously they had made up to her for all the pain they had all unconsciously given her.

She had no time to answer, for Henry was bearing down on them, gay and confident. At the two women's serious aspect, "Well?" he asked, raising his eye-brows in question.

"I have been telling Katherine not to marry you," his mother said steadily.

He stared aghast. "You have been telling her *what?*" he repeated; his tone was low, there was in every word the concentration of anger. "What does she mean?" he demanded of Katherine. "Answer me."

"There's no use asking her," Mrs. Wetherill told him simply. "I'm sorry, Henry, I had to do it. You could never have made Katherine happy."

She had told him everything he could understand.

"Let her speak for herself," Wetherill commanded sternly. "Katherine, will you marry me?" The entreaty in his voice, his anger, his very lack of under-standing, went to Katherine's heart. She was nearer loving him that moment than she had ever been. Had they been alone she realized that she must have promised whatever he wished,—and then run away. With her friend's pro-tecting arm around her she managed to falter forth,

"No, oh no!"

He turned on his mother.

"You've made mischief between us!" Anger vibrated in his low voice. "You've dared, *you, you,* to judge whether I could make her happy! *You* know whether this means anything to me! *You* know whether I've ever cared for any one else.—The first woman I care for—Oh!"—he was white with the rage and despair of it. The creature on earth he loved most had turned on him, treacher-ously. His world had gone to pieces under his feet, and he raged at it. It was the man's side of·it, old as time; and like the first man betrayed by his faithful servant, he raged against the faithlessness of women.

There was nothing mean in his anger; it didn't occur to him to try and control it because of Katherine; such as he was he showed himself. He resorted to no trick of gentleness to win her. Like his kind he had got everything through the brute force of his will, as his ancestors had got everything by might of arm. If all the protest of women from all time against the unconscious abuse of power had been his mother's story, all man's rancor against woman was in his denunciation. As his anger spent itself, he stood before the two women in very despair at his impotence. He didn't understand them; he didn't understand anything. There was not one of the many questions he put himself that he could answer. His own had turned on him. Why? He couldn't tell. The woman he loved had all but given herself to him, and then turned from him. Why? He didn't know. All he knew was the common knowledge of the men of his kind, that women were the enemies of men, creatures one couldn't understand, moved by irrational impulse, untrustworthy and fickle. And as his mother watched him she understood, she trembled for him in a very anguish of pity.

He stood before them, a tragic, lonely figure, suffering as a child suffers without knowing why; then he turned from them abruptly and left them. Katherine threw her arms around her friend.

"You shan't stand it," she cried. "Come away with me. You mustn't live with him any longer."

But Eunice Gaunt did not hear her. She watched Henry out of sight while slow tears gathered in her eyes. She breathed so low that Katherine barely heard her,—

"Oh, my poor son!" and again "My poor son!" and then,—"Oh, how could I hurt you so much?"

Why would a man use the person he loves as a punching bag? . . . Most people would say men shouldn't hit the women they love (or anyone else that they care for or who is smaller and weaker than themselves). But we've seen that historically this idea exists side by side with the traditional assumption that men should be able to control their wives by whatever means necessary. Traditional ideas die hard.

—Ginny NiCarthy, *Getting Free*

The Gold Vanity Set

MARÍA CRISTINA MENA

When Petra was too big to be carried on her mother's back she was put on the ground, and soon taught herself to walk. In time she learned to fetch water from the public fountain and to grind the boiled corn for the tortillas which her mother made every day, and later to carry her father his dinner—a task which required great intelligence, for her father was a donkey-driver and one never knew at what corner he might be lolling in the shade while awaiting a whistle from someone who might require a service of himself and his little animal.

She grew tall and slender, as strong as wire, with a small head and extremely delicate features, and her skin was the color of new leather. Her eyes were wonderful, even in a land of wonderful eyes. They were large and mysterious, heavily shaded with lashes which had a trick of quivering nervously, half lowered in an evasive, fixed, sidelong look when anyone spoke to her. The irises were amber-colored, but always looked darker. Her voice was like a ghost, distant, dying away at the ends of sentences as if in fear, yet with all its tenderness holding a hint of barbaric roughness. The dissimulation lurking in that low voice and those melting eyes was characteristic of a race among whom the frankness of the Spaniard is criticized as unpolished.

At the age of fourteen Petra married, and married well. Her bridegroom was no barefooted donkey-driver in white trousers and shirt, with riata coiled over his shoulder. No, indeed! Manuelo wore shoes—dazzling yellow shoes which creaked—and colored clothes, and he had a profession, most adorable of professions, playing the miniature guitar made by the Mexican Indians, and singing lively and tender airs in drinkshops and public places wherever a few coins were to be gathered by a handsome fellow with music in his fingers. Most Mexicans, to be sure, have music in their fingers, but Manuelo was enabled to follow the career artistic by the good fortune of his father's being the owner of a prosperous inn for peons.

Petra's attractions made her useful to her father-in-law, who was a widower. At the sight of her coming in from the well, as straight as a palm, carrying a large earthen pot of water on her head, the peons who were killing time there would suddenly find themselves hungry or thirsty and would call for pulque or something to eat. And so she began to wait on customers, and soon she would awake in the morning with no other thought than to twist her long, black hair into a pair of braids which, interwoven with narrow green ribbons, looked like children's toy whips, then to take her husband his *aguadiente,* the little jug of brandy that begins the day, and then to seat herself at the door of the inn, watching for customers beneath trembling lashes, while bending over the coarse cloth whose threads she was drawing.

In six months she had formed the habit of all that surrounded her life. The oaths no longer sounded so disagreeable to her, the occasional fights so terrifying. Manuelo might lose his temper and strike her, but a few minutes later he would be dancing with her. Her last memory going to sleep was sometimes a blow, "Because he is my husband," as she explained it to herself, and sometimes a kiss, "Because he loves me." Only one thing disturbed her: she did not like to see her handsome Manuelo made inflamed and foolish by the milk-white pulque, and she burned many candles to the Virgin of Guadalupe that she might be granted the "beneficio" of a more frequently sober husband.

One afternoon the pueblo resounded with foreign phrases and foreign laughter in foreign voices. As a flock of birds the visitors kept together, and as a flock of birds appeared their chatter and their vivacity to the astonished inhabitants. American fashion, they were led by a woman. She was young, decisive, and carried a camera and guide book. Catching sight of Petra at the door she exclaimed:

"Oh, what a beautiful girl! I must get her picture."

But when Petra saw the little black instrument pointing at her she started like a frightened rabbit and ran inside. The American girl uttered a cry of chargrin, at which Don Ramon came forward. Don Ramon, the planter, had undertaken to escort these, his guests, through the pueblo, but had found himself patiently bringing up the rear of the procession.

"These are tenants of mine," he said with an indifferent gesture. "The house is yours, Miss Young."

"Girls, do you hear that?" she cried. "This is my house—and I invite you all in."

Immediately the inn was invaded, the men following the women. Manuelo, his father, and the peons in the place formed two welcoming ranks, and the Patrón's entrance was hailed with a respectful:

"Viva Don Ramon!"

Manuelo's father looked a little resentful at these inquisitive strangers occupying the benches of his regular customers, who obsequiously folded up their limbs on straw mats along the walls. To be sure, much silver would accrue to the establishment from the invasion, but business in the Mexican mind is dominated by sentiment.

Don Ramon, reading his mind, tapped him on the shoulder with a sharp:

"Quick, to serve the señores!"

Then he clapped his hands for Petra, who came in from the back with oblique looks, and soon the guests were taking experimental sips of strange liquors, especially aguamiel, the sweet unfermented juice of the maguey plant. Manuelo tuned up his instrument and launched into an elaborate and apparently endless improvisation in honor of the Patrón, standing on one foot with the other toe poised, and swaying his body quite alarmingly—for he had drunk much pulque that day. As for Petra, she was followed by the admiring looks of women and men as she moved back and forth, her naked feet plashing softly on the red brick floor.

"I positively must have her picture!" exclaimed Miss Young.

"Of course—at your disposition," murmured Don Ramon.

But the matter was not so simple. Petra rebelled—rebelled with the dumb obstinacy of the Indian, even to weeping and sitting on the floor. Manuelo, scandalized at such contumacy before the Patrón, pulled her to her feet and gave her a push which sent her against the wall. A shiver and murmur passed through the American ranks, and Don Ramon addressed to the young peon a vibrant speech in which the words *"bruto"* and *"imbécil"* were refreshingly distinguishable. Miss Young, closing her camera with a snap, gave her companions the signal for departure, and they obeyed her as always. Don Ramon gave the innkeeper a careless handful of coins and followed his guests, while the innkeeper and his customers ceremoniously pursued him for some distance down the street, with repeated bows and voluble *"Gracias"* and *"Bendiciónes"* over the Patrón, his wife, his children, his house, his crops and all his goods. But Manuelo threw himself upon a mat and fell asleep.

Miss Young had left her guide book on the table, and Petra pounced upon it as a kitten upon a leaf. Some object in the midst of its pages held it partly open. It was a beautiful thing of gold, a trinity of delicate caskets depending by chains from a ring of a size of one's finger. With one quick glance at the unconscious Manuelo she stuck it into the green sash that tightly encompassed her little waist. The book, in which she had lost interest, she put in a drawer of the table. Then she ran outside and climbed the ladder by which one reached the flat stone roof.

Wiping the palms of her hands on her skirt, she extracted the treasure. Of the three pendants she examined the largest first. It opened and a mirror shone softly from its golden nest. A mirror! Novelty of novelties to Petra! Two things startled her—the largeness of her eyes, the paleness of her cheeks. She had always imagined that she had red cheeks, like the girls in Manuelo's songs, some of whom even had cheeks like poppies. Feeling saddened, she opened one of the smaller caskets. It contained a little powder of ivory tint and a puff which delighted her with its unheard-of delicacy. She caressed the back of her hand with it, perceived an esthetic improvement, and ended by carefully powdering the backs of both hands, even to the finger nails.

And the the third box. A red paste. It reddened the tip of her nose when she sniffed its delicate perfume. She rubbed the spot off with her finger and transferred it to one cheek, then roughed a large patch on that cheek, then one on the other, with a nice discretion partly influenced by her memory of the brilliant cheeks of the American señorita of the brave looks, the black box, and the golden treasure.

Thus did Petra discover the secret of the vanity set. But her concept of it was not simple, like Miss Young's. Its practical idea became a mere nucleus in her mind for a fantasy dimly symbolic and religious.

Her eyes—how much larger they were, and how much brighter! She looked into them, laughed into them, broke off to leap and dance, looked again in many ways, side-long, droopingly, coquettishly, as she would look at Manuelo. Truly the gold treasure was blessed and the red paste was as holy as its smell, which reminded her of church.

Where should she hide it, the treasure? She would bury it in the earth. But no; Manuelo had the habit of burying things—foolish, Indian things—and in his digging he might find her talisman. Better to leave it on the roof. And she did, wrapped in a dry corn husk, covered with a stone.

The afternoon was falling when she went down from the roof. Manuelo slept noisily on the same mat, his father peacefully on an adjacent one. Wild to be looked at, Petra lifted her husband's arm by the sleeve and shook it, but he jerked it free with childish petulance and cuddled into a deeper sleep. She laughed and, inspired with a thought of further embellishment, ran out of the house, too excited even to notice the distant approach of a storm, which at any other time would have kept her indoors praying her rosary. When she returned she was crowned with yellow jonquils, their stems wet from the brook, and in her hand was a long stalk of spikenard with which to awaken Manuelo. But first she would make light, for it was already dusk in the inn. So she lit the antique iron lanterns which hung by chains from wooden arms at the front and back doors, and two candles, one of which she placed on a window ledge and the other on the floor near Manuelo's face, and she squatted in front of the second one and held the spikenard beneath his nose, mystically tracing with it in the air the sign of the cross, until its intoxicating incense pierced his consciousness and he opened his eyes.

He blinked at the light, then blindly caught her hand and smiled with a flash of white teeth as he inhaled luxuriously with the flower against his nostrils. Then, as he was thirsty, she fetched him a jug of water, and at last he saw the jonquil wreath, and the eyes beneath them, and those cheeks of flame.

He did not speak, but looked at her for a moment, and then, with the abrupt and graceful movement that she knew so well slung forward his guitar—it never left his shoulder by day—and the words he sang to her in passionate Spanish softened by Indian melancholy were these:

> "Whether thou lovest me I know not;
> Thou knowest it.
> I only know that I die
> Where thou art not."

He had not sung her that since the nights of his serenades outside her father's adobe hut, and even then his tones had not pulsed with the magic tenderness that was in them now as he stared at her in the candle light. She crept along the floor to him and he caught her under his arm, pulling his poncho over her head, and cuddled her to him with protecting caresses which she received with the trembling joy of a spaniel too seldom petted. They were startled by a voice exclaiming:

"That our sainted Mother of Guadalupe might permit that you should always be like this, my children!"

It was the old man, whom the music had awakened. Manuelo quickly kissed the medal that hung at his waist, stamped with the image of the patron saint of Mexico. No other saint so intimately rules the hearts and lives of a people nor rewards their love with so many miracles and apparitions, and the falling of her name at that instant of love tinged with a half-felt remorse, produced a powerful effect upon the young husband. He scrambled to his feet, lifting Petra with him, and cried:

"Yes, yes, yes, my father, that the blessed Mother of our Country may hear thee!"

As he looked upward, a murmur of thunder made them all jump. They crossed themselves, and their voices mingled in a tremulous chorus of fear and piety. Manuelo, pale as a ghost, seized Petra's hand and led her with bended body before the old man.

"Thy benediction—give us thy benediction, Father mine, while I make a vow." He shook with sobs as he and the girl knelt beneath the father's benediction, and a louder rumble sounded in the sky. "I promise our blessed Mother, the Virgin of Guadalupe, that I will never again maltreat my Petrita, and if I keep not this promise may she send a thunder to fall on me!"

Petra uttered a wail of terror, and just then a withering light flashed on the world and a deafening blast of thunder shook the building and sent the three on their faces, where they remained in an ecstasy of devotion until long after the storm god had rolled the last of his chariots across the reverberating platform of the sky.

And it was by the miracle of Manuelo's vow and its answer from the heavens that Petra's mind grasped the unalterable faith that the golden treasure was a blessed thing, most pleasing to the Mother of Guadalupe.

Next morning the planter was driving his guests through the pueblo, and they were talking of many things, including the loss of Miss Young's vanity set, when they saw Petra coming toward them in the direction of her home, her great eyes looking out like an Egyptian's from between the folds of her scarf. The joy of her heart shone in her face and her native shyness almost vanished as she pulled the scarf down from her chin to give them her graceful *"Buenos dias!"* which they acknowledged with smiles. And Petra ran on singing like a bird—singing of the exceeding richness of American señoritas who can lose golden treasures of miracle-producing potency and still smile.

"One thing I'm convinced of," said Miss Young to the planter as they drove on. "That girl hasn't got my vanity set. She looked me straight in the face."

"You don't know my people, Miss Young," returned the Patrón with a heavy sigh—he was anguished because of his guest's loss. "The girl has an innocent heart—yes; but that proves nothing. These are children of the youth of the world, before the limits of 'mine' and 'thine' had been fixed. When an Indito finds lost treasure he believes that he receives a gift from God."

"It's a mighty comfortable belief, and not confined to Mexico," declared the American. "Well, if those cheeks of hers weren't their own natural color this morning, I must say that her complexion makes a stunning blend with my rouge."

Don Ramon trembled at her frankness. Not for worlds would he have smiled, or mentioned her vanity set by name. "How original!" he reflected, epitomizing the thought of all his people when they meet the people of the North.

"But why not have put the question to her right straight out?" pursued Miss Young.

"It was wiser to put her off her guard," he replied. "If these people have your—your ornament, it is probably buried in the earth. Now it is likely to be brought to light, and when I got to the inn—"

"You will take me with you?"

"I beg you not to trouble yourself. It may be painful. I—"

But she insisted, and when dinner was over at the hacienda, Don Ramon

sacrificed his siesta to drive with her to Petra's home. Taking a leaf from
Mexican tactics, Miss Young allowed the Patrón to precede her, and received
with dignified apathy the greetings of the natives who, like marionettes pulled
by one string, scrambled into rank as a reception committee. Don Ramon
ushered her through the house to the courtyard and seated her there, assigning
Petra to defend her from mosquitos with feather fan. That was part of his plan.
With Inditos one must employ maneuvers. Reëntering the inn, he caused it to
be cleared of strangers. The innkeeper and his son, questioned concerning the
missing gold, professed profoundest surprise and ignorance. Without ceremony
the Patrón searched them. Feeling a foreign object beneath Manuelo's sash he
drew forth Miss Young's guide book, which Manuelo had found in the drawer
—a thing of no apparent utility, but a treasure of a sort, possibly of occult
virtue.

This discovery, while unexpected, fell in with the Patrón's plan, which was
to stir Petra's fears through her husband—his instinct telling him that she was
the key to the problem. And Petra's feather fan fluttered to the earth when she
heard the Patrón's stern voice raised in the ringing command to accompany
him to the prefecture.

In a flash she was inside, crying in Manuelo's arms. Her Manuelo—to be
led as a sacrifice into the ominous precincts of justice, there to be interrogated
amid terrors unknown! No, no!

"No, no, Don Ramon! My Manuelo did not find the gold! It was I—I found
it!"

She sobbed, almost choking with grief. The Patrón allowed a few minutes
for her emotion to spend itself before commanding her to restore to the American señorita her property. With a piteous look she shook her head. *Caramba!*
What did she mean? Her answer was a fresh outbrust, so violent, protracted
and crescendo that Miss Young, disturbed by visions of medieval torture, ran
in to protest against further inhumanity in her name. And Petra groveled at the
American's feet, wetting the bricks with her tears for a long time. At last a
resolve came to her and with face swollen but calm she picked herself up,
turned to Manuelo and his father and motioned them toward the courtyard.

When they had gone out she shut the door. Then with bent head, speaking
to the Patrón but looking beneath fluttering eyelids at a button on Miss Young's
duster, she told the story of the miracle—of how the golden treasure had
yielded that which had made her lovely in the eyes of her beloved, of how the
blessed Virgin of Guadulupe had inspired him to vow that he would never
again maltreat her as yesterday he had before the eyes of the Americanos, of
how the saint had acknowledged his vow with much thunder, as the señorita
must have heard for herself, and of how Manuelo was so impressed with the
peril of breaking a vow thus formidably recognized that he had drunk no pulque

that day and had resolved earnestly to become temperate in his use of that beverage for the rest of his life.

All of which Don Ramon translated to Miss Young, who looked puzzled and remarked:

"Well, I just love the temperance cause, but does she want to keep my danglums to make sure of this Manuelo staying on the water wagon?"

"Certainly not!" declared the Patrón, and turned to Petra abruptly demanded the production of the gold.

She turned pale—so pale that the rouge stood out in islands streaked with rivercourses of tears, and Miss Young looked away with a shuddering prayer that she herself might never turn pale except in the privacy of her chamber. And now Petra spoke. The gold was not in the house. She would conduct the Patrón and the señorita to where it was.

So it was that a pilgrimage in quest of the vanity set sallied forth, Petra leading the way on the back of the burro, the surrey following slowly with Miss Young and her escort. Manuelo and his guitar formed a distant and inquisitive rearguard. It passed, the pilgrimage, into the populous heart of the pueblo.

"Have you any idea where we're going?" inquired Miss Young.

"No," returned the planter. "The ways of the Indito are past conjecture, except that he is always governed by emotion."

He was nervous, sensitively anxious about the impressions of his guest from the North.

"You may observe that we always speak of them as *Inditos,* never as Indios," he said. "We use the diminutive because we love them. They are our blood. With their passion, their melancholy, their music and their superstitution they have passed without transition from the feudalism of the Aztecs into the world of to-day, which ignores them; but we never forget that it was their valor and love of country which won our independence."

"They certainly are picturesque," pronounced Miss Young judicially, "and it's great fun to run into the twelfth or some other old century one day out from Austin."

Petra halted at the dark, ancient front of the Chapel of the Virgin of Guadalupe, where was inscribed in choice Spanish the history of how the saint had made an apparition to her people stamped upon a cactus plant, together with other miraculous matters. Dismounting from the burro the girl passed among the beggars and sellers of "miracles" and entered the church, uncovering her head. Don Ramon and Miss Young followed her. She knelt before a shrine at which stood the benignant figure of the national saint, almost hidden by the girls of the faithful—"miracles" of silver, of wax, of feather, of silk—and among these, its opened mirror reflecting the blaze of innumerable candles, the gold vanity set shone at her breast, most splendid of her ornaments. The gold vanity set, imposing respect, asking for prayers, testifying the gratitude of an Indian girl for the kindness of her beloved.

Don Ramon fell on his knees. Miss Young, unused to the observances of such a place, bowed her head and choked a little, fumbling for her handkerchief.

"Well, if it saves that nice girl from ever getting another beating, the saint is perfectly welcome to my vanity set," she assured herself as she left the chapel. And Manuelo, leaning against the burro, perceiving by her expression that all was well, cuddled his guitar and sang:

> "Into the sea, because it is deep
> I always throw
> The sorrows that this life
> So often gives me."

whatever any of us chooses to feel, think, or do about women fighting abusive men, women continue to fight. increasingly. the question then is not, *should this happen?*—it is happening. the question is, *how do I choose to relate to this fact of women's resistance?*

—Melanie Kaye, *"Scrambled Eggs 3"*

A Jury of Her Peers

SUSAN GLASPELL

When Martha Hale opened the storm-door and got a cut of the north wind, she ran back for her big woolen scarf. As she hurriedly wound that round her head her eye made a scandalized sweep of her kitchen. It was no ordinary thing that called her away—it was probably further from ordinary than anything that had ever happened in Dickson County. But what her eye took in was that her kitchen was in no shape for leaving: her bread all ready for mixing, half the flour sifted and half unsifted.

She hated to see things half done; but she had been at that when the team from town stopped to get Mr. Hale, and then the sheriff came running in to say his wife wished Mrs. Hale would come too—adding, with a grin, that he guessed she was getting scary and wanted another woman along. So she had dropped everything right where it was.

"Martha!" now came her husband's impatient voice. "Don't keep folks waiting out here in the cold."

She again opened the storm-door, and this time joined the three men and the one woman waiting for her in the big two-seated buggy.

After she had the robes tucked around her she took another look at the woman who sat beside her on the back seat. She had met Mrs. Peters the year before at the county fair, and the thing she remembered about her was that she didn't seem like a sheriff's wife. She was small and thin and didn't have a strong voice. Mrs. Gorman, sheriff's wife before Gorman went out and Peters came in, had a voice that somehow seemed to be backing up the law with every word. But if Mrs. Peters didn't look like a sheriff's wife, Peters made it up in looking like a sheriff. He was to a dot the kind of man who could get himself elected sheriff—a heavy man with a big voice, who was particularly genial with the law-abiding, as if to make it plain that he knew the difference between criminals and non-criminals. And right there it came into Mrs. Hale's mind, with a rub, that this man who was so pleasant and lively with all of them was going to the Wrights' now as a sheriff.

"The country's not very pleasant this time of year," Mrs. Peters at last ventured, as if she felt they ought to be talking as well as the men.

Mrs. Hale scarcely finished her reply, for they had gone up a little hill and could see the Wright place now, and seeing it did not make her feel like talking. It looked very lonesome this cold March morning. It had always been a lonesome-looking place. It was down in a hollow, and the poplar trees around it were lonesome-looking trees. The men were looking at it and talking about what had happened. The county attorney was bending to one side of the buggy, and kept looking steadily at the place as they drew up to it.

"I'm glad you came with me," Mrs. Peters said nervously, as the two women were about to follow the men in through the kitchen door.

Even after she had her foot on the door-step, her hand on the knob, Martha Hale had a moment of feeling she could not cross that threshold. And the reason it seemed she couldn't cross it now was simply because she hadn't crossed it before. Time and time again it had been in her mind, "I ought to go over and see Minnie Foster"—she still thought of her as Minnie Foster, though for twenty years she had been Mrs. Wright. And then there was always something to do and Minnie Foster would go from her mind. But *now* she could come.

The men went over to the stove. The women stood close together by the door. Young Henderson, the county attorney, turned around and said, "Come up to the fire, ladies."

Mrs. Peters took a step forward, then stopped. "I'm not—cold," she said.

And so the two women stood by the door, at first not even so much as looking around the kitchen.

The men talked for a minute about what a good thing it was the sheriff had sent his deputy out that morning to make a fire for them, and then Sheriff Peters stepped back from the stove, unbuttoned his outer coat, and leaned his hands on the kitchen table in a way that seemed to mark the beginning of official business. "Now, Mr. Hale," he said in a sort of semi-official voice, "before we move things about, you tell Mr. Henderson just what it was you saw when you came here yesterday morning."

The county attorney was looking around the kitchen.

"By the way," he said, "has anything been moved?" He turned to the sheriff. "Are things just as you left them yesterday?"

Peters looked from cupboard to sink; from that to a small worn rocker a little to one side of the kitchen table.

"It's just the same."

"Somebody should have been left here yesterday," said the county attorney.

"Oh—yesterday," returned the sheriff, with a little gesture as of yesterday having been more than he could bear to think of. "When I had to send Frank to Morris Center for that man who went crazy—let me tell you, I had my hands full *yesterday.* I knew you could get back from Omaha by today, George, and as long as I went over everything here myself—"

"Well, Mr. Hale," said the county attorney, in a way of letting what was past and gone go, "tell just what happened when you came here yesterday morning."

Mrs. Hale, still leaning against the door, had that sinking feeling of the mother whose child is about to speak a piece. Lewis often wandered along and got things mixed up in a story. She hoped he would tell this straight and plain, and not say unnecessary things that would just make things harder for Minnie Foster. He didn't begin at once, and she noticed that he looked queer—as if standing in that kitchen and having to tell what he had seen there yesterday morning made him almost sick.

"Yes, Mr. Hale?" the county attorney reminded.

"Harry and I had started to town with a load of potatoes," Mrs. Hale's husband began.

Harry was Mrs. Hale's oldest boy. He wasn't with them now, for the very good reason that those potatoes never got to town yesterday and he was taking them this morning, so he hadn't been home when the sheriff stopped to say he wanted Mr. Hale to come over to the Wright place and tell the county attorney his story there, where he could point it all out. With all Mrs. Hale's other emotions came the fear now that maybe Harry wasn't dressed warm enough— they hadn't any of them realized how that north wind did bite.

"We come along this road," Hale was going on, with a motion of his hand to the road over which they had just come, "and as we got in sight of the house I says to Harry, 'I'm goin' to see if I can't get John Wright to take a telephone.' You see," he explained to Henderson, "unless I can get somebody to go in with me they won't come out this branch road except for a price *I* can't pay. I'd spoke to Wright about it once before; but he put me off, saying folks talked too much anyway, and all he asked was peace and quiet—guess you know about how much he talked himself. But I thought maybe if I went to the house and talked about it before his wife, and said all the women-folks liked the telephones, and that in this lonesome stretch of road it would be a good thing —well, I said to Harry that that was what I was going to say—though I said at the same time that I didn't know as what his wife wanted made much difference to John—"

Now there he was!—saying things he didn't need to say. Mrs. Hale tried to catch her husband's eye, but fortunately the county attorney interrupted with:

"Let's talk about that a little later, Mr. Hale. I do want to talk about that, but I'm anxious now to get along to just what happened when you got here."

When he began this time, it was very deliberately and carefully:

"I didn't see or hear anything. I knocked at the door. And still it was all quiet inside. I knew they must be up—it was past eight o'clock. So I knocked again, louder, and I thought I heard somebody say, 'Come in.' I wasn't sure— I'm not sure yet. But I opened the door—this door," jerking a hand toward the door by which the two women stood, "and there, in that rocker"—pointing to it—"sat Mrs. Wright."

Everyone in the kitchen looked at the rocker. It came into Mrs. Hale's mind that that rocker didn't look in the least like Minnie Foster—the Minnie Foster of twenty years before. It was a dingy red, with wooden rungs up the back, and the middle rung was gone, and the chair sagged to one side.

"How did she—look?" the county attorney was inquiring.

"Well," said Hale, "she looked—queer."

"How do you mean—queer?"

As he asked it he took out a note-book and pencil. Mrs. Hale did not like the sight of that pencil. She kept her eye fixed on her husband, as if to keep him from saying unnecessary things that would go into that note-book and make trouble.

Hale did speak guardedly, as if the pencil had affected him too.

"Well, as if she didn't know what she was going to do next. And kind of— done up."

"How did she seem to feel about your coming?"

"Why, I don't think she minded—one way or other. She didn't pay much attention. I said, 'Ho' do, Mrs. Wright? It's cold, ain't it?'" And she said, 'Is it?'—and went on pleatin' at her apron.

"Well, I was surprised. She didn't ask me to come up to the stove, or to sit down, but just set there, not even lookin' at me. And so I said: 'I want to see John.'

"And then she—laughed. I guess you would call it a laugh.

"I thought of Harry and the team outside, so I said, a little sharp, 'Can I see John?' 'No,' says she—kind of dull like. 'Ain't he home?' says I. Then she looked at me. 'Yes,' says she, 'he's home.' 'Then why can't I see him?' I asked her, out of patience with her now. ''Cause he's dead,' says she, just as quiet and dull—and fell to pleatin' her apron. 'Dead?' says I, like you do when you can't take in what you've heard.

"She just nodded her head, not getting a bit excited, but rockin' back and forth.

" 'Why—where is he?' says I, not knowing *what* to say.

"She just pointed upstairs—like this"—pointing to the room above.

"I got up, with the idea of going up there myself. By this time I—didn't know what to do. I walked from there to here; then I says: 'Why, what did he die of?'

" 'He died of a rope round his neck,' says she; and just went on pleatin' at her apron."

Hale stopped speaking, and stood staring at the rocker, as if he were still seeing the woman who had sat there the morning before. Nobody spoke; it was as if every one were seeing the woman who had sat there the morning before.

"And what did you do then?" the county attorney at last broke the silence.

"I went out and called Harry. I thought I might—need help. I got Harry in, and we went upstairs." His voice fell almost to a whisper. "There he was— lying over the—"

"I think I'd rather have you go into that upstairs," the county attorney interrupted, "where you can point it all out. Just go on now with the rest of the story."

"Well, my first thought was to get that rope off. It looked—"

He stopped, his face twitching.

"But Harry, he went up to him, and he said, 'No, he's dead all right, and we'd better not touch anything.' So we went downstairs.

"She was still sitting that same way. 'Has anybody been notified?' I asked. 'No,' says she, unconcerned.

" 'Who did this, Mrs. Wright?' said Harry. He said it businesslike, and she stopped pleatin' at her apron. 'I don't know,' she says. 'You don't *know?*' says Harry. 'Weren't you sleepin' in the bed with him?' ' 'Yes,' says she, 'but I was on the inside.' 'Somebody slipped a rope round his neck and strangled him, and, you didn't wake up?' says Harry. 'I didn't wake up,' she said after him.

"We may have looked as if we didn't see how that could be, for after a minute she said, 'I sleep sound.'

"Harry was going to ask her more questions, but I said maybe that weren't our business; maybe we ought to let her tell her story first to the coroner or the sheriff. So Harry went fast as he could over to High Road—the Rivers' place, where there's a telephone."

"And what did she do when she knew you had gone for the coroner?" The attorney got his pencil in his hand all ready for writing.

"She moved from that chair to this one over here"—Hale pointed to a small chair in the corner—"and just sat there with her hands held together and looking down. I got a feeling that I ought to make some conversation, so I said I had come in to see if John wanted to put in a telephone; and at that she started to laugh, and then she stopped and looked at me—scared."

At sound of a moving pencil the man who was telling the story looked up.

"I dunno—maybe it wasn't scared," he hastened; "I wouldn't like to say it was. Soon Harry got back, and then Dr. Lloyd came, and you, Mr. Peters, and so I guess that's all I know that you don't.''

He said that last with relief, and moved a little, as if relaxing. Every one moved a little. The county attorney walked toward the stair door.

"I guess we'll go upstairs first—then out to the barn and around there."

He paused and looked around the kitchen.

"You're convinced there was nothing important here?" he asked the sheriff. "Nothing that would—point to any motive?"

The sheriff too looked all around, as if to re-convince himself.

"Nothing here but kitchen things," he said, with a little laugh for the insignificance of kitchen things.

The county attorney was looking at the cupboard—a peculiar, ungainly structure, half closet and half cupboard, the upper part of it being built in the wall, and the lower part just the old-fashioned kitchen cupboard. As if its queerness attracted him, he got a chair and opened the upper part and looked in. After a moment he drew his hand away sticky.

"Here's a nice mess," he said resentfully.

The two women had drawn nearer, and now the sheriff's wife spoke.

"Oh—her fruit," she said, looking to Mrs. Hale for sympathetic understanding. She turned back to the county attorney and explained: "She worried about that when it turned so cold last night. She said the fire would go out and her jars might burst."

Mrs. Peters' husband broke into a laugh.

"Well, can you beat the women! Held for murder, and worrying about her preserves!"

The young attorney set his lips.

"I guess before we're through with her she may have something more serious than preserves to worry about."

"Oh, well," said Mrs. Hale's husband, with good-natured superiority, "women are used to worrying over trifles."

The two women moved a little closer together. Neither of them spoke. The county attorney seemed suddenly to remember his manners—and think of his future.

"And yet," said he, with the gallantry of a young politician, "for all their worries, what would we do without the ladies?"

The women did not speak, did not unbend. He went to the sink and began washing his hands. He turned to wipe them on the roller towel—whirled it for a cleaner place.

"Dirty towels! Not much of a housekeeper, would you say, ladies?"

He kicked his foot against some dirty pans under the sink.

"There's a great deal of work to be done on a farm," said Mrs. Hale stiffly.

"To be sure. And yet"—with a little bow to her—"I know there are some Dickson County farm-houses that do not have such roller towels." He gave it a pull to expose its full length again.

"Those towels get dirty awful quick. Men's hands aren't always as clean as they might be."

"Ah, loyal to your sex, I see," he laughed. He stopped and gave her a keen look. "But you and Mrs. Wright were neighbors. I suppose you were friends, too."

Martha Hale shook her head.

"I've seen little enough of her of late years. I've not been in this house—it's more than a year."

"And why was that? You didn't like her?"

"I liked her well enough," she replied with spirit. "Farmers' wives have their hands full, Mr. Henderson. And then—" She looked around the kitchen.

"Yes?" he encouraged.

"It never seemed a very cheerful place," said she, more to herself than to him.

"No," he agreed; "I don't think anyone would call it cheerful. I shouldn't say she had the home-making instinct."

"Well, I don't know as Wright had, either," she muttered.

"You mean they didn't get on very well?" he was quick to ask.

"No; I don't mean anything," she answered, with decision. As she turned a little away from him, she added: "But I don't think a place would be any the cheerfuler for John Wright's bein' in it."

"I'd like to talk to you about that a little later, Mrs. Hale," he said. "I'm anxious to get the lay of things upstairs now."

He moved toward the stair door, followed by the two men.

"I suppose anything Mrs. Peters does'll be all right?" the sheriff inquired. "She was to take in some clothes for her, you know—and a few little things. We left in such a hurry yesterday."

The county attorney looked at the two women whom they were leaving alone there among the kitchen things.

"Yes—Mrs. Peters," he said, his glance resting on the woman who was not Mrs. Peters, the big farmer woman who stood behind the sheriff's wife. "Of course Mrs. Peters is one of us," he said, in a manner of entrusting responsibility. "And keep your eye out, Mrs. Peters, for anything that might be of use. No telling; you women might come upon a clue to the motive—and that's the thing we need."

Mr. Hale rubbed his face after the fashion of a showman getting ready for a pleasantry.

"But would the women know a clue if they did come upon it?" he said;

and, having delivered himself of this, he followed the others through the stair door.

The women stood motionless and silent, listening to the footsteps, first upon the stairs, then in the room above them.

Then, as if releasing herself from something strange, Mrs. Hale began to arrange the dirty pans under the sink, which the county attorney's disdainful push of the foot had deranged.

"I'd hate to have men comin' into my kitchen," she said testily—"snoopin' round and criticizin'."

"Of course it's no more than their duty," said the sheriff's wife, in her manner of timid acquiescence.

"Duty's all right," replied Mrs. Hale bluffly; "but I guess that deputy sheriff that come out to make the fire might have got a little of this on." She gave the roller towel a pull. "Wish I'd thought of that sooner! Seems mean to talk about her for not having things slicked up, when she has to come away in such a hurry."

She looked around the kitchen. Certainly it was not "slicked up." Her eye was held by a bucket of sugar on a low shelf. The cover was off the wooden bucket, and beside it was a paper bag—half full.

Mrs. Hale moved toward it.

"She was putting this in there," she said to herself—slowly.

She thought of the flour in her kitchen at home—half sifted, half not sifted. She had been interrupted, and had left things half done. What had interrupted Minnie Foster? Why had that work been left half done? She made a move as if to finish it,—unfinished things always bothered her,—and then she glanced around and saw that Mrs. Peters was watching her—and she didn't want Mrs. Peters to get that feeling she had got of work begun and then—for some reason —not finished.

"It's a shame about her fruit," she said, and walked toward the cupboard that the county attorney had opened, and got on the chair, murmuring: "I wonder if it's all gone."

It was a sorry enough looking sight, but "Here's one that's all right," she said at last. She held it toward the light. "This is cherries, too." She looked again. "I declare I believe that's the only one."

With a sigh, she got down from the chair, went to the sink, and wiped off the bottle.

"She'll feel awful bad, after all her hard work in the hot weather. I remember the afternoon I put up my cherries last summer."

She set the bottle on the table, and, with another sigh, started to sit down in the rocker. But she did not sit down. Something kept her from sitting down in

that chair. She straightened—stepped back, and, half turned away, stood looking at it, seeing the woman who had sat there "pleatin' at her apron."

The thin voice of the sheriff's wife broke in upon her: "I must be getting
those things from the front-room closet." She opened the door into the other
room, started in, stepped back. "You coming with me, Mrs. Hale?" she asked
nervously. "You—you could help me get them."

They were soon back—the stark coldness of that shut-up room was not a
thing to linger in.

"My!" said Mrs. Peters, dropping the things on the table and hurrying to
the stove.

Mrs. Hale stood examining the clothes the woman who was being detained
in town had said she wanted.

"Wright was close!" she exclaimed, holding up a shabby black skirt that
bore the marks of much making over. "I think maybe that's why she kept so
much to herself. I s'pose she felt she couldn't do her part; and then, you don't
enjoy things when you feel shabby. She used to wear pretty clothes and be
lively—when she was Minnie Foster, one of the town girls, singing in the
choir. But that—oh, that was twenty years ago."

With a carefulness in which there was something tender, she folded the
shabby clothes and piled them at one corner of the table. She looked up at Mrs.
Peters, and there was something in the other woman's look that irritated her.

"She don't care," she said to herself. "Much difference it makes to her
whether Minnie Foster had pretty clothes when she was a girl."

Then she looked again, and she wasn't so sure; in fact, she hadn't at any
time been perfectly sure about Mrs. Peters. She had that shrinking manner, and
yet her eyes looked as if they could see a long way into things.

"This all you was to take in?" asked Mrs. Hale.

"No," said the sheriff's wife; "she said she wanted an apron. Funny thing
to want," she ventured in her nervous little way, for there's not much to get
you dirty in jail, goodness knows. But I suppose just to make her feel more
natural. If you're used to wearing an apron—. She said they were in the bottom
drawer of this cupboard. Yes—here they are. And then her little shawl that
always hung on the stair door."

She took the small gray shawl from behind the door leading upstairs, and
stood a minute looking at it.

Suddenly Mrs. Hale took a quick step toward the other woman.

"Mrs. Peters!"

"Yes, Mrs. Hale?"

"Do you think she—did it?"

A frightened look blurred the other thing in Mrs. Peters' eyes.

"Oh, I don't know," she said, in a voice that seemed to shrink away from
the subject.

"Well, I don't think she did," affirmed Mrs. Hale stoutly. "Asking for an apron, and her little shawl. Worryin' about her fruit."

"Mr. Peters says—." Footsteps were heard in the room above; she stopped, looked up, then went on in a lowered voice: "Mr. Peters says—it looks bad for her. Mr. Henderson is awful sarcastic in a speech, and he's going to make fun of her saying she didn't—wake up."

For a moment Mrs. Hale had no answer. Then, "Well, I guess John Wright didn't wake up—when they was slippin' that rope under his neck," she muttered.

"No, it's *strange,*" breathed Mrs. Peters. "They think it was such a—funny way to kill a man."

She began to laugh; at sound of the laugh, abruptly stopped.

"That's just what Mr. Hale said," said Mrs. Hale, in a resolutely natural voice. "There was a gun in the house. He says that's what he can't understand."

"Mr. Henderson said, coming out, that what was needed for the case was a motive. Something to show anger—or sudden feeling."

"Well, I don't see any signs of anger around here," said Mrs. Hale. "I don't—"

She stopped. It was as if her mind tripped on something. Her eye was caught by a dish-towel in the middle of the kitchen table. Slowly she moved toward the table. One half of it was wiped clean, the other half messy. Her eyes made a slow, almost unwilling turn to the bucket of sugar and the half empty bag beside it. Things begun—and not finished.

After a moment she stepped back, and said, in that manner of releasing herself:

"Wonder how they're finding things upstairs? I hope she had it a little more red up up there. You know,"—she paused, and feeling gathered,—"it seems kind of *sneaking:* locking her up in town and coming out here to get her own house to turn against her!"

"But, Mrs. Hale," said the sheriff's wife, "the law is the law."

"I s'pose 'tis," answered Mrs. Hale shortly.

She turned to the stove, saying something about that fire not being much to brag of. She worked with it a minute, and when she straightened up she said aggressively:

"The law is the law—and a bad stove is a bad stove. How'd you like to cook on this?"—pointing with the poker to the broken lining. She opened the oven door and started to express her opinion of the oven; but she was swept into her own thoughts, thinking of what it would mean, year after year, to have that stove to wrestle with. The thought of Minnie Foster trying to bake in that oven—and the thought of her never going over to see Minnie Foster—.

She was startled by hearing Mrs. Peters say: "A person gets discouraged—and loses heart."

The sheriff's wife had looked from the stove to the sink—to the pail of water which had been carried in from outside. The two women stood there silent, above them the footsteps of the men who were looking for evidence against the woman who had worked in that kitchen. That look of seeing into things, of seeing through a thing to something else, was in the eyes of the sheriff's wife now. When Mrs. Hale next spoke to her, it was gently:

"Better loosen up your things, Mrs. Peters. We'll not feel them when we go out."

Mrs. Peters went to the back of the room to hang up the fur tippet she was wearing. A moment later she exclaimed, "Why, she was piecing a quilt," and held up a large sewing basket piled high with quilt pieces.

Mrs. Hale spread some of the blocks on the table.

"It's log-cabin pattern," she said, putting several of them together. "Pretty, isn't it?"

They were so engaged with the quilt that they did not hear the footsteps on the stairs. Just as the stair door opened Mrs. Hale was saying:

"Do you suppose she was going to quilt it or just knot it?"

The sheriff threw up his hands.

"They wonder whether she was going to quilt it or just knot it!"

There was a laugh for the ways of women, a warming of hands over the stove, and then the county attorney said briskly:

"Well, let's go right out to the barn and get that cleared up."

"I don't see as there's anything so strange," Mrs. Hale said resentfully, after the outside door had closed on the three men—"our taking up our time with little things while we're waiting for them to get the evidence. I don't see as it's anything to laugh about."

"Of course they've got awful important things on their minds," said the sheriff's wife apologetically.

They returned to an inspection of the block for the quilt. Mrs. Hale was looking at the fine, even sewing, and preoccupied with thoughts of the woman who had done that sewing, when she heard the sheriff's wife say, in a queer tone:

"Why, look at this one."

She turned to take the block held out to her.

"The sewing," said Mrs. Peters, in a troubled way. "All the rest of them have been so nice and even—but—this one. Why, it looks as if she didn't know what she was about!"

Their eyes met—something flashed to life, passed between them; then, as if with an effort, they seemed to pull away from each other. A moment Mrs. Hale sat there, her hands folded over that sewing which was so unlike all the rest of the sewing. Then she had pulled a knot and drawn the threads.

"Oh, what are you doing, Mrs. Hale?" asked the sheriff's wife, startled.

"Just pulling out a stitch or two that's not sewed very good," said Mrs. Hale mildly.

"I don't think we ought to touch things," Mrs. Peters said, a little helplessly.

"I'll just finish up this end," answered Mrs. Hale, still in that mild, matter-of-fact fashion.

She threaded a needle and started to replace bad sewing with good. For a little while she sewed in silence. Then, in that thin, timid voice, she heard:

"Mrs. Hale!"

"Yes, Mrs. Peters?"

"What do you suppose she was so—nervous about?"

"Oh, *I* don't know," said Mrs. Hale, as if dismissing a thing not important enough to spend much time on. "I don't know as she was—nervous. I sew awful queer sometimes when I'm just tired."

She cut a thread, and out of the corner of her eye looked up at Mrs. Peters. The small, lean face of the sheriff's wife seemed to have tightened up. Her eyes had that look of peering into something. But next moment she moved, and said in her thin, indecisive way:

"Well, I must get those clothes wrapped. They may be through sooner than we think. I wonder where I could find a piece of paper—and string."

"In that cupboard, maybe," suggested Mrs. Hale, after a glance around.

One piece of the crazy sewing remained unripped. Mrs. Peters' back turned, Martha Hale now scrutinized that piece, compared it with the dainty, accurate sewing of the other blocks. The difference was startling. Holding this block made her feel queer, as if the distracted thoughts of the woman who had perhaps turned to it to try and quiet herself were communicating themselves to her.

Mrs. Peters' voice roused her.

"Here's a bird-cage," she said. "Did she have a bird, Mrs. Hale?"

"Why, I don't know whether she did or not." She turned to look at the cage Mrs. Peters was holding up. "I've not been here in so long." She sighed. "There was a man round last year selling canaries cheap—but I don't know as she took one. Maybe she did. She used to sing real pretty herself."

Mrs. Peters looked around the kitchen.

"Seems kind of funny to think of a bird here." She half laughed—an attempt to put up a barrier. "But she must have had one—or why would she have a cage? I wonder what happened to it."

"I suppose maybe the cat got it," suggested Mrs. Hale, resuming her sewing.

"No; she didn't have a cat. She's got that feeling some people have about cats—being afraid of them. When they brought her to our house yesterday, my cat got in the room, and she was real upset and asked me to take it out."

"My sister Bessie was like that," laughed Mrs. Hale.

The sheriff's wife did not reply. The silence made Mrs. Hale turn round. Mrs. Peters was examining the bird-cage.

"Look at this door," she said slowly. "It's broke. One hinge has been pulled apart."

Mrs. Hale came nearer.

"Looks as if someone must have been—rough with it."

Again their eyes met—startled, questioning, apprehensive. For a moment neither spoke nor stirred. Then Mrs. Hale, turning away, said brusquely:

"If they're going to find any evidence, I wish they'd be about it. I don't like this place."

"But I'm awful glad you came with me, Mrs. Hale." Mrs. Peters put the bird-cage on the table and sat down. "It would be lonesome for me—sitting here alone."

"Yes, it would, wouldn't it?" agreed Mrs. Hale, a certain determined naturalness in her voice. She had picked up the sewing, but now it dropped in her lap, and she murmured in a different voice: "But I tell you what I *do* wish, Mrs. Peters. I wish I had come over sometimes when she was here. I wish—I had."

"But of course you were awful busy, Mrs. Hale. Your house—and your children."

"I could've come," retorted Mrs. Hale shortly. "I stayed away because it weren't cheerful—and that's why I ought to have come. I"—she looked around —"I've never liked this place. Maybe because it's down in a hollow and you don't see the road. I don't know what it is, but it's a lonesome place, and always was. I wish I had come over to see Minnie Foster sometimes. I can see now—" She did not put it into words.

"Well, you musn't reproach yourself," counseled Mrs. Peters. "Somehow, we just don't see how it is with other folks till—something comes up."

"Not having children makes less work," mused Mrs. Hale, after a silence, "but it makes a quiet house—and Wright out to work all day—and no company when he did come in. Did you know John Wright, Mrs. Peters?"

"Not to know him. I've seen him in town. They say he was a good man."

"Yes—good," conceded John Wright's neighbor grimly. "He didn't drink, and kept his word as well as most, I guess, and paid his debts. But he was a hard man, Mrs. Peters. Just to pass the time of day with him—." She stopped, shivered a little. "Like a raw wind that gets to the bone." Her eye fell upon the cage on the table before her, and she added, almost bitterly: "I should think she would've wanted a bird!"

Suddenly she leaned forward, looking intently at the cage. "But what do you s'pose went wrong with it?"

"I don't know," returned Mrs. Peters; "unless it got sick and died."

But after she said it she reached over and swung the broken door. Both women watched it as if somehow held by it.

"You didn't know—her?" Mrs. Hale asked, a gentler note in her voice.

"Not till they brought her yesterday," said the sheriff's wife.

"She—come to think of it, she was kind of like a bird herself. Real sweet and pretty, but kind of timid and—fluttery. How—she—did—change."

That held her for a long time. Finally, as if struck with a happy thought and relieved to get back to everyday things, she exclaimed:

"Tell you what, Mrs. Peters, why don't you take the quilt in with you? It might take up her mind."

"Why, I think that's a real nice idea, Mrs. Hale," agreed the sheriff's wife, as if she too were glad to come into the atmosphere of a simple kindness. "There couldn't possibly be any objection to that, could there? Now, just what will I take? I wonder if her patches are in here—and her things."

They turned to the sewing basket.

"Here's some red," said Mrs. Hale, bringing out a roll of cloth. Underneath that was a box. "Here, maybe her scissors are in here—and her things." She held it up. "What a pretty box! I'll warrant that was something she had a long time ago—when she was a girl."

She held it in her hand a moment; then, with a little sigh, opened it.

Instantly her hand went to her nose.

"Why—!"

Mrs. Peters drew nearer—then turned away.

"There's something wrapped up in this piece of silk," faltered Mrs. Hale.

"This isn't her scissors," said Mrs. Peters, in a shrinking voice.

Her hand not steady, Mrs. Hale raised the piece of silk. "Oh, Mrs. Peters!" she cried. "It's—"

Mrs. Peters bent closer.

"It's the bird," she whispered.

"But, Mrs. Peters!" cried Mrs. Hale. "*Look* at it! Its *neck*—look at its neck! It's all—other side *to.*"

She held the box away from her.

The sheriff's wife again bent closer.

"Somebody wrung its neck," said she, in a voice that was slow and deep.

And then again the eyes of the two women met—this time clung together in a look of dawning comprehension, of growing horror. Mrs. Peters looked from the dead bird to the broken door of the cage. Again their eyes met. And just then there was a sound at the outside door.

Mrs. Hale slipped the box under the quilt pieces in the basket, and sank into the chair before it. Mrs. Peters stood holding to the table. The county attorney and the sheriff came in from outside.

"Well, ladies," said the county attorney, as one turning from serious things to little pleasantries, "have you decided whether she was going to quilt it or knot it?"

"We think," began the sheriff's wife in a flurried voice, "that she was going to—knot it."

He was too preoccupied to notice the change that came in her voice on that last.

"Well, that's very interesting, I'm sure," he said tolerantly. "He caught sight of the bird-cage. "Has the bird flown?"

"We think the cat got it," said Mrs. Hale in a voice curiously even.

He was walking up and down, as if thinking something out.

"Is there a cat?" he asked absently.

Mrs. Hale shot a look up at the sheriff's wife.

"Well, not *now*," said Mrs. Peters. "They're superstitious, you know; they leave."

She sank into her chair.

The county attorney did not heed her. "No sign at all of anyone having come in from the outside," he said to Peters, in the manner of continuing an interrupted conversation. "Their own rope. Now let's go upstairs again and go over it, piece by piece. It would have to have been someone who knew just the—"

The stair door closed behind them and their voices were lost.

The two women sat motionless, not looking at each other, but as if peering into something and at the same time holding back. When they spoke now it was as if they were afraid of what they were saying, but as if they could not help saying it.

"She liked the bird," said Martha Hale, low and slowly. "She was going to bury it in that pretty box."

"When I was a girl," said Mrs. Peters, under her breath, "my kitten—there was a boy took a hatchet, and before my eyes—before I could get there—" She covered her face an instant. "If they hadn't held me back I would have" —she caught herself, looked upstairs where footsteps were heard, and finished weakly—"hurt him."

Then they sat without speaking or moving.

"I wonder how it would seem," Mrs. Hale at last began, as if feeling her way over strange ground—"never to have had any children around?" Her eyes made a slow sweep of the kitchen, as if seeing what that kitchen had meant through all the years. "No, Wright wouldn't like the bird," she said after that —"a thing that sang. She used to sing. He killed that too." Her voice tightened.

Mrs. Peters moved uneasily.

"Of course we don't know who killed the bird."

"I knew John Wright," was Mrs. Hale's answer.

"It was an awful thing was done in this house that night, Mrs. Hale," said the sheriff's wife. "Killing a man while he slept—slipping a thing round his neck that choked the life out of him."

Mrs. Hale's hand went out to the bird cage.

"His neck. Choked the life out of him."

"We don't *know* who killed him," whispered Mrs. Peters wildly. "We don't *know.*"

Mrs. Hale had not moved. "If there had been years and years of—nothing, then a bird to sing to you, it would be awful—still—after the bird was still."

It was as if something within her not herself had spoken, and it found in Mrs. Peters something she did not know as herself.

"I know what stillness is," she said, in a queer, monotonous voice. "When we homesteaded in Dakota, and my first baby died—after he was two years old—and me with no other then—"

Mrs. Hale stirred.

"How soon do you suppose they'll be through looking for the evidence?"

"I know what stillness is," repeated Mrs. Peters, in just that same way. Then she too pulled back. "The law has got to punish crime, Mrs. Hale," she said in her tight little way.

"I wish you'd seen Minnie Foster," was the answer, "when she wore a white dress with blue ribbons, and stood up there in the choir and sang."

The picture of that girl, the fact that she had lived neighbor to that girl for twenty years, and had let her die for lack of life, was suddenly more than she could bear.

"Oh, I *wish* I'd come over here once in a while!" she cried. "That was a crime! That was a crime! Who's going to punish that?"

"We musn't take on," said Mrs. Peters, with a frightened look toward the stairs.

"I might 'a' *known* she needed help! I tell you, it's *queer,* Mrs. Peters. We live close together, and we live far apart. We all go through the same things— it's all just a different kind of the same thing! If it weren't—why do you and I *understand?* Why do we *know*—what we know this minute?"

She dashed her hand across her eyes. Then, seeing the jar of fruit on the table, she reached for it and choked out:

"If I was you I wouldn't *tell* her her fruit was gone! Tell her it *ain't.* Tell her it's all right—all of it. Here—take this in to prove it to her! She—she may never know whether it was broke or not."

She turned away.

Mrs. Peters reached out for the bottle of fruit as if she were glad to take it —as if touching a familiar thing, having something to do, could keep her from something else. She got up, looked about for something to wrap the fruit in, took a petticoat from the pile of clothes she had brought from the front room, and nervously started winding that round the bottle.

"My!" she began, in a high, false voice, "it's a good thing the men couldn't hear us! Getting all stirred up over a little thing like a—dead canary." She hurried over that. "As if that could have anything to do with—with—My, wouldn't they *laugh?*"

Footsteps were heard on the stairs.

"Maybe they would," muttered Mrs. Hale—"maybe they wouldn't."

"No, Peters," said the county attorney incisively; "it's all perfectly clear, except the reason for doing it. But you know juries when it comes to women. If there was some definite thing—something to show. Something to make a story about. A thing that would connect up with this clumsy way of doing it."

In a covert way Mrs. Hale looked at Mrs. Peters. Mrs. Peters was looking at her. Quickly they looked away from each other. The outer door opened and Mr. Hale came in.

"I've got the team round now," he said. "Pretty cold out there."

"I'm going to stay here awhile by myself," the county attorney suddenly announced. "You can send Frank out for me, can't you?" he asked the sheriff. "I want to go over everything. I'm not satisfied we can't do better."

Again, for one brief moment, the two women's eyes found one another. The sheriff came up to the table.

"Did you want to see what Mrs. Peters was going to take in?"

The county attorney picked up the apron. He laughed.

"Oh, I guess they're not very dangerous things the ladies have picked out."

Mrs. Hale's hand was on the sewing basket in which the box was concealed. She felt that she ought to take her hand off the basket. She did not seem able to. He picked up one of the quilt blocks which she had piled on to cover the box. Her eyes felt like fire. She had a feeling that if he took up the basket she would snatch it from him.

But he did not take it up. With another little laugh, he turned away, saying:

"No; Mrs. Peters doesn't need supervising. For that matter, a sheriff's wife is married to the law. Ever think of it that way, Mrs. Peters?"

Mrs. Peters was standing beside the table. Mrs. Hale shot a look up at her; but she could not see her face. Mrs. Peters had turned away. When she spoke, her voice was muffled.

"Not—just that way," she said.

"Married to the law!" chuckled Mrs. Peters' husband. He moved toward the door into the front room, and said to the county attorney:

"I just want you to come in here a minute, George. We ought to take a look at these windows."

"Oh—windows," said the county attorney scoffingly.

"We'll be right out, Mr. Hale," said the sheriff to the farmer, who was still waiting by the door.

Hale went to look after the horses. The sheriff followed the county attorney into the other room. Again—for one final moment—the two women were alone in that kitchen.

Martha Hale sprang up, her hands tight together, looking at that other woman, with whom it rested. At first she could not see her eyes, for the sheriff's wife had not turned back since she turned away at that suggestion of being married to the law. But now Mrs. Hale made her turn back. Her eyes made her turn back. Slowly, unwillingly, Mrs. Peters turned her head until her eyes met the eyes of the other woman. There was a moment when they held each other in a steady, burning look in which there was no evasion nor flinching. Then Martha Hale's eyes pointed the way to the basket in which was hidden the thing that would make certain the conviction of the other woman—that woman who was not there and yet who had been there with them all through that hour.

For a moment Mrs. Peters did not move. And then she did it. With a rush forward, she threw back the quilt pieces, got the box, tried to put it in her handbag. It was too big. Desperately she opened, started to take the bird out. But there she broke—she could not touch the bird. She stood there helpless, foolish.

There was the sound of a knob turning in the inner door. Martha Hale snatched the box from the sheriff's wife, and got it in the pocket of her big coat just as the sheriff and the county attorney came back into the kitchen.

"Well, Henry," said the county attorney facetiously, "at least we found out that she was not going to quilt it. She was going to—what is it you call it, ladies?"

Mrs. Hale's hand was against the pocket of her coat.

"We call it—knot it, Mr. Henderson."

He liked plump women. That was the end-all of his moral debates. *Ergo,* he had murdered his wife because she had become skinny and had not, with much irritation to him, reverted, even when well-fed, to her former plumpness. He was not a fool to ask himself whether there was logic in his nerves. He knew what he liked.

—Alice Walker, *The Third Life of Grange Copeland*

When a woman kills her husband in a violent quarrel, the act is usually a desperate, final response to years of physical abuse. When a man kills his wife in a domestic setting, his act is a logical extension of the physical abuse he has been dispensing for years, an ultimate upping of the ante. . . .

A Jean Harris with a gun, like a Nat Turner with a blade, confirms the worst suspicions of the powerful about the vengeance that lies in the hearts of the weak.

—Susan Jacoby, *Wild Justice*

Sweat

ZORA NEALE HURSTON

It was eleven o'clock of a Spring night in Florida. It was Sunday. Any other night, Delia Jones would have been in bed for two hours by this time. But she was a washwoman, and Monday morning meant a great deal to her. So she collected the soiled clothes on Saturday when she returned the clean things. Sunday night after church, she sorted them and put the white things to soak. It saved her almost a half day's start. A great hamper in the bedroom held the clothes that she brought home. It was so much neater than a number of bundles lying around.

She squatted in the kitchen floor beside the great pile of clothes, sorting them into small heaps according to color, and humming a song in a mournful key, but wondering through it all where Sykes, her husband, had gone with her horse and buckboard.

Just then something long, round, limp and black fell upon her shoulders and slithered to the floor beside her. A great terror took hold of her. It softened her knees and dried her mouth so that it was a full minute before she could cry out or move. Then she saw that it was the big bull whip her husband liked to carry when he drove.

She lifted her eyes to the door and saw him standing there bent over with laughter at her fright. She screamed at him.

"Sykes, what you throw dat whip on me like dat? You know it would skeer me—looks just like a snake, an' you knows how skeered Ah is of snakes."

"Course Ah knowed it! That's how come Ah done it." He slapped his leg with his hand and almost rolled on the ground in his mirth. "If you such a big fool dat you got to have a fit over a earth worm or a string, Ah don't keer how bad Ah skeer you."

"You aint got no business doing it. Gawd knows it's a sin. Some day Ah'm gointuh drop dead from some of yo' foolishness. 'Nother thing, where you been wid mah rig? Ah feeds dat pony. He aint fuh you to be drivin' wid no bull whip."

"You sho is one aggravatin' nigger woman!" he declared and stepped into the room. She resumed her work and did not answer him at once. "Ah done tole you time and again to keep them white folks' clothes outa dis house."

He picked up the whip and glared down at her. Delia went on with her work. She went out into the yard and returned with a galvanized tub and set it on the washbench. She saw that Sykes had kicked all of the clothes together again, and now stood in her way truculently, his whole manner hoping, *praying,* for an argument. But she walked calmly around him and commenced to resort the things.

"Next time, Ah'm gointer kick 'em outdoors," he threatened as he struck a match along the leg of his corduroy breeches.

Delia never looked up from her work, and her thin, stooped shoulders sagged further.

"Ah aint for no fuss t'night Sykes. Ah just come from taking sacrament at the church house."

He snorted scornfully. "Yeah, you just come from de church house on a Sunday night, but heah you is gone to work on them clothes. You ain't nothing but a hypocrite. One of them amen-corner Christians—sing, whoop, and shout, then come home and wash white folks clothes on the Sabbath."

He stepped roughly upon the whitest pile of things, kicking them helter-skelter as he crossed the room. His wife gave a little scream of dismay, and quickly gathered them together again.

"Sykes, you quit grindin' dirt into these clothes! How can Ah git through by Sat'day if Ah don't start on Sunday?"

"Ah don't keer if you never git through. Anyhow, Ah done promised Gawd and a couple of other men, Ah aint gointer have it in mah house. Don't gimme no lip neither, else Ah'll throw 'em out and put mah fist up side yo' head to boot."

Delia's habitual meekness seemed to slip from her shoulders like a blown scarf. She was on her feet; her poor little body, her bare knuckly hands bravely defying the strapping hulk before her.

"Looka heah, Sykes, you done gone too fur. Ah been married to you fur fifteen years, and Ah been takin' in washin' fur fifteen years. Sweat, sweat, sweat! Work and sweat, cry and sweat, pray and sweat!"

"What's that got to do with me?" he asked brutally.

"What's it got to do with you, Sykes? Mah tub of suds is filled yo' belly with vittles more times than yo' hands is filled it. Mah sweat is done paid for this house and Ah reckon Ah kin keep on sweatin' in it."

She seized the iron skillet from the stove and struck a defensive pose, which act surprised him greatly, coming from her. It cowed him and he did not strike her as he usually did.

"Naw you won't," she panted, "that ole snaggle-toothed black woman you runnin' with aint comin' heah to pile up on *mah* sweat and blood. You aint paid for nothin' on this place, and Ah'm gointer stay right heah till Ah'm toted out foot foremost."

"Well, you better quit gittin' me riled up, else they'll be totin' you out sooner than you expect. Ah'm so tired of you Ah don't know whut to do. Gawd! how Ah hates skinny wimmen!"

A little awed by this new Delia, he sidled out of the door and slammed the back gate after him. He did not say where he had gone, but she knew too well. She knew very well that he would not return until nearly daybreak also. Her work over, she went on to bed but not to sleep at once. Things had come to a pretty pass!

She lay awake, gazing upon the debris that cluttered their matrimonial trail. Not an image left standing along the way. Anything like flowers had long ago been drowned in the salty stream that had been pressed from her heart. Her tears, her sweat, her blood. She had brought love to the union and he had brought a longing after the flesh. Two months after the wedding, he had given her the first brutal beating. She had the memory of his numerous trips to Orlando with all of his wages when he had returned to her penniless, even before the first year had passed. She was young and soft then, but now she thought of her knotty, muscles limbs, her harsh knuckly hands, and drew herself up into an unhappy little ball in the middle of the big feather bed. Too late now to hope for love, even if it were not Bertha it would be someone else. This case differed from the others only in that she was bolder than the others. Too late for everything except her little home. She had built it for her old days, and planted one by one the trees and flowers there. It was lovely to her, lovely.

Somehow, before sleep came, she found herself saying aloud: "Oh well, whatever goes over the Devil's back, is got to come under his belly. Sometime or ruther, Sykes, like everybody else, is gointer reap his sowing." After that she was able to build a spiritual earthworks against her husband. His shells could no longer reach her. *Amen.* She went to sleep and slept until he announced his presence in bed by kicking her feet and rudely snatching the cover away.

"Gimme some kivah heah, an' git yo' damn foots over on yo' own side! Ah oughter mash you in yo' mouf fuh drawing dat skillet on me."

Delia went clear to the rail without answering him. A triumphant indifference to all that he was or did.

The week was as full of work for Delia as all other weeks, and Saturday found her behind her little pony, collecting and delivering clothes.

It was a hot, hot day near the end of July. The village men on Joe Clarke's porch even chewed cane listlessly. They did not hurl the cane-knots as usual. They let them dribble over the edge of the porch. Even conversation had collapsed under the heat.

"Heah come Delia Jones," Jim Merchant said, as the shaggy pony came 'round the bend of the road toward them. The rusty buckboard was heaped with baskets of crisp, clean laundry.

"Yep," Joe Lindsay agreed. "Hot or col', rain or shine, jes ez reg'lar ez de weeks roll roun' Delia carries 'em an' fetches 'em on Sat'day."

"She better if she wanter eat," said Moss. "Syke Jones aint wuth de shot an' powder hit would tek tuh kill 'em. Not to *huh* he aint."

"He sho' aint," Walter Thomas chimed in. "It's too bad, too, cause she wuz a right pritty lil trick when he got huh. Ah'd uh mah'ied huh mahseff if he hadnter beat me to it."

Delia nodded briefly at the men as she drove past.

"Too much knockin' will ruin *any* 'oman. He done beat huh 'nough tuh kill three women, let 'lone change they looks," said Elijah Moseley. "How Syke kin stommuck dat big black greasy Mogul he's layin' roun' wid, gits me. Ah swear dat eight-rock couldn't kiss a sardine can Ah done thowed out de back do' 'way las' yeah."

"Aw, she's fat, thass how come. He's allus been crazy 'bout fat women," put in Merchant. "He'd a' been tied up wid one long time ago if he could a' found one tuh have him. Did Ah tell yuh 'bout him come sidlin' roun' *mah* wife—bringin' her a basket uh peecans outa his yard fuh a present? Yessir, mah wife! She tol' him tuh take 'em right straight back home, cause Delia works so hard ovah dat washtub she reckon everything on de place taste lak sweat an' soapsuds. Ah jus' wisht Ah'd a' caught 'im 'roun' dere! Ah'd a' made his hips ketch on fiah down dat shell road."

"Ah know he done it, too. Ah sees 'im grinnin' at every 'oman dat passes," Walter Thomas said. "But even so, he useter eat some mighty big hunks uh humble pie tuh git dat lil' 'oman he got. She wuz ez pritty ez a speckled pup! Dat wuz fifteen yeahs ago. He useter be so skeered uh losin' huh, she could make him do some parts of a husband's duty. Dey never wuz de same in de mind."

"There oughter be a law about him," said Lindsay. "He aint fit tuh carry guts tuh a bear."

Clarke spoke for the first time. "Taint no law on earth dat kin make a man be decent if it aint in 'im. There's plenty men dat takes a wife lak dey do a joint uh sugar-cane. It's round, juicy an' sweet when dey gits it. But dey squeeze an' grind, squeeze an' grind an' wring tell dey wring every drop uh pleasure dat's in 'em out. When dey's satisfied dat dey is wrung dry, dey treats 'em jes lak dey do a cane-chew. Dey thows 'em away. Dey knows whut dey is doin' while dey is at it, an' hates theirselves fuh it but they keeps on hangin' after huh tell she's empty. Den dey hates huh fuh bein' a cane-chew an' in de way."

"We oughter take Syke an' dat stray 'oman uh his'n down in Lake Howell swamp an' lay on de rawhide till they cain't say 'Lawd a' mussy.' He allus wuz uh ovahbearin' niggah, but since dat white 'oman from up north done teached 'im how to run a automobile, he done got too biggety to live—an' we oughter kill 'im," Old Man Anderson advised.

A grunt of approval went around the porch. But the heat was melting their civic virtue and Elijah Moseley began to bait Joe Clarke.

"Come on, Joe, git a melon outa dere an' slice it up for yo' customers. We'se all sufferin' wid de heat. De bear's done got *me!*"

"Thass right, Joe, a watermelon is jes' whut Ah needs tuh cure de eppizud-icks," Walter Thomas joined forces with Moseley. "Come on dere, Joe. We all is steady customers an' you aint set us up in a long time. Ah chooses dat long, bowlegged Floridy favorite."

"A god, an' be dough. You all gimme twenty cents and slice away," Clarke retorted. "Ah needs a col' slice m'self. Heah, everybody chip in. Ah'll lend y'll mah meat knife."

The money was quickly subscribed and the huge melon brought forth. At that moment, Sykes and Bertha arrived. A determined silence fell on the porch and the melon was put away again.

Merchant snapped down the blade of his jackknife and moved toward the store door.

"Come on in, Joe, an' gimme a slab uh sow belly an' uh pound uh coffee —almost fuhgot 'twas Sat'day. Got to git on home." Most of the men left also.

Just then Delia drove past on her way home, as Sykes was ordering magnifi-cently for Bertha. It pleased him for Delia to see.

"Git whutsoever yo' heart desires, Honey. Wait a minute, Joe. Give huh two botles uh strawberry soda-water, uh quart uh parched ground-peas, an' a block uh chewin' gum."

With all this they left the store, with Sykes reminding Bertha that this was his town and she could have it if she wanted it.

The men returned soon after they left, and held their watermelon feast.

"Where did Syke Jones git da 'oman from nohow?" Lindsay asked.

"Ovah Apopka. Guess dey musta been cleanin' out de town when she lef'. She don't look lak a thing but a hunk uh liver wid hair on it."

"Well, she sho' kin squall," Dave Carter contributed. "When she gits ready tuh laff, she jes' opens huh mouf an' latches it back tuh de las' notch. No ole grandpa alligator down in Lake Bell ain't got nothin' on huh."

Bertha had been in town three months now. Sykes was still paying her room rent at Della Lewis'—the only house in town that would have taken her in. Sykes took her frequently to Winter Park to "stomps." He still assured her that he was the swellest man in the state.

"Sho' you kin have dat lil' ole house soon's Ah kin git dat 'oman outa dere. Everything b'longs tuh me an' you sho' kin have it. Ah sho' 'bominates uh skinny 'oman. Lawdy, you sho' is got one portly shape on you! You kin git *anything* you wants. Dis is *mah* town an' you sho' kin have it."

Delia's work-worn knees crawled over the earth in Gethsemane and up the rocks of Calvary many, many times during these months. She avoided the villagers and meeting places in her efforts to be blind and deaf. But Bertha nullified this to a degree, by coming to Delia's house to call Sykes out to her at the gate.

Delia and Sykes fought all the time now with no peaceful interludes. They slept and ate in silence. Two or three times Delia had attempted a timid friendliness, but she was repulsed each time. It was plain that the breaches must remain agape.

The sun had burned July to August. The heat streamed down like a million hot arrows, smiting all things living upon the earth. Grass withered, leaves browned, snakes went blind in shedding and men and dogs went mad. Dog days!

Delia came home one day and found Sykes there before her. She wondered, but started to go on into the house without speaking, even though he was standing in the kitchen door and she must either stoop under his arm or ask him to move. He made no room for her. She noticed a soap box beside the steps, but paid no particular attention to it, knowing that he must have brought it there. As she was stooping to pass under his outstretched arm, he suddenly pushed her backward, laughingly.

"Look in de box dere Delia, Ah done brung yuh somethin'!"

She nearly fell upon the box in her stumbling, and when she saw what it held, she all but fainted outright.

"Syke! Syke, mah Gawd! You take dat rattlesnake 'way from heah! You *gottuh*. Oh, Jesus, have mussy!"

"Ah aint gut tuh do nuthin' uh de kin'—fact is Ah aint got tuh do nothin' but die. Taint no use uh you puttin' on airs makin' out lak you skeered uh dat snake—he's gointer stay right heah tell he die. He wouldn't bite me cause Ah knows how tuh handle 'im. Nohow he wouldn't risk breakin' out his fangs 'gin yo' skinny laigs."

"Naw, now Syke, don't keep dat thing 'roun' heah tuh skeer me tuh death. You knows Ah'm even feared uh earth worms. Thass de biggest snake Ah evah did see. Kill 'im Syke, please."

"Doan ast me tuh do nothin' fuh yuh. Goin' 'roun' tryin' tuh be so damn asterperious. Naw, Ah aint gonna kill it. Ah think uh damn sight mo' uh him dan you! Dat's a nice snake an' anybody doan lak 'im kin jes' hit de grit."

The village soon heard that Sykes had the snake, and came to see and ask questions.

"How de hen-fire did you ketch dat six-foot rattler, Syke?" Thomas asked.

"He's full uh frogs so he caint hardly move, thass how Ah eased up on 'm. But Ah'm a snake charmer an' knows how tuh handle 'em. Shux, dat aint nothin'. Ah could ketch one eve'y day if Ah so wanted tuh."

"Whut he needs is a heavy hick'ry club leaned real heavy on his head. Dat's de bes 'way tuh charm a rattlesnake."

"Naw, Walt, y'll jes' don't understand dese diamon' backs lak Ah do," said Sykes in a superior tone of voice.

The village agreed with Walter, but the snake stayed on. His box remained by the kitchen door with its screen wire covering. Two or three days later it had digested its meal of frogs and literally came to life. It rattled at every movement in the kitchen or the yard. One day as Delia came down the kitchen steps she saw his chalky-white fangs curved like scimitars hung in the wire meshes. This time she did not run away with averted eyes as usual. She stood for a long time in the doorway in a red fury that grew bloodier for every second that she regarded the creature that was her torment.

That night she broached the subject as soon as Sykes sat down to the table.

"Syke, Ah wants you tuh take dat snake 'way fum heah. You done starved me an' Ah put up widcher, you done beat me an Ah took dat, but you done kilt all mah insides bringin' dat varmint heah."

Sykes poured out a saucer full of coffee and drank it deliberately before he answered her.

"A whole lot Ah keer 'bout how you feels inside uh out. Dat snake aint goin' no damn wheah till Ah gits ready fuh 'im tuh go. So fur as beatin' is concerned, yuh aint took near all dat you gointer take ef yuh stay 'roun' *me*."

Delia pushed back her plate and got up from the table. "Ah hates you, Sykes," she said calmly. "Ah hates you tuh de same degree dat Ah useter love yuh. Ah done took an' took till mah belly is full up tuh mah neck. Dat's de reason Ah got mah letter fum de church an' moved mah membership tuh Woodbridge—so Ah don't haftuh take no sacrament wid yuh. Ah don't wantuh see yuh 'roun' me atall. Lay 'roun' wid dat 'oman all yuh wants tuh, but gwan 'way fum me an' mah house. Ah hates yuh lak uh suck-egg dog."

Sykes almost let the huge wad of corn bread and collard greens he was chewing fall out of his mouth in amazement. He had a hard time whipping himself up to the proper fury to try to answer Delia.

"Well, Ah'm glad you does hate me. Ah'm sho' tiahed uh you hangin' ontuh me. Ah don't want yuh. Look at yuh stringey ole neck! Yo' rawbony laigs an' arms is enough tuh cut uh man tuh death. You looks jes' lak de devvul's doll-baby tuh *me*. You cain't hate me no worse dan Ah hates you. Ah been hatin' *you* fuh years.

"Yo' ole black hide don't look lak nothin' tuh me, but uh passle uh wrinkled up rubber, wid yo' big ole yeahs flappin' on each side lak up paih uh buzzard wings. Don't think Ah'm gointuh be run 'way fum mah house neither. Ah'm goin' tuh de white folks bout *you,* mah young man, de very nex' time you lay yo' han's on me. Mah cup is done run ovah." Delia said this with no signs of fear and Sykes departed from the house, threatening her, but made not the slightest move to carry out any of them.

That night he did not return at all, and the next day being Sunday, Delia was glad she did not have to quarrel before she hitched up her pony and drove the four miles to Woodbridge.

She stayed to the night service—"love feast"—which was very warm and full of spirit. In the emotional winds her domestic trials were borne far and wide so that she sang as she drove homeward,

> *"Jurden water, black an' col'*
> *Chills de body, not de soul*
> *An' Ah wantah cross Jurden in uh calm time."*

She came from the barn to the kitchen door and stopped.

"Whut's de mattah, ol' satan, you aint kickin' up yo' racket?" She addressed the snake's box. Complete silence. She went on into the house with a new hope in its birth struggles. Perhaps her threat to go to the white folks had frightened Sykes! Perhaps he was sorry! Fifteen years of misery and suppression had brought Delia to the place where she would hope *anything* that looked towards a way over or through her wall of inhibitions.

She felt in the match safe behind the stove at once for a match. There was only one there.

"Dat niggah wouldn't fetch nothin' heah tuh save his rotten neck, but he kin run thew whut Ah brings quick enough. Now he done toted off nigh on tuh haff uh box uh matches. He done had dat 'oman heah in mah house, too."

Nobody but a woman could tell how she knew this even before she struck the match. But she did and it put her into a new fury.

Presently she brought in the tubs to put the white things to soak. This time she decided she need not bring the hamper out of the bedroom; she would go in there and do the sorting. She picked up the pot-bellied lamp and went in. The room was small and the hamper stood hard by the foot of the white iron bed. She could sit and reach through the bedposts—resting as she worked.

"Ah wantah cross Jurden in uh calm time." She was singing again. The mood of the "love feast" had returned. She threw back the lid of the basket almost gaily. Then, moved by both horror and terror, she sprang back toward the door. *There lay the snake in the basket!* He moved sluggishly at first, but even as she turned round and round, jumped up and down in an insanity of fear, he began to stir vigorously. She saw him pouring his awful beauty from the basket upon the bed, then she seized the lamp and ran as fast as she could to the kitchen. The wind from the open door blew out the light and the darkness added to her terror. She sped to the darkness of the yard, slamming the door after her before she thought to set down the lamp. She did not feel safe even on the ground, so she climbed up in the hay barn.

There for an hour or more she lay sprawled upon the hay a gibbering wreck.

Finally she grew quiet, and after that, coherent thought. With this, stalked through her a cold, bloody rage. Hours of this. A period of introspection, a space of retrospection, then a mixture of both. Out of this an awful calm.

"Well, Ah done de bes' Ah could. If things aint right, Gawd knows taint mah fault."

She went to sleep—a twitchy sleep—and woke up to a faint gray sky. There was a loud hollow sound below. She peered out. Sykes was at the wood-pile, demolishing a wire-covered box.

He hurried to the kitchen door, but hung outside there some minutes before he entered, and stood some minutes more inside before he closed it after him.

The gray in the sky was spreading. Delia descended without fear now, and crouched beneath the low bedroom window. The drawn shade shut out the dawn, shut in the night. But the thin walls held back no sound.

"Dat ol' scratch is woke up now!" She mused at the tremendous whirr inside, which every woodsman knows, is one of the sound illusions. The rattler is a ventriloquist. His whirr sounds to the right, to the left, straight ahead, behind, close under foot—everywhere but where it is. Woe to him who guesses wrong unless he is prepared to hold up his end of the argument! Sometimes he strikes without rattling at all.

Inside, Sykes heard nothing until he knocked a pot lid off the stove while trying to reach the match safe in the dark. He had emptied his pockets at Bertha's.

The snake seemed to wake up under the stove and Sykes made a quick leap into the bedroom. In spite of the gin he had had, his head was clearing now.

"Mah Gawd!" he chattered, "ef Ah could on'y strack uh light!"

The rattling ceased for a moment as he stood paralyzed. He waited. It seemed that the snake waited also.

"Oh, fuh de light! Ah thought he'd be too sick"—Sykes was muttering to himself when the whirr began again, closer, right underfoot this time. Long before this, Sykes' ability to think had been flattened down to primitive instinct and he leaped—onto the bed.

Outside Delia heard a cry that might have come from a maddened chimpanzee, a stricken gorilla. All the terror, all the horror, all the rage that man possibly could express, without a recognizable human sound.

A tremendous stir inside there, another series of animal screams, the intermittent whirr of the reptile. The shade torn violently down from the window, letting in the red dawn, a huge brown hand seizing the window stick, great dull blows upon the wooden floor punctuating the gibberish of sound long after the rattle of the snake had abruptly subsided. All this Delia could see and hear from her place beneath the window, and it made her ill. She crept over to the four-o'clocks and stretched herself on the cool earth to recover.

She lay there. "Delia, Delia!" She could hear Sykes calling in a most despairing tone as one who expected no answer. The sun crept on up, and he called. Delia could not move—her legs were gone flabby. She never moved, he called, and the sun kept rising.

"Mah Gawd!" She heard him moan, "Mah Gawd fum Heben!" She heard him stumbling about and got up from her flower-bed. The sun was growing warm. As she approached the door she heard him call out hopefully, "Delia, is dat you Ah heah?"

She saw him on his hands and knees as soon as she reached the door. He crept an inch or two toward her—all that he was able, and she saw his horribly swollen neck and his one open eye shining with hope. A surge of pity too strong to support bore her away from that eye that must, could not, fail to see the tubs. He would see the lamp. Orlando with its doctors was too far. She could scarcely reach the Chinaberry tree, where she waited in the growing heat while inside she knew the cold river was creeping up and up to extinguish that eye which must know by now that she knew.

Almost every battered woman tells of wishing, at some point, that the batterer were dead, maybe even of fantasizing how he might die. These wishes and fantasies are normal, considering the extraordinary injustice these women suffer at their men's hands. But it is equally true that the small number of women who kill their batterers do not necessarily want them dead at the time; rather, they are seeking only to put an end to their pain and terror.

—Lenore E. Walker, *Terrifying Love*

Hattie Turner versus Hattie Turner

FANNIE HURST

There was a zigzag down Hattie Turner's right cheek. Herold had put it there, or at least he had indirectly put it there, for she had fallen against a piano edge from a blow directed by him.

The duplicate of that scar lay branded against Hattie's soul, or spirit, or whatever it was that served as the backdrop against which her emotions played like heat lightning.

She could have killed Herold for that scar, and for the countless figurative ones that were nipped and tucked and hacked into her by the variety of his cruelties.

As a matter of fact, she was almost constantly rehearsing some plan for killing him. This trick of her mind frightened as much as it fascinated her. The frightening part was that she could not seem to stop herself from the grim diversion of seeking out ways and means to rid her life of the bane of the existence of Herold. Design for them lurked in the crevices of her brain. In the act of lifting a cup of tea from its saucer to her lips she would pause with it suspended, as some new map of action for the murder of Herold spread itself before her widening eyes.

"Staring jitters," Herold called it. "There you go with the staring jitters! What's the matter? See anything green?"

Yes, green and blue and black and, most of all, red. Bloody! But she dared not tell Herold that. Usually she just set the cup down untasted, or went on with whatever gesture had been interrupted by the grim pattern of her vision.

"Some day," she kept telling herself, "I'll go to somebody who knows how to write and get him to make stories for the magazines out of my ideas for murder tales. They pop into my head so. If only I was educated enough, I could make stories out of them.''

But deep down within the recesses of her, Hattie knew the truth of why they popped into her head. The getting of Herold out of her universe, out of any universe that held the peril and dread of him, was on her mind. "On her mind," scarcely expressed it. The texture of her consciousness seemed woven of the sense of her need to be free of him.

You could not divorce such a man and be free of him. That was the harrowing part. Even with the scar across her cheek, spasmodic desire for her still seemed to burn within Herold; and—oh, the terrible, the degrading, the unspeakable truth of it—desire for Herold, even while with her mind and her soul and her spirit she despised him, continued to burn like slow embers, keeping themselves alive on some apparently indestructible force within her. Not that the corresponding live embers in his eyes could not be hateful to her—those eyes that could fill with lust for her like a tumbler with cloudy waters from a contaminated source. She knew that look as it began to flow, slowly, as turbid waters must flow, muddily, and clouding up his intense blue eyes.

Usually when this happened she could almost count on his coming toward her with the gesture of tearing apart her bodice, or dragging it from the shoulder downward until it revealed what was almost invariably a fillip to his desires. Against the rise of the firm white flesh of the left of her bosom, for all the world like drops of ruddy blood fallen there, lay the small phenomena of three moles, slightly graduated in size, in color grading from the pinkish brown of the strawberry to deep and ruby red.

It was when Herold ground his kisses against them that the blue of his eyes turned milky. But even while resisting him with her strength, that indefinable sense of the surrender of her senses began to flow over her, mitigating but not detouring the rebellion of her mind against this defiler of her days and her happiness and her well-being.

It was not alone when he was wild with drink, that he smote dread and fear into her. It was in the comparative quiet of his sobriety that she dreaded almost equally what could be the refinement of his cruelties. Sober, he had a manner of sliding the edge of his glance into her flesh as if it were a razor blade. Of undressing her with those eyes of his in a manner almost as distasteful as his tearing down the shoulder of her bodice for the spectacle of the three little spots of red on her snow-whiteness. It was somehow even more humiliating to be belittled and dressed-down by Herold sober.

In the fine suburban dwelling which she had fitted out with taste and discretion natural to her, it was not unusual for him to let loose before Jimpson, their staid, middle-aged butler, who, with side-burns and implacable face looked precisely like a stage butler, or before any of the other servants, over trivialities which ranged from her choice of dinner menu to the cut of her bodice, to the size of the telephone bill, to the fancied disarray of his clothes closet.

Once when he was quite sober and had bullied Hattie at great length over a bill for repair work on an artesian well, a new chauffeur had hauled off and given it to him on the jaw. A tussle had ensued, resulting in a wrenched back and internal strain that had kept Herold confined to his bed for ten days.

During this indisposition, so unusual for him, she could not help wishing for the death of Herold. Even with self-horror for such thoughts roosting day and night upon her, desire to be rid of him rode and rode her. Free of this great bullying blusterer, who had come swooping, on an oil boom, down into the green little town of her girlhood, chances for the normal happiness of any normal woman still lay ahead of Hattie. She felt it. She beat about within herself for it.

Even eleven years back he had been the big blusterer, carrying her off against the wishes of a clergyman father who had surrendered her reluctantly from the pretty stone parsonage in which she had been born and reared.

Looking back, she saw the setting her up in this remote western town, in the hard bright square-brick house without a tree on its elaborate lawns (Harold disliked the shut-in feeling of trees), as a sort of banditry. It was as if a handsome buccaneer had snatched her to his saddle as he galloped through their town. Through her life. It had been that sudden—a Ladies' Aid Strawberry Festival on the church lawn—stranger in town—gusty, lusty, lustful. . . .

Half a dozen times, in the subsequent eleven years, the small pallid figure of her widower father had journeyed the thirty-eight hours from the parsonage to urge upon her what he knew would most probably result in his enforced resignation from his flock.

"Leave him. Come home to me, daughter. Together we will pray for the salvation of his tormented soul. But meanwhile I cannot stand by and see you, as his wife, destroyed by his cruelties. At least we can pray for the salvation of his soul. . . ."

Prayers for him. They died in her throat. She wanted to be able to pray for Herold with the consecrated meekness of her father. She wanted to be able to pray for Herold instead of simultaneously despising him for the swaggering bully he was and—oh, it was too base to be borne—even while despising him, responding with the rising nap of her flesh to his sporadic covetousness.

Shame! she cried deep in her spirit. Shame! And yet, even though she once went so far as to return to the parsonage with her father, in less than two months, and at her own initiative, she was back at the board and keep and bed of her husband once more, revolted and yet drawn there—drawn there.

Death was her only escape from Herold. His death or hers. It was of his death, however, that she constantly brooded in these two years since her return from the parsonage.

Her concentration on this subject came to resemble the concentration of a picture-puzzle or a chess addict. Day after day, alone in the big house, while he rode the oil fields and her taste for what mild social diversions the town afforded receded, she sat in the bay window of her bedroom, playing at this strange and terribly private mental game.

The game of murder. How to commit it and dispose of it without detection. True, she never admitted, even to herself, that she was plotting the doing away of a human life. Herold's. It was merely a game with which to while away the time.

She was like a woman in the throes of a strange lust, hastening through household duties that might detain her from her pastime of sitting in the bright window and planning. Plotting for stories, she called it to herself. Plots that some day she would carry to a writer to be made into a book. Plots for stories! Plots in her heart of hearts for the murder of—oh, it was too horrible, too, too horrible. She, Hattie, married to this man Herold, from whom her only deliverance would be death—his death!

There were so many seemingly foolproof methods. Really, it was a game. You needed only to realize the large proportion of murders which remained unsolved, even with the police and the detective forces of large cities spreading the immensity of their nets, to say nothing of the vast numbers of such crimes which must never come to light at all—oh, the limitless possibilities of ways and means!

With Herold dead and in his coffin—life, which had closed for Hattie like a fan snapped shut, might so conceivably open up again. Brightly. She was only twenty-seven. In spite of the scar on her cheek, which with a new preparation called Coverall she could almost powder out, much of the considerable comeliness that had attracted the blusterer to the clergyman's daughter was still her bright asset.

Even without the italicizing effect of the three moles strewn along the white rise of her breast, the texture of her flesh was still quite dazzling.

Hattie, comely, filled with the rising sap of a youth not easily defeated, wanted so passionately to be happy. And happiness meant freedom from the cruel paradox of her attraction to the flesh, and her loathing of the spirit, of Herold.

He loved to humiliate her. Sometimes he would take advantage of her slavish attraction to the animal splendor of him by tantalizing her. He would lean to kiss her and then, when he saw her eye flutter and the breath come short, withdraw suddenly and burst into immense laughter at her obvious degradation. At such times he would often snatch at a housemaid for the easy compensation of a smack against her lips before he drove off in a high-powered roadster, which he handled like an outlaw his stallion, to disappear for days into the oil camps or the resorts for which this particular wide-open town was notorious.

That there were women who fattened off his largesse, Hattie knew. Knew? Why, he was not above bringing them to the square house on the hill, flaunting them at her table, putting them up as house guests, and padding, after the household has retired for the night, through the hallways in his dressing gown to their bedrooms.

On those occasions, when Hattie allowed her mind to admit that the allegedly hypothetical victim of her murder plots was Herold, she barricaded herself with this thought: Even if I should fail in the perfect murder, no jury would convict me. The testimonies of Jimpson, the butler, or Anna, the housemaid, would in themselves be sufficient. . . .

Plots. Plots. Plots. Her head swam and sang with them. Plots for stories, of course. Some day she would take them to some one who could write. Murder plots for stories.

There was the one, to be accomplished, of course, while the victim slept, of the hatpin straight through the medulla oblongata. You held it like a dagger for straight aim and, above all, swiftness.

There had been that case of a Finnish woman who had achieved bloodless murder with such perfection that the coroner's verdict of heart failure had never even been questioned until five years later when, in the spirit of braggadocio, she had revealed the truth to a treacherous neighbor woman. Exhumation had borne out her statement. There were countless numbers of such cases. A man in Minnesota had caused his victim, by a set trap, to wrap copper cord about her own throat. . . .

There were several historic instances of a room strewn beforehand, as if ransacked, and a small-snouted gun held to the roof of the victims' mouth. (Herold slept with his mouth open! No, no, *no,* the character in the story did!) Always the verdict was one of robbery by killers who escaped. There were countless variants to this idea. The notorious one of the French woman who disposed of three members of her husband's family in a series of well-staged pretended robberies. There was the famous Stameyer case. . . .

Afternoons, while rain or shine poured down upon the square house, which, without trees, reminded Hattie of a woman without eyelashes, she would sit in her window, playing with those variants.

One popular method was to choose an evening when the victim was known, by at least several persons, to have an unusually large sum in the pockets of his trousers (there were certain days when Herold came home with quite large sums of currency) which would be flung across a chair as he slept. Robbers studied the habits of men leaving bank tellers' windows. What more natural than that Herold, leaving his bank, might be watched. No, no—the man in the plot leaving his bank!

There was one she would no more have attempted! It was out of her own head, and in her opinion better than any one of those in the occasional books on such subjects which she never ventured to bring into the house, but read at the counters of bookstores. Hattie had devised a way by which ground glass might be administered in capsules to a man who, like Herold, was constantly taking them for a digestive complaint. That, together with a guarded distribution into food, would accelerate the old and tried method of slow murder by way of pulverized glass well-known to all students of the history of crime and its motives. Now Hattie's plot ingenuity had devised a speedier way. The slow method would be too horrible and too unbearable. But better even than that perhaps would be the shot in the dark through the roof of the mouth . . . strewn evidence of robbery. . . .

It was upon this last that more and more her concentration seemed to focus. On Friday nights Herold came home with pockets well-stocked with currency, because on Saturdays he usually went to the neighboring mining town of Spear, a wide-open gambling one, where he played roulette in the house of the notorious woman of the county. Herold slept with his mouth open. No, no, the character in the story slept with his mouth open. There were two guns in the house! One, in Herold's chiffonier drawer, loaded with blank cartridges, which he fired on summer evenings to frighten away blackbirds which littered the lawns; the other a silent Maxim, which he kept wrapped in a silk handkerchief in a seldom-used sideboard drawer.

There was a book on the fingerprinting system which she would have liked to own. She had run across it one day on the counter of a bookshop and mulled through its pages. For the sake of appearances she had left it to browse among others and then, ever so idly, returned to it. But one did not bring such a book into the house. Why? No particular reason, except that one did not bring such a book into the house.

There were rubber gloves wrapped in oiled paper in the top drawer of Hattie's dressing table. She had bought them to save her hands when pottering in the garden. *Of course, she bought them to save her hands when pottering in the garden!* She intended some day to learn to potter in the garden. It was best to have them on hand. She had bought them to save her hands when pottering in the garden.

A handkerchief, preferably linen or silk, rubbed against any object removed evidence of fingerprints. Your perpetrator did not leave the scene of his activity without first rubbing a handkerchief over every object that he might possibly have touched.

It was important to become fingerprint-conscious. Herold's bed showed no metal or wooden surface. Not Herold's bed! The victim in the story's bed.

The pattern of the procedure would be almost startlingly simple. A Friday night. His trousers flung over the chair. (No wood on that chair, overstuffed and chintz-covered.) The pocket with the currency against Saturday's trip to Spear would be bulging. Herold (no, no, the character in the story) would be sleeping with his mouth open. The Maxim in the sideboard drawer was wrapped in a silk handkerchief. It would slip into the long pocket-sleeve of a Chinese kimono. It was loaded. A simple matter to strew contents of drawers and cupboards about while Herold slept. Even when sober—and almost any Friday night he was sure not to be—it was a household adage that a steam engine tearing through his bedroom could not awaken him.

Herold was known to have enemies. He was known to carry large sums of money for his loose purposes. Herold slept soundly with his mouth open. Almost the worst that could happen was the possibility of the shot being deflected downward, should the sleeper leap to resistance at the contact of the steel against his mouth. And that, if you studied the twist of the wrist and your human anatomy, might mean the alternatives of the jugular vein or the abdomen. Both equally vulnerable.

Bank notes would need to be strewn about, and, for purposes of evidence of struggle, the body dragged to the floor. That could be done. After the shot. And most important of all, before the alarm was given, that Maxim, in its silk handkerchief, must repose again in its sideboard drawer.

Hattie would be free.

He slept with his mouth open, you see. On Fridays, he was known, in anticipation of his Saturdays at the gaming table, to come home with his pockets bulging. Men hated Herold. Jilted and too easily forgotten women harbored animosities. He was not only a wife-beater, but a mistress-beater. There was that tale of the girl with the permanently injured back, whom he was compelled, by a restless public opinion, to support in a Denver Sanatarium. It seemed that she had been bent backward across a chair while her lover, in the throes of an unmentionable Sadism, pressed and pressed. . . .

"Oh God, if only I were free of him—to live the good things, now that I have so terribly lived the bad. To do good things and be done by, that way. And I can never be free for the good things until—until—"

He slept with his mouth open, you see. Rubber gloves. The silent Maxim in the sideboard drawer. He kept it loaded and wrapped in silk. The snout of the gun was small. Herold slept with his mouth open. No, no, no, the man in the plot slept with his mouth open. . . .

·　·　·

It was on the Friday of a fine week-end in April that Herold came home with his pockets bulging for what the morrow did portend. He had been drinking, she could tell it by the way the toes of his heavy shoes hit each step as he mounted the stairs, but unfortunately not enough to render him insensate so that he might be disposed of in bed beneath blankets, boots and all, while he slept it off.

This Friday he was fairly steady on his big, strong, legginged legs, and there was drawn across his face that tantalizing look which was like a red flag of defiance rippling there.

If only that face had been veined, purplish of lip, and sunken with inebriation, as the face of such a man so easily could have been, she might have found her freedom from the lure of his still powerful flesh. But Herold had the lean prowess of the fleet; firm, bold, and impudent his lips from which, when he willed, could flow laughter as appealing as his profanity could be obscene.

This afternoon, pausing before the door of his wife's bedroom of the bay window, he spun his glance ruthlessly over her person, so that involuntarily her hand flew to the shoulder of her bodice, as if to prevent it from being dragged down to reveal the three provocative little polka dots of moles that lay beneath.

She knew that look, and, loathing it, could feel her limbs begin to tremble to submission.

But there happened this day something to divert Herold.

There was lying on the light fur rug at the base of her chaise longue—lying there inadvertently, heaven knows, since she was wary of such lapses—the loose leaves of a five-page letter received that day from her father.

It must be said for Herold that whatever his contempt for the old gentleman who was his father-in-law, and however he wreaked it on his wife, his personal behavior to the Reverend Baynes had always been of a restrained, if slightly contemptuous, nature. It was as if the combination of the cloth and the extreme frailty of old age tempered his obstreperousness, but only in order that he might give vent to it where Hattie was concerned.

"Your old man dishing up some more hate, in one of those ten-page letters of his? Sitting there stewing in the juices of his hate of me?"

As a matter of fact, this particular communication from a parent chronically heartbroken over the relentlessness of the circumstances that had overtaken an only child dear to him contained no mention of the torturous subject that usually lay uppermost in his mind. On the contrary, it was a letter of local gossip, of the tidy planning of small affairs of a godly old man entering the twilight years of a godly life. To his son-in-law, whose very name the old clergyman could not write without a twist of pain, there was not even reference.

Perhaps, as Herold's eyes ran over the pages, there was resentment at the omission, or there may have stirred within the slightly inebriate Herold fresh rancor over the old score he never tired settling with Hattie—the fact that in opening the doors of his parsonage to his daughter, on that occasion of her plight, Dr. Baynes had been deliberately guilty of attempting to alienate her affections.

In any event, as he ran a cursory eye along the pages, so foul a reference to Dr. Baynes left the lips of Herold that something leaped up in Hattie which she could not control, causing her to jump to her feet and revile Herold in kind, but ending by clapping her palms across her mouth, as if to stem words that would only invoke further display from her husband.

But too late. Let slip were Herold's dogs of war which at best were kept leashed on slender chains, and there, before the servants—Anna the housemaid, Tessa the second maid, Jimpson the butler, Ella the cook—and louder still, so that even the laundress at her tasks might hear, and the gardener—flowed the invective, the drunken verbiage, the bullying vocabulary reviling her. Then, all in a breath, followed endearing names which were meant to mock her! Wench-of-my-heart. Dirty-little-flower. And on and on into an insane profanity.

Three hours of that. Three hours of bending back her fingers, one by one, until she was on her knees, and there he kissed her, delighting in feeling her tremble like a tree in a wind. Three hours of the semi-insanity of his Sadism and worse. Three hours of this minute finger-by-finger torture of a woman.

It was not the first time, or the third time, or the thirtieth. It would not be the last. At least, it would not be the last unless . . .

There were other women, whom she knew by name and, alas, from having entertained them in her home. Women whom whole communities of men knew by name. Kits. Tottie. Goldy-Meg. Madame Wray. Before the servants he flaunted these intimacies, and there would be more of this, more and more, unless. . . .

With all his wealth, he was still enough of a product of the mining camp to demand, among the gold plate and the crystal of his table, the rough-and-ready accessory of the whole bread-loaf on its round wooden plaque. Time and time again, during the meal that evening—horrible, horrible—Hattie felt her hand close over the handle of the bread knife lying beside the plaque, and her eyes rest appraisingly on the white, youthful line of his throat, where, as the wine rose higher and higher in his head, he had burst his collar open.

Her eyes, it seemed to her, must be burning with the light of a killer.

Presently, before he reached the completely drowsy stage, he would be after her again. There would be his lips against the three little apple-pits of brown moles that studded her white bosom.

This should be the night! His pockets bulged with their currency in rolls of bank notes bound with rubber bands. Satiated of her, and of drink and of food, he would be falling into his heavy sleep with his mouth open.

If only she dared make this the night.

Long after he had flung her from his couch, and, violated and trembling, she had stolen back to her room, the impulse continued to dance before her. Long after she had fallen into the deep shamed sleep that followed such an evening, her dreams were lurid with that impulse.

The Maxim in its sideboard drawer, wrapped in silk. The strewing of the objects. His box of jewelry. His mouth would be open.

Moonlight streamed over her sleep.

. . .

What awakened her first was the sound of Anna the housemaid, being hysterical. It took quite a few seconds to assemble the senses sufficiently to identify those short high barking sounds Anna made. But that was Anna all right. And then immediately there were rushing feet and rushing noises everywhere, and in a house flooded with lights and sounds of utmost alarm the moonlight was suddenly blocked out of Hattie's sleeping apartment, and in a room suddenly filled with frightened servants headed by Jimpson the butler, holding his face as if it would fall apart, Hattie sat up in bed to face the assembled horror of her household.

The face of Anna the housemaid was the worst of all. It was like a face on a gibbet, dead as a doornail.

The din of the voices. The servants all talking at once. The lights clicking on. The frantic working of the telephone hook.

JIMPSON, the butler: I'm asleep, and all of a sudden I thinks I hear a thudlike—

ANNA, the housemaid: First, I thought I was dreaming. Then I sits up. Oh my God!

ELLA, the cook: That, I says to myself, is the sound of a body falling. Glory be to God, I says to myself, it's the sound of a body falling—

JACKSON, the gardener: I says to my missis, sounds like footsteps running through the garden—

LOU, the laundress: Him laying there dead as a panel, and me as late as six o'clock this evening ironing his under-drawers for him. Him that was kissing Anna in the pantry not six hours ago—him laying there dead!

ANNA, the maid: Oh, my God.

JIMPSON, the butler: Shut up. Help the missus. We got to lay off of everything until the cops and the coroners come.

ANNA, the maid: Oh my God, I can't stop. I think I'm going to faint. . . .

ENSEMBLE: I-thought-I-heard-a-thud-Bridget-I-calls-out-to-the-missis-sounds-like-footsteps-in-the-garden-That-I-says-to-myself-is-a-body-falling-I'm-asleep-and-all-of-a-sudden-I-heard-a-thud-like—

Through all this came now to Hattie, struggling into the long pocket sleeves of her mandarin kimono, the additional craziness of the sound of motor sirens and the voices of neighbors and the paraphernalia of the uniform and brass buttons of the law.

I-says-to-the-missis-Officer-I-says-sounds-like-footsteps-in-the-garden-I-was-asleep-Officer-and-all-of-a-sudden-I-heard-a-thud-like-First-I-thought-I-was-dreaming-and-then-I-sits-up-That-I-said-is-the-sound-of-a-body-falling....

There had, it seemed, been a robbery. The body of Herold, all turned in on itself, lay on the floor in his bedroom, untouched and awaiting the coroner. There had been a tussle. His blood, in a pool on the floor, looked like mud. The shot had entered the neck. There is a jugular vein there.

Already, half a mile down the road, a suspect had been apprehended, crouching on his belly in a thicket. There was blood about his face, which he declared to be the result of a short cut homeward through brambles, but no loot was found on his person or along the road or lawns.

Herold had put up a fight. The wads of his bills lay strewn and abandoned on the floor beside his body.

·   ·   ·

The prisoner on trial for the assault and murder of Herold Laribee Turner had a head the shape of a coconut, on which the hair grew thin and straight and light brown, as on a coconut. His alleged name was Mack Metson. He was known in the nether life of the town and had several previous prison records to his name, all for robbery and assault. He had a wizened face which comprehended slowly, and which, most of the time, looked so squeezed with the effort to understand that the wrinkles seemed alive and moving.

It was a mean face, but even more than that it seemed to Hattie a sick face. Something was either lacking or out of gear behind those features. The meanness, apparently, must be the effect of some cause that had not directly to do with Mack Metson. But it was solely the effect, regardless of cause, with which the courtroom and its dreadful paraphernalia were concerned.

This man with the coconut head was on trial for his life for the murder of Herold. He had been found, not less than thirty minutes after the alarm, a half-mile from the scene of the attempted robbery. There was blood on him, although it was conceivable that it might have been from scratches—it might have been no more than would naturally result if a man had forced his way through brambles after a day of rabbit-hunting.

Thus far neither footprints nor evidence of witnesses was lifting his case out of the bothersome mire of circumstantial evidence—a slippery path along which the wheels of the law ground slowly.

Every day for a week the pattern of the courtroom had assembled itself around the pointy-headed figure of the prisoner at the bar.

Gavel. Order in the Court. Your Honor. Do you solemnly swear? Next witness. Your Honor, I object. Objection sustained. Objection overruled. Answer yes or no. Look at the defendant. Is that the man? Now, Anna, I want you to tell the Court just what happened on the night of April sixth, from the time you turned down Mrs. Turner's bed, placed a plate of fruit and a thermos bottle on the table beside her bed, and then went to your own room at the end of the hall. Your Honor, I object. Objection overruled. Your Honor, I object. Objection sustained. Order in the Court! Did you? Didn't you? Now, Ella, I want you to tell the Court exactly what you heard on the night of April sixth. How far, in your opinion, was the late Mr. Turner's bedroom from Jimpson the butler's? Was Mr. Turner in the habit . . .

For six days the figure of Hattie Turner (yes, they had dressed her up in widow's weeds) sat in the pattern of the picture, her scar, which she had forgotten to powder out with the Coverall, quivering down her right cheek, and her eyes full of shame, and something more that was indefinable, seeming much too large for her face.

A man was on trial for his life. The State versus Mack Metson. And deep down within the innermost chambers of herself, Hattie was on trial for hers. Hattie Turner versus Hattie Turner.

The terribleness of the dilemma of Hattie Turner was this: she could not be sure that the murder for which that ratlike little creature crouched there in the prisoner's chair had not been committed by Hattie Turner!

Where had she, Hattie Turner, been on that night of the alleged robbery, when Herold, coming up too slowly out of sleep, had battled with his adversary and received the shot in the neck? Dreaming, or executing that dream which for her had become almost inseparable from reality?

Had her hand slipped at its mentally rehearsed act, or had Mack Metson's? How often she had figured out just that contingency of the shot going afoul of the roof of the mouth. Had she been in her sleep when the death-dealing lead had gone pouring into the flesh of Herold, or had she been scrambling along the silent hallways to replace the silent Maxim in its place in the sideboard drawer?

If only she had taken the precaution to count the cartridges. She had meant to, ever since the afternoon, not six weeks before, when Herold had been tinkering about with his Maxim, cleaning chambers, oiling, and breaking it open time and time again as he tested the flexibility of this firearm which he kept about the house in a vague gesture of protection. And now she, who had calculated so finely, had failed in the simple matter of counting the number of cartridges in Herold's silent Maxim that had lain in the drawer.

Was that gun precisely in its place in the velvet-lined left-hand groove of the sideboard drawer, where she had regarded it as recently as twenty hours before the murder?

There were times, during that week of the trial of Mack Metson for murder in the first degree, when it seemed to those watching that the widow of Herold Turner, poor dear, must surely crack under the strain.

Poor, poor dear, she was said to be in love with the scamp who had been notorious the county over for cruelties and infidelities. Well, at least he had had the decency to die without will or testament. That left her a wealthy young widow. And a handsome one, mark you. Mope over him? She ought to toss up her cap. Probably would, once this dreadful business blew over and she turned her thoughts to the good things life would hold for her. Honestly, looking at it in one way, they ought to pin a medal on that little rat Metson, instead of sending him on his way to a gallows. Of course, society had to be protected and all that, and the fellow must hang, but by gad, it was sort of like hanging a crow for pecking out the eyes of a sheep-eating wolf. That pretty widow ought to hurry up and wipe her hands and memory of the whole dirty business, and get somewhere and start new. Lots of good things ahead for a woman like that. Coming to her, too! They ought to make her stay away from the courtroom, getting herself all harrowed like this. Darn shame!

Stay away from the courtroom where a man was on trial for a crime that she, Hattie Turner, might conceivably have committed!

Had it been in her dream, or in dreadful appalling fact, that she had tiptoed her way to that sideboard drawer? Had Herold given fight in her sleep, or in the actuality of that furiously tumbled room in which the crime had been committed? Were those her footsteps Anna claimed to have heard, and was Mack Metson, crouched in his prisoner's chair, about to be called upon to pay his life for hers?

Evidence, such as it was, seemed closing him in. Why, for instance, had he chosen an unfrequented, almost an unblazed, short cut at that time of night? Did a man without apprehensions of a serious nature throw himself flat in order to evade a few passersby? District Attorney Sinsabaugh made jeering point after point over that. Even though Metson had apparently done away with all evidence of the firearm he must have used in the crime, he was known to be a fellow who went armed. Also, Metson was known to be financially embarrassed, and witnesses revealed that debt was pressing him. Then too, there was his varied criminal record and, working indubitably against him, the furtive ratlike quality of the prisoner. The jerking nose that denoted drug habit, the darting eye, the vindictive look that darkened his face when a witness took the stand with evidence that threatened to stack against him.

Conceivably, a jury might subconsciously be rating such a man as an enemy to society on general principles.

Perhaps. But more and more Hattie was beginning to know, as terror mounted, that it was not in her to sit by while even such a life was offered in forfeit of her own.

If, on the night of April sixth, Hattie Turner, in reality instead of dream, had committed the murder of Herold Laribee Turner, then she, not Metson must—must—Oh God, had she? Had she?

There were things which, it seemed to her, she would never, never, never have done.

That horrible position of the body, for instance. She would have straightened it out. There was something inexplicably terrible to her in the doubling under of the legs and neck. That blow! Herold had apparently, even while his life's blood was flowing out, been hit against the temple with something hard and iron. The pistol, no doubt, which had not been recovered. Where was that pistol? Back in its drawer?

If only she could tear apart the opaque veiling that hung so thinly and yet so clingingly between her dream and her reality. It had the frailty of web, that veil. It had the viscosity of gum, that veil.

Had she, on the night of the murder of Herold, been in her bed, or in the act of perpetrating it herself, that fateful hour when the bullet, presumably missing its mark in the roof of the mouth, had torn its way downward through the jugular vein?

Fouler than the crime itself, Hattie told herself over and over again, would it be to permit even such poor flesh as Metson's to be sacrificed for hers. Never again would her distraught head rest on any pillow, including the one in her casket. The terrible doubt. The doubt that was jeopardizing her very sanity.

Hattie Turner to Hattie Turner: Where where you on the night of April sixth when the sounds of a scuffle and a body falling aroused the household? Asleep in your bed, or scuttling through halls to replace in its silken kerchief the object secreted in the long pocket sleeve of your Chinese kimono? Answer yourself, Hattie Turner. Answer yourself.

Oh God, where was I?

.   .   .

There would keep arising, in the various testimonies, discrepancies upon which the prosecuting attorney pounced like an angry terrier, dragging them again and again to the feet of a jury which was beginning to exhibit symptoms of wanting to be free of a case which was threatening to prolong itself into a second week.

After all, no one had actually seen Metson either cross or leave a threshold or window ledge of the Turner dwelling. The perpetrator of the crime had been heard, but not seen, on the night of the robbery and assault.

The killer's bullet, leaving the body of Herold, must have whizzed through the open window, probably lodging in the earth, the bark of a tree, or bush. Thus far searchings had failed to reveal it. What Hattie would have given for five minutes alone with that bullet! God, if you would let me have that bullet. There were two chambers empty in the Maxim in the silk handkerchief in the sideboard drawer. Would that bullet fit one of them?

Testimonies, too, were at variance. The gardener and Jimpson had testified to cross-purposes, and that had brought out in the statements of Jimpson the most damning discrepancy of all.

If, according to new testimonies finally obtained from Jimpson after he had been recalled to the witness chair for the third time, it was the sound of overturning furniture and the thud of what seemed to be a heavy falling body that had first awakened him, why, then, had he arrived on the scene at least six minutes after the gardener and the remainder of the servants were assembled there?

How did Jimpson explain this lapse of time between the exit from his sleeping room, which happened to be closest of all the servants' rooms to the scene of the murder, and his arrival in Herold Turner's bedroom? This point, according to the counsel for the defense, was one of highly debatable importance, but it was played upon relentlessly by the prosecution.

"How do you explain the fact that in order to traverse the narrow ledge of balcony along the outside of the second-story windows, a route even shorter than the one used by the other servants, it took you six minutes to traverse what at best was a two-minute distance? Your room, the only one of the servants' which opened out onto this balcony, gave you the opportunity of a short cut, of which you say you took advantage. Gentlemen of the jury, you see with what result. Only in order to arrive at the scene of the catastrophe six minutes later than any other servant of the household. Gentlemen, a testimony is as strong as its weakest link."

The jurors were getting restless. They had wives and children at home; business affairs too long neglected. The foreman had developed a severe cold. A young master plumber named Quinlin had a wife in the ninth month of family way.

Plain as the nose on your face, the guilt of Metson, and yet—and yet—now just take that matter of Jimpson. Nothing much to it, but why the devil? The jury scratched what for the most part were God-fearing heads. Plain as the nose on your face, and yet—

At the beginning of this second week, the fear that was mounting in Hattie began to take on cyclonic speed, whistling through her ears in a gale of head-noises that threatened to blow down her sanity.

Hattie, Hattie, look yourself in the eye and tell only Hattie. After that we can decide, but tell Hattie now. If you don't, all your life, all your death, the little eyes of Mack Metson will roost like scavengers upon your peace, upon your spirit, upon your soul. Hattie, look Hattie in the eye. . . .

Usually, the best way to try to get some sort of hold on herself was to rise from bed and creep down to the sideboard drawer. Was that object in its silk handkerchief in the exact position in which it had been when last she had glanced at it, the night before the murder? Or was it now in the adjoining little velvet-lined compartment, originally designed to separate knives from forks? Where had it been that night before the murder? In the right or left compartment? It was in the left one now. Had it been in the right before? Had it? Had it? More and more it seemed so. That object wrapped in silk was in the left compartment now!

And next, to her horror, she discovered that the long mandarin sleeve to her Chinese kimono had a small hole in it, as if a heavy object had burst the stitched edge. The weight of a pistol? Or was it just a rip that might occur in any garment?

Now—this minute—lying in his cell, Mack Metson, a human being, is on trial for his life. If I let him pay, his blood, even more than Herold's, will lie wet, on all my life and on all my death. Hattie, look Hattie in the eye. For God's sake look Hattie in the eye and try to tell her where you were on the night of April sixth, when it happened. For God's sake, for God's sake, tell Hattie!

But the final circumstance which precipitated decision came with accidental discovery of a trifle of a black-and-blue spot on the upper part of her arm. It was obviously a week or two old and already paling when, as she stepped out of her bath, she observed it for the first time.

How came she by that bruise? Accidentally? Possibly, but Hattie was not a person of short impulsive movements. She could scarcely, in all her life, remember previous black-and-blue spots. How came she by this bruise?

The time had come for Hattie Turner. Better now than to be discovered after she had permitted the machinery of the law to grind out the life of the innocent party.

If Mack Metson did not do it—and no one had seen him enter the house or leave it—then who did? Hattie Turner. Hattie, dreaming, scheming through all the weeks, the months, yes, even the years, to be rid of the incubus that was throttling the happiness out of her life. Hattie, dreaming to be free of one from whom her only release lay in his death. So, conceivably, she might have dreamed that act, and ultimately, one night when the border line between dream and reality faded, have committed it by crossing the hair line between contemplation and execution. Hattie Turner, look Hattie Turner in the eye. . . .

The thing to do was to allow herself just this one more morning of possibly enlightening disclosures in the courtroom, and then, immediately following recess, go to the judge, a kindly man, intercept him in his chambers before he could take off his robes to go to his lunch, and tell all. Tell all.

Quietly, Hattie, quietly. The judge will let you relate it in your own way. Inch by inch you must make him see the processes that led up to the crime of the night of April sixth. It will not be easy. But Hattie Turner, the time has come. Tell all. The evidence of the Maxim in the sideboard drawer, the ripped kimono sleeve, the bruise are the least of it. Hattie Turner, tell all.

The time had come when it was actually with a sense of unutterable relief that Hattie contemplated the hour of creeping to the judge, there to crouch beside him and with eyes closed reveal to him, inch by inch by inch, the horror and the terror and the dread out of which had been woven this monstrous web.

Hattie Turner, tell all.

The morning moved so slowly chiefly because, for the fourth time, Jimpson was in the witness chair. Poor Jimpson, he looked tired, he looked harassed, he looked beaten. More and more, pounding the fact of the time discrepancy between his response to the sound of tumbling furniture and his appearance at the scene of the murder, counsel for the defense was baiting him. Poor Jimpson. . . .

"You mean to say, Mr. Jimpson, that your final explanation of the six minutes that elapsed between the time you left your room and arrived upon the scene of the disturbance is 'I don't know'? Will you be kind enough to face the jury and repeat your reply? What explanation have you, Mr. Jimpson, of the six minutes' delay in reaching the scene?"

Every time this question came hurtling at him, deadly in its repetitiveness, the equanimity of Jimpson, faltering more and more, gave increasingly away. It had become quite pitiful to watch his trained butler's face seem to collapse into watery lines, especially in contrast with his earlier firm demeanor in the witness chair.

"How do you account for that interval?"

"I—I—you see—"

"How do you account for that interval?"

"I—I—"

"You hear, Gentlemen of the Jury. Mr. Jimpson does not know how to account for it. The blueprints have shown you the distance from his room along the narrow balcony which runs along the second story of the Turner dwelling. Obviously, it would take less than two minutes to traverse this distance, yet Mr. Jimpson does not know why it took him six minutes. Mr. Jimpson, by virtue of the fact that his window opened out on this balcony, was enabled to choose a shorter route to reach Mr. Turner's room than any of the other servants. *Yet he arrived there six minutes later than they!* Does this testimony, Gentlemen of the Jury, strike you as coming from a man sufficiently trust-worthy to influence your judgment of the life and death situation which confronts our defendant? Does it, Gentlemen? Does this smell strangely of perjury, Gentlemen? I ask you, Gentlemen, does it?"

How curious of Jimpson. Whom was he shielding? Was Jimpson shielding her? What did Jimpson know? Nothing, of course. And yet, why? What was

the strangeness surrounding him? He was a good, self-respecting man, unmar-
ried, known to support a pair of aged parents in Scotland, and of godly, simple
habits himself. Was he about to be drawn in? God, had she waited too long?
Must she, after all, jump to her feet right here in the courtroom, as they did in
motion-picture scenes, and shout out the fact that more and more surely, she,
Hattie Turner, was guilty of the murder?

"Judge!" she actually did call out, and then sat smothering her rising hysteria, for suddenly, as if the word "perjury," so cunningly reiterated day after
day by counsel for the defense, had finally snapped the last sinews of his
resistance, Jimpson was on his feet, his square face suffused with red, as the
words seemed to come rattling from under his upper lip.

"Your Honor, I'm a God-fearing man! 'Perjury' is a word I never exactly
knew the meaning of until now. I'm of white blood, God be thanked, but I
know how in America they are quick to lynch the low in station of any color
for—for crimes a man never had no thought of except—like most of us—the
crime of having desires stored away in our minds that haven't got the right to
be there!"

Jimpson! What was Jimpson knowing!

"I've respect for Mrs. Turner, Your Honor. A finer lady to work for never
drew breath. A lady for whom my heart was bleeding twenty-four hours of
every day—"

"Be brief, Mr. Jimpson."

"Those six minutes that seem to be making such a point for Mr. Lawyer
here, they are as innocent a six minutes as a man ever spent, Judge, so help me
God! But it's going to be as hard an explanation as a man, white and in his
sound mind, can be called on to give, Your Honor. You'll understand, Your
Honor, why I—I haven't come out with it before—"

"Order in the court! Proceed, Mr. Jimpson."

"The night of the—the accident, Your Honor, hearing a commotion I didn't
like the sound of, I throws on me pants and leaves me room at the end of the
corridor. Commotion seemed to come from His Nibs' room—as we in the
kitchen used to refer to Mr. Turner—meaning no disrespect, although there
was no reason, Your Honor, why any one working for him should hold him in
respect—"

"Confine your remarks, Mr. Jimpson, to what happened."

"Begging your pardon, Your Honor, I throws on me pants, and I chooses to
go along the balcony that most of the bedrooms on the second floor open out
on, because it's a short cut, and I knows every inch of that balcony, mine being
the only one of the servants' rooms that opens out on it, and it being one of my
duties to keep it swept and scrubbed clean from the doves, who dirty it."

"Keep closely to the point, Jimpson."

"All of a sudden, when I reaches the French doors that open out on the

gallery from Mrs. Turner's room, it being moonlight and bright as day, I—I—
well, I—"

Oh God! To have waited too long. To have waited until too late to confess
for herself. . . .

"Yes, it's moonlight, bright as day. You are passing Mrs. Turner's room.
The French windows are open. Proceed. Order in the court! Proceed!"

"If ever a man, Your Honor, was in a spot where he could wish the earth
would open and swallow—but knowing it's a matter of life and death, I'm
following God's will in testifying what I know—"

"Proceed, Jimpson!"

"It's moonlight—bright as day—I'm hurrying in the direction of His Nibs'
room to see what the commotion is—used as we were to commotion in that
house, from him coming home all hours and all ways, there was something
strange about that commotion—as I was hurrying along the balcony that
night. . . ."

Oh God, if only I had the strength to jump to my feet now and—tell! But
I'm paralyzed—my throat—all solid ice—God, if you love me, make me drop
dead. . . .

". . . and when I pass Mrs. Turner's room, it being a springlike night full of
moonlight, I sees laying there, through the open French windows of her room
—may God strike me dead if I sees it with anything except respect for our lady
in my heart—there I sees laying. . . ."

God, if you love me, make me drop dead. . . .

"There I sees laying—in the moonlight—"

"Order in the Court or I will have the room cleared. Proceed."

"There I sees laying in the moonlight, with the covers off, it being a warm
night—asleep like a baby, with the little lace bit she wore for a nightgown all
down off her shoulders, and her hair spreading free on the pillow, there I sees
laying in the moonlight—"

"Order in the Court!"

"It wasn't me with a bad thought in my body that stopped me, Your Honor.
So help me God, it was something I saw in the moonlight I could not make out
at first. I stopped and I kept looking, Your Honor. I thought I saw blood!"

"Order in the Court!"

"Laying there in her bed, all white in the moonlight, the coverings off'n
her, sleeping like a baby, was Mrs. Turner, and on my lady's bosom, Your
Honor, God strike me dead if my thoughts were bad, were what seemed to me
like three drops of blood, that on looking closer turned out to be three dark
spots—moles, I guess you'd call them—except that these were—well these
were like nothing I'd ever seen on a woman. I mean like nothing I'd ever
seen—"

"Order in the Court!"

"They looked like blood—hell freeze me over, if they didn't look like blood. I tiptoes, she sleeping there like a baby. I tiptoes closer, Your Honor, and what I sees close up is not three drops of blood. It's three little brown spots. Three little moles, drifting along my lady's bosom like petals from a little rose somebody might have dropped there."

"Order!"

"So help me God, Your Honor, if it's not an insult to so fine a lady, you can ask her to show them to you, to prove I don't lie. But if I'd a' had a hat on my head, I would have uncovered, that night as I stood there a'looking at my lady for what must have been those six damned minutes they are kicking up so much fuss about. May have been longer. All I know is that I stood there. If I'd a'had a hat, I'd have uncovered—looking at my lady sound asleep there in the moonlight, laying with her face sometimes puckering a bit as if dreaming something bad, laying there so beautiful and so sound asleep in the moonlight with the three little petals floating along her . . ."

"Make way there! Mrs. Turner wants out. Poor lady, having to hear that. But it's loosed up something in her. For the first time since the tragedy, she's crying, just natural woman's tears. That'll ease her."

The widespread prevalence of wife abuse suggests that it may be more a function of the normal psychological and behavior patterns of most men than of the aberrant actions of very few husbands. . . . Most psychological theories ignore the question of power. They cannot answer the question of why allegedly mentally ill men beat their wives and not their bosses, nor why impulse ridden, out of control husbands contain their rage until they are in the privacy of their homes . . .

—Michele Bograd, *"Feminist Perspectives on Wife Abuse"*

Pre-Freudian

D O R O T H Y   C A N F I E L D

I suppose, like the rest of us moderns, you have fallen into the habit of tagging human actions with psychoanalysis labels, instead of using the old folk names. You, too, probably say that the timid boy we used to call a sissy is the victim of a mother complex, and that the swaggering bully is "only overcompensating for an inferiority complex."

Did you ever happen to try plotting out on the Freudian graph paper some of the stories of older-generation doings? It's rather interesting, sometimes amusing. Not always easy to do. Just see if you can calculate the psychiatric curves of what happened to my Great-aunt Lucina.

She was really my great-great-aunt, for she was sister to my great-grandfather, and of course died long before I was born. But the family, which talked so much about her while she was alive, has gone right on talking her over in later generations. She is one of my familiars. This impression of intimacy may be helped out by the fact that I am the same size she was, and so have often worn to fancy-dress parties her huge hoop skirts, billowing flounces and lace fichus.

In her girlhood she was pretty and willful, selfish and high-spirited, and "did what she wanted, regardless!" She carried off the matrimonial prize of her time by marrying the only professional man in our small mountain community, a handsome young lawyer from Albany, just beginning what looked like a brilliant career.

In a static Vermont village there was little scope for such talents as his, and shortly after their wedding he took his bride "out West" to live. In those days this meant Western New York State, somewhere—Rochester, I think it was. It was not long before letters and occasional reports from other people who happened to see them brought the news that their marriage was not going well.

To put it mildly, at home and abroad they fought openly and without shame, like cat and dog. Lucina wrote passionately that Will had the most hateful temper in the world, and seemed to enjoy nothing in life but to humiliate her—or try to! Other people said that his young wife gave him as good as he sent.

There was not a drop of wifely meekness or submissiveness in her, they said. To a cold sneer from him, she responded with quick, fearless fury; when he made a scene she instantly made a worse one; if in a rage he deliberately broke or injured something she prized, she flew like a wild-cat to pour ink on his best shirt, or cut holes in his finest boots.

After hearing this, you—being modern—are probably not at all surprised to learn that one day, three or four years after their wedding, the stage-coach from Albany stopped in front of the Canfield house and let Aunt Lucina off, come home, bag and baggage, to stay. But although you are not surprised, her early-nineteenth-century Vermont family was—not to say appalled. For in decent families of those long-ago days, no wife left her husband unless she was literally in danger of her life from him, and often not then. In respectable settled circles there was no place for a married woman who refused to stay married. Whatever in the world could the Vermont Canfields say to people who asked —and how they would ask!—where Mrs. Upjohn's husband was?

But Aunt Lucina—by the way, that was always pronounced Lew-cye-nie— paid as little attention to this as to any other convention. To her twittering, shocked mother and sisters she said in a hard voice, "Will's a devil. I never want to see his face again!" and took possession of her old room at the head of the stairs. They were terribly embarrassed about having her there, the home people were, and hardly knew where to look when the undutiful wife sailed into church beside them, much less bothered than they by severe looks from the disapproving people in the pews. They had at least to give themselves no trouble to explain her presence. Aunt Lucina explained that to anyone who would listen, describing her husband's black furies with angry vividness, and leaving out no ugly detail of the hell on earth into which he turned their home.

One of the "exhibits" she brought back with her, and always showed as part of her indictment of Will Upjohn, still lies in a trunk in our attic. It is a beautifully embroidered collar, the fine stitchery half completed, with three round blackened holes in it, savagely burned by her York State husband, "in a rage because dinner was five minutes late. . . . Would you have gone on being a door mat under the feet of such a brute?" She used to turn violently on the mild, comfortable women around her with this question. They did not know how to answer it. They were sorry for Lucina, of course, but for the most part they were just heartily ashamed of the whole affair.

Unexpected help came to their rescue. Four or five—or was it ten?—

years after Lucina came home to live, a distant connection of the family made a special trip to our town to bring the news that he had recently been in Rochester, that Lucina's husband—Lawyer Upjohn—had grown worse since her departure, was worse all the time, and that finally the doctors of the town had pronounced him really insane. Not so much so, that he couldn't go on drawing up watertight contracts and deeds, and brilliantly advising clients. In his office and in the courtroom he was always a formidable figure, well worth having on your side. But in private life he was subject to brain-storms which went far beyond the limits of anything that could be called normal.

"Nobody out there," reported this old cousin jubilantly, "no, not even the minister of their church, blames Lucina any more. They all say there's no telling what harm he'd have done her if she'd tried to stay there." He drew a long breath of satisfaction, echoed by his listeners, and, looking around the circle of family elders, told them, "I knew 'twould make you all feel better about her being here."

He was right. It made them feel much better. It made them feel, in fact, perfectly all right about it. They looked forward with eagerness to cramming this unanswerable proof of Lucina's blamelessness down the throats of the unco guid.

But the news had the oddest effect upon Lucina herself. When she was told, "You don't say!" she exclaimed in astonishment. And again, more slowly, with a thoughtful accent, "You—don't—say!"

She asked old Cousin George to tell her some more details, and he, inno-cently thinking it would soothe her well-known hatred of the man, told her that many Rochester people were afraid of her husband, that with the exception of the clients with difficult cases who came to his office, nobody had a thing to do with him. The only servants he could get to take care of the house were drunken, thieving incompetents nobody else would hire. Alone, except for one tipsy, aged, crackbrained veteran of the Revolution to keep the fires from going out, he lived in dirty neglected rooms, taking his meals—for no woman capable of cooking was brave enough to step into his kitchen—in the tavern, at a table set apart from the others, to which nobody else ever sat down. Shaggy, haggard, gaunt, unshaven, his shirts stained with tobacco juice, he walked the streets, a solitary wreck. People who had been friends and acquaintances went quickly out of their way to avoid passing him.

"You see, Lucina, you are abso-lute-ly justified. Nobody can breathe a word against you now. They're all on your side."

Well, the next thing they knew, there was Lucina, her satchel packed, her trunk corded, waiting for the stagecoach to take her back to Rochester. You can imagine, perhaps, something of the stupefaction, turning into excited alarm, this caused her family. Their agitation on seeing her arrive was nothing to their terror at seeing her depart.

All the way down the front walk and out to the waiting coach, on the top of which her trunk was being roped in place, they followed her, talking at the top of their voices, weeping, trying to hold her back. Above all, they were bewildered.

"He'll kill you, child. He's—" "But, Lucina, you said you'd never, never—" "Daughter, I absolutely forbid this—" "But, Lucina, you've told everybody that nothing on earth would ever—" "Didn't you hear Cousin George say that Will is crazy? He'll—" "Lucina, if I've heard you say once, I've heard you say forty times, that—" "Now stop this nonsense."

To which Lucina returned but one parting exclamation. She flung her satchel in ahead of her, climbed up the steps of the coach, shut the door with a slam, stuck her head out of the window, and cried indignantly to her family, "For goodness gracious sakes, I'm married to Will, ain't I?" The driver cracked his whip, and she was gone.

He lived, Lawyer Upjohn did, for twenty years after that, till he and his wife were both well past fifty. And never again did Lucina lose her temper with him. He might storm as he would, her voice remained low and calm, her face quiet —not so much patient as waiting. She turned out the dirty, pottering man-servant, found competent women, dragooned them into service, ruled them with justice and energy, kept the house in apple-pie order, had what her husband liked for every meal and, if he threw it across the room with an oath, went on chatting cheerfully, and poured him out another cup of tea. His condition improved gradually. Though he remained moody and uncertain to the day of his death, he became much less violent, and as time went on had occasional periods when he was quiet and as peaceable as anybody. Little by little his wife made around them a normal circle of friends and associates, succeeded some-how in imposing on them the tradition that Mr. Upjohn, while odd and uncon-ventional, was very superior; created, day after day, an orderly atmosphere of regularity and health, which, more than any direct exhortations from her, in-duced him to shave, wear clean linen and smoke cigars instead of chewing tobacco. During their last years together, he read aloud to her several of Dick-ens' novels, as they came out in magazines.

"We had some real good times together," she often said in her old age. "He was a very bright man, Will Upjohn was."

For she lived on to old age, thirty years after his death, in her home room at the head of the stairs. A widow now, a decorous widow, with a long black veil. She never took off mourning, or lightened it. She wore it, she said, to show

how badly she felt for having deserted her husband when he needed her. She often spoke of her leaving him, always with sorrow and remorse, voicing the Protestant equivalent of a heartfelt *mea culpa:*

"I oughtn't to have. 'Twas a wrong, wicked thing to do. I often wake up in the night and think how wrong I acted. But I didn't know he was insane, you know. I never once dreamed he was crazy! I thought all the time it was just cussedness!"

The Club

He beat me with the hem of a kimono
worn by a Japanese woman
this prized
painted
wooden statue
carved to perfection
in Japan or maybe Hong Kong.

She was usually on display
in our living room atop his bookshelf
among his other overseas treasures
I was never to touch.
She posed there most of the day
her head tilted
her chin resting lightly
on the white pointed fingertips
of her right hand
her black hair
piled high on her head
her long slim neck bared
to her shoulders.
An invisible hand
under the full sleeve
clasped her kimono
close to her body
its hem flared
gracefully around her feet.
That hem
made fluted red marks
on these freckled arms
my shoulders
my back.
That head
inside his fist
made camel
bumps
on his knuckles
I prayed for her
that her pencil thin neck
would not snap
or his rage would be unendurable.
She held fast for me
didn't even chip or crack.

One day, we were talking
as we often did the morning after.
Well, my sloe-eyed beauty, I said
have you served him enough?
I dared to pick her up with one hand
I held her gently by the flowing robe
around her slender legs. She felt lighter than
I had imagined.
I stroked her cold thighs
with the tips of my fingers
and felt a slight tremor.
I carried her into the kitchen and wrapped her
in two sheets of paper towels.
We're leaving
I whispered
you and I
together.

I placed her
between my clothes in my packed suitcase.
That is how we left him
forever.

—Mitsuye Yamada

The Brown House

HISAYE YAMAMOTO

In California that year the strawberries were marvelous. As large as teacups, they were so juicy and sweet that Mrs. Hattori, making her annual batch of jam, found she could cut down on the sugar considerably. "I suppose this is supposed to be the compensation," she said to her husband, whom she always politely called Mr. Hattori.

"Some compensation!" Mr. Hattori answered.

At that time they were still on the best of terms. It was only later, when the season ended as it had begun, with the market price for strawberries so low nobody bothered to pick number twos, that they began quarreling for the first time in their life together. What provoked the first quarrel and all the rest was that Mr. Hattori, seeing no future in strawberries, began casting around for a way to make some quick cash. Word somehow came to him that there was in a neighboring town a certain house where fortunes were made overnight, and he hurried there at the first opportunity.

It happened that Mrs. Hattori and all the little Hattoris, five of them, all boys and born about a year apart, were with him when he paid his first visit to the house. When he told them to wait in the car, saying he had a little business to transact inside and would return in a trice, he truly meant what he said. He intended only to give the place a brief inspection in order to familiarize himself with it. This was at two o'clock in the afternoon, however, and when he finally made his way back to the car, the day was already so dim that he had to grope around a bit for the door handle.

The house was a large but simple clapboard, recently painted brown and relieved with white window frames. It sat under several enormous eucalyptus trees in the foreground of a few acres of asparagus. To the rear of the house was a ramshackle barn whose spacious blue roof advertised in great yellow letters a ubiquitous brand of physic. Mrs. Hattori, peering toward the house with growing impatience, could not understand what was keeping her husband. She watched other cars either drive into the yard or park along the highway and she saw all sorts of people—white, yellow, brown, and black—enter the house. Seeing very few people leave, she got the idea that her husband was attending a meeting or a party.

So she was more curious than furious that first time when Mr. Hattori got around to returning to her and the children. To her rapid questions Mr. Hattori replied slowly, pensively: it was a gambling den run by a Chinese family under cover of asparagus, he said, and he had been winning at first, but his luck had suddenly turned, and that was why he had taken so long—he had been trying to win back his original stake at least.

"How much did you lose?" Mrs. Hattori asked dully.

"Twenty-five dollars," Mr. Hattori said.

"Twenty-five dollars!" exclaimed Mrs. Hattori. "Oh, Mr. Hattori, what have you done?"

At this, as though at a prearranged signal, the baby in her arms began wailing, and the four boys in the back seat began complaining of hunger. Mr. Hattori gritted his teeth and drove on. He told himself that this being assailed on all sides by bawling, whimpering, and murderous glances was no less than he deserved. Never again, he said to himself; he had learned his lesson.

Nevertheless, his car, with his wife and children in it, was parked near the brown house again the following week. This was because he had dreamed a repulsive dream in which a fat white snake had uncoiled and slithered about and everyone knows that a white-snake dream is a sure omen of good luck in games of chance. Even Mrs. Hattori knew this. Besides, she felt a little guilty about having nagged him so bitterly about the twenty-five dollars. So Mr.

Hattori entered the brown house again on condition that he would return in a half hour, surely enough time to test the white snake. When he failed to return after an hour, Mrs. Hattori sent Joe, the oldest boy, to the front door to inquire after his father. A Chinese man came to open the door of the grille, looked at Joe, said, "Sorry, no kids in here," and clacked it to.

When Joe reported back to his mother, she sent him back again and this time a Chinese woman looked out and said, "What you want, boy?" When he asked for his father, she asked him to wait, then returned with him to the car, carrying a plate of Chinese cookies. Joe, munching one thick biscuit as he led her to the car, found its flavor and texture very strange; it was unlike either its American or Japanese counterpart so that he could not decide whether he liked it or not.

Although the woman was about Mrs. Hattori's age, she immediately called the latter "mama," assuring her that Mr. Hattori would be coming soon, very soon. Mrs. Hattori, mortified, gave excessive thanks for the cookies which she would just as soon have thrown in the woman's face. Mrs. Wu, for so she introduced herself, left them after wagging her head in amazement that Mrs. Hattori, so young, should have so many children and telling her frankly, "No wonder you so skinny, mama."

"Skinny, ha!" Mrs. Hattori said to the boys. "Well, perhaps. But I'd rather be skinny than fat."

Joe, looking at the comfortable figure of Mrs. Wu going up the steps of the brown house, agreed.

Again it was dark when Mr. Hattori came back to the car, but Mrs. Hattori did not say a word. Mr. Hattori made a feeble joke about the unreliability of snakes, but his wife made no attempt to smile. About halfway home she said abruptly, "Please stop the machine, Mr. Hattori. I don't want to ride another inch with you."

"Now, mother . . ." Mr. Hattori said. "I've learned my lesson. I swear this is the last time."

"Please stop the machine, Mr. Hattori," his wife repeated.

Of course the car kept going, so Mrs. Hattori, hugging the baby to herself with one arm, opened the door with her free hand and made as if to hop out of the moving car.

The car stopped with a lurch and Mr. Hattori, aghast, said, "Do you want to kill yourself?"

"That's a very good idea," Mrs. Hattori answered, one leg out of the door.

"Now, mother . . ." Mr. Hattori said. "I'm sorry; I was wrong to stay so long. I promise on my word of honor never to go near that house again. Come, let's go home now and get some supper."

"Supper!" said Mrs. Hattori. "Do you have any money for groceries?"

"I have enough for groceries," Mr. Hattori confessed.

Mrs. Hattori pulled her leg back in and pulled the door shut. "You see!" she cried triumphantly. "You see!"

The next time, Mrs. Wu brought out besides the cookies a paper sackful of Chinese firecrackers for the boys. "This is America," Mrs. Wu said to Mrs. Hattori. "China and Japan have war, all right, but (she shrugged) it's not our fault. You understand?"

Mrs. Hattori nodded, but she did not say anything because she did not feel her English up to the occasion.

"Never mind about the firecrackers or the war," she wanted to say. "Just inform Mr. Hattori that his family awaits without."

Suddenly Mrs. Wu, who out of the corner of her eye had been examining another car parked up the street, whispered, "Cops!" and ran back into the house as fast as she could carry her amplitude. Then the windows and doors of the brown house began to spew out all kinds of people—white, yellow, brown, and black—who either got into cars and drove frantically away or ran across the street to dive into the field of tall dry weeds. Before Mrs. Hattori and the boys knew what was happening, a Negro man opened the back door of their car and jumped in to crouch at the boys' feet.

The boys, who had never seen such a dark person at close range before, burst into terrified screams, and Mrs. Hattori began yelling too, telling the man to get out, get out. The panting man clasped his hands together and beseeched Mrs. Hattori, "Just let me hide in here until the police go away! I'm asking you to save me from jail!"

Mrs. Hattori made a quick decision. "All right," she said in her tortured English. "Go down, hide!" Then, in Japanese, she assured her sons that this man meant them no harm and ordered them to cease crying, to sit down, to behave, lest she be tempted to give them something to cry about. The policemen had been inside the house about fifteen minutes when Mr. Hattori came out. He had been thoroughly frightened, but now he managed to appear jaunty as he told his wife how he had cleverly thrust all incriminating evidence into a nearby vase of flowers and thus escaped arrest. "They searched me and told me I could go," he said. "A lot of others weren't so lucky. One lady fainted."

They were almost a mile from the brown house before the man in back said, "Thanks a million. You can let me off here."

Mr. Hattori was so surprised that the car screeched when it stopped. Mrs. Hattori hastily explained, and the man, pausing on his way out, searched for words to emphasize his gratitude. He had always been, he said, a friend of the Japanese people; he knew no race so cleanly, so well-mannered, so downright nice. As he slammed the door shut, he put his hand on the arm of Mr. Hattori, who was still dumfounded, and promised never to forget this act of kindness.

"What we got to remember," the man said, "is that we all got to die sometime. You might be a king in silk shirts or riding a white horse, but we all got to die sometime."

Mr. Hattori, starting up the car again, looked at his wife in reproach. "A *kurombo!*" he said. And again, "A *kurombo!*" He pretended to be victim to a shudder.

"You had no compunctions about that, Mr. Hattori," she reminded him, "when you were inside that house."

"That's different," Mr. Hattori said.

"How so?" Mrs. Hattori inquired.

The quarrel continued through supper at home, touching on a large variety of subjects. It ended in the presence of the children with Mr. Hattori beating his wife so severely that he had to take her to the doctor to have a few ribs taped. Both in their depths were dazed and shaken that things should have come to such a pass.

A few weeks after the raid the brown house opened for business as usual, and Mr. Hattori took to going there alone. He no longer waited for weekends but found all sorts of errands to go on during the week which took him in the direction of the asparagus farm. There were nights when he did not bother to come home at all.

On one such night Mrs. Hattori confided to Joe, because he was the eldest, "Sometimes I lie awake at night and wish for death to overtake me in my sleep. That would be the easiest way." In response Joe wept, principally because he felt tears were expected of him. Mrs. Hattori, deeply moved by his evident commiseration, begged his pardon for burdening his childhood with adult sorrows. Joe was in the first grade that year, and in his sleep he dreamed mostly about school. In one dream that recurred he found himself walking in nakedness and in terrible shame among his closest schoolmates.

At last Mrs. Hattori could bear it no longer and went away. She took the baby, Sam, and the boy born before him, Ed (for the record, the other two were named Bill and Ogden), to one of her sisters living in a town about thirty miles distant. Mr. Hattori was shocked and immediately went after her, but her sister refused to let him in the house. "Monster!" this sister said to him from the other side of the door.

Defeated, Mr. Hattori returned home to reform. He worked passionately out in the fields from morning to night, he kept the house spick-and-span, he fed the remaining boys the best food he could buy, and he went out of his way to keep several miles clear of the brown house. This went on for five days, and on the sixth day, one of the Hattoris' nephews, the son of the vindictive lady with whom Mrs. Hattori was taking refuge, came to bring Mr. Hattori a message. The nephew, who was about seventeen at the time, had started smoking cigarettes when he was thirteen. He liked to wear his amorphous hat on the back of his head, exposing a coiffure neatly parted in the middle which looked less like hair than like a painted wig, so unstintingly applied was the pomade which held it together. He kept his hands in his pockets, straddled the ground, and let his cigarette dangle to one side of his mouth as he said to Mr. Hattori, "Your wife's taken a powder."

The world actually turned black for an instant for Mr. Hattori as he searched giddily in his mind for another possible interpretation of this ghastly announcement. "Poison?" he queried, a tremor in his knees.

The nephew cackled with restraint. "Nope, you dope," he said. "That means she's leaving your bed and board."

"Talk in Japanese," Mr. Hattori ordered, "and quit trying to be so smart."

Abashed, the nephew took his hands out of his pockets and assisted his meager Japanese with nervous gestures. Mrs. Hattori, he managed to convey, had decided to leave Mr. Hattori permanently and had sent him to get Joe and Bill and Ogden.

"Tell her to go jump in the lake," Mr. Hattori said in English, and in Japanese, "Tell her if she wants the boys, to come back and make a home for them. That's the only way she can ever have them."

Mrs. Hattori came back with Sam and Ed that same night, not only because she had found she was unable to exist without her other sons but because the nephew had glimpsed certain things which indicated that her husband had seen the light. Life for the family became very sweet then because it had lately been so very bitter, and Mr. Hattori went nowhere near the brown house for almost a whole month. When he did resume his visits there, he spaced them frugally and remembered (although this cost him cruel effort) to stay no longer than an hour each time.

One evening Mr. Hattori came home like a madman. He sprinted up the front porch, broke into the house with a bang, and began whirling around the parlor like a human top. Mrs. Hattori dropped her mending and the boys their toys to stare at this phenomenon.

"Yippee," said Mr. Hattori, "banzai, yippee, banzai." Thereupon, he fell dizzily to the floor.

"What is it, Mr. Hattori; are you drunk?" Mrs. Hattori asked, coming to help him up.

"Better than that, mother," Mr. Hattori said, pushing her back to her chair. It was then they noticed that he was holding a brown paper bag in one hand. And from this bag, with the exaggerated ceremony of a magician pulling rabbits from a hat, he began to draw out stack after stack of green bills. These he deposited deliberately, one by one, on Mrs. Hattori's tense lap until the sack was empty and she was buried under a pile of money.

"Explain . . ." Mrs. Hattori gasped.

"I won it! In the lottery! Two thousand dollars! We're rich!" Mr. Hattori explained.

There was a hard silence in the room as everyone looked at the treasure on Mrs. Hattori's lap. Mr. Hattori gazed raptly, the boys blinked in bewilderment, and Mrs. Hattori's eyes bulged a little. Suddenly, without warning, Mrs. Hattori leaped up and vigorously brushed off the front of her clothing, letting the stacks fall where they might. For a moment she clamped her lips together fiercely and glared at her husband. But there was no wisp of steam that curled out from her nostrils and disappeared toward the ceiling; this was just a fleeting illusion that Mr. Hattori had. Then, "You have no conception, Mr. Hattori!" she hissed. "You have absolutely no conception!"

Mr. Hattori was resolute in refusing to burn the money, and Mrs. Hattori eventually adjusted herself to his keeping it. Thus, they increased their property by a new car, a new rug, and their first washing machine. Since these purchases were all made on the convenient installment plan and the two thousand dollars somehow melted away before they were aware of it, the car and the washing machine were claimed by a collection agency after a few months. The rug remained, however, as it was a fairly cheap one and had already eroded away in spots to show the bare weave beneath. By that time it had become an old habit for Mrs. Hattori and the boys to wait outside the brown house in their original car and for Joe to be commissioned periodically to go to the front door to ask for his father. Joe and his brothers did not mind the long experience too much because they had acquired a taste for Chinese cookies. Nor, really, did Mrs. Hattori, who was pregnant again. After a fashion, she became quite attached to Mrs. Wu who, on her part, decided she had never before encountered a woman with such bleak eyes.

The identity of the oppressors we face in our day-to-day lives is fluid and constantly changes. We may all oppress someone. Refusing to name persons as oppressors but instead using a remote concept means that people do not really have to be responsible for what they do, that any negative action is excusable because it's really the system's fault anyway. When your working-class white husband beats you, he is your direct oppressor. Your body is not being mutilated by the "ruling class." The ruling class of course gives full approval and support to what your husband is doing, because among other reasons they are at home beating their wives, "girl-friends," mothers, sisters and daughters too. . . . The man who beats you is a member of the ruling class in your own home.

—Barbara Smith, *"Notes for Yet Another Paper on Black Feminism"*

That She Would Dance No More

J EAN W HEELER S MITH

Ossie Lee came into the café to drink some beer. He had worked hard today. It had rained too much to do any plowing—couldn't put a tractor out in that Delta land when it was wet. The rich, loose top soil was so deep that a tractor would sink down in it. So his boss man had made him dig ditches all day, ditches that led nowhere. The man had only required the work of him in order to keep him busy. And Ossie Lee had had to dig the ditches. There wasn't much else he could do. He lived on the man's place, in his house, owed him money.

But Ossie Lee set aside his thoughts. He wouldn't worry about all that now. Just sit here and rest a while, spend the dollar he had in his pocket for some beer, and wait on his friends from the other plantations to come around. "Miss Lula, bring me a quart of Falstaff and some skins."

Miss Lula came over to the table. She was a big woman, not yet old, maybe forty-nine. She called everybody "baby." "How you doing, baby? Look like you been working hard. Got that mud all over your clothes, in your hair. A good-looking man like you ought to take better care of himself. You still young —how old are you, 'bout thirty-five?"

"I'm thirty-eight, Miss Lula."

Miss Lula raised her voice so that the rest of the people in the café could enjoy the exchange. "Well, you sure don't look a day over thirty-five. Maybe 'cause you still got a good body, strong, not all broke down like a lot of the men around here. And I always did like the way you held yourself. You know, like couldn't nobody walk over you." Miss Lula was smiling; she was pleased to be able to speak so well of him. Maybe he'd feel a little better now.

Ossie Lee appreciated her effort and replied in kind. "Well, Miss Lula, I always liked the way you carried yourself, too. It took some doing to keep the café open without even a man to help you. You a pretty good old lady, even if you are getting fat from your own cooking."

She feinted a slap at his head for this little insult and then resumed her businesslike air. "I got to see what Jimmie Lee and them want over at the bar. I'll bring you your Falstaff soon's I take care of them. I got some good neck-bones cooked in the back. You want to try some?"

"No, Miss Lula, I ate at Mama's already. Just bring me the beer."

Ossie Lee put his foot up on the next chair and looked around to see who was there. It had taken him a while to get used to the darkness. The only light came from the Schlitz beer signs, with the luxuriously dressed brown girls, and from the music box which commanded one end of the small café. Nobody was there that he knew. Well, he'd just wait. Nothing else to do. No reason to go home.

There were two girls sitting over in the corner of the café. He had not seen them before, but they looked like they might be sisters. The smaller girl was very pretty. She was black and so thin that you felt you could see everything that was happening within her, the movement of every muscle, the angle of every bone. He liked the way she looked. He figured that they were from up on Mr. Mills' place. He had heard that Mills had brought in a new family up there.

Miss Lula returned to his table. "Here, baby, here's your Falstaff." She noticed Ossie Lee's feet in her chair. Her lips tightened. "Now, why you want to mess up my chairs, putting your feet on them? Come on and do right. Always wanting me to keep this place but you-all won't help me to keep it up. You thirty-eight years old, had a house of your own, you know how to treat other people's things."

Ossie Lee was offended, but he took his feet down. He couldn't afford to get her mad with him. Miss Lula had a shotgun back there that she would put to anybody.

Seeing that she had put Ossie Lee in his place, she resumed her friendly manner. She said, "I guess you pretty lonesome now since your wife left you. I never did know what happened. What did happen?"

"Nothing much. She was messing around James Edward—you know him, he live down on Mr. Henderson's place—and I wasn't going to have that. Everytime I told her about it she tried to get smart with me. So I'd just have to whip her. She musta got tired of that. One day she went down the road to the store and just kept walking. Didn't even take her clothes."

"Yeah, well where is she now?"

"She sent three bus tickets for the children. The tickets were to Memphis. I guess that's where she is now."

Miss Lula stood quietly at the table for a moment. Then she directed his attention across the room. "You see those two girls over there in the corner? They just come over to this county. Come from up in Tallahatchie County a week ago. Some nice girls, too, named Minnie Pearl and Johnnie Mae. The thin little black one with the yellow dress on, Minnie Pearl, she loves to dance. Why don't you put a quarter in the music box. She'll dance for you."

Ossie Lee looked at the thirty cents he had left from his dollar. He weighed the value of spending it now on the little black girl against the possibility that later he might get somebody to match it and buy another quart of beer. He didn't know anything about the girl. But she did look nice. She was a pretty girl. He hadn't been getting much satisfaction from drinking beer, or from doing anything else, lately. Seemed like no matter what he did, he couldn't get satisfied. The disappointments of his life weighed heavily on him.

In fact, Ossie Lee had, for the sake of his sanity, accepted his life situation. He had yielded to it long ago, at the age of eight. The acceptance of his life style had been irrevocably forced upon him the night they came to take him.

That night they called Ossie Lee's father to the door. They were two. "Jesse, come here. Want to talk to you bout that smart-acting boy of yours."

His father turned to his mother. "Get them in the back, Sarah Mae." She hurried the children, ranging in age from eighteen years to three months, into the back of the two-room house. His father went to the front door, forced a smile to his face. "How y'all this evening?"

"We fine, Jesse. Only thing wrong with us is that boy of yours, Ossie Lee. He let one of my chickens get run over this morning. Send him out here. Got to teach him a lesson. He got to learn to take care of property, else he ain't never going to be a good hand."

Ossie Lee saw his father's shoulders drop. "Well, sir, Mr. Perry, I knew he been running too much, ain't got good sense yet. But he still young. I give him a good whipping tonight. He do better."

"No, Jesse, I think I ought to take care of this myself. He going to be working for me thirty, forty years; he got to learn how to take care of my things."

Realizing that he was in trouble, Ossie Lee slipped over to where his mother had gathered the smallest children. Perry, ignoring Ossie Lee's father, walked straight through the house and into the back. He had a long cotton sack on his arm. "Sarah Mae, give me the boy." Ossie Lee's arms went around his mother's waist. She folded him into her skirt, pressed him to her. She pleaded with the boss man, "Please, sir, don't take him off. He just a baby. Just made eight years. We take care he don't do nothing like that no more. Spare him this one time. He just a baby."

Perry did not bother to respond. Ossie Lee looked up at his mother and over to his father for help. Neither his father nor his mother could look back into his face. He began to cry, "No, Mama, don't let him take me. Mama, Daddy, Mama." In support of him, the other children set to crying. Perry seemed not to hear or to see any of them. He leaned over to Ossie Lee, pulled him from his mother and, despite the boy's kicking and struggling, forced him into the cotton sack. As Perry moved toward the door, no one offered resistance.

Ossie Lee cried hard. He knew that they must have heard him. Were they going to let this man take him away? Why didn't they run after him and pull the sack from his hands? Mama, Daddy, you always took care of me. Where are you?

Perry carried the boy out in the sack and handed him to the other man, who had been waiting in the truck. He cranked up the truck and drove away. No one came even to the porch to see in what direction their boy had been taken. As the truck moved away, Ossie Lee came to understand that his people could neither refuse to let him be taken, nor even demand the knowledge of where he would be taken. Understanding this, he himself ceased to struggle against so obviously powerful a force. His kicking subsided, his crying ceased, his muscles relaxed. He merely waited to see what they would do to him.

After riding about ten minutes, the truck stopped. Ossie Lee was pulled from the truck and emptied from the sack onto the ground. They had come to the muddy river where Ossie Lee had fished only a few days earlier. The white men stood over him. Perry said, "Boy, you been mighty careless lately, letting that chicken get run over. Don't seem like you want to be a good hand, do it?"

Ossie Lee's immediate reaction was to defend himself, to assert that he had been watching the chickens as best he could but that there had just been too many of them, that he couldn't have kept up with all those chickens. But then he checked himself; he admitted that nothing he said would matter to these powerful men, that it was their show and not his. Accordingly he replied, "That's right, sir, look like I ain't able to be no good hand."

Perry went on. "You got to learn to take care of property. That's what's wrong with you colored people now. You don't know how to take care of nothing. I'm going to give you this whipping so you'll watch after them chickens from now on. Get your britches down."

For the last time, Ossie Lee's self revolted "No, not my clothes; you can't make me take off my clothes. Daddy don't even do that. No!"

Perry stood over him. "You not going to do what I tell you? Well, I'll take them off for you." And, ignoring the last willful act that Ossie Lee was to perform in his lifetime, the white man tore off his britches and began to whip him with a corded rope.

Perry whipped him until he got tired and then the other man whipped him. They kept it up for about thirty minutes. It hurt badly and Ossie Lee cried, but he didn't really care anymore. When they finished, they shouted some words at him and left him lying by the river at which he used to play. Ossie Lee waited until they left and gathered strength to clothe himself and return home.

In another half-hour he made it home. His parents were waiting for him, in the same positions they had held when earlier they had allowed him to be carried off. His father stood by the door, alone. His mother sat in the back room. Only the smallest children looked into his face as he opened the door and entered the dimly lit house. At his arrival, the family went back to its normal activities. His mother gave the baby to Carrie, the seven-year-old, and set about cooking some bread for supper. The older children went out to get water and wood for the next morning. The little children began to harass one another.

Ossie Lee said nothing. He went over to his space on the bed which he shared with three brothers and lay down and buried his face in the quilt. His only effort was not to think, not to assess the situation which, an hour ago, had been thrust upon him. Soon after he had laid down, his mother called him to supper. She handed him two tin plates with biscuits and molasses. "Here, take your Daddy his supper too." Ossie Lee walked to the front and gave his father his supper. He sat down on the floor next to his father and began to eat. His father leaned over, took the boy's head in his hand, and gently shook him. "You alright, boy?"

"Yessir, I'm alright."

"That's just the way things is, you know."

"Yessir, I know."

The remainder of Ossie Lee's life followed the order established that night. He did carefully what he was told, never more, never less. Along with the other children, he tended the animals and chopped and picked the cotton. And when each year, after the cotton had been "laid by," it came to be revival time, he too went to the mourner's bench and got religion. When he was big enough, he was told to start driving a tractor; this he did and continued to do for the rest of his life. He learned to drink whiskey and to go with women. At some point he married and brought forth three children to share the life which had devastated him.

Through it all, there was something in him which refused the final admission that he was dirt under white folks' feet and that he deserved the dehumanization that they meted out to him. Yet he could not reject it; he felt too old to leave home and start over again. And, since his father had died and his older brothers had left for Chicago, he had to stay on the place and do the man's work so that his mother and the children would have a house to live in and something to eat. Thus, being able neither to accept nor to reject his life, Ossie Lee had constantly to buffer himself against it.

But lately things had been going badly. More closely, each week, dissatisfaction had approached his consciousness. And he no longer had the means to push it back. He still found comfort in the church and release in fighting and drinking with his friends. But not like before. Now it was hard work to "get happy." Ossie Lee had grown weary in the defense of himself.

After he had finished his beer, Miss Lula came back over to his table. She encouraged him further about the girl sitting across the room. "Go on and put your little quarter in the music box. Ain't going to do you no good sitting there." Ossie Lee looked across at the girl once more. He did like the way she looked. Under Miss Lula's prodding, Ossie Lee walked across the small room to the glowing, big bellied music box and deposited his quarter. He turned his head toward the girls. "Y'all want to come choose some records? Come get the music you want and dance for me." The girls conferred with one another for a minute and then came over to where he stood. They looked to be about twenty years old. Ossie Lee studied the little black one. She looked clean, had a pretty face. As he watched her, she looked from the music box to him, assessing her new arena of activity. Her sister asked him his name, where he lived, and all that. She said nothing, only kept time to the music until her sister would be ready to dance.

When the music burst from the music box the two girls joined hands and danced together. They danced lithely, gracefully. To Ossie Lee the little black girl, so thin in her loosely fitting yellow dress, looked especially graceful. His senses followed her and were refreshed. He followed her so closely that, for the while that she danced for him, he was able to push away the disturbing consciousness of his life. As she danced, he relaxed and leaned back on the music box to watch her. When the music ended, the girls went back to their seats, laughing and talking, breathless from their dancing.

Later, someone fed more coins to the music box. This time it sent forth blues music. Slow, pounding, insightful music, about loving and living. Ossie walked quickly over to the girl in order to reach her before anyone else. When he brought her to him to dance it was as he had expected. Her body fitted itself to him, fitted itself and then relaxed into him. As they moved slowly with the music he pulled her still closer, drinking in the ease with which she lived and moved. They danced for an immeasurable time.

When finally they sat to rest, neither spoke. He remained beside her for several minutes and, finding no words, stood up and walked over to where some friends were lounging against the far wall. They received him without comment. He too leaned against the wall, propping himself with his booted foot. He inquired of them, "That little girl got a man round here?"

One of the men answered, "No, don't think so. She ain't been here but a few weeks. And ain't none of us hit on her yet. We just been watching her. Miss Lula watches her pretty close. Miss Lula really likes that girl. Ain't let us get next to her. Say we don't mean her no good. She likes for us all to dance and have fun, but she don't want you to take that girl nowhere." Ossie Lee grunted something in acknowledgement and walked away from them. He kept walking, through the door and on to his mother's house.

His life thereafter was centered around evenings at the café. His days assumed a strange proportion. The mornings went quickly; he easily did his plowing, ran his boss man's errands, and carried the other hands home from the field to eat dinner. He was eager to make the day go by so that evening would come. But then, after dinner, when the evening was indeed near, time seemed to stand still. Every task took forever. The cotton rows seemed to be miles longer than they had been in the morning. It seemed that evening would never come. When finally the work day ended, Ossie Lee would go home and, so that he could savor every aspect of being with her, he would force himself to change his clothes in a leisurely manner and to walk slowly up the road to the café.

When, one evening, he directed her from the dance floor to the door of the café, she followed him outside. He motioned to her to get into his '56 Ford. As he cranked up the car, he turned to her. "We're going to get your things. I want to marry you. You can stay with me and Mama this week and next Saturday we'll marry. I'll get you a house soon as I can."

The girl turned to face him. "What about your wife?"

"She's gone. She knew what she was doing when she left. Do you want to marry, or don't you?"

She said, yes, she would marry.

Ossie Lee drove to her mother's three-room house. Some of the children were sitting on the sagging porch, trying to fight off the mosquitoes and to get some cool air. She went in, spoke a few words to her mother and her sisters, and gathered her things to go with him. Her mother came to the porch to see them off. As the girl climbed back into the car her mother called to her, "You know you can always come back home."

At Ossie Lee's home the girl was well received. His mother was glad to have another woman around to help in the field and to see after the children. The children liked her at once. She played with them yet took them seriously. And she danced with them, even with the baby who couldn't walk.

In the evenings, Ossie Lee took her to the café. When he told Miss Lula that they were to marry, she shook her head. She sat down at the table with them and took the girl's hand in hers. She said, "Baby, I don't know how to say this, but I don't think you should marry. It's too much in you for you to go off with some man now. I wish you wouldn't do it. I'm a old lady. I seen a lot of pretty black girls. But you got something special. Don't throw it away. I know you got to live and you got to help your mama. Well, it ain't enough work here for two, but I'll give you a job here in my café if you'll just stay on with your mama."

The girl understood. She answered simply, "I think the best thing is for me to go with Ossie Lee."

The older woman turned to him. "You a good man alright, Ossie. But you don't mean this girl no good. You ought to *let her stay home. Let her stay out where she can dance.*"

Ossie Lee chose to take her words lightly. He laughed. "You better get away from here, talking like that. Me and Minnie Pearl going to marry on Sunday. And everybody is invited to the wedding, down at Pilgrim's Rest."

Miss Lula turned back to the girl. "Remember, baby, if anything happen, you got a friend here."

The girl smiled. "Thanks, Miss Lula, I'll remember. And—I'll be alright."

They married on Sunday.

Later in the week, Ossie Lee saw his boss man about getting a house for them to live in. The man told him where he could have one, but he said it might have to be cleaned up some. Then Ossie Lee and his wife went to look at the house. It was an old, wooden, two-room house with a tin roof. Because of its age, the whole building leaned to one side. It was filled to the ceiling with hay.

Ossie Lee was slapped again by the circumstances of his life. He sat down on the broken steps and leaned his back against the wooden roof support. "That bastard expects folks to live in a place that he won't use for nothing better than hay. I don't know. Sometimes I just don't know."

His girl stood on the porch, between him and the door of the house. She said to him, "That's alright. We'll fix it up. Come on, let's go up to the café for a while."

"No, I don't want to go to the café. I don't want to go nowhere."

He walked away from the shack, his head down and his arms dangling loosely. She followed him to his mother's house. Ossie Lee came into the house, stepping over children and around beds and ducking electrical wires. He laid across the bed. She laid down next to him and tried to make him feel better.

"You'll see. It will be nice. We'll get the hay out, put in some windows, buy some curtains from the ten-cent store." He just lay there.

When he tired of the noises of the house, he sat up on the bed. "Come on, let's get out of here."

As they walked slowly up to the café, she tried to take his hand, but he shook his loose. He didn't want her hand. She couldn't help. Nothing could help, nothing could remove the fact of that hay-filled shack to which he would take his wife.

They entered the café and took seats at a table in the middle of the room. She looked around the room for her sister. Recognizing her in the back, she went over to talk with her. Soon someone put a dime in the music box and the two girls began to dance. Ossie Lee watched his girl. She danced with the same ease and enjoyment that she always had. But he could not come out to her. He could no longer lose himself in her dancing. He was held too tightly to the hay-filled shack, too closely to all the meaningless ditches he had dug. As he sat immobile in the chair, he grew angry. How could she dance like that when she had just seen that place? What kind of a fool was she to think that there was anything to be happy about, any place on earth to relax! As he watched her, his anger grew still more and his muscles stiffened. He pulled himself up and went outside to get some air. He sat down on the steps, rested his head on the wall, and looked out into the darkness.

A big hand descended on his shoulder. It was his cousin, Willie C. Willie C. was a tall, thin, brown-skinned man, with most of his teeth missing. He and Ossie had grown up together. He leaned his dirty, sweating face to within inches of Ossie Lee's. "Hey, Ossie Lee, I ain't seen you out by yourself in a long time, not since you got that little black girl from up on Mr. Mills' place. I got some old corn whiskey out in the car. Jake and Fats, they out there now drinking it all up. Come on, drink some with us, before it's all gone." He pulled at Ossie Lee's shoulder.

Ossie Lee said, "Alright, man, let's go."

They went around back of the café to where the other two men were standing. Ossie Lee helped them to finish off the pint of whiskey which they passed around. He drank quickly, thanked them, and left.

He went back around into the café and took the seat he had had earlier in the evening. His girl was at the table, laughing and talking with her sister about finding her a husband. They tried to include him in the talk, but he only grunted. When the music started, the girls once more got up to dance. She asked him, "You want to dance?" When he did not answer, she went off with her sister.

Again he watched her move and his anger swelled. He could not permit her to dance like that, not today, not in the face of that hay-filled shack. Ossie Lee held himself in his seat for as long as he could, by looking the other way, by talking to people at the next table. But he could not ignore the pounding of the music. He could not negate the sound of her laughter as she danced. He rose from his chair, walked over to his beautiful black girl and slapped her to the floor. She got back to her feet but was too stunned to hit back at him. Again he hit her, now in her stomach. She doubled over in pain.

The other people who had been dancing moved back from the couple. Only the girl's sister pushed her way over to her, screaming at Ossie Lee to stop hitting her sister. She enclosed her sister in her arms and stared back at Ossie Lee, who was readying to fight her, too. As he approached them, he was stopped by the sound of a gunshot.

The crowd moved aside for Miss Lula. She placed the barrel of the gun into his side. Her face was tightly drawn, her eyes shining, her arms holding steadily to the gun. "Ossie Lee, don't you touch that girl again in my place. If you got something to settle, take her home. But as long as she is anywhere near where I am, you can't hurt her. Now get out of here."

He turned to the girl, "You coming with me?"

She nodded yes. The two walked away from the café back to his mother's house.

At home they silently prepared for bed. The thin, black girl slipped into bed beside her husband. He took her in his arms. For hours he caressed her, aroused her, loved her. He worked with her until he felt sure that he had given her a baby, a baby which would weigh her down and destroy her balance so that she would dance no more.

"There are two things I've got a
right to, and these are death
or liberty. One or the other
I mean to have."
—Harriet Tubman

Brother
    I don't want to hear
    about
    how *my* real enemy
    is the system.
i'm no genius,
    but i do know
    that system
you hit me with
    is called
    a fist.
        —Pat Parker

To Be a Man

ANN ALLEN SHOCKLEY

Anita followed her movements in the bureau mirror as she deftly applied
pink lipstick to the full Cupid's bow of her mouth. Then pausing, she gazed
critically back at her reflection. The off-shoulder black cocktail dress fitted
snugly over her round curved hips, while the white pearl necklace and earrings
set off the creamy tan of her skin. She decided that she looked very chic and
smart.

"I'm sorry you won't go with me, Claude," she said, turning now to the
man seated at a make-shift card table desk in the corner of the bedroom.

"I got more important things to do," he grumbled sullenly, bent over the
mound of papers.

A frown wrinkled tiny delicate lines between her wide-spaced eyes as she
stared long at him. Sometimes—like now—he looked so forbidding to her with
all that fierce black hair worn stiff and high and long. Bushy hair growing
down his dark brown face into sideburns which ended in an entangled brush of
beard. With all that hair covering his face and arching above the thick full lips,

he looked like a Black Samson. A Black Samson who needed hair to give him his man-strength.

She sighed, reaching to struggle her fingers one by one into the white linen gloves. "You never go anyplace with me anymore." Not since he had gotten so wrapped up in the Movement. The Movement—almost an obsession with him now.

He lit a cigarette from the crumpled pack of Larks on the table, flicking the match into the already overflowing ash tray. "I got better things to do. Right now, the Movement—"

"The *Movement!*" she almost shouted at him. "That's all you *think* about. Hell! I believe in the Movement too, but Christ, I can't *live* the Movement. I'm also an *individualist*. A *person*. Not just a *Negro* person. I can't eat, sleep, and go to the toilet with Civil Rights and hating the white man with each breath I take. I can't *submerge* the fact that I *also* like to have *fun* once in a while. I like to enjoy a good book not soused with racism, listen to pretty music, walk in the park and admire the natural green of the grass and blue of the sky. I like to look up at the strength of the trees growing high, and I like to look down and gaze into the coolness of a spring brook. I like to *see* and *do* those things as a *person* without their being marred all the time by hating and thinking about the white man!"

She stopped, feeling out of breath like the words had drained her. Slowly she went over to him, caressing his hard broad back outlined in the colorful summer African shirt with geometric patterns of spears and masks surrounding a lion. "Can't you relax—sometimes?" It was a plea.

He tensed beneath her touch, not turning to her, not looking. "Hell no! That's the trouble now—we been relaxing too long. Your daddy and my daddy —relax—ing. Uncle Toming all those years. Letting things get tougher and tougher."

"Claude, that's not true. You know how our parents—"

"Yeah, I *know.* By buying lifetime memberships in the NAACP! *You* go on to that cocktail party with all those mealy-mouth white liberals who're going to do this-and-that for the brother until they get out in the air and back to the suburbs!"

"I *work* with those people. I can't refuse their invitations *all* the time. Besides, in my line of work, it gives me an opportunity to meet others and make significant contacts."

"Significant contacts," he sneered. "Excuses—excuses—excuses. *You* just want to be *with* them, and *act* like them, and wish you were *like* them. You can't forget your little black *bourgeois* upbringing about how great it is being *in* with white people. Like a status symbol—"

She stepped back as if struck. "You had the same so-called black *bourgeois* background as I."

"Yeah, baby, but I got *out*. That second year in that middle-class snooty college, I got out and joined the Movement. I left my doctor daddy and my social sprinting mother be-e-e-hind!"

"There *are* times when I think you're jealous because at least I *did* finish—"

His hands tightened on the chair, the knuckles showing like taut knobs through his skin. She knew the lance had pierced. Always between them now were angry, hate-filled words making them no longer one, but two, divided into sharp, brittle separate pieces blown by different winds and guided by different stars.

"Go on where you going," he muttered thickly. "I got work to do."

"Work—" she repeated bitterly, watching him shut himself away from her over the desk. Her eyes swept the papers before him, the array of pencils, and the old-fashioned battered typewriter. "What *kind* of work? *I* work. *I* keep us going. And I work because my black skin *still* doesn't deter me from liking good scotch, good steaks, living in a decent neighborhood, and seeing a good play. And it's *my* work that's doing it." She watched him puff heavily on the cigarette, knowing she had wounded this time—struck where the sore was like a cancer eating him.

Finally he laughed shortly. *"Some* work! The only nigger in a Government Job Placement Center. A showpiece to prove nobody's prejudice. A nigger behind a desk who's pretty and looks white with a forever Florida suntan. Big deal! *Me*—I'm out in the streets working *with* the brothers. Out there where the nitty gritty is fighting Mister Charlie. *I'm* going to make whitey realize I'm a *man*. I want to be treated as a man. And baby, I *am* going to be treated like a man!"

"Takes a lot to make a man," she scoffed, slamming the door hard behind her.

.   .   .

The door's slam was like a slap. A burning sting pierced the tips of his forefinger and thumb. The cigarette had burned down to a pinpoint heat. He dropped it in the burial ground of others. A sharp recurring pain streaked across his forehead, blurring his vision and the words on the paper. She had caused him to lose his thought. Just when his pencil had moved and written a wonderful spring of free flowing words. He was certain this one was *the* one—the essay that the Atlantic Monthly or New Yorker would publish. He was sure because he *knew* it was good. It was just as good as any of Baldwin's or Jones' or Cleaver's. Wasn't he socking it to whitey? Spilling out his seething hatred and venom and frustrations? Making whitey feel guilt. Making whitey want to feel punished by the hot word lava flung at him by a black writer. Now was the time for the black writer to emerge because whitey was a masochist who wanted to be verbally whipped by the black man for his guilt. Whitey *wanted* the Negro to tell him like it is. Tell him that he wasn't shit, never was shit, and never would *be* shit. But the black man *was* some shit! And even if blood had to flow, the black man would *prove* he was some *good* shit!

He stared down at the papers and rejection slip that had come in the morning's mail—the telltale slip he had tried to hide from her. The stock words swam before him: "Thank you for your submittal which we are returning to you. Please don't consider this a reflection on the quality of your work . . ."

He crumpled up the letter. Damn them! Whitey wouldn't even *give* him a chance to tell it like it is. He got up stiffly, noticing the soft summer evening rapidly fading into night. A mauve twilight streaked pink and lilac ridges across the blue sky.

What he needed was a drink. He went to the kitchen where a bottle of Cutty Sark was on the sink. He got a glass from the cabinet and half filled it with the clear brown liquid. Raising the glass to his lips, he savored the rich expensive odor of the scotch. Then suddenly, in revenge, he flung the glass across the room. It made a dull thud against the wall before crashing into pieces on the floor. The ache in his head flared anew. He closed his eyes, thinking he had to get out—away from here—if only for a while.

He had to walk a block down the neat well-kept residential street with rows of modern one-story box houses and green carpets of manicured lawns before he could board the bus. He felt the eyes upon him as he took a seat midway by the window. The people on the bus stared furtively at him because they were used to seeing clean-shaven Negro men in well-pressed suits, dress shirts, and carefully matching ties in this neighborhood. This amused him, so he always played a game with the passengers.

First he would glare at the white women: gazing boldly to frighten them through his boring eyes with all those stories about the black man's sex powers. Some of the women would look away nervously, averting the black-eyed spotlight beaming upon them, while others would squirm uneasily on their seats, as if what his gaze was divulging made them want to masturbate.

Then tiring of this, he would turn his fierce threatening look to the pale-faced, washed-out, cleanly scrubbed dickless white men, and watch them wither as they wondered if he were there to start a riot or rob them or rape their women. It was a tough, hard, funny, well-played game that he enjoyed very much.

But tonight, he didn't feel like playing. Instead of staring at them, he simply ignored them by looking out the window and down at the cars appearing like miniature bugs darting in and out of the traffic. Soon the white people began to empty the bus, and after a while, he was left alone to travel into the belly of the ghetto where the seats would then be taken by others like himself.

He felt a surge of exhilaration when the first sister got on: a large, black perspiring woman grunting up the steps, flopping down tiredly on the seat in front of him. Her hair was short and shot straight up as beads of sweat sprinkled the bare crinkled kitchen of her neck. He smelled her sweat, felt her tiredness, wallowed in her big, black brassiness, and felt suddenly hilariously drunk.

"You won't be tired long. We black men are going to take up for you," he thought he had said to himself. But when the woman turned, stared at him, and back, he wondered if he had said it aloud.

The ghetto noises began to drift in and rock with the rhythm of the bus. Flashing neon signs shattered kaleidoscopic shock waves of pawn shops, bars, furniture outlets, and all-night grocery stores. Soul music spilled from the sleazy bars and shabby, mountainous hollow eyed tenements into the streets, bouncing off the hot pavements with its loud soaring beat. Home. He wished Anita would move here where his work was, his heart lay, and where his pain could be borne with a little more ease. But no, *she* wanted to stay where they were because it was closer to her work and she liked it there.

The streets were taking on the evening's life. Men lounged on the corners cracking jokes and making passes at the pliant flashing swell of brown, yellow, black feminine pulchritude floating by in gales of teasing laughter. He breathed deeply, soaking in the fetid air and the sounds and sights. He liked it *here*.

He got off the bus and walked back to the Movement's office. A few people who knew him waved. He waved back, bracing his shoulders in a swagger, making the lion on his shirt stretch as he smiled broadly at them. The office was locked. He stood at the door for a moment, then decided to go to Tubby's Black Bar across the street.

The place was deserted except for two men in dingy T-shirts and faded pants at the bar drinking beer. An old man half-slept in a corner by the juke-box blaring James Brown's wailing blues shout. The man's muddy face sank heavily in deep valley folds. He was dressed in overalls that fell over and hid his shoes. From time to time, he would awaken, sip from a glass of beer gone flat, and nod again.

"Hi, Claude—" the shiny, dark, bald-headed man behind the bar greeted him.

"Hey, Tubby. Whiskey." He perched on the bar stool, glancing around at the shabby booths and worn wooden floor which had held and showed the weight and scuffle of many souls long gone. Friday and Saturday, there was hardly room to get in. The whiskey was set before him. It was cheap and raw and burned like a blaze going down his throat. But it warmed him and he began to feel mellow inside. He reached in his pocket and pulled out a crumpled $10 bill, the week's pay from the Movement. "Slow night," he commented, picking up the change.

"Yeah. Too hot to stir. Anyway, I got no air conditioner." Tubby's head jerked back to a lone fan in the window whirling a bee sound to make a faint breeze.

Suddenly a police siren screamed outside, reaching high above the wailing of James Brown. The two men further down the bar turned quickly, trying to peer out the dirt streaked plate glass window. A quick visible chill of fear iced their eyes. The loud whine ceased, but from the proximity of it's subsidence, they could tell it had stopped somewhere near.

Claude kept his eyes on the glass. He had to drink slowly to make the liquor and the money and companionship last. James Brown's bellow ended in a crying moan, leaving the room silent and each man's thoughts naked to the other. "Trouble—" Tubby said, frowning. "Too hot a night for trouble."

The police car's siren squealed again and faded away. The old man's eyes opened as if on signal, and he reached for the beer glass that was encircled with skimmed foam.

"Well!" Tubby smiled, relief flooding his face. "Gone. Pro'bly nothing much. Next round on the house, brothers."

Then the police's warning song shrilled again, coming closer and louder like a screaming angry hyena. The scream stopped in front of the bar. The door swung back and two uniform policemen entered.

"Everybody up and over against the wall," the big, stout one ordered, standing spraddle-legged with gun drawn in the middle of the room. "Search 'em, Ed," he said to the tall, thin young one who looked and acted like a rookie.

The two men at the bar, resembling well-trained robots, moved simultaneously to stand against the pock marked wall scribbled with countless names and addresses and epithets. The old man half stood obediently in his corner, then through no volition of his own, swayed back down in his chair, too drunk to stand.

"You too, Pops," the big officer snapped, pushing the bill of his cap back to unmask small narrow eyes. Then, moving uncannily fast across the room, he jerked the old man to his feet and shoved his dead weight against the wall. The man bent his will to blend into the scars of the wall's legacy of past histories.

"What's wrong, officer?" Tubby asked quickly. "I ain't had no trouble in here—"

"But *we've* had trouble. White man was mugged down the street. We're looking for the nigger who done it." It was then his eyes discovered Claude still sitting firmly on the bar stool. Their eyes met: the white man's cold grey steel of a winter's sky, and the angry, black man's storm of inbred hate. "Goddamnit! You get over there to that wall like the rest."

Claude steeled himself against the bar, planting his feet solidly on the rungs of the stool. Who the hell did they think they were bursting in here like this.

They had no right. That white man who got mugged had no right—being here in *their* world. Words came out, revealing his thoughts.

"What was that white man doing down here anyway? Looking for black pussy?"

The policeman's mouth opened in surprise, his thin lips folding like a tent against the flabbiness of his face. For a stilled deathlike moment, he was too shocked to say anything. Then giving an angry bellow, his meaty hands seized Claude by his shirt, ripping the African symbols and tearing the lion into shreds. Furiously he slammed him against the wall.

The hardness struck his head, stunning him for a moment. He knew he had fallen because he felt the floor and grit under the palms of his hands. Dazed, he saw the big black shoes of the policeman shift, and before he could roll out of the way, felt the hard weight of the lawman's foot plunging into his side. Pain gripped him as his body was left as breathless as a deflated balloon.

"Black bastard! I believe *you* the one done it. Get the Goddam hell up. *Get up!*"

He got up slowly, the hurt bursting through him. The room swirled in a circular motion, reminding him of the ferris wheel he rode on when he was a boy that went around and around, and when he closed his eyes, he could yet feel the revolving sensation in the blackness. He felt numbed and on another planet where there was nothing and even the nothing would not keep still. The cheap rotgut whiskey rose to his throat. He wanted to vomit. But he swallowed and swallowed the bile to keep it down. He couldn't do *that*. Not before *him*.

"Don't this one look like the one he described, Ed?"

"Naw, Bull," the young cop replied, shaking his head, eyes nervously skirting Claude. "He said the guy was little and yellow with—"

"He looks like him to *me,"* Bull growled, spittle making bubbles at the corners of his mouth. His tone became wheedling. "Now don't he to *you?"*

The young one looked down and away as if studying the thought, but said nothing. The men against the wall stood motionless like a shadow of silent ghosts.

Claude guardedly watched the cop called Bull, thinking if that white son-of-a-bitch hit him again, he'd kill him. So help him, he'd kill that white motherfucker!

"I'm goin' to take *this* nigger in—" Bull said, pointing to Claude. "Com'on. Let's go—"

Claude worked his lips. They felt cracked and he could taste the salt of blood around them. The movement of his mouth to speak hurt, but the words came out strong, not betraying the inward pain. "How you going to take *me* in? He just said I didn't fit—"

"Shut up, nigger! I can take you in for anything I Goddam got a mind to. We ought to take all you black coons in and kill ever' last one of you. Pow!

Pow! Like *that!*" He waved his pistol menacingly, shoving it into Claude's face.

Suddenly, upon seeing the beefy face and the wild grey eyes so near, the old familiar ache crossed his forehead as a rushing tide of black ancient fires of loathing seared through him. His black fist clenched, doubled hard and drew back. The white target wavered like a leering pendulum before him. It seemed like a time without beginning or end, but it was only a second before his right fist raised, ladened with the weight of his rage. Suddenly there was a weakness in his arm like a pressure was holding it back, subconsciously restraining it, making his arm not a part of him but a separate entity. The fist shot out, lightly grazing the fleshy white chin.

"Goddam black bastard!" the policeman roared.

He saw the cop's gun handle raise in the air and pause for a blinding moment before he closed his eyes and waited to go down in darkness.

He awakened in the back room of Tubby's on a hard dirty cot. A cold towel was over his forehead, and he felt the bandage behind his ear. The pallid yellow naked bulb shone above him, making him aware that he had entered the now.

"You goin' to be all right, man," Tubby said soothingly, standing above him, face anxious. "That other cop grabbed his arm just in time to keep him from *really* knockin' your brains out."

"They didn't take me in—"

"Naw. They too scared, I guess. The skinny one said sumpin' 'bout the chief wanting 'em to lay off crackin' niggers' heads for a while. Guess they scared we might start a riot—" he laughed a dim sound. "Can you make it home by yourself? I'll call a cab—" Gently he removed the towel.

"I can make it." He shifted his legs over the side of the bed, and with effort, stood up groggily. "I'm O.K.—" Aside from a pain in his head and the blood caking his lips, making them heavy and swollen. "Only thing—only thing, I sure wished I had knocked the Goddam pure white shit out of that mother-fucker—" But he hadn't. He hadn't, or was it that he *couldn't* . . .

A chilling helplessness invaded him, blown by the winds of past ancient black futility. He suddenly wanted to go home.

At home he didn't bother to wash. He simply stepped out of his tattered clothes and got between the clean white sheets in his shorts.

It was early but seemed late to him. It was early when she came home, yet seemed late to him. He closed his eyes when he heard her key, pretending to be asleep. His ears followed her movements from the living room to the bath-room where he heard the running water, the flushing of the toilet, then her foot sounds in the soft mules coming into the room. The bed dipped slightly as she slid in beside him. He could smell the peppermint toothpaste and the Avon cream she applied to her face at night, as well as the faint odor of her perfume still clinging to her. He wondered why it hadn't taken her as long as usual to go through her nightly rituals. Without opening his eyes, he knew it was because she hadn't put her curlers on—she hadn't planted the garden rows of wires to make her hair bloom round soft ringlets in the morning.

He heard her turn over on her side and sigh. Soon she would be asleep. Listening to her steady breathing, he thought: she hadn't spoken to him or even tried to awaken him and talk with him. She hadn't noticed the bloody bandage behind his ear or the cakey brown crust on his mouth. It was as though he wasn't there—wasn't there like the white policeman had acted—like he was nothing, a nameless phantom to be pushed and cursed and ignored. He was nothing at all. Absolutely *nothing.*

Suddenly he opened his eyes to shout at her as the white policeman had at him. *Make* her notice him—see him—realize he was *there.*

The darkness met his eyes first. Upon seeing it, he felt inept, frustrated in the mire of his thoughts. Somehow he knew she hadn't even bothered to turn *on* the light in the room at all. Simply undressed in the bathroom and followed her instinct around the darkened bedroom to the bed. She hadn't *wanted* to see him.

"Anita!" he shouted, sitting up angrily. *"Anita!"*

She stirred, moving a little. "What is it, Claude?" The words were even estranged from him, coming sleepy and muffled in her pillow.

He swallowed hard. What *was* it? What *did* he want? To tell her about the evening—his failure. A failure because of a yet alive age-old fear of the white man still ghosting his black mind and making him ineffectual. Was that what had caused his abortive effort to strike back the way he really wanted to? Hard, strong, like a man—not a feeble man.

"How were the nice white people?" he finally asked, the question meaningless to him, but it was an attempt, a start. For wasn't *she* there eating and drinking and laughing with *them,* while others of *them* were beating *him* up?

"Oh, God, Claude. Not tonight—again. I'm sleepy."

He moved closer to where she was lying with her back to him. A perverse anger made him want to continue: "Did you sneak out in the car with any of those faggot blonde boys who're always trying to get you in bed behind my back?"

She did not answer, her back and her silence a barrier to him.

"They almost killed a white son-of-a-bitch downtown tonight for that thing —after black women."

"Is that so—?"

"And the police thought *I* was the one who did it!" Now! Hear that? He thought gleefully. The police thought someone like *him* could do that—was capable of defending his black women.

"Well—did you?"

Had he detected a note of sarcasm in her words? The derision dipped over him like smoldering hot honey. Was it her cool contempt that made him feel she knew him too well?

"I *could* have—"

"Hum-m-m. With your black power, I suppose."

"Damnit, Anita. LOOK AT ME!" The words spewed out a belch of fire before he realized she couldn't look at him because of the darkness. Even if she did look, there would only be the dark outline of him that was a man.

"All right, Claude," she murmured in exasperation, turning towards him. "So a white man was half killed—"

"And I was involved. The police beat me up in a bar—" The words were hesitant—the story not coherent. Puzzle pieces which he couldn't put together for her. Snatches of thoughts and actions left hanging in the air.

"So? What's so new about that? The white man's been beating nigger heads since slave time and will *still* do it whenever they can get a chance. It just happened that you were there at that time in that particular situation." Suddenly her voice softened: "Claude, I'm sorry. Are you hurt bad?"

She reached for the light on the bedstand, but he stopped her. He didn't want the light. The light and its harshness would destroy the mood and the moment and turn his feelings inside out. The sudden concern of her began to anger him. But wasn't that what he had wanted? Her sympathy, kindness—the protective shelter of his black woman, as all black men had wanted and gotten at some time?

"What's there to be sorry about?" he snapped defensively. "We're all going to get bloody fighting the system. In the Movement, we *expect* those things— *welcome* them. Roll with the punches and give out some too. You dig me, baby?"

"Uh-huh," she yawned, shifting back to her side of the bed.

To him, the disdain was there in the mocking aloofness. The ache in his head began again, slowly, intensifying the pain from the cut on his head. He had been a buffoon all night—a black travesty beaten by what he was trying to beat, destroyed by what he was trying to destroy. And now, he was being 'buked and scorned by what he imagined her to be all in one: a black tribe of Amazons towering in statuesque dominance over the black male pygmies stunted by the white man's nurturing.

The ache increased as pain and heated resentment flowed hotly through his loins. The boiling blood caused his manhood to rise stiff and long. The throbbing elongated maleness of him made him passionately aware again of what he was and of what he could do. He could make babies like the white man. He could and *should* make hundreds of babies to create an army to fight the white man. Hundreds of black babies to make the white man's milk black. He *could*. He was a man. *Wasn't he?*

Uttering a harsh desperate cry, his arms reached out to grab her, to pull her savagely against him. He wanted *her* to feel and know the strength of him, the depth, the height, the power and the glory. His bruised sore lips smashed against hers.

Then tearing the flimsy material of her gown, he covered her with his stink and beard, anger and wretchedness. He entered her before she was ready and was hardly conscious of what he was doing. He heard and didn't hear her cries to cease, for him to stop, get up, get off. He had caught her by surprise.

She stiffened beneath him, trying to close the entrance to her against him. But he swelled and gloried in the battle that he fought now without gun or fist —only with the spear of him stabbing again and again into her until finally he felt her weaken and grow pliant under his warriorlike strokes to make her submissive to his will and strength and manhood. He fought and fought, marvelling at his staying power, pridefully thinking he could go on and on like this all night.

But when he felt the moistness of her beginning to receive him, bringing him into the hot deep well of her that claimed him now and made him feel caught and obliviously lost, he realized the battle was over. And in the end, he cried out in triumph—in defeat.

After a quivering moment that froze him, he rolled off her, breathing heavily, expelling the last of his strength.

Before he closed his eyes to give up to the tiredness, he heard her say in a voice that made him know she knew: "It takes more than that to be a man—"

Then he thought he never wanted to awaken again.

Most battered women of color are acutely aware of how the police routinely brutalize men of color, how hospitals and social services discriminate against men of color, and the ways men of color are more readily labeled deviant than white men. . . . For battered women of color, seeking help for the abuse they are experiencing always requires a tenuous balance between care for and loyalty to themselves, their batterers, and their communities.

—Beth E. Ritchie and Valli Kanuha, *"Battered Women of Color"*

After Saturday Nite Comes Sunday

SONIA SANCHEZ

It had all started at the bank. She wuzn't sure, but she thot it had. At that crowded bank where she had gone to clear up the mistaken notion that she was $300.00 overdrawn in her checking account.

Sandy walked into that undersized-low-expectation-of-niggahs-being-able-to-save-anything -bank. Meanly. She wuz tired of crackers charging her fo they own mistakes. She had seen it wid her own eyes, five checks: four fo fifty dollars, the other one fo one hundred dollars made out to an Anthony Smith. It *wuz* Winston's signature. Her stomach jumped as she added and re-added up the figures. Finally she dropped the pen and looked up at the business-suited/ cracker sitten across from her wid crossed legs and eyes. And as she called him faggot in her mind, watermelon tears gathered round her big eyes and she just sat.

Someone had come for her at the bank. A friend of Winston's helped her to his car. It wuz the wite/dude who followed Winston constantly wid his eyes. Begging eyes she had once called em, half in jest, half seriously. They wuz begging now, along wid his mouth, begging Sandy to talk. But she couldn't. The words had gone away, gotten lost, drowned by the warm/april/rain dropping in on her as she watched the car move down the long/unbending/street. It was her first spring in Indianapolis. She wondered if it wud be beautiful.

He was holding her. Cryen in her ear. Loud cries, almost louder than the noise already turning in her head. Yeh. He sed between the cries. He had fucked up the money. He had . . . he had . . . oh babee. C'mon Sandy and talk. Talk to me. Help me babee. Help me to tell you what I got to tell you for both our sakes. He stretched her out on the green/oversized/couch that sat out from the wall like some displaced trailer waiting to be parked.

I'm hooked he sed. I'm hooked again on stuff. It's not like befo though

158

when I wuz seventeen and just beginning. This time it's different. I mean it has to do now wid me and all my friends who are still on junk. You see I got out of the joint and looked around and saw those brothers who are my friends all still on the stuff and I cried inside. I cried long tears for some beautiful dudes who didn't know how the man had em by they balls. Babee I felt so sorry for them and they wuz so turned around that one day over to Tony's crib I got high wid em. That's all babee. I know I shouldn't have done that. You and the kids and all. But they wuz dudes I wuz in the joint wid. My brothers who wuz still unaware. I can git clean babee. I mean I don't have a long jones. I ain't been on it too long. I can kick now. Tomorrow. You just say it. Give me the word/ sign that you understand, forgive me fo being one big asshole and I'll start kicking tomorrow. For you babee. For the kids. Please say you forgive me babee. I know I been laying some heavy shit on you. Spending money we ain't even got—I'll git a job too next week—staying out all the time. Hitting you fo telling me the truth bout myself. My actions. Babee it's you I love in spite of my crazy actions. It's you I love. Don't nobody else mean to me what you do. It's just that I been acting crazy but I know I can't keep on keepin' on this way and keep you and the children. Give me a whole lot of slack during this time and I can kick it babee. I love you. You so good to me. The best muthafucking thing that done ever happened to me. You the best thing that ever happened to me in all of my thirty-eight years and I'll take better care of you. Say something Sandy. Say you understand it all. Say you forgive me. At least that babee. He raised her head from the couch and kissed her. It was a short cooling kiss. Not warm. Not long. A binding kiss and she opened her eyes and looked at him and the bare room that somehow now complemented their lives and she started to cry again. And as he grabbed her and rocked her she spoke fo the first time since she had told that wite/collar/cracker in the bank that the bank wuz wrong.

The-the-the-the bab-bab-bab-bies. Ar-ar-ar-are th-th-th-they o-o-o-okay? Oh my god. I'm stuttering. Stuttering, she thot. Just like when I wuz little. Stop talking. Stop talking girl. Write what you have to say. Just like you used to when you wuz little and you got tired of people staring at you while you pushed words out of an unaccommodating mouth. Yeh. That wuz it she thot. Stop talking and write what you have to say. Nod yo/head to all of this madness. But rest yo/tongue and nod yo/head and use yo/hands till you git it all straight again.

She pointed to her bag and he handed it to her. She took out a pen and notebook and wrote that she wuz tired that her head hurt and was spinning and that she wanted to sleep fo a while. She turned and held his face full of little sores where he had picked for ingrown hairs the nite befo. She kissed them and let her tongue move over his lips, wetting them. He smiled at her and sed he wud git her a coupla sleeping pills. He wud also pick up some dollies fo himself cuz Saturday was kicking time fo him. As he went out the door he turned and sed lady, you some lady. I'm a lucky mothafuka to have found you. She watched him from the window and the sun hit the gold of his dashiki and made it bleed yellow rain drops.

She must have dozed. She knew it wuz late. It wuz dark outside. The room wuz dark also and she wondered if he had come in and gone upstairs where the children were napping. What a long nap the boys were taking. They wud be up all nite tonite if they didn't wake up soon. Maybe she shud wake them up but she decided against it. Her body wuz still tired. She heard footsteps on the porch.

His voice wuz light and cracked a little as he explained his delay. He wuz high. She knew it. He sounded like he sounded on the phone when he called her late in the nite from some loud place and complimented her fo understanding his late hours. She hadn't understood them, she just hated to be a complaining bitch. He had no sleeping pills but he had gotten her something as good. A morphine tablet. She watched his face as he explained that she cud swallow it or pop it into the skin. He sed it worked better if you stuck it in yo/arm. As he took the tablet out of the cellophane paper of his cigarettes, she closed her eyes and fo a moment she thot she heard someone crying outside the house. She opened her eyes.

His body hung loose as he knelt by the couch. He took from his pocket a manila envelope. It had little spots of blood on it and as he undid the rubber bands, she saw two needles, a black top wid two pieces of dirty, wite cotton balls in it. She knew this wuz what he used to git high wid.

I-I-I-I-I don-don-don-don't wa-wa-want none o-o-o-of that sh-sh-sh-shit ma-a-a-a-a-n. Ain't th-th-th-that do-do-do-dope too? I-I-I-I-I just just just just wa-wa-wa-nnnt-ted to sleep. I'm o-o-o-kay now. She picked up her notebook and pen and started to write again.

I slept while you wuz gone man. I drifted on off as I looked for you to walk up the steps. I don't want that stuff. Give me a cold beer though if there's any in the house. I'll drink that. But no shit man, she wrote. I'm yo/woman. You shudn't be giving me none of that shit. Throw the pill away. We don't need it. You don't need it any mo. You gon kick and we gon move on. Keep on being baddDDD togetha. I'll help you man cuz I know you want to kick. Flush it on down the toilet. You'll start kicking tomorrow and I'll git a babysitter and take us fo a long drive in the country and we'll move on the grass and make it move wid us cuz we'll be full of living/alive/thots and we'll stop and make love in the middle of nowhere and the grass will stop its wintry/brown/chants and become green as our black bodies sing. Heave. Love each other. Throw that shit away man cuz we got more important/beautiful/things to do.

As he read the note his eyes looked at hers in a half/clear/way and he got up and walked slowly to the john. She heard the toilet flushing and she heard the refrigerator door open and close. He brought two/cold beers and as she opened hers she sat up to watch him rock back and forth in the rocking chair. And his eyes became small and sad as he sed half-jokingly, hope I don't regret throwing that stuff in the toilet and he leaned back and smiled sadly as he drank his beer. She turned the beer can up to her lips and let the cold evening foam wet her mouth and drown the gathering stutters of her mind.

The sound of cries from the second floor made her move. As she climbed the stairs she waved to him. But his eyes were still closed. He wuz somewhere else, not in this house she thot. He wuz somewhere else floating among past dreams she had never seen or heard him talk about. As she climbed the stairs, the boys' screams grew louder. Wow. Them boys got some strong lungs she thot. And smiled.

It wuz eleven thirty and she had just put the boys in their cribs. She heard them sucking on their bottles, working hard at nourishing their bodies. She knew the youngest twin wud finish his bottle first and cry out fo more milk befo he slept. She laughed out loud. He sho cud eat.

He wuz in the bathroom. She knocked on the door but he sed for her not to come in. She stood outside the door, not moving, and knocked again. Go and turn on the TV he sed, I'll be out in a few minutes.

It wuz thirty minutes later when he came out. His walk wuz much faster than befo and his voice wuz high, higher than the fear moving over her body. She ran to him, threw her body against him and held on. She kissed him hard and moved her body over his until he stopped and paid attention to her movements. They fell on the floor. She felt his weight on her and she moved and kissed him and moved and kissed him as his hands started to move across her small frame that wuz full of red/yellow/motions that reached out for Winston's yesterdays to turn them into tomorrows. Her body wuz feeling good and she culdn't understand why he stopped. In the midst of her pulling off her dress he stopped and took out a cigarette and lit it while she undressed to her bra and panties. She felt naked all of a sudden and sat down and drew her legs up against her chest and closed her eyes. She reached fo a cigarette and lit it.

He stretched out next to her. She felt very ashamed as if she had made him do something wrong. She wuz glad that she culdn't talk cuz that way she didn't have to explain. He ran his hand up and down her legs and touched her soft wet places.

It's just babee that this stuff kills any desire for fucking. I mean I want you and all that but I can't quite git it up to perform. He lit another cigarette and sat up. Babee you sho know how to pick em. I mean wuz you born under an unlucky star or sumthin? First you had a niggah who preferred a rich/wite/bitch to you and blkness. Now you have a junkie who can't even satisfy you when you need satisfying. And his laugh wuz harsh as he sed again, you sho know how to pick em lady. She didn't know what else to do so she smiled a nervous smile that made her feel, remember times when she wuz little and she had stuttered thru a sentence and the listener had acknowledged her accomplishment wid a smile and all she cud do wuz smile back.

He turned and held her and sed stay up wid me tonite babee. I got all these memories creeping in on me. Bad ones. They's the things that make kicking hard you know. You begin remembering all the mean things you've done to yo/family/friends who dig you. I'm remembering now all the heavee things I done laid on you in such a short time. You hardly had a chance to catch yo/breath when I'd think of sum new shit to lay on you. Help me Sandy. Listen to my talk. Hold my hand when I git too sad. Laugh at my fears that keep popping out on me like some childhood disease. Be my vaccine babee. I need you. Don't ever leave me babee cuz I'll never have a love like you again. I'll never have another woman again if you leave me. He picked up her hands and rubbed them in his palms as he talked and she listened until he finally slept and morning crept in through the shades and covered them.

He threw away his works when he woke up. He came over to where she was feeding the boys and kissed her and walked out to the backyard and threw the manila envelope into the middle can. He came back inside, smiled, and took a dollie wid a glass of water. He fell on the couch.

Sandy put the boys in their strollers in the backyard where she cud watch them as she cleaned the kitchen. She saw Snow, their big/wite/dog come round the corner of the house to sit in front of them. They babbled words to him but he sat still guarding them from the backyard/evils of the world.

She moved fast in the house, had a second cup of coffee, called their babysitter and finished straightening up the house. She put on a short dress which showed her legs and she felt good about her black/hairy/legs. She laughed as she remembered that the young brothers on her block used to call her a big/legged/momma as she walked in her young ways.

They never made the country. Their car refused to start and Winston wuz too sick to push it to the filling station fo a jump. So they walked to the park. He pushed her in the swing and she pumped herself higher and higher and higher till he told her to stop. She let the swing come slowly to a stop and she jumped out and hit him on the behind and ran. She heard him gaining on her and she tried to dodge him but they fell laughing and holding each other. She looked at him and sed I wish you could make love to me man. Then she laughed and pushed him away and sed but just you wait till you all right Winston. I'll give you a work out you'll never forget and they got up and walked till he felt badly and they went home.

He stayed upstairs while she cooked. When she went upstairs to check on him, he was curled up, wrapped tight as a child in his mother's womb, and she wiped his head and body full of sweat and kissed him and told him how beautiful he wuz and how proud she wuz of him. She massaged his back and went away. He called fo her as she wuz feeding the children and asked for the wine. He needed somethin' else to relieve this saturday/nite/pain that wuz creeping upon him. He looked bad she thot and she raced down the stairs and brought him the sherry. He thanked her as she went out the door and she curtsied, smiled and sed any ol time boss. She noticed she hadn't stuttered and felt good.

By the time she got back upstairs he wuz moaning and turning back and forth on the bed. He had drunk half the wine in the bottle, now he wuz getting up to bring it all up. When he came back up to the room he sed he was cold so she got another blanket for him. He wuz still cold so she took off her clothes and got under the covers wid him and rubbed her body against him. She wuz scared. She started to sing a Billie/Holiday/song. Yeh. God bless the child that's got his own. She cried in between the lyrics as she felt his big frame trembling and heaving. Oh god she thot, am I doing the right thing? He soon quieted down and got up to go to the toilet. She closed her eyes as she waited fo him. She closed her eyes and felt the warmth of the covers creeping over her. She remembered calling his name as she drifted off to sleep. She remembered how quiet everything finally wuz.

One of the babies woke her up. She went into the room and picked up his bottle and got him more milk. It wuz while she was handing him the milk that she heard the silence. She ran to their bed/room and turned on the light. The bed wuz empty. She ran down the stairs and turned on the lights. He wuz gone. She saw her purse on the couch. Her wallet wuz empty. Nothing wuz left. She opened the door and went out on the porch and she remembered the lights were on and that she wuz naked. But she stood fo a moment looking out at the flat/Indianapolis/street and she stood and let the late/nite air touch her body and she turned and went inside.

For most of the twentieth century, it was the study of combat veterans
that led to the development of a body of knowledge about traumatic disorders. Not until the women's liberation movement of the 1970s was it
recognized that the most common post-traumatic disorders are those not of
men in war but of women in civilian life.
—Judith Lewis Herman, *Trauma and Recovery*

The Day My Father Tried to Kill Us

PAT STATEN

Nightmares have plagued me all my life. When I was young, ten or earlier,
I began to look on them as a natural ailment I must learn to accept. Just as
some people were born deaf or lame, I was born with nightmares (I wisely
concluded). Actually, they were so much a part of my life, so routine, that I
rarely thought about them at all or questioned why I had them. As I got
older the nightmares at least decreased in frequency, though not particularly in
intensity.

When I was small I would wake up in the old Kansas farmhouse I grew up
in and cry out for my mother. As I got older, I felt foolish about such childish
displays of weakness and would not cry out—except in my sleep when I had
no conscious control over it. I would wake up—covered with sweat, panting
like a scared, exhausted animal, too terrified to cry out, and finally after minutes
of forcing myself to consciousness the fear would begin to lessen. Sometimes
I would wake myself with my own screams, sobs, pleas. The lights would go
on and my mother would be standing at the door. She wouldn't come to the
bed to hold me or console me. She would simply stand by the door, her hand
near the light switch.

"All right now?" she'd ask.

"Yes."

"Want the light on?"

"Yes."

"You turn it off later?"

"Yes."

She would look at me for a second before she turned to leave the room. I
grew in time to understand that look. It was a look of worry, concern, a certain
painful expression of helplessness, as though she wanted to reach out to help
me but didn't know how, as though she wanted to say something to me but

didn't know where to begin—or maybe she was waiting for me to say something, to reach out to her, but I never could. I often wanted to sob my heart out on her breasts but something always made me pull back, unable to go on.

She never mentioned my nightmares the next day. No reference was ever made to the nightmares in the family. They were a sort of accepted fact. Occasionally a sister would complain if I had kept her from a good night's sleep.

And no one had any knowledge of Freud or the subconscious or dream symbolism. My family existed a couple of centuries behind the sophisticated, educated world. I even thought they existed apart from the rest of the world. They were farmers. Generation after generation had been farmers. Uneducated, untraveled, and incredibly innocent or ignorant of any larger world beyond the plains of western Kansas.

A television arrived late at the farm, as we could never afford it, and when we did finally get one it only picked up one station and that poorly. Books were unknown in the house. The local newspaper was all the reading done in the family and generally that remained unopened. My parents had no friends. My brother and two sisters did not invite their friends to the house. Relatives did not visit, though we had quite a number of them.

The plains stretched to all sides of the farmhouse. Flat, empty, uneventful. Always that huge expanse of blue sky over the flat horizon. Only the clouds ever seemed to change—rolling in over the plains like prehistoric monsters, transforming themselves to gods and goddesses, to the friends I was too shy to make in real life, to the mountains and skyscrapers I had never seen. The clouds brought the winds that howled outside my bedroom window at night and the storms that popped and rolled and thundered across the endless miles of wheat fields and prairie.

If we hadn't been so isolated on that farm, perhaps I would have had some gauge of what we were all living with—but I didn't. I would have understood why the sister three years older than I had emotional, almost epileptic fits—a kind of hysteria that nearly choked her—why the oldest sister had married at fifteen and left home, why my brother left the farm at fourteen to live and work on a neighboring farm and never again returned home to live.

Through it all, it was my mother who held me together. She was always there—not with kisses or great displays of affection or even words because she was never a woman comfortable with words or exaggerated gestures. She was there simply, with a silent presence, solidarity, a completely inarticulate strength. Without her, I'm sure none of us would have survived those years as whole as we eventually turned out to be.

But as much as I loved her, depended on her, needed her, there was frequently a distance between us. A distance I never quite understood. I never talked to her about my father. I never once thought I could just go to her and say, "I'm afraid of my father." And if I cried out for her at night during my nightmares, she quickly learned not to touch me, as I would pull violently away from her, and even I didn't understand that particular reaction in myself.

And so, at fifteen, when it began, I didn't tell her about it. I spoke to no one about it. At first I thought it was a dream because it came to me as an incident that had happened somewhere outside the usual realm of daily reality. It was a moment suspended outside myself and what I thought the "real" world to be. A funhouse image in which all the people became distorted and grotesque nearly beyond recognition.

And though I thought it must be a dream, it was not like my other dreams. Suddenly in the middle of the day—I could be at school or walking home or waking up in the morning—a part of a scene would flash into my head. I would feel a veil was slowly lifting over something, then falling back again. I would feel a light was passing through some darkness inside myself, and for a second it would hit on something, then pass on before I could really see it. The light would be gone. The veil would fall. I did not know what I had seen. But it nagged at me, disturbed me in a way my nightmares had never disturbed me.

I am fifteen and it's spring. I just got off the school bus and am walking toward the house on the mile-long dirt road. As I near the house, my eyes wander to the large red barn near the house. I've never liked the barn. In fact, I do everything I can to avoid going in it at any time. I've never asked myself why, but now as I'm looking at it, again, for a second it happens. The veil lifts. The light passes. I quickly shrug it off. Today I want nothing to do with this disturbing sensation. Today I must block myself off and I have already begun the process before I reach the house.

My father has been drinking solidly for three days. It's not unusual. It's as routine as my nightmares, and given the same peculiar acceptance. His ritual from the time I can remember is to drink three days, sleep three days. Occasionally there will be a day, if he's lucky, of being sober and not asleep during which he tries to work. I dread his sober days more than the others. His nerves are so raw, he yells at you for any minor thing. I welcome the moment I see him dig the bottle out. I can at least calculate his states of inebriation.

The first day of drinking he's relatively calm. Relaxed. He talks a lot about the "great" past and the "great" war. Always his war memories. He was an infantryman during World War II. At first the stories will be funny and full of practical jokes. Then heroism and patriotism. Even into the second day he is frequently humorous, good-natured, and tells stories that make me laugh till my sides ache. He is full of warmth and light-hearted teasing. He makes up games for us kids to play and joins us with all our childlike enthusiasm and total belief.

But gradually, usually into the third day, the horror stories begin. Shooting people against walls. Turning people into human torches. My father relives

each episode as he talks about it, although often his sentences are so discon-
nected and incoherent it's difficult to make out any concrete incident behind
his ravings.

He calls me as I step into the house. I expect it. I go to the living room
where he sits surrounded by beer cans, overflowing ashtrays, half-eaten food
on dirty plates. He's spilled food on his shirt. His hair is uncombed.

He tries to appear jolly. "Patty Sue, you come here!"

I sit down in the chair opposite him. "Hi, Dad."

"What'd you learn in school today? Huh?"

I shrug. No matter what I answer he will not hear. He's somewhere else. He
barely knows I'm there.

"Nothing." I say.

He suddenly tries to struggle out of his stupor. "Huh?"

"Nothing."

"Nothing! Goddamn! Nothing!"

In a way it's comical. If he were in another mood I would laugh and he
would laugh with me. But not now. I can't laugh. If I do, I risk my life. One
swing from his powerful arm can knock me unconscious. I watch him closely.
I say nothing I must know when to move, when to escape. I must know when
that blank look enters his eyes. My existence depends on knowing each precise
change in his mood. In fifteen years, I've learned the art well. I have never
miscalculated. I know that for a while I am safe. He is in the numb, half-asleep
stage. He will be at that stage till at least the time my mother comes home.

Suddenly his eyes clear for a second. "I've killed men! Did you hear? Do
you understand? I've killed men!"

I nod my head. A huge repressed fear nearly grabs me but I hold it down.
My expression must show nothing.

"Blow the bastard's head off! . . . Son-of-a bitch . . . he came out of there
like a bat out of hell . . . but I blew the bastard's head off. One shot! That's all
it takes! One shot!"

The words do not shock me. I don't even really hear them any more. I've
been hearing such things for years. It has reached a level of total unimportance
with me.

My father looks at me. "Kid. Just a kid. Never seen anything. Take my
advice—you stay here on the farm—the good life—never see what I seen . . ."

He drifts off again and for a second I think he has fallen asleep. I study him
as he sits in the chair, his head nodding to one side. He is a big man. Six foot
three, with powerful muscles he developed from his youth as a farmhand. Even
the years of drinking have not given him the usual soft look of drunks. I saw
pictures of him when he was young, and he had once been a handsome man
(even now I see he has not lost his good looks). In the picture he had wavy red
hair, penetrating blue eyes, sharp sensitive features. I saw a picture of him

during the war. The sensitivity was still there, but changed, masked by a fierce expression. While, before, his gaze was penetrating, now it seemed similar to the look of well-trained dogs, ready for attack.

He comes awake abruptly. "You hear?"

"Yes."

A sudden direct intensity in his gaze. I am always shocked to suddenly encounter this penetrating, deadly sober, commanding look in his eyes. It happens without warning.

"You hear good! You stay where you belong! You stay on the land—they'll kill you. Those bastards kill everything! I seen girls like you—" He stops for a second, then continues. "Bunch of mad animals. Got to break 'em! Kick-the bastards in the teeth! They won't do that to my kids! No sir, not my kids. I love my kids . . . all my kids . . . something they never touched . . ."

His mind wanders and I see that beaten, defeated expression cross his face.

"You forgive me, Pat?"

I look at him and say what I always say when he asks this.

"Yes."

He nods gratefully and falls asleep, sitting in the chair.

But I do not forgive him. I hate him. And much deeper than my hatred, I fear him.

After I am sure he has fallen asleep, I slip out of the house. I walk the dirt road from our house to the main highway. Mom works at the Boeing Airplane Plant in Wichita and each night the plant bus leaves her off at the highway. And each night I wait for her. It is a ritual I established years earlier when she first took the job. Dad loses job after job and even when he can work he misses so many days his check is never substantial. We've lost all of the farm over the years but the barn and main house. There is nothing left to farm but a big plot for a garden. We still have a few chickens. But it's impossible to live off the land, so Mom took the job at the factory. Putting parts of machinery together all day. Standing on her feet eight hours. Then the two-hour trip back and forth to the plant on the factory bus.

I wait by our mailbox. The bus pulls up and stops. Mom steps off. I am always proud when I see her step off the bus. No other woman on the bus is as pretty as my Mom. Even the rich women in town with new clothes and makeup and fancy hairdos cannot compare with my mother.

She is small. Five foot two. (At ten I was as tall as she and by fifteen I've already leaped up to five eight.) She never wears anything but the same cheap dresses. Even if she had the money, I doubt that she would spend it on clothes. She is dark. Dad says she is part Indian but, if she is, she never mentions it. In the summer her skin tans to a golden bronze. Her red-auburn hair is cut at her shoulders, ending in a natural wave. She has soft, light blue eyes. And if her beauty can be called in any way startling it's in the summer when the clear blue of her eyes contrasts with her dark skin. But it is not a flashy beauty or even a beauty she is aware of possessing. I'm sure she never thinks of herself as beautiful—particularly at a time when the idea of good looks seems to depend on lots of makeup and chemical curls. She hasn't the time or money for any of this. There is nothing superficial or phony or imposed about her. It is a completely natural beauty and part of it lies in her soft grace, her strength, the gentleness and warmth in her eyes. And her smile.

She smiles, seeing me as she gets off the bus. This is the only time I have with her alone. At the house there are always my father and the other children and work to be taken care of. She has no time there. But this one-mile walk back to the house each evening is reserved for me alone. She asks me about school and I tell her and I ask her about work and she always says, "Oh, it's the same as always."

It is an unusually warm day for this time of year. A strong southerly wind. As we start toward the house, Mom takes her shoes off. Unless it's cold, she will frequently do this. Mom seems to have an innate dislike of shoes. Sometimes she points out a butterfly or a flower or notes if there will be an early winter or a late summer that year.

She was raised on a farm. Born to a family of nine children. Pioneer stock. She spent the summers of her youth walking barefoot behind a horse and plow, farming the fields. Nature is still her real home. She understands it. She draws strength from it. She doesn't like the factory. It cuts her off from something essential in her life—her roots in the earth. This walk is her time to get back in touch with it.

This walk is also an important ritual in my life. It builds the bond between me and my mother, though we rarely talk of anything outside the trivial. Occasionally I will build myself up to some huge confession. But she constantly surprises me with her reaction. Her look is undisturbed, unreproachful, sometimes even amused. It's a look of: "I knew that years ago and now you're just getting around to telling me but I'm not surprised."

Not that she was without bad moods or a tired irritability at times. As she is tonight. She has been up almost constantly for two days. The weariness shows in the circles under her eyes, the tension in her face. We do not discuss my father, if he's drinking or not. She knows he is. We never discuss my father.

I know she needs time alone tonight so I begin to walk ahead of her. We are halfway to the house. I turn to look at her. She's standing right in the middle of the dirt road, her arms spread wide, her head thrown back. She sees me looking at her and turns her face into the last rays of afternoon light.

"Do you feel that wind?" she says. "Lord, do you feel that wonderful wind!"

Since my mother is rarely given to outbursts of any sort, I stand and feel the wind. I think it must be different for her to get so excited. Just a little warmer, an early spring wind. But aside from that, I decide it's the same old wind and keep walking. I hear her laughter behind me. I turn and look at her and realize how much she puzzles me. How much she has always puzzled me.

I don't understand her. I don't understand her joy, her strength, her endurance, her loves or her drive. I don't understand why she stays with my father. I don't understand how she can work all day, then come home to stay up most of the night with him. I don't understand her silent ability to endure day after day.

Why does she put up with this sort of life? The worry. The poverty. His drunks. The beatings. Is it her Puritan upbringing that suffering is good? An old-fashioned sense of duty? Or maybe she is so concerned with just surviving, so preoccupied with paying the bills and feeding the children that she long ago stopped thinking there was any other way to live.

I saw a picture of my mother soon after she was married. Both my parents look so young, neither twenty yet. There is a freshness and sensitivity to both of them. And in that picture my mother is happy. Genuinely happy. Outside that picture I have never seen my mother so happy. She is beautiful and young and holding the arm of a man she obviously loved. That picture is all that comes close to explaining something to me I've never understood—her relationship with my father.

We reach the house. Dad calls Mom into the living room. I go to my room and shut the door. It will begin now. The very worst period of his three-day drunk will begin now.

I look on these periods as something that must be endured, and my main method of endurance is fantasy. I withdraw into elaborate stories of beauty and love in exotic lands far from this shabby farmhouse and a broken man's ravings. But even my complete withdrawal into a world of make-believe does not work in those few hours when he hits his peak of violence and terror.

I lie awake and even if the night is freezing I throw all the covers off, sleep with my jeans and shirt on, make quick decisive plans of escape, keep the window half opened, calculate how long it will take me to get from the bed out of the window, across the roof, and finally into the open area beyond the house. And all the while, I am sure that when he comes I will be too terrified to move.

Sometimes, if he gets particularly bad, Karie will help me barricade the door with a dresser. Karie is the sister three years older than me, and I share the bedroom with her. Usually she puts the radio to her ear or pulls the pillow over her head and falls asleep. I never understand how she can sleep then. I could no more fall asleep then than you can fall asleep on your way to the gallows.

It begins late at night. Two or three in the morning. First he listens to music. Then he talks about the war. The sound of his voice rising through the house —words so blurred, vicious I can rarely understand them. He begins to yell at my mother. Then he begins to beat her. Dishes crashing. Furniture overturned. The sound of her body hitting the walls or floor. She never cries or screams during these beatings. And the next morning there will be no sign the beating happened—aside from a large bruise or cut she will try to hide with makeup or clothes.

He stops beating her. I lie awake. Listening. Waiting. My ear tuned to every sound in the house. Silence. Only the wind howling outside and the creak and groan of the old boards in the house. I wonder if she's dead or alive. I think she is dead. I listen for any sound she might make. But I don't hear her. I think that tomorrow morning I will find her dead. But now I am too frightened to move, to help her even if she needed me. I am paralyzed with fear.

Silence. Listening to my father's footsteps downstairs. Waiting for him to climb the stairs. Waiting for him to come up and kill the rest of us. Waiting. But he never comes, and I never go through one of those nights without believing this time it will happen, this time he will kill us, this time I will not fall into exhausted sleep when the dawn comes.

But the dawn comes and I fall asleep. Mother's voice wakes me for school. She has a bruise on her forehead. She covers it with makeup. No one discusses it. No one acts as though it had ever happened.

But that day, perhaps because I'm so tired, the dream begins to come to me again. And today I have much more difficulty shaking it off than ever before. Today something is determined to come awake in me, despite all I do to ignore it.

That evening I'm in the kitchen helping Mom do the dishes and I decide to mention it.

"Mom, I keep having this dream. . . ."

The words fade. I can't go on.

My mother is exhausted from the night before and the factory. She isn't paying much attention to what I'm saying. Her lack of attention makes it easier for me to continue.

"But I don't know if it's a dream. I mean, I sort of remember it like it was a dream—you know, you wake up and you can remember parts but not all— but every day now I remember a little more of this dream. Ain't that funny?"

My mother stops washing the dishes and glances at me.

"What's the dream about?"

"Oh, it's crazy. Don't make no sense."

"You want to tell me what you can remember?"

"Well, first a door slamming. It's hot and bright. I'm real little. I'm sitting under the big tree in the front yard, playing. And this door slams—I think it's the door to the porch—the screen door—and you come running out and you're real scared and you tell us all to run but I don't know why. . . ."

That part of the dream is gone so I stop. My mother hasn't stopped washing the dishes but I sense something about her then. She's waiting for something to happen. She's waiting for me to say something. But I don't know what.

I continue: "Then it's dark and I'm alone. That don't make no sense. It was bright and hot and suddenly it's dark and cold. Must be a dream, huh?"

My mother says nothing.

"I can't remember nothing else," I say.

"Nothing?"

"Well, a line—all of us are in a line in the barn and I'm last."

My mother stops washing the dishes.

"That's all?"

I nod yes.

She touches me on the arm, saying, "Off you go now."

"Don't you want me to finish drying these dishes?"

"I'll finish. You go on now."

I put the dish towel down, happy to get out of a task I hate. But as I go to my room, I think it's odd. It was my turn to dry the dishes and Mother has broken one of her strict rules of discipline by letting me out of it. But I'm too relieved to think much more about it.

It's a few days later in school that it really begins. I've had a slight headache all day. We're having our history lesson. My mind is wandering. I can't concentrate. A cold feeling begins to come over me and I wonder if I'm getting sick. But the cold isn't a kind of cold I've ever felt before. I sit at my desk, struggling with the feeling, trying to hide it. Afternoon. Sitting in a classroom with thirty other students. The teacher's at the blackboard, talking. I'm trying to listen to what she's saying but I can't.

All of reality seems to be retreating from me. It's not a literal hallucination. It's a feeling of being connected with nothing. I'm cold. The sun streaks through the window and falls across my desk. I suddenly look up at the sun, that blinding white light burns into my eyes.

I remembered then.

I'm little. No more than five years old. It's summer. The farm. A hot day. The hottest part of the day has arrived. A clear day. Not a cloud. The sky is an empty, pale blue. Only that huge ball of fire above us. The fields are burned brown. The color seems bleached out of everything, even the trees and earth.

I am with my brother and sisters in the front yard. My brother and oldest sister are playing with sticks, pretending they're swords. Karie is sitting on the steps of the porch with her doll. I'm sitting alone under the tree, playing with a toy car in the dirt. Mom's inside the house. My father is gone. He's been gone for a few days.

I look up through the branches of the tree, directly at the sun. Mother has often punished me for looking at the sun like this. She says I'll ruin my good eyes. But it fascinates me. And if I stare at it long enough it becomes a dark ball and throbs, like a big heart in the sky.

I finally look away and see black spots everywhere. The black spots begin to fade when I see the dust rising off the road to our house. The car enters the area in front of the house. The ground is hard and dry and when the car goes over it the scales of dried mud crack and pop under the tires like broken glass.

The car skids to an abrupt halt. My father gets out. Something's wrong with him. I think he must be drunk because I'm used to seeing him drunk. But there's something different this time. He does not greet us children or respond to our greeting. In fact, he doesn't even seem to notice we're there, though he walks within a few feet of us to get into the house. He walks like a blind man or someone who has had all his side vision eliminated.

I feel it then. A split second of childish premonition. A distinct feeling of something not being the same as usual (even the usual of his alcoholism, which at that age I accepted as the norm). But I'm old enough to understand or react to the feeling. I go back to playing in the dirt. My older brother and sister continue their sword fight. Karie plays with her doll.

Remembering the scene then, I thought it odd that I could not remember any of the usual sounds of children playing. Only a heavy silence and the hot sun. A slow-motion film with the sound off.

How long did we continue to play in the front yard? I don't remember.

The front-porch door slams, like a pistol shot. I look up from where I'm playing with a sense of terror, like an alerted animal. My mother (then a young woman) runs down the steps of the porch. She grabs Karie's hand, knocking the doll out of her grasp, and pulls her to her feet, all in one swift uninterrupted gesture.

For a second my mother scans the yard, then realizes the children are too scattered to grab them all. She must grab the ones nearest her and hope the others will follow. She already has Karie in one hand. My brother is near her so she grabs his hand. None of us know what is happening, why suddenly the day is interrupted with this blind terror. I have not moved from under the tree. I am startled and bewildered at my mother's panic.

Then my mother screams, "Run! Run! Follow me!"

My older sister grabs my hand and pulls me to my feet and we follow my mother. For a second my mother glances frantically around, not sure of her direction, then starts around the house. With one sister and my brother held by each of her hands, they half stumble, then catching her panic, run after her. My older sister and I run too, but not nearly as fast. We don't know what we're running from. My sister seems to have some clearer understanding of it than I do. I can barely keep up with her. My mother keeps looking back at us, to make sure we're following. Of the five of us, I'm the last.

We round the corner of the house. I fall. My sister stops and without words grabs me to stand up and keep running. Then I look up from the ground where I have fallen and back. My father is walking toward me. Already a huge man, from my vantage point on the ground he seems gigantic. His trousers are wrinkled and worn and his white shirt dirty, half-open, sweat-stained. His face is pale. His expression is completely blank. He hasn't even seen me fall. He simply keeps advancing with that same powerful, unhindered, slow methodical gait. He's carrying an army rifle.

From the day I remembered it to now that image has never left my mind.

I struggle to my feet and run after my sister toward the barn.

The memory fades here. I have no idea how I end up under the barn, crawling through the small foot-and-a-half space between the floor of the barn and the earth. I'm crawling farther and farther back from the light. Chicken dung. Smell of animals. A few pieces of hay. Cold earth. I don't know where the rest of the family is. Somewhere in the barn.

Crawling. I'm as far back as I can go. I stop, lying flat on the earth. Suddenly the world is cool and dark and still. I do not think of my father. I wonder where my mother is. I am alone in the darkness. I can't think of anything.

(Years and years later, my early twenties, I was in the Haight-Ashbury, tripping on LSD, and I thought I heard a dog panting. I searched and searched for the dog but couldn't find it. The panting continued. It was as though the dog were right over my shoulder. By then I knew enough about drugs to know that if I was hallucinating there was a reason. Then I remembered that I frequently awaken from nightmares with the same heavy, terrified, short-breathed panting. I forced myself to think of the reason. With a sudden flash of insight I realized it was my own panting I had been hearing all these years, the panting of a five-year-old child trapped under a barn.)

Five years old again. Under the barn. The darkness is everywhere. I'm shaking from the cold. Trying to catch my breath. Trying not to breathe so he won't hear me. But he knows I'm here. I am hiding in this darkness waiting to die. I am five years old and the monumental, crushing realization that I will not live out another day of a short life hits me. Not an intellectual realization because all thoughts have stopped. It's in the coldness in my limbs, the blackness in front of my eyes, the stark terror that has paralyzed my whole body. There is nothing I can do. In this darkness smelling of chicken dung I will live out my last moments.

My father is going to kill me.

Another blank space. My sister would fill it in years later. I have no memory of it and can only relate it as she told it to me.

While we are hiding, my father fires the gun. I have no memory of a gun going off. My brother is hiding in the hayloft in the barn. My father fires into it three times. My brother is hit—a slight skin wound on one leg. He's crying out for my mother.

My memory begins again only when I hear my mother's voice: "It's all right now. You can come out now."

The nightmare's ended. It's over. Dear God, it's over! I begin to feel warm again. I can breathe again. I crawl out from under the barn. I see my sisters appearing from under the barn too though they went in at other places. I'm not afraid any more. Mother has said it's all right. It's finished.

So I and my sisters walk to the open doors of the barn, where my mother has called us from. She is telling us to come into the barn. I can't see my father. We enter the center area, where the trucks come in to unload grain.

And all of us are quietly, without protest, lined up against the wall, I don't remember if my father or mother lined us up. Since the line is arranged chronologically and I'm the youngest, I'm at the end of the line. First my mother. Then my brother. Then my oldest sister. Then Karie. Then myself. We are a good foot from one another. There's no physical contact between any of us. I don't even remember noticing that my brother is hurt, though he must have been.

My father is sitting on the barn stool, loading the gun. After we are all in position, he walks up to my mother and raises the gun. I think he will shoot her then, though I will not look. I refuse to look. I stare off through the open doors of the barn to the empty plains. I play with the grain under my feet. I'm not afraid now. It has gone beyond fear. It is just waiting.

But I don't hear the shot. It should have come by now. I turn and look at my mother. The gun barrel is pressing into the skin of her forehead. She stands straight, erect. She has the same stillness, firmness, I've always seen in my mother. She does not tremble or cry or plead. She is willing to die.

I look at my brother and sisters. I later thought it was odd that none of us made any attempt to run. Maybe we instinctively knew we couldn't. We knew we could not break that silence. We knew our lives depended on that moment. That space of time my mother stood with a gun at her head.

If she had weakened for one instant, or if her glance had wavered, or if even an involuntary tremble had passed over her, I sincerely believe to this day my father would have pulled the trigger and then proceeded to kill us all one by one, then himself. I have absolutely no doubt that he would have done that. She reached him. By her very stillness, her direct, unflinching strength, she was able to reach through the blur of his insanity; she was able to pull him far enough back to see what he was doing.

I went through a period of doubting how much my mother could have loved any of us to play Russian roulette with our lives, and I felt betrayed that she had said it was all right and we had come out to be lined up against a wall and executed. Then I thought she had risked us all to save my brother—that to stop my father from shooting at him she had come out and said she would bring all the children out and he could kill us all. And she had done it.

It took me years to understand the decision my mother had made. She knew that by hiding, trying to run, we were doing exactly what would cause our deaths—that my father (trapped in the madness of a war memory) would simply have shot us all one by one where we were hiding. If he had gone far enough to shoot at my brother, eventually he would have killed him and all of us. My father was a crack shot. He had learned how to kill in the war. He could do it. It would not be the first time.

My mother took a terrible chance. Today I am not much younger than my mother was then and I doubt that I would have the courage to take such a chance. She staked her life and the lives of her children on her own strength and her belief that face to face he would not go through with it. And she won. She took the chance. She made the decision. And she won.

But at five years old, standing in a line waiting to die, I do not even vaguely think of any of those things. I only know this is the end of my life. A strange gratitude comes over me when I realize that, being the youngest, I will die last. He has to kill four people before he gets to me. I think I am very lucky. I have that much more time than the rest.

How long did my mother stand with that gun at her forehead? I don't know. Seconds. Minutes. I don't know.

Finally my father lowers the gun. He sits down on the stool again. The gun rests at his side. None of us move. He begins to cry. The bright sun streams through the door, silhouetting this huge man bent over in sobs, his hands over his face.

I can't remember anything else. It's ended.

But now I'm fifteen and sitting in a history class. The sun has gone behind the tree outside the the window. It's drawing patterns across my desk.

"Pat—."

I hear the voice from far away, like the end of a tunnel.

"Patricia! Three times is enough for anybody!"

I look up at the teacher. She's asked me a question. I don't know what it was. I don't know where I am.

The teacher is staring at me. "Are you sick?"

I don't reply. What's she talking about?

"You're white as a sheet."

I continue to stare at the teacher. I can't even think of her name now.

The teacher walks back to her desk. "Go see the school nurse."

I stand up. I feel like a robot. I walk out of the class and down the hall to the nurse's office. The nurse takes my temperature and my pulse. Not finding anything else wrong with me, she decides I'm having my first period and should be taken home. (Actually, my first period has come some months earlier). The nurse drives me to the farm.

I come into the house. My father is not there so I'm left alone. I go up to my room but I can't sleep. I'm not sick but I can't eat. I feel nauseous.

In a few hours, my sister comes home from school. She comes into the bedroom.

"Hey, I heard you come home early today."

"Yes."

"What's wrong? You sick or something?"

"No."

"Then why'd you get out of school early?"

"The nurse thought I was sick."

"That dumb nurse."

My sister sits down and begins to paint her nails. Makeup has lately become a whole ritual with her.

"Hey, Karie, can I ask you something?"

"Ask away."

She continues to paint her nails. When she was little she was known for her tantrums. Now, no matter what happens, she always "plays it cool," as she says. Nothing disturbs that surface placidity.

"Karie, did something happen when we was little?"

"What you talking about?"

"I been having a dream—"

My sister's impatient. "Oh, you and your nightmares. You know you woke me up last night—scared me to death, you crying out like that."

"No, this is different. I keep having this dream that Dad lined us up in the barn to shoot us—"

My sister starts to laugh. She thinks I'm as naive as they come.

"If that's a dream, you and me been having the same bad dream, kid."

"Well, it ain't truth, is it? Got to be a dream," I say.

"Ain't no dream, you dummy."

I stare at her. She isn't fazed. To her it was an unimportant thing that happened. Nothing earthshaking.

She looks at me and stops painting her nails.

"Well, what you so big-eyed about? It happened a long time ago. No use getting excited about it now. You was just a kid."

I continue to stare at her, wordless.

"Don't look so stupid! All the rest of us remember. Why don't you?"

"I thought it was a dream. . . ."

"It's no dream. It's fact. Happened. Right out there. He flipped out. Cracked up. Had a breakdown, the doctors said. Bang—bang. Sure. Dad don't remember nothing about it, but ask Mom."

She goes back to painting her nails.

"Don't it bother you none?" I ask.

"Why should it?"

I don't say anything as she continues to paint her nails.

"Ah, I knew he wasn't going to do it," she says. "Shoot us all just like that? He wasn't going to. Just trying to scare us."

"I thought he was—"

"Nah, he wouldn't do that."

"When he tried to kill us, when you called us out—called us out so he could line us up and kill us."

My mother doesn't say anything. She stands up and goes to the window. She looks out at the early evening, one hand on the old white curtains.

"Answer me!" I yell.

My mother turns and looks at me. It's hard for her to talk. She never discusses what she feels—her regrets, her hopes, her fears or her loves. She is a silent woman when it comes to emotions or explanations. She lives. She acts. She decides. She survives. She does not discuss any of these things. To her there's no point to endless verbal analysis. It consumes energy and time and solves nothing.

"Why don't you say something? Why you acting like you didn't hear?"

"I didn't think you'd ever remember," she says. "I thought you'd forgot and sometimes I thought it best you'd forgot."

I continue to scream out my rage. "We could have all died! He was going to kill us! Didn't you understand that?"

"I couldn't hide in the dark and listen to my children dying one by one."

"I trusted you!"

That hurt. I see the wound pass deep into her eyes.

"I did what I thought I had to do. If I was wrong, I'm sorry."

But how could I say she was wrong? I was alive. Alive enough to be furious at her in this moment, alive enough to be outraged over something that happened ten years earlier and that I had just remembered for some subconscious reason I would never guess. She was right. I was alive. I could not say she had been wrong. Yet I felt she had been wrong. I could not blame her for a decision that proved right. Yet I did blame her.

"Why didn't you leave him?" I ask.

"That first year after the hospital I couldn't."

I remember the year my father returned from the Veterans' Hospital. He was in bed most of the time. When we got home from school, we had to take our shoes off before we could come into the house. He couldn't stand the noise our shoes made on the floor. In the winter we'd come home and make a fire in the wood stove. He was so helpless then, he couldn't make a fire to keep himself warm during the day, but stayed curled up all day in bed like a baby. But that year passed. He drank more and more and over the years we all became accustomed to his drunks and semi-insanity.

"Why didn't you leave him later then?" I ask. "When he was well."

My mother says nothing. I see she is never going to answer this question for me.

"Why didn't you make them keep him in the Veterans' Hospital?" I ask.

"They said there wasn't anything they could do."

"He's crazy. He should be locked up."

"They gave me this piece of paper to sign. They said it was just so he would be taken care of. But I read it and it had this word—'frontal lobotomy.' I didn't know what that word meant so I asked. They said it was just an operation to make him better. I asked what kind of operation. They said it was on the brain —finally they said they would cut away part of his brain and that's all that could make him well again."

"Then he should'a had the operation," I say.

"Maybe."

"Then why didn't he?" I ask.

My mother goes to the other side of the room. She is searching for the words to explain something to me.

"There was men there had the operation. They was peaceful enough. Talked, made sense. But they seemed . . . I don't know . . . when you cut the pain out do you cut out part of the soul?"

For a second I don't hear the question. It's a thought far beyond anything I've considered in my fifteen years. But I'm more surprised because it's not the sort of question I had thought my mother capable of asking. Yet she has. With such clarity and directness I'm taken aback.

I have no answer so I say nothing.

She continues. "One doctor there was doing those operations all day long. Just slicing off part of the brain. I never met such people. They was educated, intelligent. Big words I didn't understand. But I never met such people that'd do something like that, not half knowing what they was doing. So maybe they could make him quiet, not somebody we'd have to be afraid of. But I couldn't do it. I couldn't sign that paper for them."

"They could'a give him some other treatment," I say. "They could'a done something else for him."

"They said they couldn't. Said they had too many veterans there after the war already. Said there wasn't no way to make them forget. Lots of veterans was having the operation. I had to agree or there wasn't nothing they could do, just release him again."

I think for a while. I don't know anything about a frontal lobotomy. I've never heard of it before.

But I say, "Well, maybe the operation was okay if it made them all better."

My mother is silent again. She's searching for the words to explain something I doubt she has ever verbally tried to articulate even to herself. She uses the words and images she understands.

"You know that old river down on the lower forty—the one you kids love to go swimming in in the summer—"

I'm paying little attention. I don't know what on earth this has to do with the subject.

She continues. "Well, let's pretend that river turns wild one day—always overflowing, ruining crops, maybe even drowning people—a mean, wild river sometimes. And someone comes up to you and says I can do something to that river to make it always quiet, no matter how bad the storm, never wild no matter how much rain falls. They say you sign this piece of paper and we'll change that river. But it won't reflect the blue sky no more and it won't sparkle and dance in the sunlight no more and it won't bring joy when it laughs and jumps over the rocks—"

"It ain't the same!"

My mother stops. "No, it ain't the same."

Abruptly I say, "You love him more than us, don't you?"

My mother is startled at what I've just said.

"I never compared the kind of love I had for him and the kind I got for my children."

"But you brought him home again."

"Yes." She says it without shame or guilt.

I am outraged at this admission.

"What about us?"

"I knew he wouldn't try to do that again. That was all broken."

I stare at her. Is she talking herself into lies to justify what she did?

"What about him beating you and getting drunk?"

"Has he ever beat you?" she asks.

"No."

It was the truth. He never had. I am silent for a moment, then stumble, trying to say something. "But—"

"But you're afraid."

I don't answer that. She needs no answer. Silence. In that silence I see the guilt in my mother's face.

Then she says, "He loves you children more than anything in this world."

I stare at her in total bewilderment. Love! A man who has inflicted this kind of psychological torture on us for years.

I don't even try to restrain the words: "Like hell!"

"You forget the good times."

"What good times?" I ask.

I shouldn't have asked that. There had been good times—when Dad told us funny stories, when he dressed up in a sheet like a ghost and went out with all of us in the middle of the night to milk the cow and we laughed and laughed when the cow ran all over the pasture with Dad chasing it, when he danced with my mother all over the kitchen and without even any music playing, when he made up rhymes to go with our names, when he spent all the money he had on toys for us even when we were over our heads in debt, when he found out about the mean old woman five miles away who always sicked her dog on us everytime we came by and Dad went over in the middle of the night with some paint and wrote in big letters on the side of her barn THE GODS ARE GOING TO GET YOU—when he worried if one of us was sick. Yes, my father loved us. But I had two fathers. One was gentle and warm and light-hearted. The other was tormented, violent, frightening—a madman.

"Do you love him?" It was hard for me to ask that. I had to force myself.

Again, I know my mother will not answer.

My mother knows what I'm feeling when she says, "Don't you think I'd like you to have the father he was before he went to war? Don't you think I'd like you to see that big-hearted, laughing, strong man I married? The other kids knew him then—they was born before the war—but you didn't. You was born during the war and when he got back he was already crippled, in his mind and heart. If he'd come home without an arm or leg, you could understand. Anybody could understand. It wouldn't make him less the man he was. But he come home crippled some other way—in his soul. You children never understood the things that crippled him."

"Do you?" I ask.

My mother is silent for a few moments. "I never been to war. I don't know what it means to have to kill people, kill children like your own children. I don't know the guilt and hate and torment you got to live with all your life. He didn't make this world."

"I don't think that's no excuse for nothing."

"Maybe not. Maybe there ain't no excuses for him or me. I don't try to find the excuses no more."

"Mr. Jackson went to war and he ain't crazy like Dad," I say.

"Lord, child, don't you understand people ain't the same?"

"But if the war was so awful, why ain't he crazy?"

My mother is irritated, close to anger. "Yes, and Mr. Jackson's the one that goes out of his way on the highway to hit a stray dog and thinks it's funny when the high school boys poured gasoline all over that poor monkey in the town zoo and set it afire."

"But Mr. Jackson never tried to kill his family," I say.

My words stop her. She stands up, moving away.

"Besides," I say, "Mr. Craig went to war too and he's a good man."

"Yes, he's a good man."

She's standing on the dark side of the room. The afternoon sun has totally disappeared by now. Only the small light on near my bed. I have to listen hard to understand everything she begins to tell me.

"When your father was young, not even twenty, and he come to my parents' farm for a job—it was hog-butchering time. They'd slit the hog's throat, put a bucket under it till most of the blood was out, then string it up till it bled to death. All the time the hog screaming. The other men was going to teach your father how to do it. Your father tried but he couldn't. And the other men laughing and making jokes, him such a big man and he acts just like a woman, can't stand to see a hog die. But then your father picks up the knife and quick slits the hog's throat. He walks out of the barn and I follow him. He's so sick he's throwing up, shaking like a child."

She pauses, then says, "So he went to war and instead of hogs it was people."

There's a long silence before I ask, "Did he have to go?"

"No," she answers.

"Then why did he if he didn't have to?"

"Oh, they was making big speeches then and having parades. All the other men joined. He wanted to wear a uniform, be a hero. And I guess he was restless on the farm—wanted to see the world and come back covered with medals. He didn't know what war meant. I didn't either. I kissed him goodbye just like they did in the movies and I thought, just like in the movies, when it's over the bad guys will be dead and the good guys will still be good. The lights will go on and we'll all walk out of the theater and go back to our normal way of living with nothing changed."

I say nothing, waiting for her to continue.

"And the war ended and he come home. Still handsome. More handsome. Filled out. A man now. He come home with medals and bragging and drinking too much, like the other men. With suitcases of toys for you kids, new dresses for me. When he sees you for the first time, he grins like it was all Christmas. And that night in bed he's full of jokes and stories about Paris and all them places I never been. But I know something's wrong. He's too loud. He won't look right at me, not deep in the eyes the way he used to. Just keeps talking and laughing. He tells me some story and laughs—and all of a sudden he turns and slams his fist into the wall. He hits it so hard the plaster gives way—his fist has gone half through the wall. He turns and walks out and I don't see him again for a week, when he comes home drunk."

I say nothing. At that age I have little understanding of what my mother is trying so desperately to communicate, wants so badly for me to begin to understand.

"What did he do in the war?" I ask.

My mother looks at me but does not answer.

I ask again. "What did he do?"

"He killed—like everybody else."

"But our teachers say we was right in World War Two."

"Right? I don't know what that means any more."

"The Germans was bad."

"Yes."

"That was a awful thing they did to the Jews."

"Yes, that was awful."

"The Germans couldn't win."

"No."

"Then he had to go and he shouldn't be crazy for killing people we was supposed to kill, for killing bad people."

"No, he shouldn't."

A silence. My mother's face is drawn.

"Then why?" I ask.

My mother says nothing. She doesn't know the answer.

"The Nazis was trying to take over the free world. Somebody had to stop them," I say.

Suddenly my mother says, "They were going to court-martial him."

"Dad?"

I'm surprised. Dad court-martialed? Only traitors or cowards were court-martialed. But Dad had been brave. He hadn't run. He killed people.

"Your father was the biggest man in the outfit so they made him carry the flame-thrower. They was going through Germany. They took this village. Just farm people like us living in this village. They were hiding in the basement of the church. The sergeant tells your father to burn out the basement—that there's enemy hiding in there. But your father won't do it. He says they're just women and kids. Sergeant says it don't matter—they're Germans, ain't they? But still your father won't do it. The sergeant puts a gun to his head and says either he kills the Germans or gets killed—"

"Did he do it?"

"Yes."

An image flashes through my head. My father standing at the top of the stairs to a basement. Women and children huddled together at the opposite side of the basement. A sudden streak of orange-red flame across the basement. And again. Another streak. And again. But not even a vivid imagination can show me the agony and horror of people being burned to death. It is a scene I am incapable of visualizing, do not want to visualize.

Silence. Finally I say, "But if he did what he was ordered, why did they want to court-martial him?"

"The next day he found the sergeant and beat him till the sergeant ended up in the hospital. I guess even that they was willing to let pass with some time in the brig. But then he started losing every flame-thrower they gave him, getting drunk all the time. But they didn't court-martial him cause after that he was the best man in the outfit—killed more Germans than anyone. So instead of a court-martial he got a medal."

A strange expression comes to my mother's face. It's not bitterness or even disbelief. Just a tired familiar astonishment.

She gets up to leave. She has said what she wanted to say. She won't try to explain any more to me. She has tried to make me forgive and understand my father. But I can't. I can't even begin to understand at that age. If I do, I will begin to weaken. If I let myself love him, he will hurt me more than he has. And even if I could understand the reasons, it does not make the terror less for me. It does not diminish the fear. It does not erase that day from my memory.

Suddenly I say, "If he did that, he should have died in the war."

I am standing. My mother turns to face me. Though I'm six inches taller than she is, she slaps me hard across the face. It's the first and last time she ever hit me.

Tears well in my eyes as she walks out of the room.

I do not forget that slap for days. But finally one evening I go to meet the bus again. We have barely spoken to each other since the discussion. I say nothing as I stand by the highway and she gets out of the bus.

We begin to walk home. Not speaking. Separate. I'm ahead. Finally I drop back, walking beside her though still at a distance.

"How was school?" she asks.

"Okay."

We continue to walk separately. She looks off across the fields and says something about the irrigation the neighboring farmer is running to one of his fields. I nod without much response. I pay little attention to anything that has to do with crops and land. I'm not like my mother. I will not stay on the land. I will go to the cities. I only live for the day I can leave this country and never come back.

We are near the house. I stop in the middle of the road. I don't look at her when I say it.

"I'm sorry." The words barely get past my lips.

I do not look at her to see her reaction.

"Ragmuffin."

It's a term of affection she has not used since I was a child. We resume walking to the house. And for the next three years, until I'm eighteen and leave, I will meet her each night at the end of the road. The ritual is re-established. But we never again discuss the day my father tried to kill us.

I was home two years ago. My visits never last more than a couple of days at the most. My father had a heart attack a few years back so now he's a complete invalid. They draw a small social-security check and something from the Veterans' Administration but it's not enough to live on, so Mom still works at the same job at the factory. The house is looking a little better these days and they bought back an acre of land near the house so Mom has extended the garden. My father still drinks but his insanity has cooled. He doesn't have the physical strength to back it any more.

The children have all left home, scattered to all parts of the country. My two sisters are married, with large families, living in big cities. My brother joined the military as soon as he was of age and has become a career man. At the time of my visit he was in Vietnam. I finished college—the only one in the family that went to college. But I never seemed to find the place I fit in. I dropped out in the sixties. Drugs. Haight-Ashbury. Berkeley. The East Village. Protested. Saw the big cities.

Last time I noticed how my mother had aged. She is middle-aged and her beauty has long ago died in beatings and drunken nights and year after year in the factory. Her face is lined, aged, tired. She suffers from frequent headaches, though she did finally go to a doctor and get glasses. I always think it's amusing how she treats those glasses like a prize possession. Cleaning them, carefully putting them away at night.

I am sleeping upstairs in my old bedroom. I hear my mother get up a little before dawn. Her usual six o'clock. She always gets up at that hour even if she's been up half the night with Dad.

I hear her in the kitchen talking to the dog. She's recently found this funny mutt of a dog and, when she thinks there's no one around to hear her, she talks to it just as though it were a person.

"There now. There now. You silly dog. Don't know why I keep you. Just a big pest."

I am half awake in bed, listening to her. In this half-dream state, I begin to remember something.

Again, it's the day my father lined us up in the barn. He has dropped the gun. He's crying. He reaches in his pocket and hands Mom the keys to the car. There is no verbal exchange between them. . . . She takes the keys and, helping him stand, leads him to the car, where he sits in the passenger seat. He does everything without complaint. His entire body seems to have crumbled. He stares out the car window like a child.

Then she comes back, kneeling by my brother to look at his leg. She tells him to get in the car so she can take him to the doctor. My brother refuses to get in the car with my father. He seems more angry than anything else. The wound is hardly more than a slight skin cut. My brother makes an angry exit to the house. My sisters are sobbing. My mother embraces each of them, saying something to them. They go toward the house, still crying.

Then my mother turns to me. I'm standing in the same place I was during the lineup. I have not moved. My mother says my name, standing at the entrance to the barn. I do not respond. She walks toward me, then stands in front of me for a long while.

"Cry."

I can't. I don't look at her. I stare out across the plains. I don't want to look at her or anyone.

She grabs me by the shoulders. "Cry."

I pull away from her, without looking at her. I would cry if I could, but something in me is too far away for tears. When I look at her there's a faint rim of tears in her eyes. It's the only time in my life I've ever seen my mother cry. She takes her hands from my shoulders. I don't say anything to her. I barely know she's there. I turn and walk away from her.

I should have cried that day. I should have sobbed my heart out as my sisters did. I should have clung to her as I wanted to, but I couldn't. The tears, pain, fear, betrayal were buried so deep inside myself it was ten years before I could even remember that day happened.

But that's past. It's morning. I'm twenty-five. I get out of bed, still hearing my mother in the kitchen with the dog. I go downstairs. It's just sunrise. I stand at the kitchen door and look at Mom.

She's sitting on the back step with a cup of coffee. The little dog is beside her, wagging his tail. She pets his head now and then. The dawn catches my mother's profile—the years have revealed a strong, straight nose, high cheek-bones and firm mouth. Although she is partially gray now, the sun catches some strands of still-auburn hair around her face. I think my mother is beautiful then—in a way more beautiful than I had thought she was when she was a young woman.

I sit down beside her on the front step.

"Want some breakfast?" she asks.

"I'm okay."

"Leaving today?"

"Yes."

She will not ask me where I'm going. If I volunteer the information, that's one thing, but she makes absolutely no attempt to pry into my life. She doesn't ask me about drugs or how I'm living. She doesn't condemn my long hair and sandals. If I want to talk about my life, my plans or hopes, she will listen but she will not question me.

We sit and watch the sunrise together. I had forgotten how much I miss the plains, how deeply they had become a part of me. The sun has already broken over the bare, slight curve of the horizon. The plains seem endless now; yet I know that by that afternoon I will reach the towering peaks of the Rocky

Mountains. Shadows begin to streak across the flat land. A slight wind comes up, moving the leaves of the trees near the house. The birds begin. It will be a beautiful, clear summer day.

We do not speak or touch. But I have never felt so close to my mother.

Then I hear my father's voice from inside the house. "I'm dying. . . . I'm dying. . . . Where are you?"

My mother stands up and goes to him.

I hear her voice. "You're always dying, old man. Guess we'll just have to bury you soon."

"That's what you want! You want to bury me! You want to kill me! It's dark —it's dark—"

"Morning's coming. . . ."

"It's dark."

"It's a beautiful morning coming."

My father says nothing. A silence comes over the house. He has fallen back to sleep. I only hear my mother's footsteps as she begins her day's work.

I am not at all the typical Mexican woman. I saw my ma get beaten and have to work to support the family, because my father would take off. I knew, even when I was young, that I didn't want to live that way. I figured that, someway or other, I would get out of that kind of life.

—Esther Serrano, *"Barefoot and Pregnant"*

No estás sola. Tanto como la mitad de todos los matrimonios en los Estados Unidas experimenta violencia entre familiares en algún tiempo. Estudios indican quo 1.8 millones de mujeres son golpeadas por sua maridos cada año. La mitad do todos los homicidios en la familia ocurren entre el esposo y la caposa. Es muy común que unos empujones y unas cachetadas o bofetadas se conviertan en patadas, golples y hasta estrangulación o violatión. El abuso no para allí, sino que también incluye insultos y acusaciones falsas—lo que seguido se considera el abuso mental.

Las Dos Hermanas

ROSALIE OTERO PERALTA

I watched my aunt Marcelina tie the traditional embultorio. I couldn't remember a time that I hadn't carried cariños from one sister to another. Poor though they both were, they always shared the little they had . . . a few tortillas, fresh eggs, biscochitos or a prized can of golden peaches . . . tied up neatly in a bleached muslin dishcloth. But today Marcelina absently brought the corners together in a neat knot. She was sadly quiet. I stood as tall as my eight year old body would reach and tried to look big and responsible. I sensed that I musn't add my share to her troubles.

I scrambled up the hill and straight home . . . even the ditch didn't look inviting. As soon as I entered grandmother's kitchen, I breathlessly began, ". . . Nina was so sad . . . and . . ."

Grandmother quickly dismissed me and the entire matter in her "children should be seen and not heard" manner. It was little by little that I grew to realize the importance of the decision, and awe at the love and faith of the two sisters.

The following Sunday, catching sight of my aunt's blue hat, I skipped down the dirt pathway to meet her. By the time we reached each other, Grandmother was already shouting her welcomes from the doorway, "Cuidado con el gallo colorado, Marcelina . . . he's a mean rooster . . . he'll run your nylons . . . look what he did to my leg yesterday . . . Margarita, shoo him away from your tía!"

I grabbed a rock and pursued the old rooster clear to the hen house whereupon he turned with ruffled feathers . . . that was his territory . . . it was my turn to back off. A few minutes later when I reached the kitchen, Grandmother and Aunt Marcelina were still discussing the old gallo, but already the embultorio lay opened on the table. Nina had brought us apples, some golden-crusted home-made bread and a slab of bacon. I knelt on the chair leaning my elbows on the table and regarded each woman in turn as the conversation shifted.

My Grandmother, Teresina, was the dominant one, her dark hair neatly intertwined into a braid that she wound into a chignon and pinned to the back of her head with large bone hairpins. Today, being Sunday, she had waved the sides of her hair with her old curling iron and donned her silver filigree earrings. As she talked, her penetrating hazel eyes would capture the minutest detail through green tinted wire-framed spectacles. She still wore the customary black dress of a widow, although Grandpa had been dead for five years. I watched her walk from the table to the cupboard clicking her heels. Grandma always wore black oxfords, size five, triple A . . . years later when sickness and old age had taken her weight and shrunk her size, Teresina still insisted on size five, AAA.

Marcelina was the younger. Grandmother said she was only fifty, but to me she looked much older. She had wispy hair much grayer than grandmother's and she had more wrinkles, too. But sometimes when she was sitting near a window the sun would lighten every line and her face would appear smooth and beautiful. Her hands were rough and red and gnarled with rheumatism. Only last Sunday I had watched her slip on a pair of gloves in order to put on her sheer stockings.

"So that I don't run them, hijita," she had explained. Now those hands were gently cleaning her rose-tinted eye-glasses.

I loved hearing them talk . . . Teresina's resounding vociferous tones mingling with Marcelina's almost gentle humming . . .

"That was Juanita Cruz, daughter of José and María from Vallecito."

"Cousin to Martina Padilla?"

"Yes, María and Pablita were sisters by Don Joaquin's first marriage."

"Oh, sí, and then he married his first cousin . . ."

"Yes, well, you know how people talk."

"No wonder she had to move away."

"Doña Francisca even told her she could no longer be a member of the Altar Society."

"Bah, as if she was so lily white with that illegitimate boy of hers."

Their voices would rise and fall tracing geneologies and sharing the latest gossip of the village.

But today Marcelina sat quietly listening to Teresina's chatter about the rooster and watched her bustle about the kitchen. Teresina brought out some tortillas and then put them away again. When she wrapped the bacon twice, I giggled. With a worried frown she handed me an apple, "Margarita, go play outside." Then, without noticing that I had shrunk into the pantry near the doorway, Teresina turned to Marcelina and half-whispered, "Marcelina, did you go see the Padre?"

"Speak to my right side, Tere, I didn't bring my hearing aid today." Marcelina dragged the chair closer to her sister.

"I don't see why you save it. That's the least he can do, buy you new batteries once a year." Teresina scolded with that outraged voice intended for the villain, not the victim. And again, "Did you see Father O'Shaw this morning?"

"Sï, he is such a holy man . . . but so very thin. He's coming to see me Wednesday. Maybe you can come to help me get ready for him."

"Sï, I'll go and take along the beautiful doilies Juanita send me and my statue of the Sacred Heart."

"I don't know what to do. It's becoming so hard to dissimulate."

"Well, I warned you about marrying him. He was twice your age . . . viejo calbo, fiero . . . and all those children. Everytime I think of your wasted youth with that sin verguenza and how he repays you now, I could kick him."

I pictured my Uncle Flavio, a tall ruddy-faced bald man surrounded by ten babies and standing beside a beautiful young bride. Grandmother set a jar of capulïn jelly on the table with such vehemence that it startled me out of the imaginary wedding. Aunt Marcelina was weeping softly while Teresina continued her ranting.

"Vagamundo, ese tal! Someday he will realize what a good woman you are. He can never point an accusing finger at you. You have been an example of such loyalty and goodness all these years. What he wanted was a maid, not a wife . . . he'll rot in hell! And you, mi hermanita, will be rewarded by Our Father and His Blessed Mother."

I stopped chewing on the apple and remembered the day Grandma and I had stopped to see my aunt Marcelina after Mass. Uncle Flavio was there. He was usually at his brother's ranch in Northern New Mexico or in Wyoming herding sheep. But that Sunday he was home.

"Teresina, cómo estás? Come in," he politely invited. Then he swooped me up by the waist. He reeked of the familiar smell of Beechnut chewing tobacco.

"Put her down!" the icy command from my grandmother interrupted my giggles. I was glad; any moment he would have rubbed his whiskered face against mine. I hated that!

Grandma hurried me into the bedroom, leaving Uncle Flavio standing there in his suspendered trousers and yellowed undershirt.

Aunt Marcelina had been crying . . . her eyes still red and swollen.

"What's the matter?" Grandmother began and as if she knew the answer continued, "When did he return?" indicating the kitchen with her head.

"Juana came home Friday so I knew he was due soon. Sure enough, he arrived last night about two."

I couldn't understand why Doña Juana, my aunt's next door neighbor had anything to do with my uncle's coming home.

My aunt's whispered voice continued, ". . . began bragging about his good times in Wyoming . . ."

Uncle Flavio's entrance interrupted her. "Qué ya está chuchando? Already she's telling you her lies and suspicions?" It was a sarcastic loud voice that left "suspicions" echoing in the room.

My grandmother turned and faced him, her eyes flaming. Lines of anger were forming around her eyes and along her forehead. I shrunk into a corner.

"You coward . . . tormentor . . . haven't you done enough to this woman? She was a beautiful young woman and too naive to know what you were really like! You took advantage of her . . . now look at her. You never even gave the proper mourning period for your first wife . . . you needed an immediate maid for your ten children! And now you dare call her the LIAR!"

"Tere . . . Tere, stop . . ." a pitiful plea from my sobbing aunt.

I could feel my heart beating faster and terror tightening my throat. My uncle's almost purple neck and face bulged out hate-filled eyes, his jaws working, tightening and loosening and tobacco juice escaping from the sides of his twisted mouth. Then, pointing a large hairy arm and hand toward the kitchen door, he hissed, "Get out of my house!"

Grandmother stood her ground. "So that you can hit Marcelina like you know how to do so well?"

Uncle Flavio stood pointing for what seemed to me endless seconds. Then with one quick movement he grabbed his hat off the chair, spit a black tobacco cud at my grandmother's feet and lurched toward the kitchen door slamming it behind him.

"Why didn't you go? He might have hit you!"

Teresina embraced her sister, "If I had gone he might have killed you. Let's go home with me. You don't have any reason to remain. Before, you used the children as an excuse . . . now the children are all gone . . . you've done your duty . . . you don't have to stay on with that sin verguenza, vagamundo!"

My aunt gathered some of her things and the three of us started up the hill. I carried the embultorio.

Aunt Marcelina stayed with us a few weeks. As soon as she heard that Uncle Flavio had returned to his brother's ranch, she went home. My grandmother wanted her to remain, but Aunt Marcelina explained, "What will people say,

'Tan buena Católica y divurciada,' " mimicking the squaking tones of Doña Francisca.

Doña Francisca was the president of the Altar Society. On Sundays she always was up front lighting and rearranging candles and thought it her duty to shush at the choir girls who sat in the first pew. Everytime she passed in front of the tabernacle, which was often, she would genuflect on her left knee and make three tiny crosses on her forehead, nose and throat followed by an enormous one from the top of her hat to both shoulders and ending with a loud clap between her large breasts.

The imaginary clap became a realistic whop as the pantry door hit the kitchen wall and grandmother stood over me.

"Margarita, what are you doing in here? I said outside!" I dropped the browning apple core as she pulled me up and out by one arm.

Wednesday I went with Grandma to prepare for Padre O'Shaw. About two that afternoon, when Father was due, I was sent to the parlor for its final inspection.

"... and when you see Father coming let us know?" Grandmother commanded.

I liked my aunt's neat parlor although I wasn't allowed to be in there very often. Today I surveyed the white freshly calcimined walls, the picture of the Good Shepherd holding the stray lamb, a larger oval gold frame enclosing a wedding photograph and near the window, a replica of Our Lady of Guadalupe. Just below her painting stood my grandmother's Sacred Heart surrounded by fresh white and violet lilacs I had picked that morning. The strong fragrance of the lilacs made me aware of the blue and pink flower patterns on the carpet, worn into gray disfigured spots at the entrance and directly in front of the settee and the two maroon wing chairs. Using the pink roses as stepping stones I danced a criss-cross pattern in the room stopping before the wedding picture. It was my aunt Marcelina and Uncle Flavio. She looked so beautiful . . . her wedding veil and train draped over the chair in which she was sitting, her hands holding a small bouquet of pink-tinted flowers and a pearl rosary. It was like looking at a princess in silks and lace. He, too, looked beautiful . . . so tall in his dark suit and white shirt and had so much hair then!

Footsteps and a soft knock took me at a run to the kitchen . . . "He's here . . . he's here!" I ran back to the parlor door and stood there waiting for my aunt to open it. She moved slowly; her navy blue dress made soft swishing noises and barely noticeable was the colorless cord running from the right side of her neck and hiding behind her ear.

"Good afternoon Mrs. Trujillo . . . Margaret! What are you doing here?" Father's clean-shaven face smiled at the both of us. I had never seen such blue eyes.

"Hello, Father. Come in . . ."

Father sat leaning forward in one of the maroon wing chairs, his hands folded together. Aunt Marcelina sat primly on the brown settee; her small rough hands playing with the solid gold band on her left hand.

My grandmother's "Maaarrgaritaaaa!" interrupted my move to the rocker. Reluctantly I left the guest with his hostess.

Long after Father O'Shaw had gone, Marcelina sat in the parlor. I had crept back quietly, but the pathetic slight figure of my aunt bent over, her voice coming and going, disjointed, unclear, paralyzed me in the doorway.

". . . the Church agrees to separation, no divorce . . . But I loved him . . . Why God? Why? The children . . . Tere was right! Oh Tere! ! . . . Mis hijos . . . My home . . . what punishment . . . what evil did I commit? Aye Diós . . . Now that I'm old . . . where would I go if it weren't for Tere . . . Oh, my God . . . the scandal . . . But I just can't live with him anymore . . . I just can't go on pretending that nothing is the matter . . . Oh my God! The scandal!" Her tears mingled with tears. Her handkerchief had long since drowned in a crumpled ball in her hand. I watched her walk slowly to her wedding photograph and take it down leaving the naked nail sticking out conspicuously.

Saturday I rose early, dressed and helped grandmother with last minute errands. I was excited . . . my aunt Marcelina was coming to live with us. Grandmother had promised it would be forever. I went to wait for her at the old apricot tree. It formed a natural bench. Grandma had told me that it had been split by lightning many many years ago.

I thought of my aunt. I understood she was leaving Uncle Flavio and that it had something to do with Doña Juana. I pictured her . . . a large nose with a hairy mole on the left side, and squinty eyes underneath thick glasses. And she always wore a wide-brimmed red hat. I remember overhearing Doña Francisca whispering that Don Flavio had brought it for Doña Juana from Wyoming. I didn't understand. Perhaps he had brought it home and Marcelina had sold it to her or given it away because she didn't like it.

I spotted Aunt Marcelina through the apricot leaves, jumped down from the tree and ran at a gallop to meet her. I took the large white embultorio from her and we chattered our way to the house.

She no longer looked the small pitiful aunt we had left on Wednesday . . . she looked resolute and determined. I thought this must have been the way she looked when she defied everyone to marry Uncle Flavio. I remember Grandmother's words, "We warned you against marrying that viejo . . . but no . . . you knew better . . . you were determined to go with him despite his age and all those children . . . AND our warnings!"

When I was almost twelve, Aunt Marcelina became very ill. We had to take her to the hospital, but even then the doctor gave us little hope. She had been with us almost four years.

That evening I asked my grandmother why Aunt Marcelina had come to live with us. "Did it have anything to do with Doña Juana?"

Grandmother's eyes moistened and her voice quivered. "Your Aunt has had a hard life, hijita. Flavio had bad women everywhere. Yes, Doña Juana was one of them. At first he tried to hide it, but after your aunt found out, he'd even brag to her about them."

"When did my aunt know? How did she find out?"

Grandmother began to speak softly occasionally wiping her glasses and eyes almost in simultaneous movement. Sometimes her voice would rise in angry tones and then fall to a soft pitying murmur. It was like she was delivering lines from a play she had been rehearsing a long time. "It was a terrible night. The snow had steadily fallen all that day. By six, Marcelina was frantic, your cousin María still wasn't home from school. Marcelina thought perhaps the bus had been held up by the storm. She decided to go next door and ask Doña Juana if Gilbert had come home. So she wrapped herself in her woolen shawl and went next door. She stood in the snow knocking for a long time. Finally Doña Juana opened the door and I imagine with a shocked expression asked Marcelina in. Marcelina began to explain her visit . . . that María had not come home and wondered if Gilbert had since they both rode the same bus. All of a sudden she noticed Flavio's denim jacket, boots and trousers on the chair next to the stove and became conscious of the strong tobacco smell. Marcelina said she doesn't remember what happened or how she got home. The next thing she remembered was the door crashing open. She found herself still wrapped in her shawl sitting near the fireless stove. Flavio had begun yelling at her . . . things like, 'Why were you spying on me? . . . What was the idea of busting into a lady's home . . . like Mrs. Juanita?' Imagine the sin verguenza calling Juana a lady to your aunt! Marcelina tried to explain but he called her a liar. The fight went on for hours. He admitted to his women and threatened Marcelina. Pobrecita mi hermanita."

"But why didn't she just come to stay with us then?"

"Rosa, José and María were still living at home and she thought it was her duty to stay and take care of them. Anyway, he was gone much of the time."

"Well, I'm glad she finally did leave him!"

"Sĭ, although she was so worried about the scandal it would cause. But Father O'Shaw was good to her and between the two of us, we convinced her she no longer had obligations to Flavio."

I slept in snatches that night. My dreams were flooded with wide-brimmed red hats, huge cavernous mouths chewing tobacco, my Aunt Marcelina and Teresina wrapped together in a black shawl in a field of snow.

When I awoke, Grandmother was already dressed and hurrying me.

We were going to the hospital. I dressed quickly. Then, taking a fresh muslin dishcloth, I wrapped up my favorite statue of the Immaculate Conception which

I had received for perfect attendance at school, a pearl rosary I had saved for Grandmother's birthday . . . she wouldn't mind, and a small box of chocolates, my Aunt's favorites.

We were only allowed to go in one at a time and the nurse had said we were to stay in there only one minute. I would be last. The dreams of the night still haunted me.

My turn. I walked slowly down the antisceptic white hall and into my aunt's room. She looked so small, so frail, her wispy hair smeared on the pillow. She smiled weakly. I kissed her and handed her the small embultorio.

How well she works a room: the spotlit
sequins on her white gown
irradiate her curves as she moves
from couple to couple, man
to man, her gaze direct
and knowing. But when she bends
low notes around her body and the words
implode, she startles
even herself. Some of the women
sit straight: She sings
of us, they think to themselves,
not for the men.

—Meg Schoerke

bertha schneiders existential edge

ANDREA DWORKIN

first I gave up men.

it wasnt easy but it sure as hell was obvious. you may want to know, woman
to woman, what it was that made me decide. well, it wasnt the times I was
raped by strangers. I mean christ you do the whole trip then, nightmares, cold
sweats, fear and trembling and a not inconsiderable amount of loathing as well
—but one thing you cant do is take it personally. I mean I always figured that,
statistically at least, it had nothing to do with me, bertha schneider.

now the two I knew a little bit, that was different. I mean, I felt there was
something personal in it. the man from Rand, that well-mannered smart ass,
and some starving painter who limped for christ sake. I mean, I figure I must
have asked for it. I mean, Im always reading that I must have asked for it, and
in the movies women always do, and theyre always glad. I wasnt glad goddam
it but whod believe it anyway. the painter told me that if I didnt want it my
cunt wouldve been locked and no man couldve penetrated it. I told him I wasnt
a yogi though I was seeing the value of all that oriental shit for the first time. I
figure thats why there arent too many women yogis in India, they dont want
them locking their cunts which is obviously the first thing they would do.

it wasnt even being married for 3 years. it wasnt the time he kept banging
my head on the kitchen floor (hard wood) so that I would say I really did like
the movie after all. I mean, lets face it, I just dont like Clint Eastwood and if
thats a fatal flaw, well it just is. it wasnt the time he beat me up in front of my

mother either. it wasnt the time he threw me out on the street in my nightgown and called the police. it wasnt even the time he brought home 4 drunken friends, one of whom kept calling me kike, and they tied me to the bed and fucked me until I passed out and thank god I dont know what happened after that. after all, that was only 4 events in 3 years which is 1,095 days. besides, I loved him. besides, I didnt have anywhere else to go.

I never exactly made a grand exit. I mean, I could have. for instance, running away with another man wouldve been a grand exit. it also wouldve required presence of mind and a basically unbruised body. I couldve changed the locks and gotten a court order, except, frankly, and I know this for a fact, no one wouldve believed me. I know that thats true from the time I went to a doctor after he bashed my head against the kitchen floor. I was, I admit, hysterical. what I kept trying to explain to the doctor was that if someone had bashed his head against a hard wood kitchen floor because he didnt like Clint Eastwood he would be hysterical too. my fatal flaw wasnt regarded kindly by him either. he told me that they could have me locked up or I could go home. then he gave me some valium. I considered it but I guess I was more afraid of the nuthouse than I was of being beaten to death.

anyway, finally 2 events led to my final departure. first I went shopping and he tried to run me over with his car. the police came at the point where he had gotten out of the car after backing me against a wall and was strangling me and screaming obscenities simultaneously. I refused to press charges. I kept thinking that he was confused and had made a mistake. I thought that every time which, for an educated woman, was quite an accomplishment. then I went home and cried and told him I loved him and would do anything for him and sucked his cock and made dinner. then the next day I got a stomach virus and had terrible diarrhea and vomiting and when I asked him to drive me to the doctor he kicked me in the leg midway between the knee and ankle. the kick sent me flying across the room whereupon I hit my shoulder against the wall, he went back to sleep, and I shit in my pants. I lay there for a long time and when I did finally get up, I limped, dripping shit, into the sunset.

I never did get revenge or anything like that. his new girlfriend moved in with him right away. I had provoked him she said which, for an educated woman, was quite an accomplishment. he got tearful whenever he saw me on the street and asked, bertha, why did you leave me. that is, until our day in court. on that day he beat me up, called me a whore, and told me that he always finished what he started.

oh, I fucked around for a while after I left. in fact I was one big fuck around. I had that look men love, utterly used. I had that posture men lust after, flat on my back. also I was poor and usually hungry and fucking was the only way I knew to get a meal.

I didnt actually *decide* to give up men until almost a year and a half later. I took a lot of acid and on those nights, or even on afternoons, looking into the void which was located precisely between my legs, I would simply shake and tremble. for 8 hours, or 12 hours, or however long the acid lasted, I would shake and tremble.

I also had nightmares. somehow all the feelings I didnt feel when each thing had actually happened to me I did feel when I slept. I hated going to sleep because then I had to feel. I felt him hit me, and I felt what it felt like, and christ it felt awful. I would sleep, sometimes with my eyes open, and I would feel it all over, and most of it for the first time. I didnt understand how I had not felt it when it was happening, but I hadnt, I had felt something else. I had felt almost nothing, which was something else. when I was sleeping each thing would happen to me as it had happened and I would feel what I had not felt.

then I began to feel it when I was awake.

then I decided that though I might never feel better, I didnt want to feel worse. that was my decision to give up men.

women were the next to go. now that may sound a little nutty since Im nuts about women. it all began when I was very young, 13 to be exact, and I had many an amorous night well into adulthood and even past it. sometimes when he beat me up I went to my next door neighbor who comforted me kindly with orgasm after orgasm but I couldnt stay there or think anything through because she was married to a man she hated and he was usually there. there didnt seem to be any rest or happiness anywhere in those troubled times.

to tell the truth I gave up women after some very bitter sweet love affairs which got fucked up because I was still fucking men and was still very fucked up by men. I was, to tell the truth, one running, festering sore, and I didnt do anyone much good. a lot of women were good to me and I fucked them over time and time again because I couldnt seem to get anything straight. finally I figured that since I couldnt do anyone any good I might at least stop doing monumental harm.

little boys were the last to go. 18, 19, 20. not prepubescent, certainly not. all long and gangly and awkward and ignorant. they never beat me up but they didnt stay hard long either. soon I came to appreciate that as some sort of good faith. finally though it hardly seemed worth the effort.

now I was in what all those men writers call "an existential position." that, contrary to the lewd images that might be evoked because Im a woman, is when youve given up everything youve ever tried, or havent tried but definitely had planned on. in my case, being quite taken with the arts, that included having mustard rubbed into whip wounds (Henry Miller), fucking Norman Mailer (Norman Mailer), and being covered in chocolate and licked clean by a horde of Soho painters (me).

now the problem with telling you what it means for me, bertha schneider, to be in an existential position is that I dont have Sartres credibility. I mean, theres just no emotional credibility that I can call on. look at Jackie Kennedy for instance. there she was, John dead, her very very rich, and she didnt have emotional credibility until she married Onassis. I mean, we all knew right away that she had done the only thing she could do. I mean, if De Beauvoir hadnt been Sartres mistress, do you think anyone would have believed her at all? or look at Oedipus as another example of emotional credibility. suppose he and his mother had fucked, and it had been terrific, and they had just kept fucking and ruling the kingdom together. whod believe it, even if it was true. or look at Last Tango in Paris. when Maria Schneider shot Brando most people didnt believe it at all. how is it possible, they asked, why did she do that? me I believed it right away.

so look at me. here I am, bertha schneider, someone not so special as these things go, right with my heels on the existential edge and my toes curling over the abyss. no men, no women, no boys. and what I want to tell you, though you wont believe it at all, is that its better here than its ever been before. bertha schneiders existential position is that shes not going to be fucked around anymore. now maybe that doesnt sound like much to all of you but I call it Day One. I figure that when my mind and body heal its my mother Im going to get it on with after all. I always did have a high regard for that woman although it did get obscured by the necessities of daily life. when I think of bliss, not to mention freedom, frankly its my ma and me alone somewhere kissing and hugging and sucking like God intended. and despite the obvious pressures I will not have second thoughts, or be unfaithful, or gouge my eyes out. thats my promise to posterity.

as for my ex-husband, well I didnt have Marias good sense. Im told he suffered a lot when I left. oh I dont kid myself. it wasnt out of love or regard or anything like that, whatever he called it. it was more like when a limping person dripping shit leaves you, you figure youre in real trouble and even a Clint Eastwood fan has to notice. I mean, when the baseball tells the bat to fuck off, the games over and I for one am never going to forget it.

for right now Im reading a book that says women can reproduce parthenogenetically. its a biology book so I have reason to hope for the best. frankly Im just going to curl up with that book in any existential position I can manage and concentrate on knocking myself up. I never did like that crap about the child being father to the man.

How many Black women, in the course of our lives, could unequivocally withstand the assaults on our very existence? The message we're getting is that it's commonplace to beat, stab, burn, mutilate us and literally take our lives away. . . . Black women are feeling scared, humiliated, angry, and depressed. In, and out of, therapy they share their own untold herstories of violence against them—even women I thought I knew.

A basic premise in Black feminist thought is that the personal is political. . . . What causes a Black woman to continue to struggle with Black men for mutual love and respect, in the face of overwhelming abuse, neglect, and misunderstanding?

Given the origins . . . of Black people in this country, collective strategies for survival have always been the essence of our existence.
—Eleanor Johnson, *"Reflections on Black Feminist Therapy"*

Ghosts Like Them

SHIRLEY ANN TAGGART

I. AUNT AMANDA JANE

Dear Amanda Jane, she writes. But she is too ashamed and guilty to continue. Ashamed of her contempt and fear of Amanda Jane, of the name Amanda Jane itself, the way it makes her think of black women in white kitchens, of Aunt Jemima. Although, she herself had loved Aunt Jemima once; as a little girl. A little girl dreaming on her aunt's front porch. Dreamed Aunt Jemima into the kitchen to bake special cakes for Angela Powers. But Aunt Jemima always turned in those dreams and viciously locked the oven door, so that she, Angela, would have to watch all the cakes turn black and burn to ashes. But when she woke up crying, Aunt Amanda Jane, sitting on that porch with her, would take Angela into her big arms and tell her sternly that bad dreams was God's reminder to sinners to make their peace with the Lord, and you was never too young to make your peace, to drive off the devil.

So how can she write Miss Amanda Jane Powers, Natchez, Mississippi, without feeling her soul burning and going to hell, without seeing her Aunt Amanda Jane with her straw hat and the Bible she couldn't read, rocking on an old weathered rocking chair on her front porch. Her Aunt Amanda Jane with her old black eyes fumbling in their yellow sockets, grabbing at Angela's face, her thin body, saying, "Amen, girl, Amen. I been there and back. Yes, Lawd, I been there and back." An old heavy black woman who is neither particularly impatient nor particularly peaceful with all her flesh, just a little tired of it, a little bored with it. "But it jes a house, Angela Ann, jes a house, honey, and the Lawd seen fit to give me a big one and if He seen fit to do it, then I seen fit to keep it."

Yesterday from Philadelphia, Pennsylvania, Angela Powers said, "How is she?" Her mother in Mississippi said, "She's an old woman, Angela." Her mother sighed into the telephone not in sympathy or resignation, but just as a habit. "But you don't think she'll die, do you Mama?" And she imagined her mother shaking her head, sad and intense and tired herself, before she said, "Honey, that old woman's been dead a long time now, her body just ain't believed it yet."

Ten years ago, she, Angela Powers, had sat on that old rotting front porch with her. A skinny nineteen-year-old from a poor Mississippi family of eleven children, all younger than her, yet home from college in those summers not to teach the children, but the aunt (who even then was well into her eighties, well into dying). A promising young woman on a full scholarship to a northern university, mysteriously compelled home into that fiercely hot summer sun in Natchez, to teach her aunt that the Lord didn't give her a fat body, a tired body; that, she, herself, made her body fat, made it tired.

Going off every day to her aunt's porch until her mother had said, "Lawd, child, what do you want with that old woman?"

And she would shrug her awkwardly tall and thin body and say, "I don't know, Mama."

But she had refused dates to sit on that porch with her, refused offers to drive into town with the tall predatory young men and sometimes older men, that hovered around her aunt's front gate, its broken-down condition, its peeling paint.

"I ain't never read me no books," was all her aunt had said, "and girl I ain't about to now." And then she sang, "Ain't about to leave you, Lawd. Ain't about to."

But Angela, always patient and polite, would continue sitting there reading out loud; sitting with her hair pulled painfully and neatly straight back from her high-cheekboned face, her continually washed and creamed face. Whose aunt had even said she could smell the mothballs and cleaning liquids still on Angela's sweaters and skirts. An old aunt whose voice would come on with a sudden power like a radio left on high, violently plugged in, and would sink into Angela's ears, anchor in her heart. "You stink, chile. You stink like a new bicycle and you gonna rust, chile. I knows, chile. I knows."

So sometimes she had hated her, her Aunt Amanda Jane; rocking there on that front porch that looked out over nothing now but broken rhubarb stems and ghosts of cotton plants. Hated that old woman singing and rocking there; picking at her decayed teeth between songs, and tapping on her chair a different beat from whatever songs she sang; as if there was such a multitude of songs, such an urgency to sing them, that they had had to appear in pairs, multiples. And how that had confused Angela, tangled up her words, until her aunt, alert to sounds, their patterns in space, had said, "Don't mumble, girl."

Yes, and hated her aunt's laziness too, her preaching from a rocking chair she never left to know one way or another what she was preaching about. Angela's mother had told her that Amanda Jane had been a flirt, a tease, but that men sensed that stubborn density of her soul, its competence and independence too; the Amanda Jane Powers who could go out in a heavy storm, her hair all done up for a date and a new dress just sewed; could go out and direct all her brothers and sisters to getting the animals inside and who brought in the last pig herself. So she had plenty of proposals, although one sweetheart was killed, but she said she wasn't about to marry him anyway, so who knows. But she never did get married, never did anything past 25, when her father died and left her in the house; had brothers and cousins and then nephews and then great-nephews to look after her. Took right to the porch, sewing in the beginning, and talking about opening a sewing place, selling her quilts and dresses, but then after a while, just rocking and remembering. So, of course, Angela couldn't help pitying her, pitying the way her life slipped into the wood she rocked in; but pitying her from far away exactly like she thought some white northerners with a brand new color TV might, tuning in to a documentary on the south, taking time to sigh and shake their heads before turning the channel. But then she would feel ashamed. Because, really, she loved her aunt.

But couldn't write to her. Even said she didn't have time to visit her the last time she was home. Said she didn't have time to see an old woman rock and sing and not even know you're there; an old woman who might even die right there, right in front of Angela herself. Although her mother had laughed that same mournful trying to be joyful sound of her aunt's songs, and said, "No, honey, you ain't about to see that." But when her mother had turned back to washing down the kitchen floor, she had said, "Then you wouldn't have to worry about death no more, child. You'd have to worry about the resurrection."

No, wasn't going over to see her aunt six months ago when she was home, until her mother had leaned her own deep, dark face into Angela's and said, "You my daughter, girl, my flesh and blood; but girl, you as cold as the north you live in." So it was fear that got her over those three-hundred yards to her aunt's porch; guilty and ashamed in that hot stagnant Mississippi air.

Was it fear of her aunt dying, she had thought, or fear of an aunt who at ninety-five, wouldn't die?

Yet she loved her.

And was afraid of her. Of the way she sang, so loud and uncontrolled. Afraid of the wrinkles in her aunt's face, the wrinkles even in her faded white socks pulled down below her heavy black ankles. And Angela would become a little dizzy at this loss of moisture and life in her aunt's skin, even mirrored in her aunt's clothes, as if the woman herself had already left them, routinely and unsentimentally abandoned them, moved inward. Her Aunt Amanda Jane turning inward upon herself like a dead star in space.

In the last summer before she graduated from college, she had gone over to see her aunt and her aunt had said, "A woman's got to be saved, chile. She was His second thought and He wasn't yet done with her when the world got started. So she need a man, honey."

But she hadn't needed those men in Mississippi, men who hung around on a broken gate, smelling of chewing tobacco and a boisterous camaraderie. "Good afternoon, Mizz Angela. Ain't it a good afternoon, Miss Angela. Now ain't it just a real fine afternoon?" Dragging out the word fine with their wide mocking toothy grins.

Her aunt said, "If a woman not saved by love and childruns, her soul jes dries up and dies, chile. Dries up and dies. Oh Lawdy, you can hear it crack. Yes, Lawd. Happened to women I knows. Women, I knows, chile."

So in the late summer afternoons of 1967 Angela dreamed she saw images in the haze off her aunt's front porch. Of her savior who would be the strongest, blackest man she had ever seen. One day washing dishes with her sisters she thought she saw him coming through the field in the back. But up close, she recognized him as a preacher and saw him put his arms around their mother who had run out the back door drying her hands on her dress. Angela stood stiff and still when her mother came back inside. "Was it. . . ?" And she was surprised at her panic, her fear, and her coldness. "Why honey, no," her mother had said startled, guessing her question. "It was Grandma Powers who went with the Lord." And she wondered how she could have forgotten her Grandmother Powers deathly sick in her bed and still reciting her tales of Mississippi that Angela's brother Latent, at 16, convinced of his pending importance and superiority, had generously vowed to write and publish. So that later, the preacher had said she had died slightly frantic, angry at the Lord for taking her too soon, right in the middle of that final story. The end lost forever in ordinary Mississippi dirt and rock.

But her brother, Latent, believed in ghosts, in his grandmother reappearing, in the ending being revealed to him. He believed in ghosts, more than in her, his sister, who he admitted was exceptionally bright, but who he was convinced would get lost, become anonymous and harmless in marriage and fertility, like so many other sisters, all the sisters he had ever known. Impotent with their big bellies and their big breasts, he had said. But it was all right. Acceptable for women. Only men needed to commit suicide.

In the late summer evenings her savior committed murder and theft. In the movies downtown. Breaking up rocks on a chain gang with Sidney Poitier. Or maybe even Sidney Poitier himself. A man so strong she imagined she could smell his sweat, like hot burnt rubber, all the way through the paper movie screen in the concrete church basement on Farm Street. Heard his cry through the giggling and whistles, when he finally broke the rock, when he said in that fierce amplified whisper, his black face blazing with sweat, "God, I can't stay here. These men are dead. And I'm still alive." And when he was sentenced to die she dreamed that she was the woman he saw in that movie, the woman who turned his soul to love and repentence; and mystically, magically this saved her. She was saved.

II. ENRIQUE JONES

In real life she was also finally saved. His name was Enrique Jones, a tall, exotic looking black man who wore hand embroidered Swedish shirts and vests sent to him by a sister in Scandinavia, so that he almost looked like a shepherd, lost in the wrong land, the wrong contour of the earth, in the mountainless, flat, sea-level city of Philadelphia. Enrique Jones, her savior. His mother was Spanish and his father was black and the combination of strange bloods never quite jelled, so that Enrique never quite understood Spanish and never quite identified with blacks, with any of their rallies, their tears, their rage. He only understood rage in a purer, more impersonal sense and when he broke Angela's nose with his fist, he had cried. Gently and lovingly he tried to persuade her that it wasn't personal, that it wasn't even because he hated his job, hated collecting people's trash, because, he joked, even those rich, smart-assed politicians had to do that, all that wealth and power and they still had to take people's trash every day! And they couldn't even punch out at 4:00 either. Enslaved forever with other people's trash! And he would laugh heavily, heartily, at this irony until he had had too much beer or until his friends left or until he felt sick. And then he might hit her again, punch her in the stomach. But it wasn't personal, he would tell her; he loved her, god how he loved her. And then he would watch television, watch people in new clothes wander into ski lodges and unwrap fancy bottles of booze in front of a fireplace, and over their heads, wooden rafters, that someone could have rubbed their skin, their goddamn soul out polishing. And through those big glass windows was new snow; all white and clean like those faces, all those contented, uncluttered white faces smiling at him. And on another channel, doctors staring seriously, thoughtfully at patients; prescribing perfect treatments, exercises, love. White male doctors. Over 40. Fatherly and respected. And then suddenly they were younger. And then women. And now black. But all with the same smiles, all pointing fearlessly, confidently, to the remedy, the cure. But he could never quite focus on the cure, never quite concentrate on those prescriptions because he would be trying to remember when it started. When he first saw them. Those doctors. And it gives him a headache, a pounding and throbbing in his head trying to remember all those puffy, broken-up streets in his old neighborhood; his youth in those potholes, those bars, so cloudy and noisy with the same people, the same dudes, the same friendly slaps, the same angry punches. But the TV was always going, he remembers that, remembers the exact day they got color TV's downtown, has a good memory; but there were never black doctors, never, he would have noticed. And he can't imagine who snuck out, Jesus Christ, who would even think of sneaking out and masquerading as a doctor?

So he broke her nose, and her glass Christmas tree ornaments, and their daughter's wrist. When she left, he said it was personal, it was personal now. Very personal. He said, "Woman, I'll kill you if you leave." He said, "You hear? You hear that woman?" And his rage had finally taken shape, crystallized. But when she was out the door he ran after her, yelled from the sidewalk to her, "Get your fucking little ass out of here, woman. And don't you come running back. Don't you ever come running back."

And she could feel him behind her, watching her, trying to hypnotize her with his eyes, trying to pull her back to him. So she didn't turn around once. Not once. And then what? And then nothing.

III. ANGELA POWERS JONES

She just walked straight ahead and didn't look back. Walked into this apartment with Mandy, her nine-year-old daughter, and signed the lease, signed him out of her life, and she didn't cry once. Since then she hasn't seen him, doesn't want to, but hasn't bothered with a divorce the way the people in this neighborhood don't always bother with marriage, with written laws; the powerful inertia of all those words and papers that drive educated men to horror movies and roller coasters, to get going again, to get their blood moving again.

But she still lives in Philadelphia, a city with historic landmarks, the Liberty Bell. The cracks in the bell for when freedom starts to break apart, break down into slavery again. But when she married Enrique and had a child, there were things she had to do, meals she had to cook, love she had to give to a man who was her husband. And she didn't cry when he hit her, hardly moved at all. He said she was so good, even her body was so good, not crazy and out of control like his body; and then he would start to cry and she would comfort him. Other times he caressed her and said, "How do you live with me? How are you so brave?"

Didn't whimper or scream like her sisters did, five sisters still in that shack at home on that burned-out farmland in Mississippi with a hundred kids and animals and lovers running over them, keeping their faces down so close to the dried-up useless soil that they wouldn't leave because it wouldn't feel right, because that was their home. But with no way out for them anyway; no scholar-ships and no beauty. Their mother had said Angela was the only one about to get anywhere. And if she didn't get anywhere, her mother had said, no one she knew in the whole world would.

But once when he slapped her, slapped her hard, and then looked right into her face, into how hard she tried not to change that face, not to remember that slap, he had gotten angry and said, "Je-sus, woman. Are you human?" But she was always in love with him. She doesn't remember a time when she wasn't in love with him, just a time when she had to go away and not look back. Like going away to college had been. And now she dreams of walking in tunnels. Of doors being slammed shut. And this bothers her. Because wasn't leaving home, going to college, leaving a husband who beat her, weren't these good decisions? Wise decisions? Wouldn't psychiatrists agree with this, applaud her; so many people couldn't do that well. Couldn't just walk out of a life like that. Like she did.

But she still lives in the same kind of neighborhood, a neighborhood that is a little worn-out and neglected. A neighborhood starting to shrivel, crack, like old photographs kept too long, kept in too much light; as if the light from the city was too powerful for neighborhoods so close and unprotected. A neighborhood that could burn and turn to ashes, like something in a childhood nightmare that she can almost taste, that makes her uneasy.

So she sits on guard at her window on the fourth floor. Looking out for whole days while Mandy's in school. At the holes in the streets. The broken bottles and old tires in yards, wherever there are yards. At the collapsed build-ings. The condemned buildings. At the collapsing wooden fence around a vacant lot across the street with "Jarcy and Jimmy '77" in big awkward red letters, and in a corner on that same fence, in piercing angular black print: "You die, man."

In the afternoons she watches the adolescent boys stand around and pass out plastic bags of drugs and put them in their jackets. Watches them push each other against the fence and laugh, imitating violence, but not violent yet, not ready in the daylight to try and blast the souls out of their own or each other's bodies yet; but excited, desperate to get out, to take off, to get away finally from so many people so close screaming into each other's hearts, or on hot nights, all vegetating in crowds outside on their steps like colonies of seals. She thinks that's what it looks like from up here, from her window.

And in the mornings she watches the prostitutes come home in their flashy clothes and heavy make-up. And the old men and old women asleep or drunk on someone's front steps. The most harmless people in this neighborhood and yet these are the ones that panic her, like dead fish washed up on beaches always do, as if there was some disaster just out of the corners of her eyes that could suddenly move in and destroy her. But she knows these old people are not dead, not even very dramatic, just lonely and tired. But she would like to take their pulses, listen to their hearts; shake their old bony shoulders right out of their skins just to make sure they are still there.

But most of the time she watches the strangers, well-dressed strangers not from this neighborhood, who walk quickly from block to block, absorbed and entranced by their destinations, seeing nothing.

Her destination today was the supermarket, the welfare office. But she tells herself it's all right, the welfare, the food stamps, won't always be like this, things will change, get better, after all she has a college degree, a diploma, something magic, the first in her family. So she has to remember that. "But in history?" An employment counsellor had said, astonished, but a very familiar, routine astonishment. He had said, "Well, you know you can't do anything with that." And then he asked her what machines she could operate, was she familiar with any of the machines on this list?

But one of the employment counsellors was friendly, sympathetic. She was a little older than Angela, a white woman, pretty, but a woman who wore a little more make-up, a little more force in her smile than Angela. She studied her a minute and then said, "Your boyfriend made a bad husband and you got a couple kids, right? And you don't know what to do. Oh, honey, I know." She took her hand. "I know. And look at this, you graduated from college. But honey, I got a kid in here today with a master's degree in something you couldn't even pronounce, and I don't want to discourage you, but she was useless, good lord, didn't know anything you need to know to live, to keep alive."

And good grades. Angela always had good grades, and good grades must mean something. She was convinced of it. She must be able to do something. Her mother said she could come home, that's what she could do. She said Latent was working in a plant in Birmingham part-time, "but he still thinking about his ghosts, still waiting for Grandma's ghost to finish that book of his. Amanda Jane has a touch of the flu, been in bed all week, nothing serious, but wants to hear from you. Keeps asking if there's a letter from Angela Ann. Keep the Lord in your heart and come home. Love, Mama."

She tears up the letter. She didn't believe in ghosts, she didn't even believe in her fear of ghosts, only Aunt Amanda Jane believed in that. She would tell Angela's stiff little body, "Now don' you worry bout them ghosts Latent tell you bout, he ain't gonna conjure up no ghosts. Even if he could, oh, Lawdy, help us, they never hurt you honey, cause ghosts is the soul. Theys not the body that does, theys the soul that is. Ghosts like them, they might wanna scream up the grass in the winna, and oh, Lawdy, they in pain, yes, Lawd; but ghosts like them, chile, they jes can't do nuthin. They jes can't."

She throws the pieces of the letter into a wastebasket in her living room.

Her living room is a greenish-brown, with a little blue. A couple of worn blue tweed chairs and the wallpaper is light green with brown dancing women who have cried the whole way down one wall, the wall that faces that street, the rain and the snow. She asked the landlord about the leaks, said he was letting his own apartment depreciate, it wasn't her wallpaper after all. He had smiled, the kind of smile babies smile by accident, with a burp. He had said, "Yes." Just yes. So she let them cry, all those women who lost their limbs, their faces. Good, she thought that they should be mutilated by nature and not by men. But how did it happen? How did her husband break her nose? And how could she know when even Sidney Poitier on a chain gang, a convicted murderer, gave her such a gentle, loving look? Her mother agreed with Enrique's gentle soul; she had said, "You treat this man good, honey." Of course Angela had known Enrique had gotten into fights, knifed someone once. A long time ago. But his life with her would be different. Saved by their love. Protected. Yes, she admitted she was tired and needed protecting. But wasn't that her privilege, after all, as a woman? No, those were someone else's words. She, Angela Powers Jones, advocated equality. And in their marriage they both had had an equal chance to escape, to die gracefully.

Dear Amanda Jane, she writes from an old round kitchen table with a formica top. Writing Dear Amanda eternally, she believes, into her one hundredth year of life. One hundred sheets of her daughter's tablet paper crumpled up and stuffed under the exposed pipes of her kitchen sink, although later she would dig them out and count them and find that, really, there were only 15. Dear Amanda Jane, she writes, but a friend of hers from college, whom she hasn't seen since college, comes over and interrupts her with her good clothes, her good job, her advanced degrees; she takes her hand and says, "Oh, Angela." Her friend's face is disappointed, compassionate, going out of control. But Angela's face, her perfect smile, her perfect bone structure and perfect teeth are convincing, persuasive. She says, "It's not so bad, really. It's just the wallpaper. It's such an awful color." Later, her friend, brave in her expensive dress, her neatly sculptured afro, her solid gold hoop earrings, asks, "But a man like that, Angela? A man who would physically abuse you?"

Angela shrugs. She looks out the window at the buildings. Buildings like her building. Old and dirty with small cement yards. And she thinks that some place else in Philadelphia things must be growing, coming alive. She thinks of trees and grass and flowers, and she feels suddenly deserted, angry.

Her friend makes an effort to sit neatly in one of Angela's sagging chairs, not to get stuffing on her dress. She says, "Angela Powers. Our social conscience. That Angela Powers shrugs?" She makes another effort to laugh, to joke about this. Then enthusiastically she says, "Angela, remember that paper you read in sociology? About our people struggling to get up north where the cold air will revive them, but with the cotton still caught under their fingernails. Remember? And about their new life in the north, how ironically it wasn't new at all, but the same. The same rats and the same weariness to be white, so that they felt cheated, as if they had been purposefully distracted at that moment when things were going to change. Remember that? God, Angela, we couldn't believe it was you . . . you were always so quiet. And remember our professor, Miss Dover, a white conservative woman, a little sickly, and how we swore she turned even whiter, embalmed right there at her own familiar worn desk she had written a poem about. Do you remember that? A poem about a *desk!* But anyway, your paper and Miss Dover, god, I've remembered that all these years!" Angela says nothing and after a minute her friend leans out of her chair and reaches over and touches Angela's hand again. She says, "If you ever want to talk about it. . . ." Angela doesn't move, she thinks only how hot it is. As hot as Mississippi. And it's only April. Only spring and still expected to be pleasant, comfortable.

She gets up and opens the window, feeling a little dizzy, a little tired. But in her mind she sees that her sociology professor does turn a little whiter, paler, behind that solid mahogany desk. A little shocked on such a routinely drowsy late May afternoon. And Angela feels that this, this must be something.

Her friend says, "Angela. . . ?" She says other things also, but Angela is only aware of the beat of that other black woman's voice, aware of the beat of the tires, the horns outside, a faster, more demanding beat that continually assaults and wears down the streets and eardrums of her neighborhood. And she wonders what the beat is like in Africa in 1978, the Africa she sees on the news, and whether the beat of a thousand guns and bodies being pounded into the ground will destroy their forests; their jungles. But secretly, she wonders how really this has anything to do with her.

Her friend says, "Angela, can I help you? Is there any way I can help?"

"You help them," a skinny, angry young college woman of the 1960's says in her mind. "You help them set up programs. You give them food. And yet they deceive you, they cheat you and your government. They take your money and watch your televisions, your dreams. Because their dreams aren't so visible, so concrete. Surely you know that. And your dreams are too expensive, too impossible for them. And they know this, they smell this like they smelled those sweet suffocating lilacs, that wet cotton and oily sweat that permanently opened, widened their nostrils."

Words rehearsed over and over in a life she can hardly remember so it is a surprise they are still there, still in perfect order. She looks out the window and the bricks in the building across the street make her feel dizzy and confused, the way she felt dizzy for two months before her freshman year in college, alarming her parents. What was she just thinking about? Suddenly she can't remember. But who was that vicious accusing college girl with all those white faces staring at her, and four black ones too, all staring blankly at her. And who was this woman now who stared out her window all day, rocking on a rocking chair. No, that at least, wasn't true, she didn't have a rocking chair. And she did do something, she did take care of her daughter, of course, and she does have a college degree. . . .

Her friend comes over to her, concerned with her silence, her appearance of nausea and sickness, concerned also with the dust that makes her cough, blown in from somewhere she can't see. But she manages to ask Angela if she is all right. Is she all right? Angela, her mind blank now, not dizzy anymore, assures her she is fine, fine in her strong thin, handsome black body, she is just tired. Saw her lover last night, not a violent man either, not very violent at all. And her daughter will be home from school soon. And the dishes have to be washed, and the roaches chased off the counters; her daughter is very fussy, squeamish; not good at all in the role of a poor minority child. Her friend says, "God, Angela, look at me. You can do better, girl. Girl, you can do so much better." Angela says of course, she plans on it. She smiles and says, "Don't worry about me, Rennie." She stares at her hands, so long and thin and graceful. "I think I'll become a doctor. Enrique hated doctors. Was scornful of them. Scornful of healing itself." She says, but today she is just so tired. Her friend nods, and they walk together to the door. Her friend hugs and kisses her goodbye. She says, "But you still look good Angela. Fantastic. Remember that. You still have a chance."

When her friend leaves, she falls asleep and dreams she is in a jungle in Africa and a tribal chief whom she knows is a murderer, insists she is his wife. She is attracted to him and thinks maybe this is true, but she somehow feels she is married to someone else, although she can't remember him, can't picture him at all. And then she thinks of her Aunt Amanda Jane and she can't remember if she is dead or alive, but surely if she were dead, surely she would remember the funeral? So she comes to the conclusion in the dream that she must have amnesia. And in her amnesia married the tribal chief. A handsome man who treats her gently. So why should she strain to remember a life she's already forgotten? And she can't think of a reason why. And yet she feels uncomfortable. And is glad to wake up.

Since it is 1:00 in the afternoon she fixes herself a light lunch. Some lettuce and tuna fish. She thinks about her dream and laughs because the tribal chief looked like Sidney Poitier, although she is a little ashamed to have dreamed herself so easily married to a murderer.

Sitting in a light cotton dress at her kitchen table, having finished eating now, and absent-mindedly peeling the formica off the top of the table. White and black formica, although the white has yellowed a little. Has given up writing to an old inert woman furiously trying to rock away her life on a porch in Mississippi that won't quite collapse and give up like that fence across the street; and not even Angela, Angela's elevation and rise into the mystical white forests of the north could save her. And of course Angela's marriage didn't work out, couldn't save anyone.

She cuts her thumb peeling the formica, but stubbornly she keeps peeling it, breaking it off in her fingers. And yes, it's true, she is ashamed of her aunt, an old ignorant woman who won't move and won't listen and won't die. Yes, so ashamed of her aunt, that she can't even write to her when she is sick in bed, a ninety-five-year-old woman of her own blood sick in bed, waiting to hear from her and she can't even tolerate her name, Amanda Jane, and yet she named her own daughter Amanda. Ashamed of her shame.

At 2:00 she gets up and goes over to the window and looks out, vaguely daydreaming, vaguely watching for her daughter to come home from school. She has been waiting, watching at this window for such a long time, so many months, and nothing has happened. A "dangerous, high risk" neighborhood where, after all, there is no danger, no risk. A disappointment. Disappointing that the women on this wall cry, suffer, for only bad weather, too much spring rain. So she is surprised when there is an accident outside in front of her building, and her heart is pounding. A man hit by a car! A black man in a gold suit, hit and thrown to the sidewalk. Two men run away, quickly, deftly, and other people gather, press against each other, greedy for a better view. Kids run over and circle the area, kicking aimlessly at the garbage and then pushing and jostling each other to see the man.

Angela watches this from her window. She watches the people move slowly closer to that man lying on the ground not quite twisted out of shape, out of their reach. And she thinks of insects. Insects around a light. Swarms. Swarming. But the movement, the whispers, are choked off suddenly by sirens, police cars, an ambulance. And then someone yells. A thick, heavy voice, heavy with rage, pain, yelling, "He's dead so get the fuck out of here."

But they come anyway, the police, the ambulance. Two men bring out a stretcher. They cover the man on the ground with a white sheet. And Angela dreams of ghosts rising from the sidewalk, of white socks on black legs. And she wonders where this dream comes from and where it goes from here, wonders if she is going crazy finally, when there has never been any sign of it, no hint at all. They put the stretcher in the ambulance. They close the doors and drive away. She is shaking. Violently cold on such a warm spring day. Ashamed. Guilty. Almost sick. But she can't quite cry. She can't quite cry with the hundred other women in this apartment. A hundred brown women crying. And one who isn't. But after all she didn't even know him. "I didn't even know him," she says to no one of them in particular.

The Short Song of What Befalls

—for Robin Wells

What just happens, the mystery of that,
what comes about apart from trying.
Accidere: to happen, generally
of misfortunes. Perhaps better, to befall.
By the Interstate I saw one red
high heeled shoe and wondered did she lose it
running from the car very late at night,
did she try to escape what was happening to her?
Was she walking on the shoulder,
did the car run her down,
and the shoe was left behind in the accident?
Did she throw it at the driver's head
in a rage and miss and lose the shoe
out the window, like that? So her misfortune
was just losing the shoe. On a radio interview
I heard a woman, one of five
struck by lightning in Ohio,
whose eyes changed instantly from blue
to grey. This befell her
in the late afternoon. Now she lives on
in terror of the rain,
she knows what any storm can do.

—Karen Fiser

Woman Waiting for Train at Dusk

CONSTANCE PIERCE

It is almost dusk on a perfectly normal evening. Across the rocky field, beyond the milkweed and Queen Anne's lace, the many bungalows and the few larger structures of the town have settled into a cluster of squares and triangles against a lavender sky. Here and there a telephone pole rises in a cruciform, here and there a parabola of elm or maple, and the steeple of a small church pricks at the evening like the point of a very sharp pencil. In the immediate foreground, the train station stands deserted behind its concrete platform, where down at the end, just before it drops off into the rubble of paper and tin and gravel, a woman sits alone on a green slatted bench.

The woman has settled a large purse on her lap and an old-fashioned wicker suitcase near her feet. She is in profile: a small straight nose and round chin thrust up slightly against the light, an erect and motionless posture. Her dress, a mauve silk with a high neck and long sleeves, reaches down to her feet, which are neatly crossed in their quaint shoes and tucked beneath the bench. Over the dress she wears a dark jacket, cropped at the waist. There is enough light to see that her hair, rolled back into a bun pinned low on her neck, is chestnut and that her eyes are dark and unblinking, fixed on the air above the train tracks in front of her almost as if she were a mannequin. But the skin on her face looks real enough, like lavender cream. Since the light is falling further, much must be imagined: the tracings of vein in the cheek, the creases in the furl of underlip, the small blue shadow that clefts the space beneath it. No, she is real all right, but she has a very fetching Other look, is the conclusion.

Inside the hair (and this is where you come in): you think you can see a pearly ear, curled nautilus-like around the opening to a long black tunnel that seems to go on and on, subsuming the station, the town, the sky beyond. Within that tunnel, a dim light slowly spreads to a sepia glow, revealing a bedroom with flowered wallpaper and the heavy carved furniture of the most indulgent phase of the last century. The high-backed bed rises in a swirl of ebony roses from a tangle of sheets and pillows, and to the side, the woman, dressed in a thin gown, seems to be protesting something. Her hands are raised in front of her, the fingers bent not very gracefully at all to repel something or someone, and her hair has fallen out of its bun and travels in loose frantic waves about her shoulders. The face seems to have knotted up to protect itself, the eyes squinting, the cheeks tight and contorted. The lips move, but there is no sound.

Suddenly a man steps sideways into view, his huge back toward you. He is dressed in some kind of uniform, but very old-fashioned, with epaulets and thick fringe. You cannot see his face, but the rigid posture tells you he is angry. He looms against your eye, and further away the woman, still protesting, has backed up and settled against the bed's wooden roses. She looks very small, compressed between the bulk of the man and the bulk of the furniture. Her eyes are still frightened, but you think you see a suggestion of resignation. As the man moves toward her, for a moment you want to step forward and identify yourself, struggle with the brute, save the day. But beyond his shoulder, the long window reveals you slipping out a side door and scuttling across the garden (you coward!), breaking into a sprint as you cross the street.

While you were occupied, the train has arrived without a sound, a series of dark windows segmented by bands of steel, something like a strip of film. Turning to look at it more closely, you are fascinated by these immense frames and the impressions they are generating from even the dim light remaining. Forgetting the woman, you watch these and follow the long segmented tail as it stretches back into the dark, only vaguely aware of the metallic rumble of doors opening and closing nearby. Then the windows begin to roll by, and you turn again to watch the train go, curving up to the right of the town, shrinking lower and lower until it hardly makes a bump on the wide, wide plain.

Back on the platform, the woman is gone. You feel a mild disappointment and unease, though you are unsure why you should, and since it is so mild, you are not inclined to pursue it to its source. The green of the bench has disappeared into the dark, and when you squat to tie your shoes, you glance between the slats and see, in the last wisp of light, the little town across the field, a solid geometry against the night.

The batterer who threatens to kill himself, his partner, the children, or her relatives must be considered extremely dangerous. . . . The batterer who threatens suicide should be considered potentially homicidal. The coupling of homicide with suicide is a frequent occurrence with men who kill family members. . . . A batterer who is obsessive about his battered partner—who either idolizes her and feels he cannot live without her or believes he somehow owns her because she is his wife—is likely to act more dangerously to keep his partner. The man who keeps telephoning a battered woman, who works hard to track her down, who stalks her, or who feels that if he cannot have her no one else will, may be potentially lethal. . . . Clearly, access to the battered woman is an important factor in predicting lethality. If the batterer cannot find her, he cannot kill her.

—Barbara Hart, *"Beyond the 'Duty to Warn' "*

"I Don't Believe This"

MERRILL JOAN GERBER

After it was all over, a final detail emerged, one so bizarre that my sister laughed crazily, holding both hands over her ears as she read the long article in the newspaper. I had brought it across the street to show to her; now that she was my neighbor, I came to see her and the boys several times a day. The article said that the crematorium to which her husband's body had been entrusted for cremation had been burning six bodies at a time and dumping most of the bone and ash into plastic garbage bags, which went directly into their dumpsters. A disgruntled employee had tattled.

"Can you imagine?" Carol said, laughing. "Even that! Oh, his poor mother! His poor *father!*" She began to cry. "I don't believe this," she said. That was what she had said on the day of the cremation, when she had sat in my back yard in a beach chair at the far end of the garden, holding on to a washcloth. I think she was prepared to cry so hard that an ordinary handkerchief would never have done. But she remained dry-eyed. When I came outside after a while, she said, "I think of his beautiful face burning, of his eyes burning." She looked up at the blank blue sky and said, "I just don't believe this. I try to think of what he was feeling when he gulped in that stinking exhaust. What could he have been thinking? I know he was blaming me."

She rattled the newspaper. "A dumpster! Oh, Bard would have loved that. Even at the end he couldn't get it right. Nothing ever went right for him, did it? And all along I've been thinking that I won't ever be able to go in the ocean again, because his ashes are floating in it! Can you believe it? How that woman at the mortuary promised they would play Pachelbel's Canon on the little boat, how the remains would be scattered with 'dignity and taste'? His mother even came all the way down with that jar of his father's ashes that she had saved for thirty years, so father and son could be mixed together for all eternity. Plastic garbage baggies! You know," she said, looking at me, "life is just a joke, a bad joke, isn't it?"

Bard had not believed me when I'd told him that my sister was in a shelter for battered women. Afraid of *him?* Running away from *him?* The world was full of dangers from which only *he* could protect her! He had accused me of hiding her in my house. "Would I be so foolish?" I had said. "She knows it's the first place you'd look."

"You better put me in touch with her," he had said, menacingly. "You both know I can't handle this for long."

It had gone on for weeks. On the last day, he called me three times, demanding to be put in touch with her. "Do you understand me?" he shouted. "If she doesn't call here in ten minutes, I'm checking out. Do you believe me?"

"I believe you," I said. "But you know she can't call you. She can't be reached in the shelter. They don't want the women there to be manipulated by their men. They want them to have space and time to think."

"Manipulated?" He was incredulous. "I'm checking *out,* this is *IT.* Goodbye forever!"

He hung up. It wasn't true that Carol couldn't be reached. I had the number. Not only had I been calling her but I had also been playing tapes for her of his conversations over the phone during the past weeks. This one I hadn't taped. The tape recorder was in a different room.

"Should I call her and tell her?" I asked my husband.

"Why bother?" he said. He and the children were eating dinner; he was becoming annoyed by this continual disruption of our lives. "He calls every day and says he's killing himself and he never does. Why should this call be any different?"

Then the phone rang. It was my sister. She had a fever and bronchitis. I could barely recognize her voice.

"Could you bring me some cough syrup with codeine tomorrow?" she asked.

"Is your cough very bad?"

"No, it's not too bad, but maybe the codeine will help me get to sleep. I can't sleep here at all. I just can't sleep."

"He just called."

"Really," she said. "What a surprise!" But the sarcasm didn't hide her fear. "What this time?"

"He's going to kill himself in ten minutes unless you call him."

"So what else is new?" She made a funny sound. I was frightened of her these days. I couldn't read her thoughts. I didn't know if the sound was a cough or a sob.

"Do you want to call him?" I suggested. I was afraid to be responsible. "I know you're not supposed to."

"I don't know," she said. "I'm breaking all the rules anyway."

The rules were very strict. No contact with the batterer, no news of him, no worrying about him. Forget him. Only female relatives could call, and they were not to relay any news of him—not how sorry he was, not how desperate he was, not how he had promised to reform and never do it again, not how he was going to kill himself if she didn't come home. Once, I had called the shelter for advice, saying that I thought he was serious this time, that he was going to do it. The counselor there—a deep-voiced woman named Katherine —had said to me, very calmly, "It might just be the best thing; it might be a blessing in disguise."

My sister blew her nose. "I'll call him," she said. "I'll tell him I'm sick and to leave you alone and to leave me alone."

I hung up and sat down to try to eat my dinner. My children's faces were full of fear. I could not possibly reassure them about any of this. Then the phone rang again. It was my sister.

"Oh, God," she said. "I called him. I told him to stop bothering you, and he said, *I have to ask you one thing, just one thing. I have to know this. Do you love me?*" My sister gasped for breath. "I shouted *No*—what else could I say? That's how I *felt.* I'm so sick, this is such a nightmare; and then he just hung up. A minute later I tried to call him back to tell him that I didn't mean it, that I did love him, that I *do,* but he was gone." She began to cry. "He was gone."

"There's nothing you can do," I said. My teeth were chattering as I spoke. "He's done this before. He'll call me tomorrow morning, full of remorse for worrying you."

"I can hardly breathe," she said. "I have a high fever and the boys are going mad cooped up here." She paused to blow her nose. "I don't believe any of this. I really don't."

Afterward she moved right across the street from me. At first she rented the little house, but then it was put up for sale, and my mother and aunt found enough money to make a down payment so that she could be near me and I could take care of her till she got her strength back. I could see her bedroom window from my bedroom window—we were that close. I often thought of her trying to sleep in that house, alone there with her sons and the new, big watchdog. She told me that the dog barked at every tiny sound and frightened her when there was nothing to be frightened of. She was sorry she had got him. I could hear his barking from my house, at strange hours, often in the middle of the night.

I remembered when she and I had shared a bedroom as children. We giggled every night in our beds and made our father furious. He would come in and threaten to smack us. How could he sleep, how could he go to work in the morning, if we were going to giggle all night? That made us laugh even harder. Each time he went back to his room, we would throw the quilts over our heads and laugh till we nearly suffocated. One night our father came to quiet us four times. I remember the angry hunch of his back as he walked, barefoot, back to his bedroom. When he returned for the last time, stomping like a giant, he smacked us, each once, very hard, on our upper thighs. That made us quiet. We were stunned. When he was gone, Carol turned on the light and pulled down her pajama bottoms to show me the marks of his violence. I showed her mine. Each of us had our father's handprint, five red fingers, on the white skin of her thigh. She crept into my bed, where we clung to each other till the burning, stinging shock subsided and we could sleep.

Carol's sons, living on our quiet, adult street, complained to her that they missed the shelter. They rarely asked about their father and only occasionally said that they wished they could see their old friends and their old school. For a few weeks they had gone to a school near the shelter; all the children had had to go to school. But one day Bard had called me and told me he was trying to find the children. He said he wanted to take them out to lunch. He knew they had to be at some school. He was going to go to every school in the district and look in every classroom, ask everyone he saw if any of the children there looked like his children. He would find them. "You can't keep them from me," he said, his voice breaking. "They belong to me. They love me."

Carol had taken them out of school at once. An art therapist at the shelter held a workshop with the children every day. He was a gentle, soft-spoken man named Ned, who had the children draw domestic scenes and was never once surprised at the knives, bloody wounds, or broken windows that they drew. He gave each of them a special present, a necklace with a silver running-shoe charm, which only children at the shelter were entitled to wear. It made them special, he said. It made them part of a club to which no one else could belong.

While the children played with crayons, their mothers were indoctrinated by women who had survived, who taught the arts of survival. The essential rule was *Forget him, he's on his own, the only person you have to worry about is yourself.* A woman who was in the shelter at the same time Carol was had had her throat slashed. Her husband had cut her vocal cords. She could speak only in a grating whisper. Her husband had done it in the bathroom, with her son watching. Yet each night she sneaked out and called her husband from a nearby shopping center. She was discovered and disciplined by the administration; they threatened to put her out of the shelter if she called him again. Each woman was allowed space at the shelter for a month, while she got legal help and made new living arrangements. Hard cases were allowed to stay a little longer. She said that she was sorry, but that he was the sweetest man, and when he loved her up, it was the only time she knew heaven.

Carol felt humiliated. Once each week the women lined up and were given their food: three very small whole frozen chickens, a package of pork hot dogs, some plain-wrapped cans of baked beans, eggs, milk, margarine, white bread. The children were happy with the food. Carol's sons played in the courtyard with the other children. Carol had difficulty relating to the other mothers. One had ten children. Two had black eyes. Several were pregnant. She began to have doubts that what Bard had done had been violent enough to cause her to run away. Did mental violence or violence done to furniture really count as battering? She wondered if she had been too hard on her husband. She wondered if she had been wrong to come here. All he had done—he said so himself, in the taped conversations, dozens of times—was to break a lousy hundred-dollar table. He had broken it before, he had fixed it before. Why was this time different from any of the others? She had pushed all his buttons, that's all, and he had gotten mad, and he had pulled the table away from the wall and smashed off its legs and thrown the whole thing out into the yard. Then he had put his head through the wall, using the top of his head as a battering ram. He had knocked open a hole to the other side. Then he had bitten his youngest son on the scalp. What was so terrible about that? It was just a momentary thing. He didn't mean anything by it. When his son had begun to cry in fear and pain, hadn't he picked the child up and told him it was nothing? If she would just come home, he would never get angry again. They'd have their sweet life. They'd go to a picnic, a movie, the beach. They'd have it better than ever before. He had just started going to a new church that was helping him to become a kinder and more sensitive man. He was a better person than he had ever been; he now knew the true meaning of love. Wouldn't she come back?

One day Bard called me and said, "Hey, the cops are here. You didn't send them, did you?"

"*Me?*" I said. I turned on the tape recorder. "What did you do?"

"Nothing. I busted up some public property. Can you come down and bail me out?"

"How can I?" I said. "My children . . ."

"How can you *not?*"

I hung up and called Carol at the shelter. I said, "I think he's being arrested."

"Pick me up," she said, "and take me to the house. I have to get some things. I'm sure they'll let me out of the shelter if they know he's in jail. I'll check to make sure he's really there. I have to get us some clean clothes, and some toys for the boys. I want to get my picture albums. He threatened to burn them."

"You want to go to the house?"

"Why not? At least we know he's not going to be there. At least we know we won't find him hanging from a beam in the living room."

We stopped at a drugstore a few blocks away and called the house. No one was there. We called the jail. They said their records showed that he had been booked, but they didn't know for sure whether he'd been bailed out. "Is there any way he can bail out this fast?" Carol asked.

"Only if he uses his own credit card," the man answered.

"I *have* his credit card," Carol said to me, after she had hung up. "We're so much in debt that I had to take it away from him. Let's just hurry. I hate this! I hate sneaking into my own house this way."

I drove to the house and we held hands going up the walk. "I feel his presence here, that he's right here seeing me do this," she said, in the dusty, eerie silence of the living room. "Why do I give him so much power? It's as if he knows whatever I'm thinking, whatever I'm doing. When he was trying to find the children, I thought that he had eyes like God, that he would go directly to the school where they were and kidnap them. I had to warn them, 'If you see your father anywhere, run and hide. Don't let him get near you!' Can you imagine telling your children that about their father? Oh, God, let's hurry."

She ran from room to room, pulling open drawers, stuffing clothes in paper bags. I stood in the doorway of their bedroom, my heart pounding as I looked at their bed with its tossed covers, at the phone he used to call me. Books were everywhere on the bed—books about how to love better, how to live better; books on the occult, on meditation; books on self-hypnosis for peace of mind. Carol picked up an open book and looked at some words underlined in red. *"You can always create your own experience of life in a beautiful and enjoyable way if you keep your love turned on within you—regardless of what other people say or do,"* she read aloud. She tossed it down in disgust. "He's paying good money for these," she said. She kept blowing her nose.

"Are you crying?"

"No!" she said. "I'm allergic to all this dust."

I walked to the front door, checked the street for his car, and went into the kitchen.

"Look at this," I called to her. On the counter was a row of packages, gift-wrapped. A card was slipped under one of them. Carol opened it and read it aloud: "I have been a brute and I don't deserve you. But I can't live without you and the boys. Don't take that away from me. Try to forgive me." She picked up one of the boxes and then set it down. "I don't believe this," she said. "God, where are the children's picture albums! I can't *find* them." She went running down the hall.

In the bathroom I saw the fishbowl, with the boys' two goldfish swimming in it. The water was clear. Beside it was a piece of notebook paper. Written on it in his hand were the words *Don't give up, hang on, you have the spirit within you to prevail.*

Two days later he came to my house, bailed out of jail with money his mother had wired. He banged on my front door. He had discovered that Carol had been to the house. "Did *you* take her there?" he demanded. *"You* wouldn't do that to me, would you?" He stood on the doorstep, gaunt, hands shaking.

"Was she at the house?" I asked. "I haven't been in touch with her lately."

"Please," he said, his words slurred, his hands out for help. "Look at this." He showed me his arms; the veins in his forearms were black and blue. "When I saw that Carol had been home, I took the money my mother sent me for food and bought three packets of heroin. I wanted to OD. But it was lousy stuff; it didn't kill me. It's not so easy to die, even if you want to. I'm a tough bird. But please, can't you treat me like regular old me? Can't you ask me to come in and have dinner with you? I'm not a monster. Can't anyone, *anyone,* be nice to me?"

My children were hiding at the far end of the hall, listening. "Wait here," I said. I went and got him a whole ham I had. I handed it to him where he stood on the doorstep and stepped back with distaste. Ask him in? Let my children see *this?* Who knew what a crazy man would do? He must have suspected that I knew Carol's whereabouts. Whenever I went to visit her at the shelter, I took a circuitous route, always watching in my rearview mirror for his blue car. Now I had my tear gas in my pocket; I carried it with me all the time, kept it beside my bed when I slept. I thought of the things in my kitchen: knives, electric cords, mixers, graters, elements that could become white-hot and sear off a person's flesh.

He stood there like a supplicant, palms up, eyebrows raised in hope, waiting for a sign of humanity from me. I gave him what I could—a ham, and a weak, pathetic little smile. I said, dishonestly, "Go home. Maybe I can reach her today; maybe she will call you once you get home." He ran to his car, jumped in it, sped off. I thought, coldly, *Good, I'm rid of him. For now we're safe.* I locked the door with three locks.

Later Carol found among his many notes to her one that said, "At least your sister smiled at me, the only human thing that happened in this terrible time. I always knew she loved me and was my friend."

He became more persistent. He staked out my house, not believing I wasn't hiding her. "How could I possibly hide her?" I said to him on the phone. "You know I wouldn't lie to you."

"I know you wouldn't," he said. "I trust you." But on certain days I saw his blue car parked behind a hedge a block away, saw him hunched down like a private eye, watching my front door. One day my husband drove away with my daughter beside him, and an instant later the blue car tore by. I got a look at him then, curved over the wheel, a madman, everything at stake, nothing to lose, and I felt he would kill, kidnap, hold my husband and child as hostages till he got my sister back. I cried out. As long as he lived he would search for her, and if she hid, he would plague me. He had once said to her (she told me this), "You love your family? You want them alive? Then you'd better do as I say."

On the day he broke the table, after his son's face crumpled in terror, Carol told him to leave. He ran from the house. Ten minutes later he called her and said, in the voice of a wild creature, "I'm watching some men building a house, Carol. I'm never going to build a house for you now. Do you know that?" He was panting like an animal. "And I'm coming back for you. You're going to be with me one way or the other. You know I can't go on without you."

She hung up and called me. "I think he's coming back to hurt us."

"Then get out of there," I cried, miles away and helpless. "Run!"

By the time she called me again, I had the number of the shelter for her. She was at a gas station with her children. Outside the station were two phone booths. She hid her children in one; she called the shelter from the other. I called the boys in their booth and I read to them from a book called *Silly Riddles* while she made arrangements to be taken in. She talked for almost an hour to a counselor at the shelter. All the time I was sweating and reading riddles. When it was settled, she came into her children's phone booth and we made a date to meet in forty-five minutes at Sears, so that she could buy herself some underwear and her children some blue jeans. They were still in their pajamas.

Under the bright fluorescent lights in the department store we looked at price tags, considered quality and style, while her teeth chattered. Our eyes met over the racks, and she asked me, "What do you think he's planning now?"

My husband got a restraining order to keep him from our doorstep, to keep him from dialing our number. Yet he dialed it, and I answered the phone, almost passionately, each time I heard it ringing, having run to the room where I had the tape recorder hooked up. "Why is she so afraid of me? Let her come to see me without bodyguards! What can happen? The worst I could do is kill her, and how bad could that be, compared with what we're going through now?"

I played her that tape. "You must never go back," I said. She agreed; she had to. I took clean nightgowns to her at the shelter; I took her fresh vegetables, and bread that had substance.

Bard had hired a psychic that last week, and had gone to Las Vegas to confer with him, taking along a $500 money order. When Bard got home, he sent a parcel to Las Vegas containing clothing of Carol's and a small gold ring that she often wore. A circular that Carol found later under the bed promised immediate results: *Gold has the strongest psychic power — you can work a love spell by burning a red candle and reciting "In this ring I place my spell of love to make you return to me." This will also prevent your loved one from being unfaithful.*

Carol moved in across the street from my house just before Halloween. We devised a signal so that she could call me for help if some maniac cut her phone lines. She would use the antique gas alarm our father had given to me. It was a loud wooden clacker that had been used in the war. She would open her window and spin it. I could hear it easily. I promised her that I would look out my window often and watch for suspicious shadows near the bushes under her windows. Somehow neither of us believed he was really gone. Even though she had picked up his wallet at the morgue, the wallet he'd had with him while he breathed his car's exhaust through a vacuum-cleaner hose and thought his thoughts, told himself she didn't love him and so he had to do this and do it now; even though his ashes were in the dumpster; we felt that he was still out there, still looking for her.

Her sons built a six-foot-high spider web out of heavy white yarn for a decoration and nailed it to the tree in her front yard. They built a graveyard around the tree, with wooden crosses. At their front door they rigged a noose and hung a dummy from it. The dummy, in their father's old blue sweat shirt with a hood, swung from the rope. It was still there long after Halloween, swaying in the wind.

Carol said to me, "I don't like it, but I don't want to say anything to them. I don't think they're thinking about him. I think they just made it for Halloween, and they still like to look at it."

An irony is that among Third World people biological determinism is rejected and fought against when it is applied to race, but generally unquestioned when it applies to sex. . . . Black and other Third World women are sexually oppressed every day of our lives, but because we are also oppressed racially and economically, sexual oppression has not been considered a priority. It has been rendered falsely invisible. . . .

The phrase "men are not the enemy" dismisses feminism and the reality of the patriarchy in one breath and also overlooks some major realities. If we cannot entertain the idea that some men *are* the enemy. . . . then we will never be able to figure out all the reasons why, for example, we are being beaten up every day, why we are sterilized against our wills, why we are being raped by our neighbors, why we are pregnant at age twelve and why we are at home on welfare with more children than we can support or care for.

—Barbara Smith, *"Notes for Yet Another Paper on Black Feminism"*

Minerva Writes Poems

S A N D R A   C I S N E R O S

Minerva is only a little bit older than me but already she has two kids and a husband who left. Her mother raised her kids alone and it looks like her daughters will go that way too. Minerva cries because her luck is unlucky. Every night and every day. And prays. But when the kids are asleep after she's fed them their pancake dinner, she writes poems on little pieces of paper that she folds over and over and holds in her hands a long time, little pieces of paper that smell like a dime.

She lets me read her poems. I let her read mine. She is always sad like a house on fire—always something wrong. She has many troubles, but the big one is her husband who left and keeps leaving.

One day she is through and lets him know enough is enough. Out the door he goes. Clothes, records, shoes. Out the window and the door locked. But that night he comes back and sends a big rock through the window. Then he is sorry and she opens the door again. Same story.

Next week she comes over black and blue and asks what can she do? Minerva. I don't know which way she'll go. There is nothing *I* can do.

Linoleum Roses

SANDRA CISNEROS

Sally got married like we knew she would, young and not ready but married just the same. She met a marshmallow salesman at a school bazaar and she married him in another state where it's legal to get married before eighth grade. She has her husband and her house now, her pillowcases and her plates. She says she is in love, but I think she did it to escape.

Sally says she likes being married because now she gets to buy her own things when her husband gives her money. She is happy except sometimes her husband gets angry and once he broke the door where his foot went through, though most days he is okay. Except he won't let her talk on the telephone. And he doesn't let her look out the window. And he doesn't like her friends, so nobody gets to visit her unless he is working.

She sits at home because she is afraid to go outside without his permission. She looks at all the things they own: the towels and the toaster, the alarm clock and the drapes. She likes looking at the walls, at how neatly their corners meet, the linoleum roses on the floor, the ceiling smooth as wedding cake.

How does a mother talk to her daughter about the feel of her husband's fist against her cheek? About the corrupt, aching silence in darkened bedrooms in the aftermath? Is there a language for this?

—Marita Golden, *"Walking in My Mother's Footsteps to Love"*

The number one issue for most of our sisters is violence—battering, sexual abuse. Same thing for their daughters, whether they are twelve or four. We have to look at how violence is used, how violence and sexism go hand in hand, and how it affects the sexual response of females. We have to stop it . . .

—B. Y. Avery

Noises

JANE BRADLEY

Connie remembered how for months after Trisha was born, she would wake in a panic suddenly in the night. She would swear she had heard something: a gasp, a cough, or even too much silence, but something screamed "Danger!" and Connie would bolt from her bed and run to her daughter's room. She would touch the baby's face, lift an arm, jostle a shoulder, do something that would make the baby stir and let her mother know that yes, of course, she was still alive and safe.

Looking at her grown daughter's face Connie remembered that old panic, but now there was a reason. At twenty-six, Trisha was filthy and so drunk that her words slurred and spit flew when she talked. Her bottom lip was cracked, caked with dried blood, and her eye was bruised, her cheek swollen, her nose smeared with blood and dirt. Connie reached for her.

"That's it!" Trisha said. "He's done it this time, by god." She leaned back on the couch and slowly exhaled smoke from her cigarette.

"I hope you mean it," Connie said, knowing the old line repeated, "I'm leaving," then the loneliness of leaving, the running back, the constant running back again.

"Of course I mean it," Trisha said. "I've had enough. I told him. I said, 'You hit me one more time, Jimbo Jones, and I'm leaving, I swear.' Then he hit me again! See?"

"I see it," Connie said. She reached for her daughter, pulled her close to her chest, smelled the oil in her hair, thought, "How did my little girl get so dirty?"

Trisha jerked away. "It hurts my neck when you do that." She started to cry. "I've been hurt enough already. Just leave me alone."

Connie sat back on the couch. "You don't have to live with him. You've got a home right here if you want."

Trisha shook her head. "Don't you have any cold beer or nothing?"

Connie got up and made Trisha a Coke. She wanted to kill this Jimbo Jones who used to love her daughter. He did love her until she got drunk, then he got drunk, and they started circling each other like two dogs finally released from their chains. Connie put the tall cool glass on the table in front of Trisha. "He'll kill you one day," she said.

Trisha stared at the floor, took a sharp breath. Connie watched her hand clench into a fist, saw the fist beat softly one, two, three into the cushion of the couch. "He won't kill me," she said. "He loves me. He's just crazy sometimes."

Connie went to the door to make sure it was locked. Nobody ever doubted that he loved Trisha. Anybody could see it in the way his face went soft and warm when he watched her do something as simple as scramble an egg. Connie remembered watching him watch Trisha make potato salad for the Fourth of July picnic. It was supposed to have been a good day, a day when they both promised not to drink, not to fight. They had promised. And it had started to be a good day, in Connie's kitchen with Connie frying chicken, Trisha making the salad, and Jimbo sitting at the table, drinking coffee, smiling, peaceful as a prince. "He's a prince," Trisha had said. "I finally got me a prince, Mom." And that day he did seem like a prince, so calm, so happy, so soft and warm when he watched Trisha move across the floor, looking so sweet Connie couldn't help saying, "You really love my girl, don't you, Jimbo."

He nodded once and looked at his coffee. Connie said, "He couldn't live without me, Momma. He told me. Couldn't get up in the morning if he didn't have me."

"Shit," he said. But he was grinning, that strange grin, the way Larry used to grin when he looked at a poker hand, knew he was losing, knew he couldn't let that loser's hand show. But Trisha was peeling potatoes and didn't see it. So Trisha said, "It's true, Jimbo, you said it. You couldn't live without me."

"Like hell." He looked at Connie. "She's good in the mornings, but you get her out drinking, she's nothing but a goddamned whore."

Trisha had stared at the potatoes. She wouldn't cry, but Connie could see that she could break any second from the way she held her mouth set tight and closed, while her hands moved like there was nothing else in the whole world but peeling potatoes.

Connie knew that game. It was an old game that Trisha's Daddy had played. Connie had called it the black turn game. She had seen it a hundred times before, and now she saw it in Jimbo: that soft look of a boy in love turn in a second to something mean. The man could be happy as a prince until you said the wrong word, made the wrong sound that could make a man in love swoop like a hawk ready to grab anything that dared to move across the ground.

Connie could hear the old words screaming, "You asked for it!" Larry had always said that just after the hit. Now Jimbo said the words. Now even Connie said the words when she was shaking Trisha by the shoulders, yelling, knowing that Jimbo wouldn't hit Trisha if she would just behave. "You asked for it!" Connie had said to her own daughter who stood there bleeding, saying, "Momma, he did it again."

Now she looked at Trisha, wondered, "Did anybody really ask for that?" She reached for her daughter's hand. "He's gonna come for you," Connie said. He would come crying, want to talk, make up, then he'd buy her flowers, a new sweater, buy something as a promise, the old promise: "If you be good, I'll be good," then they would start all over. That was the only promise. They would go round and around and around, mad dogs circling again.

Now Trisha was laughing, holding her hand to her mouth to sooth the torn lip. "Damn right he'll come for me," she said. "As soon as he finds I'm gone. He thinks I'm locked in the bathroom. Guess he forgot about windows." She smiled and tapped her head with her finger. "He might be good-looking, but he ain't too smart. I climbed out of that window like a ten-year-old boy. Good thing I'm tough. I'm too tough for him, right Momma?"

"Right," Connie said, thinking, "Wrong," feeling in her chest that old panic at the wrong sound in the night. Trisha would never say the right thing, and as long as Trisha said the wrong thing, took the wrong step, Larry would be there to swoop down and grab her and squeeze until she bled in his hands.

"Why don't you get some sleep," Connie said. "I got to clean the kitchen."

"I hurt too bad to sleep. Don't you have a cold beer?"

"No." Connie stood and turned off the lamp. Trisha sighed and lay down. From the door of the kitchen, Connie watched as Trisha groaned and shifted her body on the couch. "At least she's here," Connie thought. She stood and listened to Trisha's breath rise and fall. The living room was dark except for the new street light that shone through the curtains. All around the house stretched silence and darkness except for the one light that made Connie happy because it meant that the city was growing toward her house where there was nothing but woods, rabbits, birds, and a black-top road that was hardly used.

From where Connie stood, Trisha looked like a child who had fallen asleep in front of the TV. There was her baby girl, the girl who once left wild flowers in a vase at the front door and a card to Connie signed "Love, Elvis." Trisha who was once always trying to find a way to get her momma laughing. They both had loved Elvis, spent afternoons together in the front-porch swing, rocking, singing "Love Me Tender," the only song they both knew well enough to sing all the words. Connie took a blanket from the closet to cover Trisha, and as she leaned she smelled the stale cigarettes, sour whiskey, and a faint musky body odor that made her wonder when Trisha last had a bath. Trisha snored softly, and Connie wanted to kill Jimbo Jones who once broke her daughter's nose.

She went to the kitchen, ran the water hot, and filled the sink to wash a few dishes. She thought she should mop the floor or clean the shelves. She wanted the smell of bleach, ammonia, lemon, pine. She wanted to be strong enough to throw Trisha in the shower and lock her in with the soap and steam until Trisha could stand straight, smell sweet, and smile.

Connie remembered how Trisha used to be so pretty with those brown eyes and dark skin like her daddy, her daddy's girl all right with those eyes flashing and the sad way of getting wild after just one beer, that one beer that could make most people happy, but made Trisha, like her daddy, throw her head to the side a little and say something loud and mean.

Yes, Connie believed it when Jimbo said Trisha would start on other men when they were out drinking. Yes, Connie believed Trisha would grin at other men, say Jimbo didn't make enough money, Jimbo snored at night, say Jimbo couldn't get it up, say anything to let Jimbo know he didn't own the words that could fly from her mouth. Sometimes even Connie thought Trisha deserved getting smacked. Who could blame him? But when she had seen Trisha's face, the lip torn, eye swelling, the purple, yellow welt spreading across her skin, she had thought, "Nobody asks for that."

Connie could hear the voice again, someone's voice, rushing, rumbling, cracking like a summer storm, "You asked for it!" Larry screaming, her own voice screaming "Larry, please," then Trisha, crying "Please, Jimbo, stop hitting me." Connie heard it, the sad wailing scream, "Please."

Jimbo could be polite. "He's a prince," Trisha had said. And even Connie thought he might be that day she first met him in the hospital room. They had thought she was dying then, and everybody was polite when they thought you were dying. Jimbo was sweet as a puppy that day Trisha brought him to the hospital, "This is Jimbo, Momma," she had said. And he stood at the foot of the bed smiling, wrapped his long arms around her daughter, said, "Don't you worry, Mrs. Jenkins, I'll take care of your little girl."

And with the way he smiled back then, anybody would believe him. He took good care of them both for a while, sneaking fried catfish dinners and hot fudge sundaes up to the hospital room. Sometimes she thought she would have given up if it hadn't been for Jimbo. There he was smiling, saying he'd take care of her girl. And he had kept them laughing with his stories of how he could walk into Penney's and walk out carrying a television, a rug, a bicycle if he wanted, right under the cashier's nose. Connie couldn't help laughing, couldn't help sitting back in her bed, couldn't help asking, "How do you do it, Jimbo?"

And he had grinned, said, "You just have to look like you know what you're doing. You just look like that little color TV belongs in your hand and you walk out that door, and that big-eyed little check-out girl just watches, while you say, 'Have a nice day ma'am.' And she says, 'Thank you.' " He had laughed, nudged Trisha's shoulder just a little too hard. Connie didn't like that laugh. He brought flowers and catfish and hot fudge sundaes, but she had heard that laugh before, knew the sound of danger, so she fought to keep on living to take care of her girl.

Connie finished the dishes and went back to the living room. Trisha lay flat on her back with the blanket pulled up and tangled around her neck. Connie carefully straightened the covers and pulled off Trisha's new shoes and took them to the closet so if Trisha wanted to leave, she would have to ask for her shoes. Connie picked up the leather jacket to hang, and thought of Trisha all dressed the way Jimbo dressed her like something out of a magazine: silk shirts, good leather, wool sweaters, and designer jeans. Whenever Connie complained about Jimbo, Trisha always said, "But Momma, look at all my pretty things." Now she heard Trisha snore, then mumble the slurred tangled words of a little girl dreaming. "Just sleep," Connie thought. She had always loved her baby most when she was sleeping.

Connie unplugged the phone and went to the kitchen. She decided to clean out what she called the junk drawer. Everything in the house that had no place to go found its way there: coupons, pencils, nails, string. She emptied the drawer on the table and sat with a fresh cup of coffee.

She wondered how so many odd things could wind up in the drawer, as if they had sneaked in there of their own will: the imitation pearl earring she thought she had lost months ago, the piece of dried-up macaroni that must have slid off the counter, toothpicks, a perfume bottle, a hickory nut, the sample of fabric softener she got who knows when in the mail. She never remembered putting things in there, but somehow they piled up till one day she opened the drawer, looked in, thought, "How in the world have I been living around such a mess?"

She had always prided herself on keeping a good house. Even back when Larry kept her so scared she couldn't see straight, she had always found a way to keep the floor waxed and the windows clean. But a mess in a drawer always grew somehow, like a spider's web in a corner you couldn't reach. She leaned back from the table, closed her eyes, felt that old tangle of voices rise up in her head. She could hear him screaming, "Shut up, god damn you!" She could hear her own crying, "Stop, please, Larry!" She could see her little girl running in circles, shaking her hands like she was flinging something hot. She could hear that scream.

Connie sat up in the chair and tried to think of something else to clean. The house was still, quiet as a well, but all those voices kept screaming. She thought, "It's all right. It's all right. Your girl is sleeping, and the only real sound you hear is the refrigerator." She forced her mind to listen to that easy hum.

She heard Trisha moan. "Momma, Momma, I'm sick." Connie hurried to help Trisha to the bathroom. She sat by the toilet and soothed Trisha's head with a cold cloth while she vomited and cried.

Connie washed Trisha's face, helped her into a flannel nightgown, and led her back to the couch. "Water," Trisha said. Connie made a tall glass of ice water, placed it carefully between Trisha's hands, then sat in a chair and watched Trisha drink.

"You don't have to live like this," Connie said. She wanted to shake her, wanted to throw her against the wall and scream, "Why do you do this!"

"You think I'm happy?" Trisha said. "I know he'll do it again." She was crying. "He says he won't. He don't mean to hurt me, Momma. He loves me. He kisses me, Momma. When he kisses me sometimes, it's like sinking my mouth in a bowl of whipped cream." She covered her face with her hands. "You'll never know what I mean."

Connie reached for her, tried to rock her like a baby. Oh yes, she remembered those kisses before the black turn, kisses that spread across your mouth like cream. Connie gave her a tissue to wipe the lip that was bleeding again. "We aren't giving him another chance," she said. "You're leaving for good, this time. Remember?"

Trisha dabbed at her lip. "I guess I'll have to see him sometime." She looked at the floor. "He's got all my stuff. My clothes. My boots. My plants."

Connie stood to take the empty glass to the kitchen. "I'm coming with you this time," she said. "We'll walk in there together, get everything that's yours, right down to the knives and forks."

She held Trisha tightly, but Trisha shrugged her shoulders and pulled away. "He loves me, Momma. We have a real good time, sometimes. Like the other night he went out for pizza just because I was hungry. So we sat up in bed and ate pizza. See, Momma, he loves me." Trisha shook her head and stared at the floor. "He'd die for me, Momma. He said that once, he said, 'I'd die for you, girl. Would you die for me?' And he tickled me till I said yes. Oh Momma, you don't know how he can get me laughing. He tickled and tickled till I couldn't breathe, till I said, 'Yes, oh yes, Jimbo, I'd die for you.' And I would, Momma, 'cause I know he'd die for me."

"He's lying," Connie said.

Trisha sat back on the couch and pulled the blanket up around her. "It's your fault," she said. "If you weren't so sick, I wouldn't need Jimbo. I wouldn't need somebody to take care of me."

"I'm not sick!" Connie said.

"But you will be," Trisha said. "We all know it. You'll get sick again. And you'll die one day."

Connie reached for her, held her again, thinking she could hang on. She would hang on forever for Trisha. She owed her life to Trisha. It was Trisha who saved her that night when Larry had beaten her so badly she was passing out on the floor, and he started kicking, aiming for her head. Trisha had screamed and grabbed his leg, and he had tried to shake her off, but she held on until he grabbed her and threw her across the room.

That night Connie had taken Trisha and left, thinking, "You can hit me, Larry, but not my girl." She had hoped that by leaving the man she could leave it all like a bad dream, but he put his mark on Trisha. Trisha was still wearing the mark of a fist like a brand. A voice hissed in her head, "It's you, Larry. You're the reason my girl is sitting here on my couch bleeding." Connie stroked Trisha's hair. "I did all I could," she thought. "It was him that did this. I just loved a man who could hurt me." She took Trisha's hand and pulled it as if they were walking and Connie could pull her to the right way. "Don't love anybody that can hurt you, honey," she said, thinking, "The only safe love is a mother love." But she wouldn't say that because she knew better. Any kind of love was a danger.

She looked up and saw a face peering in the window, and she pulled Trisha close. She heard a rustle outside, then a step on the front porch.

Trisha sat up. "It's Jimbo," she whispered.

"Hush!" Connie said. She covered Trisha's shoulders with the blanket, then left the room to get the .38 out of her top drawer. She was ready. She would not let him win now. She wasn't sick and wouldn't die for a long time.

"Trisha!" Jimbo said. "I didn't mean to hurt you so bad, honey."

Trisha ran to the door, leaned against it and yelled, "You get away from me!"

Connie pulled Trisha from the door and turned on the porch light. "Leave her alone, Jimbo."

"This ain't your business," he said.

"I got my .38 pointed at the door," she said. "I can use it."

"No!" Trisha screamed.

"Don't fight her, Trisha," Jimbo said. "The gun might go off. She won't shoot."

Connie took a breath and stared at the gun in her hand, suddenly wondering if she really held a weapon. She thought, "How can he talk like that, so easy, like he was saying, 'Don't bump her arm, she might spill her coffee.'" Like being careful had nothing to do with staying alive. She yelled through the door. "You don't know me!" She waved her empty hand at Trisha, said, "Get over there and sit down."

"Now, Connie," Jimbo said. "You know I love Trisha. You know I don't want to hurt your girl."

She wouldn't listen to his words. She yelled, "Get away, Jimbo!" She thought, "Careful, don't let him get started on love." She forced her words over his deep, heavy voice. "Stay away from my girl!"

Trisha was pulling Connie's arm. "He just wants to talk." She leaned next to the window. "I'm listening, Jimbo. Just tell me you love me, Jimbo. Just say you love me, please."

Connie tried to pull Trisha's hand from the curtain, but Trisha wouldn't move. She and Jimbo stared at one another through the glass. Trisha's mouth was bleeding again, and Jimbo stood there, his handsome face calm, his dark eyes just a little bit worried, just sad enough to make you think he was sorry, just gentle enough to make you think he was safe. He was too good-looking, Connie thought, to get so mean.

She saw blood smeared on his green shirt with the alligator stitched on the front. He always wore those shirts and designer jeans. He liked to brag about those shirts he stole. She looked at his face, thought he looked like a sad little boy trying to look brave, the back straight, standing tall, but the mouth tight, the eyes looking down at some scary thing just there in the air between them. She forced her eyes to look at the blood on his shirt, not at the face of a sad boy. She stared hard at the dark stain of Trisha's blood on his shirt.

Trisha cried, "Go on, Jimbo. Tomorrow I'll come back and we can talk."

"I want you now!" he yelled. "I drove all the way out here!" He slapped his hand against the window. "God damn it, Trisha, you know I've been good to you."

Connie stepped back from the window, moved back toward the center of the living room to get away from the sight of that stain on his shirt, knowing if she looked long enough she would kill him. The gun was heavy in her hand, so heavy it pulled her arm, her shoulder, her whole body to a deep heavy place in the center of the room. Even if the house were burning down in that instant, she wouldn't be able to move. She saw Trisha reach, open the door, and heard the word "No!" jump from her mouth like a quick hard breath. The gun was so heavy. She tried to pull it up, hold it steady with both hands.

Jimbo stepped back from the open door. "Easy now, Connie. I'm not coming in." Trisha stood there holding the door knob, half leaning out toward Jimbo, but holding back to be safe from where his hand could reach. "Look at my face, Jimbo. Look what you did to me."

"I know what I did," he said in the quiet voice Connie hated. It made her shiver to hear a man talk as if he had the power to do anything, as if he were something more than a man that walked the earth on two legs and lived and died like everything else. But he did have a power with that voice. She had heard it in Larry, that deep man's voice that could make you put down the telephone when you were calling for help, that voice that wrapped around you like a rope, pulled you down, yanked at your chest while your feet carried you across the floor. Connie looked at Trisha, saw the voice work as her baby girl leaned against the door and cried.

Connie grabbed her under both arms and pulled her to the center of the living room. She felt strong, stronger than his voice as she turned and looked Jimbo in the face and said, "You leave her alone. I swear I'll blow your head off and tell the cops I thought you were a thief."

He looked down, shook his head. "I don't have to come in," he said. "Ask Trisha." He looked straight at Connie. "Ask Trisha if she wants to go."

Trisha was crying, crawling across the floor, looking for her shoes. Connie put the gun down in the corner of the room and gripped Trisha's arm and sat down beside her on the floor. She held her shoulders and tried to look into her daughter's eyes. She saw a swollen blotchy face that wasn't Trisha but some strange girl that stank with sweat and blood. "You don't have to go," Connie said. "In a few minutes he'll be gone, and I'll buy you all new stuff. I promise I'm gonna live a long time. I can do it, honey, I can live. Even the doctor said it's a matter of will."

Trisha shook her head and fought to get to the door. Connie looked up and saw Jimbo's face staring down at them. He looked peaceful. Even with the blood on his shirt, he looked happy as a man sitting on a bench and just watching the clouds change. He would wait all night if he had to because he knew he had the power. Connie cried, "Trisha, please!" She cringed at that old word, "Please," the sound that tore from her throat just before Larry had slammed her head against the wall. Trisha yanked her hands free, ran to the door, and was gone.

Connie sat on the floor and stared at the open door. Trisha had run off barefoot, with her nightgown flapping around her jeans. Connie saw the gun lying in the corner where she had put it down, out of the way, where it would do no harm. She had never even pushed back the safety catch.

She looked up at the door thrown open wide to the dark night. The house was still now. She couldn't remember when her head had felt so empty of human sound, those talking voices tangled and rushing, the old constant noise. She was empty now. Still. She heard tires screech somewhere in the distance. She heard crickets chirping loud and strong, the sound mixing with the pulse beating in her head, and she wondered if they had been singing like that while she and Trisha were screaming and Jimbo was talking so easy and winning just as he knew he would. The sound of the crickets filled the air, the house, her head, growing stronger, then fading, then stronger again, and she wondered how long had their song filled the night and how long would they sing. Connie strained to hear a human noise. Connie heard her heartbeat. She heard an owl scream in the trees.

If It Weren't for the Honeysuckle . . .

ESTELA PORTILLO TRAMBLEY

El Nido was one of many little villages lost deep in barranca country along the Sierra Madres in northern Mexico. Along a cluster of desert mountains, every so often a green hill rose and sank among mountains thick with dry brush, strewn with red stone, nearby muddy streams, and grass-covered crags. The village of El Nido lay on the eastern slope of a hidden mountain. Houses, huts, stores, a placita, and one large, abandoned mansion dotted this desert side, going down, down, until they reached low ground. A long time ago flash floods from a river on the western slope had driven people to high ground. But now the river was gone, dried up. Signs of a river existing in the past were visible where water still narrowed to dry patches surrounded by mud and arbustos polvorosos. Close to the top of the eastern slope a huge white church towered high and was visible from the western slope. From an ancient grove of wild elms, a footpath led for three miles from one side of the mountain to the other. The old riverbed on the west was banked by huge cottonwood trees, deep-rooted weeds of a primitive life. They were staunch and demanded little else than feeding from a deep subterranean river, for the source of life.

The only house around on this side of the mountain had been built on the dry surface of the riverbed; it was cradled in a world of greenness. One wall of the house was invaded by profuse honeysuckle vines. The house belonged to Beatriz. It had been built by Beatriz, who was now digging in the garden. She was a slender, small woman with wisps of brown hair and watery blue eyes. Her mother had had seven children. Two of them had died at a very young age, so Beatriz did not have a memory of them. But she had grown up with four older brothers. There had been many "fathers," so her mother claimed, but she remembered only one who had been a gachupín. She was the only fair-skinned child, so her mother had concluded that the wandering gachupín must have been Beatriz's father, but she wasn't sure. Beatriz as a child had been full of shame when her mother repeated the story as a joke, so she had run to her abuelita, who loved her and made her feel that she mattered in the world. But that had been many years before, in a distant village. Now she was a woman of thirty-nine. Past her youth, she had become part of the riverbed, the honeysuckle, and the giant trees. Together they were the music of a symbiotic breathing. Her desires and her dreams were like the intricate patterns of underground roots, a silent wildness.

It was a cool early morning and she had worked with total concentration around the tomato plants in her thriving vegetable garden. She was content like the fragrance of the moist earth. She worked a while longer, then leaned her body back to rest. Squinting, she looked out to the steeple of the church. Sometimes she imagined the steeple was looking over the mountain to see how she was doing. She made a mental note of things she had to do. She would take her vegetables into the village to sell. With the money she could buy a pane for the broken window. She had to wrap the brown sugar melcochas she had made for the kermes tomorrow at the church . . .

The voice of Sofía broke her reverie. "Mofi! Mofi! Come back—Mofi . . ."

Beatriz watched Sofía limp toward the cottonwoods, then stop, calling piteously, "Mofi! Mofi! Where are you?"

Beatriz wanted to tell her that her cat was never coming back, but she didn't have the heart. Sofía looked over to Beatriz with big, dark, liquid eyes that pleaded. "Do you think he'll come back?"

"I'll get you another cat," Beatriz consoled.

Sofía shook her head. "No. I want Mofi. I miss him so."

The younger woman looked hopelessly at Beatriz who many times felt an impatience with Sofía's fearful dependency. If only she had a little courage. Beatriz had grown to feel protective of Robles's other "wife." Robles's victim was more like it; Sofía, in her early twenties, looked thin and gaunt, her pretty face lined with worry. Her shoulders hunched, she clasped and unclasped her hands and began to whimper.

"Mofi's chasing butterflies somewhere." It was a wish more than a lie, and Beatriz said it only to stop Sofía's distress. It did make Sofía feel better. She imagined, "You think so?"

"Cats do that sometimes."

"I—I hope he's happy."

Beatriz wondered what Sofía knew about happiness, poor thing! The girl stiffened again and her face became distorted with fear. Beatriz asked, "What's the matter now?"

"You know he's coming today. Aren't you afraid?"

Beatriz's voice was steady and sure. "Not anymore." What she felt was loathing.

Sofía clutched Beatriz's arm, her eyes pleading for denial. "Today—he's coming today. I marked each day off on the calendar. The afternoon—he always comes in the afternoon."

"Or the middle of the night. Try to put it out of your mind. You make yourself miserable. Just keep out of his way."

"I'm so afraid . . ."

"I know . . . I know . . ." She reached out and held the younger woman to comfort her. Beatriz could feel the frail body tremble. "He wants you to be afraid. It gives him pleasure, don't you see?"

Sofía shook her head. "He broke my hip. A year ago . . ." She began to sob hysterically.

"The doctor said it can be fixed. You just wait and see. You'll be as good as new."

Sofía was wringing her hands; now she clasped them until her knuckles went white. Beatriz firmly unclasped them. "Listen to me . . ."

Sofía was not listening, still encapsulated in memories that terrified. Beatriz took her by the shoulders. "Look at me—I said look at me! I will not let him harm you—do you hear? Not anymore. What's going to kill you is pure fright. Do you know people have died of fright? Now, do as I say. Look out there, look at the trees, the sky, the climbing honeysuckle. Look! Everything is still wet from the rain, the tears that wipe us clean. Now, breathe in and smell the world . . ."

Sofía was responding to the world about. She was holding tight to Beatriz's hand. "Now, let go of my hand and let's go over there where I was digging. Yes, over there. Sit down. Here, beside me. Look . . ." Beatriz took a handful of moist, sweet earth and put it in Sofía's hand. "Smell it. Isn't it wonderful? When I do that it fills me with a gladness."

Sofía did exactly what Beatriz prescribed. The lines of worry were now gone from her face—the beginning of peace. Beatriz laughed softly. "This place will be ours forever, and our lives will be good. Our days are already good, aren't they?"

"Except when he comes . . ." Sofía's voice was edged with fear.

Beatriz quickly reassured, "He's not going to be around forever. He's tired, sick, old, and drink will be the end of him. Forget him; listen to the river sing . . ."

"You always hear it singing. I can't."

Beatriz began a song that came from earth, wind, and sky; it flowed like light in currents, deep currents of a glad heart. Sofía's fears were temporarily stilled.

After a while Sofía spoke in an almost hopeful voice. "I'll make breakfast."

She limped her way back to the cool kitchen. Beatriz tidied her hair, then she went to look at the wide, profuse tendrils of honeysuckle forming a geography of their own, vines extending in all directions. The tendrils crept in and out of the trellises Beatriz had made for their support. It had rained for three days and nights, making the greenness shockingly bright and heavy with sweetness. She looked up to the heavens, watching the clouds move with the secrets of rain-drops. The tapestry of earth and sky spelled out such a beautiful order to her, and she loved order above all things.

She had clipped and trimmed the honeysuckle so that it wouldn't choke itself. Its breadth was free to reach for the sun. But now she noticed that she had neglected the bottom growth close to the ground. Here the honeysuckle tangled chaotically. There were no ins and outs, but an overlapping and an entanglement that made her decide to clip and trim it that very afternoon. Six years before, she had planted the honeysuckle, two years after the house was finished. The joy of her house!

What had life been before the house? She remembered the little village of San José. She remembered four brothers and a mother. Most of all she remem-bered the grandmother who had bought old, tattered books for her to read. She recalled how she had met Robles through her brothers. At fourteen she had ridden her little donkey to town during la feria. The fair was held every year, and every year she and her brothers dyed turkey feathers to make headdresses to sell. Her grandmother had been dead a year, and she was not happy at home where she washed, ironed, and cooked for the family. She was a good work-horse to the family and nothing else. When she reached her brothers' booth she noticed an older man drinking with them. She listened to him talk about all the places he had been and was impressed because she had never been anywhere. How stupid she had been at fourteen! The forty-year-old Robles talked about all the things he would buy for her and all the places he would take her if she ran away with him. Her brothers, half-drunk and unconcerned, had kidded Robles. "Hey, leave her alone. You like them young, eh? Apestoso, you have a wife in every pueblo."

All of this had meant nothing to Beatriz. The prospect of a new dress and travel, the flattery of attention, and the thought that she would no longer be a slave to her coarse brothers and a mother—who cared little for her because she was only a girl—it was enough for her to take up Robles on his offer. At fourteen, there had been no thoughts about consequences.

The lunacy of being a woman! She had run away with Robles in his vegeta-ble truck; for three years she had lived in the back of it. Yes, he had bought her a dress, the only thing he ever bought her. Three years of utter misery, for Robles was worse than her brothers. He went into violent rages when he was drunk. He beat her and raped her at intervals, and there was nothing Beatriz could do. From village to village, three years of sleeping on dirty vegetables or piles of manure, with no cover against rain or freezing weather. She planned to run away, so she memorized how to start the truck and drive it—all in her head. One time he had left her on the outskirts of a pueblo while he visited one of his "wives." She stole the key without his knowing and took off in the truck. But as fortune would have it, she had driven the truck straight into a tree. Dazed and bleeding, she tried to flee on foot, but Robles caught up with her and beat her unconscious.

She lay bruised and swollen in the back of the truck without food or water, wishing she could die, while he drove for two days along a road she had never seen. When she felt better, hunger became an awful gnawing in her stomach. She raised herself up to a sitting position and reached for some turnips to eat. Her mouth was parched and she longed for a drink of water. Robles was driving down a road following a dry riverbed. As they reached the bottom of the hill, she noticed that the world had turned green. Suddenly the truck stopped.

Robles got out of the truck and walked to a broken-down, skeletal shack in the middle of the riverbed. Beatriz, spying a little stream snaking through cottonwoods, found her way to the water. She was washing her face after a long drink when Robles came up behind her and announced, "This is my land."

"Your land? You mean you own it?" She could not believe it; an excitement began to grow. "You mean we're home?"

He laughed disdainfully, as if he had heard a bad joke. "Home? What home?"

Beatriz was beside herself. She ran to the shack, touching its walls, walking into the windowless, doorless, single room that lacked even a roof. "Home ..." She savored the word as if it were holy.

He laughed his cruel laugh again and ordered, "Get back in the truck. We're leaving."

"Why did you bring me here?" she demanded.

"To show you I am a man of property. It's good land. The river's underneath. But I don't stay in one place. You know that. Let's go."

"I'm staying. I'm going to build a house right here."

"You're crazy." He spat out the words. "Stay—I don't care. When I come back, I'll find only your bones. You'll be a good meal for the coyotes up in the hills." Then he had left.

She ran back to the truck to salvage her grandmother's Bible. That night she had prayed to the Virgin Mary. In the dark she visualized the kind face of her grandmother who had truly loved her. She remembered the thin, veined hands that had held the Bible, the wisps of white hair that had escaped a tight bun at the nape of her neck. She remembered the smell of the old woman's apron as she had laid her head against her abuelita's breast while being taught to read. Oh, the warmth of that love! Oh, the magic of words! Her only possession was her grandmother's Bible, but she had also left her a legacy—a passion for reading. Alone, in the cold, dark shack, when the wind moaned and coyotes howled in the hills, she held the Bible close to her heart and envisioned la anciana who had loved her so. It warmed her; courage glowed.

On the second day, hunger made her go into the village to find work. She had found work in a taquería, washing dishes, then later becoming the cook in the small restaurant. There was enough money now to take care of her small needs and a few extra pesetas to save in a glass jar. When she had saved enough, she began to buy wood, nails, adobe, a hammer. It had gone so slow, so slow, the building of her house—never enough pesetas, never enough time for building. But she never stopped, never gave up. It was the only thing with meaning in her life.

She shook herself free of the memories. There was too much to do. She went back to the house and found Sofía busy in the kitchen. Lucretia was asleep on the cot. Over the wall hung a calendar with a picture of the Virgin wearing a painted smile, passive and calm. Beatriz stared at the bright aura around the saintly face and wondered if she heard their prayers every night, prayers for the safety of the girl-child sleeping so soundly, so innocently. She must never be another victim.

Sofía was pouring water into a pan for cereal. She stood waiting for the water to boil, staring at it with a numb, forlorn look on her face. When it began to boil, she poured in some dry cereal and stirred it round and round. So many things baffled Sofía, so many terrors invaded her life, that Beatriz understood these moments of blocking out existence, this floating into a nothingness. All dreams had been beaten out of Sofía.

She had come into their lives furtive and lost. Robles had found her on a mountain road. She had crossed Snake Mountain and its terrors. Suffering from exposure and starvation, Sofía had taken the liquids given to her by Beatriz with the frozen look of death on her young face. But she had recovered, and recovered quickly, but not soon enough so that Robles would stay to abuse her and use her for his pleasure. Sofía had been the first victim Robles had brought to her. Beatriz had ministered to her needs with patience and compassion for she had been a lost creature in the world herself.

Sofía had become very attached to her. In time she had told Beatriz her story. She had lived in a poor farm in San Angelo with her parents, two teenage brothers and a three-month-old baby sister. They all had died violently. Her father and two brothers had been killed in a feud over the piece of land where their house had stood. The killers had burnt down the house, but Sofía, her mother, and the baby had escaped. They had found themselves crossing La Montaña de las Víboras. The mother had made the choice out of hysteria and desperation. It was a deadly mountain, a mountain of stone and poisonous snakes. But it was the dead heat of the days and the cold of the nights that had given the mother a fever, driving her to her death. The baby had died of hunger when there was no more milk from the mother. Sofía dug their graves with her hands and buried them; she had wanted to dig a grave for herself, to lie in it and wait for death. Instead she had fallen asleep in total exhaustion. She slept a long, long time; then, half out of her mind, she made the perilous climb to the top.

Beatriz listened to the story of the sixteen-year-old with tears in her eyes and a wanting to protect the girl from Robles. He had ordered Beatriz to clean her up so he could take her for a "wife." The older woman shuddered at the horror awaiting the girl. She had to be warned. "Sofía, the man who brought you here is a beast. He wants you for his 'wife.' You know what that means?"

The girl nodded. "Are you his wife?"

A bitter laugh from Beatriz. "He has women all over. Victims, like you and me. Go, go, while you can."

"Why do you stay?"

"This is my house. My house. I built it. But you can still escape. I'll take you to the village. Sometimes he stays away for a long time. When I was building this house, he stayed away for five years. He never goes to the village. A long time ago he cut up a man badly in a bar fight, so he stays away. I'll help you find a job there."

But Sofía had found a protector in the world. She felt safe in the house with Beatriz. She could not be convinced. So it had happened, as it had happened to Beatriz so long ago, the violation, the cruelties. Somehow Sofía had survived it all, but she had been crippled in body and spirit by Robles and had become totally dependent on Beatriz.

Sofía shuffled over to the sleeping Lucretia, and Beatriz knew she was thinking the same thing: "How are we going to save her from him?"

She looked at Beatriz beseechingly. "He's coming this afternoon. What are you going to do?"

Always, she had to have the answers; always she was to be the buttress. She loved Sofía and pitied her helplessness. She had no solution. Yet there must be a solution. Ways came to her mind. "We can tell him she died."

"Of cholera?" Sofía was not satisfied.

"That's the way he brought her to us. He expected her to die."

"Yes, he did . . . yes, he did." There was a tinge of hope in Sofía's voice.

"We'll get her out of the house." A plan was growing in Beatriz's mind. "We'll send her to the church to help with the booths for the kermes. Señora Acosta can feed her supper at the rectory. I'll send a note to Father Ruiz asking him to put her to work until we get there."

"Get there?"

"For rosary services this evening."

Doubt hovered in Sofía's voice. "He won't believe us. What if he goes to the village?"

"He never goes to the village."

Sofía sat down, her body quivering. "He'll kill us. Everytime he comes, I tell myself today is the day, the day we die."

Beatriz s face tightened with impatience as she pulled Sofía out into the garden. "Now stop it. You want to awaken her? Frighten her?"

Sofía remembered. "She doesn't even know about Robles . . ."

"Do you see how important it is to get her out of the house? It's the beginning of a plan. I'll work out the rest. Right now let's do something sensible. Work puts things together, makes things clear." Beatriz really believed it. It had been a point of salvation in her life. "We're out of herbs. Let's cut some herbs."

Beyond the vegetable garden was her bed of herbs growing profusely. Beatriz knelt down and started to loosen the earth around her plants. There was altamisa and estafiate for stomachache, carcomeca for cleaning out the body, masta for the nerves. Beatriz began to cut the té de tila from the mountain of the Yaqui seers. Sofía recognized it. "Isn't that the tea you brew for Robles?"

"Yes. It numbs pain and relaxes the body. Here, taste it. It's sweet."

Sofía took a leaf and put it in her mouth, chewing it slowly. Again, a thought. "I wish it were poison."

"We'll make him some tila to make him sleep."

If only he would sleep forever, thought Beatriz. There must be a way . . .

Lucretia appeared at the kitchen door. "Why did you let me sleep so late?" Then she reminded the two women, "You left the cereal on the stove. It boiled over."

Beatriz stood up, her apron full of herbs, and walked up to Lucretia. She kissed the girl's cheek. "I don't feel like eating cereal anyway. We can have fruit, bread and butter, and a good cup of coffee. How does that sound?"

Lucretia laughed. "Oh, yes!"

Beatriz and Sofía looked at the girl-child with soft blowing hair and bare feet, a child of god, full of love, full of trust. Beatriz and Sofía looked at each other. Their eyes said, Our child is happy and content. Garden, sun, morning, birds—all were a symphony of peace.

Beatriz led the way into the kitchen. "Let's make some breakfast then."

· · ·

Lucretia had been informed about her day helping out for the kermes.

"All day?"

"Yes, they'll need you all day. Give Mrs. Acosta my note, and she'll fix supper for you and Father Ruiz."

"Why can't you come?"

Beatriz fumbled for an answer. "Sofía needs help with the dolls she's making for the kermes."

Lucretia searched Beatriz's face with a question. "Where did you get all the books you have?"

Beatriz was somewhat startled by the question. "Books?"

"Yes, you have so many."

"Why do you ask that?"

"Because Father Ruiz told me you have read more books than all the people in the village, including the doctor. You told me you never went to school. Where did you get them?"

"I got them." Beatriz's words were strained and tight. She changed the subject. "Time to get started, before the sun gets too hot."

"I'll wait for the both of you before rosary," Lucretia remembered as she made her way up the path toward the road. She waved at the approaching Sofía who had been out looking for her cat. Both women watched her until she disappeared behind the bend of cottonwoods. Sofía brought Beatriz back to the reality of Robles. "He'll come soon."

Robles, a man who crushed souls between his teeth. Robles who came in kicking furniture, breaking things, cursing, full of drink. The rage had to be vented. He would find his favorite victim, Sofía. In the beginning, Beatriz would interfere when he beat Sofía, so he had turned on her, until she could no longer endure it. Again and again she warned Sofía, "I can't come between you and Robles when he's in a rage. Go—hide—don't let him see you. If you're not around, I can calm him down much better."

"I can't leave you alone with him." Sofía didn't understand.

"He's afraid of me," Beatriz explained. "But he smells your fear like an animal. It excites him. He's rotten."

Sometimes Sofía disappeared into the woods when they heard his truck on the road. But there were other times when he caught them unaware. Poor Sofía! Nothing could stop him when the rage was high. Soon Sofía lay crumpled and whimpering on the floor. Beatriz would step in when the rage was nearly spent. She would place a firm hand on his arm and say ominously, "No more."

He would stare with incredulous, bleary eyes but, with a slobbering, hanging mouth, he would obey. And she knew why. There had come the day when she could no longer take his blows. After beating her, he had fallen asleep in a drunken stupor. Beatriz had taken the small, sharp ax she used to cut vines and jumped on the bed, straddling his bloated belly. She grabbed him by the hair and beat his head against the headboard until he came to his senses, bleary and stinking of panic. Full of hate, holding the ax high over his head, she had threatened, "If you ever lay a hand on me again, I'll split your head." Gulping his astonishment and fright, Robles looked into the eyes of a woman who would not hesitate to kill. She had hissed menacingly, "I can do it while you're asleep—any time."

But now, at the mention of his name, Beatriz shared Sofía's dread. It crawled through her skin. How could they save Lucretia? She would never allow the filthy animal to take the child's innocence. It was up to her. It was always up to her.

Sofía's face flushed darkly. "Let's go away. The three of us. The city—he'll never look there."

Beatriz felt a rush of anger. "To beg in the streets? To sleep in alleys? To starve? This is my house!"

Sofía was relentless. "Your house is on his property. Everytime he comes, he claims the house—says it's legally his. Let's just leave. He's going to throw us out anyway."

"Didn't you hear? This is my house! My house!" The fury in Beatriz's voice made Sofía cringe.

"My house is my life," reasoned an anguished Beatriz. "It's my self. It's my reward for suffering, for the pain of degradation. It's my haven, my ordered world." How could she make Sofía understand that she would never leave it? Leave the house? Struggle out in the world without anything? Never again. "Out there, Sofía, it's no different from the mountain where your mother died, no different from the violence of the men who killed your family. It destroys the spirit inside. This house, it's our haven, our peace, our order, a place to raise our girl, to see her go to school, even make a good marriage."

"A good marriage . . ." Sofía savored the words without really understanding.

Beatriz continued, "The earth beneath my feet wants me here. The house wants me here. I gave up my soul for this house."

"Your soul? Sofía held her breath in disbelief, expelling it with the same self-question, "Your soul?"

"Hurricanes die down, floods recede, and volcanoes stop vomiting their fire. Somehow, I don't know why, an order comes about afterward, and flowers grow, like honeysuckle, sweet as the breath of heaven."

"Are you all right?"

"I'm fine. So many terrible things have happened to me, to you. Don't you see? We deserve this place, this peace."

The sudden clatter of birds' wings reminded Beatriz of things to be done, of finding a way out of a hell called Robles. She must keep busy to dispel a growing fear, a fear that could overwhelm. Work, put something in order, then things would be clear, and hope would find some kind of solution. She had to trim the honeysuckle. Oh, the greenness of the world! There she could find a wondrous tranquility, a good clean impartiality, for a little while. She approached Sofía, put her arm around the frightened woman, promising, "I'll find a way. I'll make things right."

She felt some of the tenseness leave Sofía's body. Beatriz told her, "I'm going to keep busy. That's when I can sort things out. I have to trim the bottom of the honeysuckle."

Sofía walked to the kitchen door, stopped, turned, and asked in soft compliance, "Shall I make something?"

"He'll expect food. What do you have? Oh, I know, the chicken."

"I already cut it up for soup. He likes chicken soup."

"Let's both keep busy then." She repeated the words to herself. Beatriz had no doubt there was salvation in work. She picked up her ax and a rusty spade and made her way to the honeysuckle vines. She examined the bottom and found incrustations growing in a wilderness. Traces of three days' rain everywhere. Her strokes with the small hatchet were swift and trained. The vines could hardly breathe. She set about to give the bottom of the vines some kind of space, a path for the vines to find the sun. She worked in full absorption for a while. The church bell had announced the noon hour as she came to the side of the wall where there was little sun. Moisture was visible on leaves and petals. She lifted the vines to find the main artery, the one to lie salvaged when the rest were cut away. In the cool darkness of the undergrowth she saw a whiteness gleam.

Three white, fruiting, amanitas, full blown, forming the usual fairy ring. The ring was completed by smaller stumps of spores that had failed fruition. But the three, the three, these beautiful three were a blown reproduction of a whiteness found in dreams. Beatriz stared in fascination. An excitement grew in her and her blood found a song, "I shall find a way, a way ..." She looked up at the climbing honeysuckle and felt its triumphal presence. A breathing, smiling god looked down at her, the vestal maiden. The honeysuckle had given her a gift, an answer to her problems. She did not doubt; she touched the white glories with a growing assurance. But she had to be careful, for the pollen of the amanitas burned the skin. She swiftly cut them with the ax and put them in her apron pocket. Then she went back to her work, cutting the small, overlapping vines away from the main stem. The flowers on the honeysuckle vines had a brilliant timbre—trumpets of freedom, trumpets of freedom. She had to tell Sofía. She went back to the coolness of the kitchen and found Sofía cutting up cilantro and garlic. The chicken was already simmering in a pot. Sofía looked furtively toward the door when Beatriz entered.

"We're going to have an abundance of squash and onions this season," Beatriz informed Sofía as she made her way to wash her hands.

"He'll come anytime now. Are we going to do it? Tell him Lucretia's dead?" Sofía's questions were thick with doubt.

"Yes, died of cholera. We couldn't save her. She died like the rest of her family."

"The plan will do for today, but what about the next time he comes?"

"There won't be a next time." Beatriz's words rang clear, mixing with the soft shadows in the room. When she heard the impossible, Sofía turned and looked at Beatriz intently, narrowing her eyes in disbelief. "No next time?"

"I've found the answer. How we can rid ourselves of the beast."

"Rid ourselves?"

Beatriz reached into the pocket of her apron and took out the three amanitas. "They are the gift of the honeysuckle."

"Poison mushrooms?"

"Yes."

"For Robles?"

"Yes . . . the fruit of freedom."

"No, not that way . . ." Sofía recoiled at the thought.

"Then what way, Sofía? You asked me to make things right. Well, this plan was fated by the gods."

"What gods? Don't talk like that. You frighten me."

"I need your help."

"I can't." Sofía was crumbling again.

"You rather he rape Lucretia? Throw us out of my house? Beat you to death? He can, and he will one day. This way is so easy, Sofía."

"To take a life?" Sofía asked righteously.

"To kill the dragon with seven heads."

"It's murder, Beatriz."

"Listen to me! I'm tired of picking up the broken pieces. You snivel and cry and grovel in fear all day long, clinging to my skirts like the coward that you are. You left it up to me, remember?"

"Not this way, please, not this way!"

"For once in your life, be brave. The gods are on our side."

"There are no gods on our side. You're thinking crazy."

"He's forcing our hand. It's his doing, Sofía. He comes into our lives like a bellowing wounded pig, destroying everything in his path, maiming. He's so miserable. You really think he wants to live?" Beatriz had to defeat Sofía's convictions.

"Everybody wants to live," Sofía answered lamely.

"Like Mofi?" Beatriz knew this was her trump card.

"What do you mean?"

"I saw him kill Mofi. He grabbed Mofi by the tail and smashed her head against the wall after you ran out, after he beat you."

"He killed Mofi?" Sofía's stricken face refused to believe.

"He'll do the same to us." Beatriz knew she had won.

"Killed Mofi? Killed my furry ball of love? For no reason . . ." The weaker woman folded in pain.

"Robles? Reason?" Beatriz's voice was strident with scorn. Sofía's eyes were wild, all the terror in her life welled. She was full of the energy called hate. She walked up and down, all moral convictions were pushed away, giving place to rage.

"You're right! Dragon with seven heads! No, no—he's a scorpion. I used to kill scorpions in the fields. They would leave me with the babies, the women who gave birth out in the fields. I was just a girl then. I would wrap the baby and cover it with sand up to the shoulders, always under a shade tree. The cool sand would keep the baby alive. The mother would go back to work in the fields. It was my job to kill any scorpions that came near the baby. I killed them with a rock. I can kill a scorpion."

Then Sofía floated into a pain all her own. She sang her pain for Mofi. "No, no, no, no . . ." Beatriz waited quietly for the pain to spend itself. Then she broke the silence. "How else can we save our child?"

.   .   .

Beatriz had cut flowers for the table. The chicken soup was simmering on the stove. She removed the pot from the fire and set about to washing and slicing the amanitas. When they formed a little heap on the cutting board, she stared at the brownish-white pile. Mixed feelings were mounting. A kind of wary anticipation, a tinge of fear, but there was no sense of guilt. Why don't I feel any guilt? she asked herself. She pushed the thought aside as she looked for a smaller pot to pour the portion of chicken soup that was to be Robles's. She poured it into a blue enamel pan, then she threw in the mushrooms. She glanced over at Sofía who sat immobile, numb. She knew her companion was paralyzed by fear and guilt. She was waiting for the sound of Robles's truck. After watching the pieces of mushroom float and dance in the liquid, mixing well with the cilantro and small potatoes, Beatriz sat down at the kitchen table and faced Sofía. She knew why she felt no guilt. She knew too well and she had to tell someone. "I know it's wrong, Sofía, I know it'll work, and I know why I feel no guilt."

"I wish I could be calm like you." Sofía's tearful voice wavered. "Look at you! You even put flowers on the table. Why did you put flowers on the table?"

Beatriz knew it was an accusation. It didn't matter. She smiled at Sofía as she explained. "I feel as if we have been caged for a lifetime, and now we have the key to open the door to freedom. Don't you feel that?"

Sofía shook her head. "Free? What about the weight of the guilt I'm feeling?"

Beatriz confessed. "I only feel this—this pleasure in my guts. The thought of seeing Robles dead . . ."

"Stop!" Sofía clenched her hands and lowered her head.

"Sofía, is there something wrong with me?" Beatriz reached out and put her hands over Sofía's. "I feel as if there were something unholy and heartless in me. Maybe, maybe because it isn't the first time—the first time I've taken a life.

"You've . . . you've . . ." Sofía dared not even think it, much less say it.

"Don Carlos. You know that big mansion, the one that's all boarded up in the village? That was his house. I used to work for him."

"I heard he died of a heart attack. Didn't he?" Sofía's soft eyes were pleading for an answer.

Beatriz was caught in painful memories. "Day after day after day, the exhaustion, the defeat. I would fall asleep with a saw in my hand, nails in my mouth. I could not stop, I could not rest—the house, the house had to be built. Many times I went hungry; I bought adobes instead. I would forget I had not eaten for days and went on working and working on the house. It was like a fever that kept me going, never stopping, until my body just collapsed. I would pass out, then come to, deluding. In my head—or maybe I really saw it—I imagined it, so real, so real. I'd see the house completed—windows, walls, doors, all finished. Delirium? Perhaps. Deep, deep down I knew I didn't have the strength, the money, or the time to build it by myself . . ."

"But you did it."

"No, no—not by myself. I went to work for Don Carlos as a housekeeper. The job paid a little more than what I made at the taquería. I had heard that Don Carlos was a wise and learned man. When I saw his study, with books covering wall after wall, I knew it was true. In the winter the long walk from here to his house left me frozen. I would make the walk before sunrise so I could go into the house early on these cold mornings, make myself a cup of tea, and then go to his study and read and read and read. He slept late into the morning, so the old man never knew. It was so wonderful, all the worlds that opened up to me . . ."

"The books in your room. That's where they came from?"

"They were his."

"He gave them to you."

"No." Beatriz's face was taut with bitter memories. "He knew about the house. He would make jokes about it, not in a vicious way. But he knew I would never be able to do it by myself. One day he handed me this paper to sign, an agreement, he said. If I promised to stay for one year and do everything he said, he would give me enough money for materials and workers to help me finish the house. Of course I signed it. I never imagined . . . I thought he was a man to be respected for his years and his position in the town. One day I was changing the bedding in his room when I saw him at the door, watching me. I knew what he wanted. He told me to take off my clothes and lie on the bed.

Oh, the obscenity of that bed! It was his playpen and I became his plaything. I felt so unclean, so worthless."

Beatriz covered her mouth as if to stifle a scream, her body shuddering with remembered disgust. He hurt my body, maimed my soul. Two months later, he caught me reading. For some reason he awakened early and found me in his study. He grabbed the book from me and hit me across the face. He was enraged. How dare I read his books! My mere touch defiled them; to him I was no more than an animal. Then he laughed. A joke, he said, a joke! How did I learn to read, a nothing like me? He threw me out of the room and had a locksmith put a lock on the door. The only key hung on his key chain. Oh, he was old and feeble and had a bad heart. When I went to work for him he had given me careful instructions about his medicine. Oh, the gods are just! The very next afternoon, after the lock had been put in, he was playing like an idiot with my naked body when he started to choke and his face turned purple. I knew it was a heart attack. He pointed a bony finger toward his medicine, his eyes pleading. I did nothing. Then, while he watched helpless and dying, I found his key chain, took the key that unlocked the study, dangled it before his face, and walked away. I had mercifully refused him his pitiful life."

Sofía was moaning, "I'm so sorry, so sorry . . ." Beatriz was by her side, comforting. "It happened a long time ago. It's all gone now. I remember going down to the study, opening the door, and taking book after book. There were so many. While he lay dead on his bed, I found some boxes, packed the books. I paid a boy to take them to the rectory. Days later, they found him dead and closed up the house. Little by little I brought all the books here. They never questioned me about his death or about the books. So you see, I helped him to die. I felt the same pleasure then as I feel now. I feel no guilt. Absolutely no guilt . . ."

The sound of Robles truck broke the silence of the outside world. Sofía's eyes widened in terror. "It's h—him."

Beatriz went to the door, then gave rapid, short orders to Sofía. "Wipe that look from your face. Don't say anything. Keep out of his way. Whatever you do, for our sake, don't break down, understand? Let me handle him."

Sofía was looking around the room in desperation, as if trying to find a place to escape to. A wild question came to her lips. "Where's Mofi? Did you bury Mofi?" She moaned, her hands clenched in prayer, eyes tightly closed to erase the world. "It's him—it's him . . ."

Beatriz took Sofía's face in her hands and observed harshly, "He's clever, he can read what's on your face and you're going to get us killed. Is that the way you want it?"

Sofía's horror mounted with the truck door's slam and the sound of heavy trudging steps coming to the door. The uneven steps were muffled by loud cursing. Fungus of the world, thought Beatriz. He was drunk, but that was in

their favor: he would be dull witted, thick tongued, and wanting sleep. Yes—
yes, it was better that way. The swollen poison stood in the doorway. Beatriz
felt no fear.

Robles was breathing hard and his face was pale. His eyes were unseeing.
He made his way unsteadily to a chair and slumped down heavily. His head
fell forward into his hands as he made deep retching sounds. He was going to
vomit, Beatriz was sure. Yes, he stood and headed for the bathroom. He pushed
Beatriz roughly aside, then disappeared into the other room. Soon the sounds
of heaving and vomiting filled the room. Beatriz motioned to Sofía to stay in
the shadows while she sat at the table calmly until he emerged from the
bathroom. He looked like a sick animal as he tried to focus through his bleari-
ness.

"I feel sick."

Beatriz smiled. "Want to lie down?"

"Eh?"

"You should lie down. I'll get you a cold compress."

Robles nodded, stumbled to the cot, and fell heavily on it. In the dark corner
Sofía grimaced and closed her eyes tightly. Beatriz quickly and efficiently rose
to get a basin which she filled with cold water, then she found a wash cloth and
made her way to the cot. She sat down by his side, wrung out the cloth, and
placed it on Robles's forehead. She did it several times until he mumbled his
satisfaction. "Ahhh."

Beatriz motioned to Sofía with her head. "Put the tea kettle on. A cup of
tila tea will settle his stomach. It'll help him relax. That's what you need—
your cup of tea."

He groaned his answer. "Awww."

Beatriz turned to Sofía who was already lighting the stove. "Take out the
whiskey." She wiped Robles's face again. "You'll feel much better. I'll even
put a little whiskey in it."

He opened his mouth, exposing rotten teeth. "Ahhh."

Beatriz informed him, "We have a whole bottle of whiskey, don't we,
Sofía?"

Sofía stuttered, "Y-y-yes."

"Whiskey?" Robles showed signs of interest.

It's better than the tequila you've been drinking all day." She had to find
out how much he had drunk.

"Beer," was the sullen response.

"Beer? You must have finished a barrel." Beatriz calculated the alcohol in
the man.

"Uh-huh," was his thick response.

He'll fall asleep—he'll fall asleep right after we feed him the chicken soup.
He'll give us no trouble, thank God. Beatriz relaxed, coaxing, "I'll take off

your shoes, bring you a basin with warm water and baking soda to soak your feet."

"Vieja." A tinge of suspicion in his voice.

"¿Sí?"

"You're still getting out of my house, you and that cripple!"

Her mind clicked—the injustices of the world—men had decreed that living things were not equal. Men had decreed that women should be possessions, slaves, pawns, in the hands of men with ways of beasts. It had been decreed that women should admire a manhood that simply wasn't there.

Beatriz gave no answer to his threat. She just sat by his side, her face carved in hate. She had to help Sofía with the tea. She made her way to Sofía who was already pouring the tea into a cup, the cup precariously sliding on the plate held by her trembling hand. Beatriz took the whiskey bottle and poured some into the cup, then took it to Robles, saying, "It'll make you feel so much better."

Robles, slumped against the wall on the cot, turned to face her, groaning and moaning. He sat up shakily, with great effort, then stood, reeling, his body swaying in a circle. "I can drink it myself, cabrona. Give it to me!"

He snatched it out of her hand, spilling the tea all over his shirt. The drunk let out a howl like a maddened bull and struck Beatriz across the face. The blow froze her. Robles glared at her, his eyes wondering why she had taken the blow without a word. Sofía fell into a chair, head in hands, swaying back and forth, whimpers writhing out of her throat. Robles taunted, "Beatriz, where's your ax, eh?"

Beatriz smiled resignedly. "I'll get you another cup."

She went to the stove and filled the cup again, pouring whiskey with a steady hand. With a subservient gesture, she offered it to him again. He gulped it down, then threw the cup against the wall, screaming his demand, "Give me the whiskey!" Without a word, Beatriz handed him the bottle. As he took it, he glared at her warily, then drank, slurping, as it ran from the sides of his mouth. He looked around the room. "Where's the girl?"

Sofía was sobbing now. Beatriz had to be careful. He might not believe her. "Lucretia died, Robles."

"Died?" He would not believe it. Sofía's wild sobs angered him. "Shut up! Shut up! You cripple!" He glowered with disbelief, repeating, "Died, eh?" He grabbed Beatriz's arm. "You're lying, you piece of shit!"

Disdainfully, she removed his fingers from her arm. She felt her senses floating in a great calm. There is no storm, no storm. Again a power suffused her, the same feeling as when she had denied Don Carlos his medicine . . . a savoring of revenge. Now, to function on volition, deliberate machinations, to appease him, to dull his senses, a mortal gesture against the kind of death Robles brought with him every time. Any fear in her had dwindled away.

Robles was screaming in her ear, "Where is she? Don't you try to fool me, you slut!"

"Don't you remember? She was so sick when you brought her to us. You told us her whole family had died of cholera. How could she survive?"

"When did she die?"

"About a week after you left her here."

"I know a lying whore when I hear one," he hissed vehemently. Suddenly he turned on Sofía. "I'll get the truth out of that sniveling coward!" He made a grab for the cowering woman, dragged her by the hair, then, twisting her arm, he brought her to her feet. Sofía screamed in pain. "The truth, you garbage!"

A long scream of pain came from her throat. "She's d-e-a-d!"

He twisted her arm as if to break it. Sofía was choking in her own pain. She could stand no more. "She's in the village . . . the . . . village . . ."

He threw Sofía to the floor to confront Beatriz. But Beatriz did not give way: she looked him in the eye. "We did it for you."

"For me?"

Beatriz saw bewilderment on his face. She continued, "Look at you! You want Lucretia to see you like this? Is that the way a bride-groom should look? You need a shave and a bath and, above all, rest—so you can be at your best for your new bride. I have a clean shirt for you. Don't you want her to be proud of her husband? She's waiting for us to fetch her."

There was a mixture of confusion and anticipation on his face. He couldn't believe, but he wanted to believe, his feelings and thoughts in disarray. She smiled at him with unafraid eyes. He asked, "Waiting?"

"Yes, Sofía and I are going for her when you're ready. Now you tell me, you don't want her to see you like that. You want to be in your full manly vigor when you take her. To have that kind of strength, you need food and rest, then you'll be like new."

She could tell 'he liked what she was saying. She continued the coaxing, easy and calm, for she knew she had the upper hand now. The beast would eat out of her hand. "I made a pot of chicken soup for you. I know you haven't eaten for days. I made it just the way you like it, with small potatoes, celery, garlic, cilantro. You eat and rest. It's three miles to the village. By the time we come back with her, you will have rested."

Sofía picked herself up while listening to Beatriz as if it all were happening in a dream. She was caught, mesmerized by the confidence Beatriz exuded. Beatriz pulled out a chair for Robles. "Now you sit down, and I'll get you a bowl of delicious soup. Then I'll go look for your shaving things."

Robles sat down at the table. There was what might have passed for a smile on his face. When Beatriz brought him his soup, he inquired, "Pretty, eh, after you cleaned her up?"

"Beautiful! Eat your soup. Doesn't it smell delicious?" She turned to Sofía, asking with a lightness in her voice, "Bring glasses. We have to drink to Robles and his future bride."

Still dazed by Beatriz's euphoric state, by her daring, Sofía did as she was told. Beatriz poured some whiskey in each glass, then handed one to Robles and another one to Sofía. She raised her own. "To you, dear Robles. May the future bring all you deserve."

The three drank the whiskey, then Beatriz sat opposite Robles and watched as he took the first mouthful of soup. "It's not too hot, is it?"

Robles savored the first spoonful, then commented, "It has mushrooms. You forgot to tell me it had mushrooms."

Sofía could not stand it anymore. She silently slipped out of the house. Beatriz knew the poor woman was repelled by the smiling cat playing with the mouse. Robles had eaten his bowl of soup too fast. "Here I'll fill your bowl again, then I'll leave you to enjoy your food. Remember, it's a long way to the village. So you have time for a nap. You can clean up afterward, long before we return."

He merely nodded and continued eating. At the kitchen door, Beatriz turned to look at him one last time. Lucretia had been saved from the pestilence. Her skein of order would be maintained, with no more furies to defile it. She stepped into the yard, breathing in the brightness of the sun.

. . .

The waiting had created new tears. Sofía asked desperately, "How long does it take?"

"I looked in and he had gone to bed. He's sleeping peacefully."

"Maybe he's dead already. I don't believe it. It was too easy."

Beatriz assured her, "It'll be soon. He probably passed out with all that drink in him."

"Isn't there any pain, any symptoms?"

"Usually there are cramps, dizziness, vomiting. He's snoring like a pig."

"Aren't you afraid?"

"Of what?"

"Of going to hell . . . after what we've done."

"A merciful thing, Sofía. He's old and tired and so miserable."

Beatriz knew Sofía did not believe her. Their two different worlds were forever bound by a single action. Hell? wondered Beatriz. I don't believe in a hell. Words from the Bible began to run in her head. They fell from her lips with joy. " 'And the earth was without form and void, and darkness was upon the face of the deep. Then God divided the light from the darkness and He said, "Let the earth bring forth grass, the herb yielding seed, and the fruit tree yielding fruit after its kind." ' Oh, Sofía, look at all the gladness God made. This house, this yard, is a piece of his heaven."

"I don't think you believe in God," Sofía accused. Still, she asked, "Do you?"

"I don't know, Sofía. I believe in the greenness of the earth. Listen! The river's singing again. Can't you hear it?"

"No. It's only a dry riverbed."

"I will teach you how to listen. I have such plans for us. First, our trip to the city to fix your hip. Then Lucretia must go to school . . ."

"I don't want to hear them now. How can you be so sure he's going to die?"

"I'm sure."

"You sound so evil."

"No, Sofía, not evil. I love order around me more than anything. Yes, there's a wildness in me from all the things that have happened in our lives, the sadness, the loneliness, the violences. They grow inside us—mix—and become something I cannot explain. Remember when we were walking home from church one Sunday evening and we saw a couple in the park? They were kissing—remember?"

"Yes. You said the moon hurt so much."

Beatriz replied in sweet cadence, "It wasn't the moon. It was not knowing the love of a good man. Maybe that's what happens: we cannot love or believe —for a while. We'll have to learn, Sofía."

"You really think there are good men in the world?"

"Oh, Sofía, there must be—somewhere."

The sun was deep in the west now, the sky a darker blue. They sat on the sweet grass, listening. No sounds came from the house. But the sounds of the world combined into a distant and shadowy beginning. The steeple of the church shone with the setting sun. Beatriz intuitively knew it was time now. She stood up, then cleaned off her skirt and tidied her hair, a ritual. She put out her hand and helped Sofía to her feet. Together they walked toward the house with fresh momentum, a sturdy confidence. Beatriz went straight to the cot where the figure of Robles lay. Sofía followed her. Sofía whispered, "Is he dead?"

"Not yet. He's in a coma."

Robles eyes were wide open, and his mouth had a slight twitch that looked almost like a smile. Suddenly, the death rattle cut the silence like a filament of hollowness, something without roots, something lost in the course of evolution. For the two women, peace wore a bright design. Beatriz came to the next order of things. "We have to bury him."

"Bury him?"

"Yes, and I know exactly where. Where I found the amanitas, in that soft dark corner, underneath the honeysuckle vines. I'll get the shovel."

They dug for a long time, using the shovel and a bucket. They finished when the dark had fully cloaked the light. They wrapped him in sheets, dragged him out, and laid him gently in the moist earth where a fairy ring had once grown. Then they covered up the grave, an offering to a god dressed in honeysuckle vines.

Later, as they walked along the road leading to the church, they heard the vespers bell. They hurried to meet Lucretia for rosary services.

Isolation is the most effective way to set the stage for brainwashing, since once the victim is away from emotional supports and reality checks, the rest of the process is relatively easy. . . . Women who are battered are often kept from contact with almost everyone except the person who batters, so that the self-interested, demeaning or threatening messages can saturate her senses.

The abused woman, whether lesbian or heterosexual, may be allowed to see people, especially if the abuser wants her to work, but the isolation may still occur on a more subtle, emotional level. For instance, she is not allowed to speak of what is done to her behind the closed doors, and she may be terrified of the abuser's violence if she inadvertently lets someone know what she is subjected to. To be on the safe side, she becomes unnaturally silent or superficial. She may also be convinced that if her friends or colleagues knew about the violence they would believe it was her own fault. Under those circumstances she is emotionally and socially isolated from everyone, because she hides her feelings, her thoughts and the pattern of her life from them and they don't really know her.

—Ginny NiCarthy, *Getting Free*

Women in the Trees

PAT MURPHY

"This is our new place," your husband says. "We'll be happy here."

A white farmhouse with peeling paint, far from the nearest neighbor. Behind it, golden hills roll away into the distance. Trees crowd closely around it, sprawling oaks that grow outward as much as they grow upward. Their leaves are small and brittle; their thick branches are gnarled and twisted with age.

Your husband takes your hand and you stand very still, like a deer frozen in the headlights of an oncoming car. He kisses your cheek and squeezes your hand gently. "We'll be happy," he says again, as if repeating the words will make them come true. You hope that he's right this time.

That afternoon, after the movers have come and gone, you are unpacking clothes in the bedroom. You are putting your husband's shirts in the drawers of the dresser. You place each shirt with its collar toward the back of the drawer, the buttons facing up. His shirts must be right or you don't know what will happen.

You look up from the drawer and for a moment you forget about your husband's shirts. The leaves of the oak tree that grows outside the window filter the sunlight; the bare mattress of the bed is dappled with bright spots that shift and move with the breezes. You look out the window into the leaves of the tree. In the shifting patterns of light and dark, you see faces. Women's faces, looking back at you. When the leaves flutter in the breeze, the women laugh to see you in the bedroom, worrying about your husband's shirts.

Your husband didn't mention the women in the trees when he told you about the house, but then it makes sense that he would miss them. You are accustomed to watching for tiny signals that others might not see: the tightening of a muscle in your husband's jaw, a sudden straightening of his shoulders, an involuntary movement as his hand begins to clench to form a fist. When you can see the beginnings of a frown from across the room, spotting women who live in the trees is simplicity itself.

You hear your husband's footsteps and look away from the window. He stands in the doorway, with one hand hidden behind his back. "Daydreaming again?" he asks in a playful tone. "What were you watching out there?"

You lie automatically. "A blue jay in the tree," you say. "It flew away."

"I brought you something," he says. From behind his back he produces an enormous bouquet of scraggly wildflowers, an assortment of California poppies, yellow mustard flowers, and dandelions. As he holds them out, yellow petals fall to the carpet, each one as bright as the spots of sunlight on the bed.

When you take the bouquet, he puts his arms around you and kisses you on the neck. You are glad that this is a day for kisses. He sweeps you up in his arms: he is not such a big man, but you are a small woman, a frail woman, barely twenty years old and light enough for him to carry. He lays you on the bare mattress and kisses you again, so gently, so sweetly. You know just now that he loves you; you are sure of it.

Your body responds to him, responds to his hand on your thigh, to his lips on your breast. His hand strokes between your legs and you moan and press yourself to him. Your body is fickle; it forgets the other times so quickly. He pulls you to him, and you cry out with each thrust, the pleasure coming in waves. Then he relaxes on top of you, and it feels good to have him near.

You look up at his face. His expression is distant, as if he is remembering something. He is looking down at your arm. On the pale skin of the upper arm there are bruise marks, left by four fingers and a thumb. Gently he touches the injury, matching his thumb and fingers to the marks. A perfect fit.

You push the thought away and look into the trees to see the women laughing. If he were to ask what you were thinking, you would lie.

You have acquired the habit of lying, the habit of covering up. To do otherwise would be admitting to failure. You have failed as a wife; you have failed as a woman. Your man is not happy and his discontent is your fault. On some level, deep down where your mother's voice is stronger than your own, you know this.

Your husband beat you for the first time just a month after your wedding. He was angry because one of his shirts had lost a button in the laundry, and you had forgotten to sew another on in its place. He yanked the shirt from the drawer, threw it at your face, and then came at you with his fists, punching you in the ribs, in the breasts, in the belly.

After it was all over, you lay on the bedroom floor, gasping for breath. You heard him weeping in the living room and you went to him. His face was wet with tears. He begged for your forgiveness. He said that he would kill himself if you left him. It would never happen again, he said. Never. You rocked him in your arms and the two of you wept together. He loved you and you loved him. How could it happen again?

A week after the beating, you still felt a stabbing pain with each breath. Solicitous and concerned, your husband drove you to the doctor's office.

In the examination room, the doctor asked you what had happened. How had you hurt yourself so badly? You looked at the doctor, an older man with a stern face. "I fell," you said. "I was getting a bowl down from a high cupboard and the chair slipped. I fell."

He studied your bruises. The purple marks had turned to a sickly yellow-green. Both arms were mottled where fingers had grabbed you, where fists had struck you.

"I see," he said. In his report he wrote, "Accident." And then he told you that you had two broken ribs.

Yes, you thought, it was an accident. Surely your husband would never have broken your ribs intentionally. He loved you. He said that over and over. He brought you flowers and gifts. He promised you it would never happen again.

And then, after a while, he said, "If only you wouldn't do these things that upset me."

If only you wouldn't flirt with other men. So you stopped smiling when you walked down the street, because a smile could be flirting if your husband was watching. If only you wouldn't neglect his needs. So you told your sister not to call in the evening when your husband was home. If only you wouldn't talk back. So you stopped stating your opinion, and he called you stupid because you had nothing to say.

He doesn't hit you often. And when he does, he strikes where the bruises will not show. Oh, sometimes he slaps you, but more often he uses fists. He doesn't use his fists on your face, because that would leave marks that you could not easily hide. He punches you in the ribs, in the breasts, in the belly. If you try to block his punches, he strikes the arms. He knows that you will wear long sleeves rather than reveal your failure, your shame, the bruises that are marks of dishonor.

• • •

At night, that first night in the new house, you hear the oak trees scratching against the roof. The branches of the one nearest the house rattle against the windowpane, tapping like fingernails on the glass, trying to get your attention. "Over here. We're over here." It's a comforting sound.

In the morning, your husband says that the damn branches scraping against the window kept him up all night. You know that isn't true: he was snoring while you lay awake. But you say nothing. The women in the trees will understand. You can't speak out.

After your husband leaves for work, you go outside and wander among the trees. Though the morning is hot, the shade is cool. Insects trill in the grasses, a soothing sound. Squirrels scold you from the branches, then fall silent, recognizing that you belong here. When you squint up at a squirrel, you see a woman's face staring back at you. Her eyes are blue, like the gaps between the leaves where the sky shows through. The wind blows and the woman vanishes. She is shy, easily frightened—you understand that. No doubt she has reasons for hiding. You catch a glimpse of another woman, or perhaps the same one. You move suddenly, and she disappears.

The women in the trees are like those puzzles in children's magazines: "Find all the things that are hidden in this picture." When you searched diligently, you discovered a cocker spaniel in the patterns of the wallpaper, a hammer and saw among the flowers in the flowerpot, a high-heeled shoe in the window curtains. You know you must observe carefully; if you are quiet and attentive, you will see things that other people miss.

Though you walk quietly, you don't see the women again. But on your way back to the house you find a bright blue feather, and you know that they have left it for you as a sign. They are watching. They will take care of you.

Just as you get back to the house, the landlord drives up in his pickup truck. He has come to see that everything is okay. You are wearing a sleeveless shirt. He notices the bruises on your arms and asks about them. You shake your head, looking away so that he can't see the lie in your eyes. "I'm so clumsy," you say. "Always banging into cupboard doors and counters." The cupboard doors are too high to bruise your arms and the counters are too low, but the landlord says nothing more. People believe what they want to believe; people see what they want to see.

You give him coffee to drink. Your husband would not like having this other man sit in his kitchen, even though the landlord is an older man, potbellied and unattractive. Your husband would not like it, but it seems harmless enough and you are lonely. You ask him about the oak trees. He tells you that they are California live oaks, tough trees that flourish under difficult conditions.

"How long have they been there, so close to the house?" you ask him.

"A long time," he says, "a very long time." They were old when his grandmother was growing up. His grandmother had lived in the house alone for many years, after his grandfather had died.

You nod. You like the thought of a woman living alone in this house, happy among the trees.

"I offered to cut back the oaks for her," the landlord says. "They need trimming, sure enough. But she didn't want me to. Had a thing about them, she did."

You smile, understanding his grandmother across the years. She knew about the women in the oaks. You think you would have liked his grandmother.

You have lived in the farmhouse for two weeks when your husband decides that you must celebrate the two-week anniversary of the move. He calls you from work and tells you not to make dinner. He brings home a pepperoni pizza, turns the lights low, and puts an old Elvis Presley album on the stereo. Together, you eat pizza from paper plates, and he talks and jokes. He tells you about his boss, imitating the way the man puffs out his cheeks when he talks and making you laugh.

When Elvis sings "Love Me Tender," your husband takes your hand and pulls you up off the couch. He holds you close. As you dance, he sings along with Elvis, his voice deep and loving. When the song ends, he kisses you.

In the sudden silence, you hear the wind rattling in the branches outside. You ignore the sound. Your bruises have faded and you are happy. You think right now that you will always be happy.

When you were a child, your family moved a lot. Your father worked as a mechanic in a garage, and he could get work anywhere. When he didn't like his boss or the house or a town, he moved. Sometimes you stayed in one place for six months; sometimes, for three; sometimes, only for two. You and your sister were jerked from school; you packed your things in the cardboard boxes that your mother never bothered to throw away, and you drove to a new town, a new house, a new school. You had no choice.

Sometimes, you would cry about leaving your friends. Once, you ran away and tried to stay at a friend's house, reasoning that your parents might leave without you, they just might. But they didn't. Your father found you, and you moved again.

After that, your parents never warned you before a move. You would notice an odd tension around the house, a peculiar feeling of activity even when everything was still. Then one morning, you would wake up and your mother would be wrapping the dishes in newspaper and packing them away in boxes.

After a while, you stopped making friends. What was the use when you knew you would be moving in a month, in two months, in half a year? No use. No use at all.

You swore that when you were grown-up you would live in one house. You would stay there with your husband who would take good care of you. You would live in the house all your life and never move. That's why you like thinking about the landlord's grandmother—an old woman living in the house that was hers, making friends with the trees. You like that.

You have been in the house for a month when your husband brings home a hammock made of colored twine. "Perfect for this place," he says. "It will look great hanging between the trees."

He takes a beer from the refrigerator. He's been drinking more and more beer lately. He says that he needs it to relax after the long commute. He has been late to work a few times, and his boss is on his back. He doesn't like his job. You try to be sympathetic and understanding.

When he goes out to hang the hammock, you go with him. He wanders from tree to tree, looking for two that are the right distance apart. The hammock came with some rope, but not much. None of the trees seem to be positioned right. This pair is too widely separated; this one, too close together.

As he searches for the right tree, your husband is getting angry. He carries his beer in one hand and the hammock in the other. He does not like the oaks —you know that. They have deep roots. He does not like things that are stronger than he is.

"What about these two?" you say. "They look about right."

"Too far apart," he says impatiently.

You look up into the leaves where the women live. You can't see them, but you know they are there. You can feel them all around you. They will help you if they can.

"I think it might fit here," you say. He glares at you and throws the hammock at you in exasperation. You catch it, smiling as if he were doing this in fun. You pretend. You lie—to yourself and to him and to the women in the oaks. You don't fool anyone, but you do it anyway. It's automatic now.

The distance between the trees is perfect. The rope just reaches. You think gratefully of the women in the oaks as you tie the rope around the tree, stringing the hammock a few feet off the ground. Your husband is watching, angry that you succeeded where he failed. You speak to him softly, trying to placate him. You tell him that this will be a wonderful place for him to rest on weekends; you tell him that this is a fine house, that you are so happy, that he is so wise. He turns away as you are tying the rope and goes to the kitchen for another beer.

You test the hammock, lying down under the trees. The sun is gone and the first stars are out. You don't want to go back to the house, but you know that the longer you put it off, the worse it will be.

The sun is setting. In the leaves above you, the women are dancing. You can

only catch glimpses of them, but you make up the rest. They are beautiful—
slim and young, about your age really. You hear them calling to you; they know
your name. Perhaps they overheard it when your husband was yelling at you.
Your name sounds different when they say it—softer, gentler, like wind caressing leaves, like summer rain on the grass.

Your husband calls to you from the porch. Reluctantly, you leave the hammock and go toward the house. "Where's dinner?" he grumbles, and you smile
as if he is just joking. As you go toward him, you see that he is holding a beer
in one hand and a saw in the other. He's on his third beer: you see two empty
bottles on the counter.

"It'll be on the table in just a minute," and you hear echoes of your mother's
voice saying "Yes, dear. Of course, dear," while your father shouts about
something or other.

"I'm going to take care of that damn branch that's been keeping me awake,"
he says, stepping off the porch and heading toward the oak nearest the house.
You stand by the porch and watch as he climbs the tree. The branch that scrapes
against the bedroom window grows off a sprawling trunk that is as thick around
as your waist. He straddles the trunk and saws at the branch awkwardly. He is
clumsy with the saw, a little drunk, you think. The tree in which he is sitting
trembles each time he jerks the saw. You can hear the leaves rattling, the oak
women talking excitedly among themselves.

"Be careful," you say. You are not sure what you are warning him against:
the sharp saw, the oak women, the danger of falling. Or perhaps you are
warning the women. You are not sure, but you know there is danger somewhere
nearby.

He drags the saw toward him and the branch creaks, a high cry of alarm. It
dips lower to rest against the ground. Only a thin strip of bark and wood holds
the branch to the tree. He pushes the saw forward and the bark gives way
suddenly. The branch falls and the saw slips through the gap, striking his leg.
He cries out. The crash of the branch hitting the ground is like a burst of sudden
laughter.

You bandage his cut, a ragged gash. The blood and pain have calmed him,
and he submits to your attention willingly. At times like this, he is a small boy,
grateful to be taken care of. You baby him and bring him his dinner, happy that
the earlier tension has somehow dissipated.

That night, when he is asleep, you slip out of the house and lie in the
hammock. From the woods, you can hear the creaking of insects, the rustle of
small animals in the underbrush, the low hooting of an owl. When you were a
little girl, a teacher read the class a story about an enchanted forest. Dryads
lived in the trees, coming out to dance and sing in the moonlight. One day, a
little girl went to the forest and met the dryads.

You don't know what happened next. Your family moved the next day and you never heard the end of the story. In your mind, the little girl is still living in the enchanted woods, never leaving, growing up among the dryads and learning their ways.

You lie in the hammock and wait to see if the women will sing, but you do not hear them. After a time, the moon comes up, and you go back to bed.

You have a red notebook, like the one that you carried to classes during the one year that you went to community college. Sometimes you write in your notebook, trying to tell the truth. You write, "I love my husband." You consider the words, remembering your broken ribs. You cross the sentence out, then write again. "I hate my husband." You cross that out too. The truth is a slippery thing, as elusive as the women in the trees.

The summer goes along. You try to take care of your husband. Small things anger him: He sees a letter from your sister and he says that she never liked him. You smile at the checkout boy at the grocery store and your husband says you are a slut. You ask him to take you to town so you can go to the library, and he insinuates that you think you are better than he is, you think you are so smart. But these are all minor complaints. You soothe him, you comfort him, you make him dinner.

Your mother writes you letters, telling you the family's latest address and asking how you are doing. You write back cheerful notes that say nothing. You have nothing to say. The first time your husband hit you, right after you were married, you asked your mother if you could come home. She was packing the dishes for another move and she said that you must stay with your husband. Make your husband happy, she said. In your letters, you tell her that your husband is happy.

When your husband is at work, you walk in the woods. You feel strong when you are among the trees. On a warm day, you kick off your shoes and climb a tree. High in the foliage, you find a place where two branches come together to make a natural seat, as comfortable as a rocking chair. When you look down, all you can see are leaves. You are alone at the top of the tree, hidden from view.

For a while, you sit and listen to the jays squawk and the squirrels chatter. The leaves rustle, fluttering in the breeze. When you squint your eyes, the flickering light looks like sunlight on water.

You fall asleep and the oak women gather around you. In your dream, you smile at them. "This is a beautiful place," you say.

They murmur to you, their voices no louder than the whispering of the leaves. "Stay. Stay with us." They stretch their hands out to you.

You look around. "I can't live in a tree."

They mutter reassuringly. "You can do anything."

You shake your head, knowing they are wrong.

Their eyes are shaped like almonds; their hair is the color of new grass; their fingers are slender and graceful. The smallest one, a young girl with a sweet smile, whispers, "You are beautiful."

You look down at your hands. You have been biting your fingernails again. Your wrists are so thin you can see the bones. Your hair is thin and stringy. You are ugly.

"You are not seeing clearly," she whispers. "Truly, you are beautiful."

The rumble of an engine drowns out her voice. A car is coming up the driveway—your husband is home. Startled, you clamber out of the tree and hurry home to greet him.

You call to your husband as you walk in the door. "Dinner will be ready in just a minute." You can hear him in the bedroom, changing out of his work clothes. You hear his footsteps crossing the living room. From the sound, you try to judge how angry he is that you weren't home when he got there.

He stands in the kitchen doorway for a moment, watching you slice tomatoes for salad. He gets a beer from the refrigerator, throws the bottle cap in the general direction of the wastepaper basket. He misses. The cap rolls across the floor, but he doesn't pick it up. "This place is a sty," he says. "Sometimes I don't know why I even bother to come home." He turns away and you hear the television go on in the living room. By the time the lamb chops are done, he is drinking his third beer. He eats half the chop and leaves the rest. As you wash the dishes, you can hear gunfire from a cop show on the television.

That night, you wake from a bad dream. You dreamed of a time past that you would rather forget. Your husband had his hands on your throat and he was choking you, shaking you, cursing you for something you had done. What was it? Smiling at the postman, maybe, or folding one of his shirts incorrectly. It doesn't matter. All that mattered was the air and the pain. He released the pressure just before you fainted. You gasped, "I'm sorry. I'm sorry." You didn't even know what you were sorry for, but whatever it was it must have been bad, very bad to make him so angry. You had to wear a scarf around your throat for two weeks until the bruises went away.

You wake and your husband is asleep, lying on his back with his hands at his sides. A fold of blanket is pressing lightly against your neck and you push it away. You can't go back to sleep and you are afraid that you will wake your husband with your tossing and turning. As quietly as you can, you slip from the bed and go outside. In the moonlight, the trees are beautiful.

You are on the porch when you hear footsteps. The door creaks open. Your husband sits beside you on the steps and for a moment you let yourself think that everything will be all right. You listen to him breathing beside you.

"I couldn't sleep," you say. "I came outside so I wouldn't wake you up."

"You woke me up by getting up," he says. He isn't looking at you; he is gazing out toward the oaks.

"I'm sorry," you say automatically.

"If I'm late again, that bastard will have my ass," he says, and somehow it is your fault. You are responsible for the long commute, for the unreasonable boss, for your husband's state of mind. He will be late to work and you will be to blame.

"Let's go back to bed," you say. "You need your sleep." Moving carefully, you reach out and take his hand. You lead him back to bed.

He falls asleep quickly, but you lie awake beside him, listening to him breathe.

You do your best. You have dinner ready on time. You serve his favorite foods. You keep the house very clean. But even so, there are small signs—you watch for them and you notice them. He stops complaining about the traffic and his commute to the city, although you know neither one has improved. He stops complaining about the boss who is picking on him, always on his back. You watch and wait, knowing that something is coming.

You try to make sure that everything is perfect. Everything must be perfect. If it isn't perfect—but you don't want to think about that. This time, you will follow all the rules. You will put all the shirts in the drawer just so. You will not say anything that makes it sound as if you think you're smart. You will not smile at anyone. And you will watch him, noticing the slightest signal.

Even though you are very good, sometimes you slip away to your place in the trees when he is at work. Once, when he has had too much to drink and falls asleep, you risk sneaking out at night, finding your way in the darkness. You are lucky. You don't get caught.

He is silent much of the time. When he gets home at night, he watches cop shows on TV. He drinks steadily, watching you over the rim of the glass. Sometimes, you catch him watching you. Something is coming, but if you can keep everything perfect, it will not come.

Your husband is at work when the landlord and his wife stop by. The Lions Club is having a pancake breakfast at the local high school and they want to sell you tickets. They want you and your husband to come; they say you will have a good time; they say you should get out more. Your landlord's wife says you need some meat on your bones.

You buy two tickets. You know, even as you buy them, that your husband will not go. But you smile and buy them to be polite. And you think about what it would be like if he decided to go and be charming. He could be charming. He could be sweet. You picture yourself in a sundress. You have no bruises on your arms and your husband is smiling at you the way he used to before you married.

You tell the landlord and his wife that you can't talk long. You must get dinner started. Your husband will be home soon. But they keep talking until the shadows stretch across the valley. When they finally leave, you make a pot of stew, a big green salad. Your husband is late and you're glad. Dinner will be ready when he gets home. Everything will be perfect.

It's dark. You see his headlights first, sweeping across the trees and spotlighting the house. You stand on the porch, ready to greet him. "Dinner is ready," you call to him.

He has been drinking. You can smell whiskey and cigarette smoke on his clothes. He pushes past you into the kitchen and you follow him, still trying to smile. He glares around the kitchen. The stew bubbles on the stove and it smells good. Surely he will be happy now: good food, a nice clean home.

"What's wrong?" you ask. You know as soon as you speak you have said the wrong thing. There was no right thing to say.

"That son of a bitch I work for fired me," he says. "Are you happy now?"

You can think of nothing to say. Are you happy? No, you're not happy.

He sees the tickets to the pancake breakfast. Carelessly, you left them on the table. He snatches them up and reads what they have to say.

"You spent money on this shit?" he says. He throws them down on the floor. Before you can speak, he grabs your hair and tries to slap you—once, twice, three times. You block his hand once, twice, but the third blow knocks your arm aside. You try to pull away, but he strikes again with the back of his hand, rocking your head to one side.

"I'll teach you a lesson," he says, and you remember other lessons that your husband taught with his fists. You bring your arms up to protect your face and he swings his fist low and buries it in your stomach. Lesson one: whatever you do, it's wrong. You double over, wrapping yourself around the pain, and he slams a fist into your head. Lesson two: the same as lesson one.

You fall to the floor and try to crawl away. He grabs your ankle and you turn on him, slapping at his hand. He grabs your wrist. Desperately you bite him, tasting blood and sweat and cigarettes. You have never fought him so hard before. You have grown stronger during your time among the trees.

When you bite him, he lets you go, and in that instant you are running—out the door, off the porch, into the protective darkness beneath the trees. You know your way. You can hear him behind you, clumsy in his drunkenness, shouting that he will kill you, you bitch, you stupid bitch. He is cursing you, screaming that you are useless and stupid, a burden to him, a drag on his life.

The wind is up and the oaks are alive. You run among them, ducking beneath the low branches. The women are calling to you in high thin voices like leaves in the wind. Behind you, you hear your husband trying to follow. The branches slap at him, clawing at his eyes. The roots trip him. You can hear him grunt as he falls.

You are far ahead of him when you reach your secret place and you climb quickly, knowing your way by touch. The oak women help you, their cool hands clutching your wrists, soothing your pain, urging you on. You find your place and you sit there, very still.

You hear your husband searching for you. He shouts your name, curses you, slams his fist into trees as he passes. He tells you that you must come out.

You sit very still, listening to your own heart pounding. For a moment, you think, "I'd better go back. It will only be worse later." But you remain still. After a time, you think, "I didn't do anything wrong."

A flashlight beam darts across the tree trunks. You can see if flickering through the leaves, but he can't see you. You are as invisible as the oak women. You blend into the picture, becoming part of the branches, part of the leaves. No one can find you here. As he crashes through the underbrush, you fight the urge to laugh. He is not strong, with all his bashing and crashing. You lean back into the fork of the tree, listening to the oak women soothing you. "Hush," they say. "Quiet."

Finally, he goes back to the house. In the distance, you hear the sound of breaking glass. The kitchen window, you guess, but that doesn't matter now. He can break every window and burn all your things. You don't care.

Your body is stiff and you are starting to wonder what to do. "Leave it," the oak women say. "Come with us." The first light of dawn is rising. Birds are starting to sing.

"Come on," the youngest one says impatiently. She reaches out her hand, and you take it. She smiles and tugs on your hand. It happens so easily. You stand up and look back at the small body, curled up in the fork of the tree. So thin, so beautiful. You feel the wind in your hair.

Your husband will never find you here. You will watch him from the trees. Sometimes you will drop twigs on his head. Sometimes, remembering the good times, the times when he was sorry, the times when he danced with you and treated you well, you will miss him.

But you will not be sorry, not sorry ever again. Eventually, you will forget how to lie. And then you can come back down.

The risk of attempted suicide becomes almost five times greater for battered than for nonbattered women . . . after the onset of abusive injury. . . . Domestic violence may be the most significant precipitant of female suicide attempts yet identified. Yet, after medical treatment, battered women who attempted suicide were significantly more likely than nonbattered women to be sent home and/or to receive no referral of any kind after a suicide attempt.
　　　　　　　　—Demie Kurz and Evan Stark, *"Not-So-Benign Neglect"*

The Man Who Loved His Wife

JANET LAPIERRE

"Off!" The dog hesitated, growling softly, and Alma Linhares kept her right hand on her holstered revolver while she considered the options. She didn't want to blow away somebody's pet, even one this ugly, should have kept her butt in the car except that boredom and curiosity had gotten to her.

"Nice doggy," she muttered, and was not surprised to get another, deeper growl in response. Okay, when the chief sent her to keep an eye on the son of a bitch who apparently owned this mutt, he didn't exactly say it had to be from cover. "Mr. Berquist?" she sang out. "Could you call off your dog please?"

The front door of the house opened, and a tall figure clad in Levi's and a white T-shirt shambled out onto the porch. "Caesar!" He shaded his eyes with one hand as he peered down into the yard. "Caesar, go to your house."

The dog, a leggy, grizzled beast with German shepherd somewhere in its ancestry, lowered head and tail and slunk off. "Sorry," Arnold Berquist called. "He's confused, he misses Celia and the kids." Moving across the porch and down the steps, Berquist carried his gaunt frame with hunched caution, as if a misstep might awaken a pain somewhere. His face was haggard and unshaven, colorless except for reddened eyelids. Hand half extended, he stopped and frowned at her. "I don't know you, do I?"

"No, sir. I'm Officer Linhares, Alma Linhares." She had never met the man, but the Berquists kept having troubles of the kind that brought them to public notice. A gust of wind pushed his smell at her, sweat and booze. Grief might be a good excuse for hitting the bottle, but guilt was just as likely; and she personally wasn't convinced that Celia Berquist had committed suicide.

"Ah." He looked at her, and then past her, toward the chainlink fence and the thick stand of brush that screened his property, five acres as she recalled, from the road. Behind him, the narrow two-story house showed no lights although this late October afternoon was darkly overcast.

"So." He focused on her once again, with a nod and a grimace probably meant as a smile. "Everything is straightened out, and I can proceed with arrangements."

"No, sir, not yet. Chief Gutierrez asked me to stop by, since you don't have a phone. He had to go to Ukiah this afternoon. He should be back before long and he'll come straight here."

"Don't you people care that you're driving me crazy?" He lifted clenched fists and hammered them down against empty air, nearly losing his balance with the force of the gesture. "There can't any doubt about what happened, it was . . . it's Celia's family, isn't it? Trying to make trouble?"

"I don't really know, sir." Alma saw the shine of sweat on his forehead, saw him shiver. So far as she knew, she was out here as a kind of baby-sitter, and the chief would probably be seriously pissed if she let the baby catch pneumonia. "Could we go inside? The wind is getting real sharp, might even be an early rain on the way."

"Oh. Yes, of course." He nodded and reached out as if to take her elbow; Alma stepped aside and gestured for him to precede her. Always a good idea to make clear who was in charge, and besides, she didn't want his hand on her.

It was an old house, pinched and charmless, as if its builder had grudged every board and pane of glass. But the paint was fresh, the narrow staircase and the living-dining room thickly carpeted against noise and drafts. Sofa, several stuffed chairs, a rocker, tables. Pictures on the walls, flowers and land-scapes. Big television set, and a spinet piano against the far wall. Most of the furniture sat askew, and flat surfaces bore a thick film of dust.

"Sit down, please. I'm sorry. . . ." He looked around the room and shrugged. "I've never been much of a housekeeper. And to be honest, Celia pretty much gave up this past year on anything but the kids and that committee."

A brick fireplace was centered on the outer wall to the left, its maw filled now by a black iron stove. Alma went to inspect a row of framed photographs on the mantel and found Celia Berquist: cheerleader, cornsilk hair and sky-blue eyes and sexy pout; bride, wide-eyed and ethereal; madonna from a church painting, round-bellied and demure.

Then Celia the mother, holding a baby, trailing a toddler, supervising a crowded sandbox. In the last frame, thinner now with hair dimmed to light brown, Celia stood with two freckled little boys and a skinny girl, holding on her hip the baby of a year or so that had to be poor Amy. The photos were clearly the work of a loving amateur with a steady hand and a good camera, probably Berquist; remembering similar displays in the homes of her sisters, Alma thought it odd that there were no separate shots of the kids.

"In a way I do blame myself." Berquist's voice was rough, as if his throat hurt. "I was thirty . . . aah, no, that's a lie. I'd been teaching for twelve years and I was thirty-five years old. Celia was seventeen and beautiful as a sunrise, she made my whole world glow." As he turned to smile at Alma, she caught behind the lank grey-streaked hair and bleary eyes a glimpse of the man who'd been able to charm the socks . . . or anyway the pants . . . off that gorgeous girl.

"Seventeen," she said, and stopped just short of saying that she, too, had been crazy in love at seventeen with a teacher, a man she hadn't thought of in years. Mr. Corey, who told her she had beautiful eyes and five feet seven wasn't too tall and someday a nice man would love her as much as he, Mr. Corey, loved his wife. Too bad Celia hadn't encountered a Mr. Corey.

Berquist's eyes narrowed and his mouth made a grim down-curve. "Some people, the woman I'd been going out with for instance, saw Celia as a randy teenage girl seducing an older man for the challenge. Girls do that sort of thing, you know; any male teacher who's reasonably young and attractive could tell you endless tales.

"Then of course others—most people, including Celia's family—insisted I'd either brainwashed her or more likely raped her, right there in the class-room."

Alma made a little murmur, something between shock and sympathy, and he shrugged. "So the principal fired me and assured me that I'd never teach again in a California public school. Celia's parents tried to force her to leave me, to have the baby and give it up for adoption. But we loved each other. We knew God meant us to be together forever."

He swung away from the mantel abruptly, dropped to the couch and put his head in his hands. "I'm sorry. I've been alone out here going quietly nuts, nobody to talk to or . . . Could I ask you, Miss . . ."

"Linhares. Alma."

"Ah. A pretty name, is it Spanish?" He lifted his head to look at her.

"Portuguese."

"Alma, I haven't had a decent cup of coffee in days; I can't seem to make it come out right. Would you mind making a pot?"

"Okay." And you owe me one, Chief Gutierrez, she told her boss silently. Probably turn out to be more than one. Berquist stayed where he was, hunched forward over his knees. As Alma turned away, she found there was a picture inside her own head that belonged there on the mantel: Celia one day at the police station, right after her loving husband had beat the shit out of her.

The kitchen, an awkward square of a room with too few windows, contained all kinds of nice shiny appliances, including a Krups coffee maker. Alma located an open can of coffee and set the machine to work. Big garden outside the back door, most of it dried up now or gone to seed. A shed and run for chickens beyond the garden, looking empty. Sinkful of dirty dishes, more dishes littering the table against the wall. A couple of cardboard boxes under the table, and a telephone, not connected. She pulled open a flap on the nearest box, to find a stack of flyers: "Find the Children."

The coffee maker spat and sputtered to a finish; she poured a mugful and carried it in to set it on the low table before the couch.

"Thank you." He sat up, blinked hard and squared his shoulders. "Aren't you having some?"

"I'm not much of a coffee drinker," she lied, preferring to keep her hands free. As he lifted the mug to his mouth, she sat down in the rocker. Her survey of the lower floor had revealed no toy trucks or dolls or sports gear, no children's books or crayoned drawings from school; perhaps Celia's kids had spent all their time upstairs. Or perhaps they had taken along, to their grandparents' home where they were staying, everything they owned.

"Something wrong with the coffee?" she asked as Berquist set the mug down after two swallows.

"Just . . . needs a little something." He lurched to his feet and set off toward the kitchen. Back door, she thought, and got up quickly to follow. His truck was out back, and a lot of open country; if he got away or maybe even killed himself, Chief Gutierrez would eat her alive and spit out the bones. Berquist reached not for the door but for a cupboard high over the sink, to retrieve a bottle; Alma released held-in breath, returned to her chair and sat there watching him top off his coffee with bourbon. Jim Beam, from a 750-milliliter bottle now down slightly more than half.

"So what brought you and Celia to Port Silva?" she asked him. Wife-killer or not, he clearly liked to talk, and it might slow the drinking.

"You ever been to Yuba City?" He didn't wait for an answer. "Hot as hell, dusty, only job I could find was in my Uncle Earl's plumbing shop where I'd worked summers during high school and college. We had this stuffy little apartment, and Celia was sick practically the whole nine months; I think that's when her depression really began. And her mother and sisters and about a dozen cousins were always hanging around. We needed to get away, get ourselves some privacy."

This was private, all right. Five acres of scrubland at the very edge of a chilly north-coast town. Half a mile to the nearest neighbor, five or six to the grocery store.

"So I found a job here, Mazzini's Plumbing. And I bought this place. Room for a garden, chickens, we got a calf to raise. Celia was safe here, and she could send the kids outside to play without worrying that they'd get run over." He reached for the bottle and poured more bourbon into his cup.

"You said her depression began years ago," Alma remarked. "Did she ever see anybody, a doctor, about that?"

"No. We aren't—weren't—believers in psychologists and therapists and that lot. We believe in hard work, and prayer, and trusting in God. And in talking to your pastor; I know Celia drew great comfort from her visits with Pastor Kilgren."

Alma had met Pastor Kilgren of Port Silva Southern Baptist and had found him well-meaning if sanctimonious, and not very smart. Put her on the battle lines, she'd a whole lot rather have Father Lucchesi beside her. On most issues, anyway. "Mr. Berquist, excuse me for asking this, but I come from a big family, brothers and sisters and nieces and nephews. I know kids can really wear you down. Didn't Celia ever want to do something else for a change— get a job, maybe?"

He sat up and glared at her. "She had a job, right here. Oh, she wanted to help out, she tried part-time stuff a couple of times. But James and Ellen hated day care, and the baby got sick, and I developed an ulcer. We needed her at home."

Celia had her fourth child at, let's see, twenty-four years of age. Alma suppressed a shudder and reminded herself that her own mother had had five children by the age of thirty. God. She sighed, got slowly to her feet and stretched—to ease tight muscles and to cast a glance out the front window. Dusk coming quickly up to dark, no traffic. Where was the chief, anyway?

"So we were just fine," Berquist went on mournfully. "Celia got a small inheritance from her grandmother and I let her buy a little car. Before that she'd been getting up early to drive me to work on days she wanted to keep the truck. Besides, she was pregnant again and the truck wasn't big enough anymore, not in bad weather."

He took a big mouthful from the mug, set it down, and reached for the bottle.

"Let me get you more coffee." She snatched up the mug before he could protest, carried it to the kitchen and filled it.

"Well. Thank you." He took a gulp that must have burned his mouth, took a second and then tipped in whiskey to the brim. "Anyway, pretty soon Amy was born and things were just fine for, oh, quite a while, a couple years."

Alma, shoulder-propped beside the mantel, kept her eyes down and her whole body still, in a tension that apparently communicated itself across the room.

"Of course you know about that, the police know. The time I lost my temper and that's why I'm being treated this way now, I understand that." Berquist's speech was losing its crisp edge to the whiskey; he licked his lips and spoke more slowly.

"You see, my wife, my wife didn't talk to me about it, or to her pastor either. She just drove herself to Santa Rosa and went to a clinic and had an abortion. Without her husband's permission, I didn't think a wife could do that. I was upset."

And Celia filed a complaint and then withdrew it the next day. Like any poor dumb broad would who had no education, no job and four kids.

"I never hit her again," Berquist said hoarsely. "I argued with her, and I tried to make her understand that I loved her and wanted her with me, that kids need a full-time mother. But as God is my witness, I never again laid a hand on her in anger. Not even last year, when she went off and left me, left us."

⋅ This was all a matter of sad record. Celia Berquist had hired a baby-sitter, a woman recommended by a church friend. Celia had then set off for a three-week study conference at the University of California at Santa Cruz, a program intended to prepare women for a second chance at higher education. While Celia was away, three-year-old Amy disappeared and was never seen again. The baby-sitter, an illegal from Central America, had disappeared as well.

"She just never got over losing Amy." Berquist sniffed and wiped a forearm across his eyes. "I said we should have another baby. I let her work with that lost-children committee until she wore herself out, then I made her quit for her own good. Took the phone out, told those other people to leave her alone. I loved her. I never blamed her for Amy, she thought I did but I didn't.

"Hey." He wiped his eyes again and peered up at her owlishly. "If you don't drink coffee, how about a little bourbon? No, that's right," he said as she shook her head. "Cops don't drink on duty, huh? Especially not lady cops, I bet. What do you suppose has happened to that boss of yours?"

"I expect him any minute."

"And what did he send you here for, anyway? To shoot me if I try to run away?"

"You're not under arrest, Mr. Berquist. I think he was worried about you, out here all by yourself."

"And he sent me company. What a friendly fellow he is. Listen to me!" He planted his feet and thrust his head forward. Gaunt and grey, he still had an impressive breadth of shoulder, and corded muscles ridged his forearms.

"I swear to God I did not kill my wife, my wife that I loved more than anything on earth." His lips trembled, and tears began to spill from his eyes in a slow trickle that he ignored. "Three days ago my beautiful Celia took the kids to a friend from church. Then she got into a bathtub full of water and cut her wrists. When I got home from work I found her there floating in her own blood, and I found the note that said she was just too tired to go on. *Shit,* why am I even talking to you?"

"Mr. Berquist, I'm not here to upset you. If you want me to, I'll leave."

"Sure you will, and you'll go about as far as the end of the driveway. A suicide watch, is that it? Listen, I loved my wife, but I'm not going to kill myself." He sank to the couch, stretched his long legs out wearily and took a gulp from the mug. After perhaps ten seconds of silence, he said, "Pretty."

"I beg your pardon?"

"I said you're pretty, a pretty girl. Thick shiny black hair, beautiful eyes." He drank again. "Nice big boobs under that ugly brown shirt, make your husband happy, feed your babies. Pretty girl like you shouldn't walk around with a badge and a gun."

Sure, asshole. Alma kept her breathing even and hoped her anger did not color her face. Sure, spend my days cleaning up after some prick like you, my nights making babies. Probably poor Celia *was* just tired to death, thought suicide looked like a good long rest.

"Almost as pretty as Celia. I didn't kill my Celia." He pulled his legs close, planted his feet with care and rose. "Pretty lady, soft pretty lady. Believe me?"

Actually, she did. "Yes, I believe you," Alma assured him as she began to back toward the door. She couldn't shoot this weeping drunk, and she wasn't confident that she could take him out any other way, not in this narrow, furniture-cluttered room. Not when he had about seven inches on her and those long arms. Let's get this out-of-doors.

He came slowly around the table, swaying slightly, arms wide as if to embrace her. She moved sideways, felt the door handle behind her, pulled the door open and backed around it.

"Officer Linhares?"

"Jesus!" She'd backed right into Gutierrez, practically knocked him down. "Sorry, Chief. I was just . . . trying to defuse the situation."

"Good." Gutierrez stepped into the room. Alma followed close on his heels. Berquist looked blearily at them, nodded, backed up and sat down.

"Chief. Chief Gutierrez, I'm glad to see you. I bet you have the coroner's report, and the handwriting report, and all that stuff, right?"

"Right."

"So you know that I did not kill my wife. I didn't kill Celia."

"Correct, I know that. But what about Amy?"

Berquist squinted, opened his mouth, closed it and swallowed. "I don't understand."

"Before killing herself, Celia Berquist wrote a note."

"I know *that*. I found it for God's sake."

"Another note, more of a letter. She wrote a letter to the Port Silva Police Department, to me, and went out and mailed it and then came home and climbed in the bathtub."

"No."

Alma watched Berquist shrink into himself, shoulders high and tight and quivering, bent knees up close like a barricade to hide behind. She turned to look at the man beside her and flinched. Gutierrez's dark face was hard as a clenched fist, his lips drawn tight in a white-toothed snarl. Alma took a quick step sideways.

"Listen. 'Dear Chief Gutierrez. My husband Arnold Berquist killed our daughter Amy Berquist, age three. I am sure about this, I worked it out from things he has been saying to me recently.' "

Jesus, Mary and Joseph. Alma put one hand across her mouth, the other on the butt of her revolver.

"That's not true." Berquist shook his head. "Absolutely not true. Celia was depressed, suicidal. She kept having terrible nightmares about Amy, and she came to see them as real."

"There's more. 'I have tried to think where he put her after killing her, and the only place would be his fishing place, up near the Lost Coast on a creek called Usal Creek. I have never been there, but one of the men he works with has, Peter Benoit. I believe you will find my daughter Amy Berquist buried there. Thank you for your help. Celia Berquist.'

"I got the letter this morning," said Gutierrez. "Peter Benoit took me to the place on Usal Creek. I found Amy."

Alma, feeling her lateish lunch rise to press at the back of her throat, turned from Gutierrez's frozen face to stare at the man who loved his wife.

Berquist frowned into space, let his shoulders slump and his hands fall loose. "But I had to show her what terrible things could happen if she left us."

Since the beginning of the battered women's movement in the mid-seventies, women have learned there is nothing as helpful to them as a group of women who have been in situations that are similar to their own. The group can be in a shelter or at a community center, it can be a formal arrangement with a professional leader or just three women trading stories at a laundromat. . . . Battered women are confiding in each other during office and factory coffee breaks, at university sororities, at neighborhood coffee klatches and church socials. If you've been battered . . . you want to know how other women were able to leave dangerous partners and stay away.

—Ginny NiCarthy, *The Ones Who Got Away*

Wild Turkeys

BETH BRANT

Violet smiled when she saw the sign: Welcome to Fairview, Wild Turkey Capital of Michigan. The sign had been there for as long as she could remember, the same tired old bird peering out from behind the letters. Over the years the vivid colors of the bird's feathers had dulled to a light brown, and the black lettering was now a washed-out grey. Violet had lived nearby before she ran away. But she remembered the sign and remembered the wild turkeys.

She was six or seven when she'd seen them. While playing in the field near her home, she came across them pecking for food and moving silently on the ground. She thought they were ugly birds until they spread their wings and skittered away from her. Then the rich reds, rusts, and browns were displayed for her to see. They flew low over the field, not reaching any great height, almost as if it were a struggle to get off the ground. She had run home to tell her mom about the birds. Her mom told Violet a story.

"In the old days, sweetie, the turkey used to fly real high. Almost as high as a hawk. There was an animal, a porcupine, who got jealous of the turkey's pretty colors and the way she could fly. See, the porcupine was kinda ugly. One night when the turkey was sleeping, the porcupine sneaked up and clipped her wings with his sharp claws. After that, the turkey couldn't fly very far or very high, but she still kept her pretty feathers. The porcupine made the Creator so mad, he gave him those long, sharp quills so nobody would go near him anymore."

276

"That's sad, Mom."

"Well, lots of things are sad, Violet. But the turkey kept her feathers and she's still alive. I think that's the important thing."

Slowing down the car to get a good look at the sign, she saw another across the street: Rita's Diner. She didn't remember the diner; it must be new. She was hungry and needed some coffee to fortify her for the two hours of driving she still had ahead of her. She pulled into the lot and sat for a few minutes, checking her money supply and cleaning her glasses. She had spent more than she'd planned on this trip back to see her grandmother. She had bought a birdhouse for Grandma who loved to sit and watch the birds that came to visit her yard. The birdhouse was a fancy one, handmade, with dozens of small holes for the birds to nest. Violet had set it up by the front window where Grandma spent most of her day, looking out at the trees and rose bushes.

"Can't you stay longer, Violet? It's been so long since I seen you. Talking on the phone's not the same as having my best girl here."

Violet had looked at her grandmother's old, lined face, the brown eyes full of life and curiosity. "I'm starting my new job tomorrow, but I promise I'll come back more often, Grandma. I'll be making more money so I can afford the travel as long as the car holds out. If it weren't for you and the money you've given me, I don't know what I would have done. But I'll be back. I'm not scared anymore."

"You shouldn't be. He's long gone, can't hurt you no more. And the money," Grandma waved away the hundreds of dollars she had sent to Violet, "what have I got to spend it on?"

"You don't have that much, Grandma."

"I don't need much. Now that I got this fancy birdhouse, I got everything I need," and she had pulled Violet to her and kissed her.

Violet entered the diner, noting the smallness and cleanliness of the place. There were only a few tables, no booths, and the walls were painted a sun yellow. Red-and-white checked curtains hung at the scrubbed windows. She sat down at a table and looked around the space, grinning when she saw the stuffed turkey mounted on a wall. Turkeys were evident most everywhere. Turkey salt-and-pepper shakers were sitting on each table. Her napkin, aligned in front of her, had knife, fork, and spoon lying on top of a foolishly smiling turkey. There were photographs and paintings of wild turkeys hanging on the walls.

A waitress with improbable red-lacquered hair came over and poured coffee into the thick white mug resting beside the smiling turkey. Violet noticed the woman's hands were chapped and red. She looked up and smiled her thanks. The pin on the woman's yellow uniform said Rita. Violet looked around the room as she sipped her coffee. A group of men were sitting at a table by the window. Across from her, a woman was eating from a plate of french fries, her black hair pulled back into a ponytail, secured with two beaded barrettes. The woman smiled shyly at Violet and resumed eating her fries.

"You hear about Rosie?" the waitress inquired to no one in particular. "After all these years she finally left that bastard."

Violet tensed in her chair and drank her coffee.

The men acknowledged they'd heard the news. "Wonder where she went?" one of them asked, an expression of boredom on his face. The other men shrugged.

Rita said, "I don't know, but I tell you, I wouldn't say even if I did know. That Billy's a mean son-of-a-bitch. He'd go after her and probably kill her this time."

Violet felt a wave of fear flush through her body. She sat like a rock, afraid to move.

Rita continued. "That Billy come in here looking for Rosie. Said she stole his money and took off. Butter wouldn't melt in his mouth when he was talking to me. Like I don't know what kinda man he is. Son-of-a-bitch. As if he ever made a dime on his own, the lazy bum, living off of Rosie and her wages here."

Her mouth bleeding, Violet tried to reach the door. He pulled her back and smacked her face again. Hot tears stung her eyes and she couldn't see where the next blow was coming from, but she felt it, landing on her nose. A new flow of blood to add to the rest. "Lazy bitch. Can't even have my dinner ready when I get home. You know I like my dinner on time." The blows were coming from all directions now. How could one man have so many hands? The thought snapped across her mind as she struggled to get free. Don't fight him, he'll just get meaner. She tasted the blood in her mouth and bent over to retrieve her glasses. Broken. Again. A last kick to her butt. "I'll get your dinner."

Violet's hand trembled as she picked up her mug and drank the cooling liquid. Rita came over and poured more coffee. "You want anything to eat, honey? Our special is meat loaf sandwich, lots of gravy. I make the pies myself, so I know they're good." Rita's face was heavily made up: beige foundation, rose-colored rouge, blue eye shadow, black mascara, and red lipstick. Her face was kind and tired.

Violet wanted to leave but felt like she was welded to her chair. "I guess a piece of pie would be nice."

"Apple, cherry, pumpkin, strawberry, blueberry, or chocolate?"

"Cherry, please." Why did she always sound so meek? She cleared her throat. "I changed my mind. Apple."

"You're entitled," Rita said, as she went to get the pie. Bringing the slab of sugared crust leaking with fat slices of apples and cinnamon, Rita continued her tirade against Billy. "That man! Thought I never noticed Rosie's black eyes, her bruises. And that broken arm. Fell down the stairs, my foot! He probably pushed her. Twenty years married to that bum. Thank god, they didn't have any kids. I told her, I said, 'Rosie, you can't let him do that to you.' Said it so many times she must have got sick hearing me. More coffee, Cheryl?" Rita held up the pot and looked toward the woman eating the french fries.

"Yes, I could do with another cup," Cheryl's voice was soft. She glanced at Violet and smiled again. "You from around here?"

"I used to live near here. I'm just up visiting my grandma. I'm on my way home right now." Violet wanted to leave. She lurched from her chair and it made a loud scraping sound on the floor. The men turned to look at her. She fled to the washroom.

Broken arm. "I think my arm's broken. Please, I think you broke my arm." A kick to her stomach. "That right? Maybe I'll break the other one, bitch. You know I like starch in my shirts. Can't you do anything right?" The fist on her back, pounding on her back. Blows on her head. The arm dangling at her side, her useful one raised to stop the fists. Burning pain in her arm. She couldn't breathe from the pain. The fists pounding on her back, her shoulders. It stopped. "Get me a beer. Better go get that arm fixed. Dumb bitch." She'd get her arm fixed. Fell down the stairs. Again. How many times can you fall down the stairs before someone notices how accident-prone you are? Dumb bitch. She'd better think of a new excuse from now on.

Violet looked in the mirror of the washroom and rubbed her arm. He always called her dumb and ugly. She stared intently at the image in the mirror. Her new haircut took her by surprise. The short hair where there used to be a long, brown tangle. She adjusted the glasses on her nose. She wasn't ugly. Dumb maybe, for staying with him so long. She smiled at her reflection. I got away, didn't I?

She came out of the washroom and noticed that the men had left. She sat down to eat her pie. Cheryl was watching Rita clear the table where the men had been.

Rita stacked the dishes and carried them into the kitchen. She came out immediately. "I'll get to those later. Those old farts," she jerked her head to indicate the empty table. "They could care less about Rosie. Probably side with Billy. I tell you, men are all alike. Think a wife's there to get screwed and clean up their messes." She shook her head, the stiff red helmet of hair not moving an inch. "You married, hon?" she inquired of Violet.

"No."

"Smart girl. You get married and they just think they can boss you around to suit them. I guess you, me, and Cheryl's the only smart women left in this town. A couple of bachelorettes, that's us." Rita snorted and went back to the kitchen.

Violet finished her pie. She had wanted cherry, but the apple was good and filled the hollow space inside. From the kitchen came the sounds of dishes clattering and water being run. "Damn that Billy! Lost a waitress and I have to put up with him, sneaking around here and asking questions."

Cheryl said, "Rita's mad. Not about losing a waitress but about losing a friend. Rosie was a good woman."

"You act like she's dead," Violet said angrily. "More power to her, I say."

Cheryl looked surprised. "I know. I think the same as you. It takes guts to do what she did."

Guts. "I hate your guts, bitch." The slap in the face, the punch in the stomach. Her glasses flying off her face. "I don't know why you can't do anything right. Jesus Christ, this place is a pigsty. But that figures, a pig like you. Squaw. Can't even keep a man's house clean." She hurried to pick the newspapers off the floor and stacked them neatly on the table. "Come here." "No." "Come here!" Of course she went. His hands on her body, his mouth forcing hers open, his tongue pushing down her throat. "Bitch." As he raped her on the floor, her eyes wandered to the neat stack of newspapers sitting on the table. She looked at the table while he pushed and shoved inside her, her arms outflung at her sides. Finished. She lay on the floor, not sure of what he expected of her now. "Get me a beer."

"You O.K.?" Cheryl asked, concern on her face.

"Yeah. I was thinking of . . . nothing."

Rita came bustling out of the kitchen, carrying pies that she carefully set in the plastic covered containers by the coffee pot. Getting a rag, she began washing down the tables, checking the ketchup and mustard bottles, realigning the salt-and-pepper shakers. "Can I get you girls anything?"

Cheryl held up her mug to indicate more coffee.

Rita poured. "I tell you, I was just in the kitchen thinking about Rosie, wondering where she was. Do you think she went to one of them shelters? But how could she get there? And why didn't she call me? I would have driven her anywhere. Billy never let her drive his car, and she didn't have one. *His* car. As if her money didn't pay for it. God, I hate that man! Never could stand the sight of him. Strutting in here like some prize package. I never knew what she saw in him in the first place. Me and Rosie go way back together. Do you think she'll call me when she gets settled? You don't think she'll come back, do you? I'd sooner never see her again than think she might go back to that bastard." Rita's face was worried.

"No, I don't think she'll come back," Cheryl answered.

"Well, how do you know she won't? I remember one time she ran away and was staying with me. We had the best time together, then he comes crawling up to the door, begging her to come home. 'I didn't mean it,' he says, in that spineless voice of his. She looked at me like to say, what can I do? I know what she could have done. Stayed with me.

"Billy was afraid of me. Oh, he hated me, it was plain on his face, but he was scared of me just the same. She went back and he musta beat her real bad that time 'cause she called in to say she got the flu and wouldn't be in to work for a few days. I says to her, Rose Helen, I'm coming right over there to get you. But no, she wouldn't hear of it. I just got the flu, she says. So I let her be."

Rita wrung the cloth in her hands, the strong tendons standing out like ropes. "I'm glad she got away. Too bad she didn't shoot him and burn the house down, like that woman a few years back. Oh, Rosie." Her eyes became bright and wet, and she turned away and went into the kitchen.

She ran away, but she didn't have anywhere to go. She thought of calling Grandma, but Grandma didn't know the things he did to her and he might hurt Grandma if she took Violet in. She called in sick to work and took a bus to Traverse City. She wandered the streets, looking in shop windows, looking into people's faces. Nobody knew her here. Nobody knew what he did when the door was closed. Nobody knew. She pretended she was someone else. Just a woman going shopping, leisurely, taking her time, enjoying a day out. The freedom. The freedom of walking up the street. She was another person, not the dumb, ugly squaw he said she was. Even her body felt different. Like it belonged to her. *Her.* What would happen if she stayed here? She couldn't. She didn't have any money, only the clothes she was wearing, no place to stay. What was she thinking of? Not possible, not possible. She took the bus home. Of course he knew she had run away. She should have known he would find out. He cried this time. Promised he wouldn't hurt her anymore. Said he was scared she had left him for good. Promised he wouldn't hurt her anymore. She believed him. What else could she do, a dumb, ugly bitch like herself? Later that night he stomped on her feet and legs as if to punish the very limbs that dared to go walking, like a *real* person, up the street in Traverse City.

Violet looked up from the table. Cheryl was watching her, a look of sympathy in her lively brown eyes. "So you were visiting your grandma? Do you have other family here?"

"No. My mother died when I was twelve. My dad . . . I don't know where my dad is. I went to live with my grandma after Mom died. I haven't been back here for a while, about a year. My grandma's getting old, and I like to check on her, you know, see for myself how she's doing. I'd like her to come and live with me. She says she'll see, but I think that means no. She wouldn't like the city unless I could find a place that had a little grass or some trees. But I'm looking for a new place. Right now, I'm living in kind of a dump." Violet stopped. She could feel her cheeks getting hot. She never talked this much. "Are you from around here?" she asked Cheryl, anxious to get the conversation away from herself.

"No, I'm from Peshawbestown, the reservation past Traverse City. I'm just here for the summer, working in a place for women and children. We're starting something similar in my community, and I'm here to learn the ropes." Cheryl's full lips curved into a smile. "Naturally, our place will be more 'Indian style.'"

"My mother was from there."

"No kidding! What was her name? Maybe I know your family," Cheryl asked eagerly.

"I don't know her maiden name." What a stupid thing to say, Violet thought. What possible harm could come from telling Cheryl her mother's name? Was she going to live like this forever, afraid to tell people anything?

Rita hurried out of the kitchen. "Thought I heard the door. Must be going crazy! For a minute there, I thought it was Rosie. Didn't know whether to be mad or glad. You get my age, you start imagining things." She smiled weakly.

Cheryl said, "Your age indeed. You don't look a day over thirty-five."

Rita touched her hair. "Well, the dye job helps, don't it? Thirty-five, my foot! Thought I was the snow-job queen around here."

Cheryl and Rita laughed. Even Violet joined in, though her laugh was rusty and unused.

"I'll get you girls more coffee, then I think I'll join you and have a cigarette. Trying to quit," she said ruefully to Violet, "but it's only my second one today."

She brought the pot over and gestured to Violet. "Come on over here and sit with us."

Violet pulled out a chair and sat stiffly holding her coffee cup, pretending this was the most natural thing in the world for her to do—sit with women, share stories, share life.

"Well, this is nice," Rita took a deep drag from her cigarette and blew the smoke out gustily. "Just us girls. I can't get my mind off Rosie. Two days she's been gone and not a word. Not that I expect her to be rushing to a phone to call me. I expect this is the first time in her life she's had some breathing space. But I do want to hear from her.

"Ever since we was kids I've been worrying about her. Her dad was the biggest drunk in town. I know he used to beat Rosie's ma. I heard my own folks talking when they thought I wasn't listening. Rosie used to tell me things too. I won't repeat them. The woman's gotta have some dignity. It just got to be a natural thing. I'd think up ways to get Rosie out of that house, away from her dad. She slept over our house so much, my ma said she might as well adopt her. Oh, I prayed for that to happen, I did. We were like twins, never apart.

"And when we were teens, didn't that big, ugly Billy Claymore come into our lives and spoil everything. What she saw in him I just don't . . . well, I guess he was good to her for a while, made her think he'd take care of her. I saw right through him, but she wouldn't listen to me."

Rita puffed angrily at her cigarette and tapped the ashes into a metal tray. "She wouldn't listen to me. I was maid of honor at her wedding. Not much of a wedding, just standing in front of the justice of the peace. I helped her pick out her dress. It was pink and had a full skirt. We starched her crinolines so the dress stuck out real far. She looked so pretty. And happy. I'll guarantee that was the last happy day she had with that man. First and last!" She stubbed out her cigarette and lit a fresh one. "I cried. Told her I always cry at weddings. She would have believed anything on that day.

"She had on this cute little hat. White, with a veil that came down to her nose. She gave me that hat some years back. Said it just took up space in her closet. It looked like hell on me, but I kept it anyways. Girls, it's a terrible thing when you can't help a friend." She stubbed out her second cigarette with force.

"It sounds to me," Cheryl said, taking Rita's hand, "like you helped her all you could. You were a good friend to her. Most women don't have that."

"That's right," Violet blurted. "Women like that . . . we . . . they don't have any friends. Too scared or ashamed . . . or something." Her voice trailed away.

Rita squinted her eyes and gave Violet a long look. "You think she'll be O.K.?"

Her mother didn't have friends. "Just you and me, Violet. You're the best friend a mother ever needs." But she couldn't be the kind of friend her mom needed, the kind that would protect her from the jealous rampages of a husband. She was a little girl, not a grownup who could stand up to her father. And after her mom died from the cancer, he came to her and wanted to touch her, wanted to do things to her. What had she done to make him want to do things that only grownups are supposed to do? Was it because her body had matured so fast? She had started her period when she was eleven and her breasts got bigger and she started to grow hair under her arms and on her private place. *Private place.* That's what her mom used to call it. Was that why her dad wanted her to do things that she wasn't supposed to do? And then Grandma, her precious grandma, had come to take her to live with her. "You're not fit to raise this child," Grandma had told her father. "You're not fit." She had never told Grandma about the grown-up things dad had wanted her to do. Did she know? But if she'd known, would she have wanted Violet anyway? Violet never told, fearing the answer to the question she carried in her twelve-year-old heart. And it settled in her heart that it must have been her fault—her mother's beatings, her father's seductions—and she vowed to be a good girl from now on. Try to please everyone. Try very hard to please.

Cheryl was talking. "I bet she went to a shelter. They'll take good care of her there. She'll call you when she's got herself together, I'm sure of it."

"A while back I saw this TV show," Rita lit up another cigarette. "There was a woman on there from the shelter. She talked about women hating themselves and thinking they deserved the beatings they was getting. I thought, that's my Rose Helen. No matter how many times I told her she was worth something, that she was a wonderful woman, *she* didn't believe it, so why would she believe me? At the end of the show they gave some numbers to call. I copied them down and gave them to Rosie. What's this? she said. I told her they was phone numbers for women shelters. A woman could go there and get away from her husband and they'd keep her safe. She gave me a look, I tell you, I don't ever want to see that look again. Like a whipped dog. Like she was ashamed 'cause her own husband was beating on her. Like it was all her fault! I tell you, girls, I like to die to see that look on my Rose Helen's face." Rita's mascara was running in dark rivers down her face, and she lifted a hand to wipe away the black smudges. Violet handed her a napkin, the smiling turkeys a malicious joke against Rita's pain-filled face as she wiped her eyes. "I'm not a praying woman, but I pray that Rosie's safe and learning how to love herself. Like I love her."

Love yourself. Her counselor had brought that incredible, unthinkable idea to Violet. It took her days to sort through the thoughts that were making a mess in her brain. Wasn't it enough that she had found strength to leave her husband? Finally making that call to the shelter, to her grandma, who had saved her once and now had to do it again. Must she think about loving herself? A dumb, ugly bitch? A squaw? A pig? A woman who couldn't make dinner on time, starch his shirts right, pick up newspapers that she dared to read and leave lying on the floor? Her self? Love? Slowly, so slowly, she started to put the little scraps together, the bits of herself that she could love. Like piecing together a quilt, she basted the parts in her mind with fragile thread. It wasn't finished yet, but someday the cloth would be whole and she would cover herself with the multicolored blocks.

"My mother's name was Johnson." Violet looked at Cheryl and smiled.

"I know so many Johnsons, it'll take us forever to figure it out," Cheryl laughed, touching Violet's hand delicately with her own.

Violet reached for her coffee and relaxed in her chair. Cheryl gave her hand a last pat and asked, "You ever gone back to where your mom came from?"

"No, but I've thought about it. You know, just to see where she lived when she was a girl. She used to talk about it, and so did my grandma. They moved from there when my mom was just a kid. Maybe the next time I come here, I'll drive up that way and take Grandma too."

"You do that, honey," Rita piped in. "And when you do, be sure to stop by here and see me." She blew her nose and got up, gathering the ashtray and coffee mug. "Just help yourself to more coffee, girls. I'll be in the kitchen doing up the dishes. Maybe I'll put together more pies. Supper crowd's gonna be coming in soon." She made her way to the kitchen, turning to smile at Cheryl and Violet. "You girls sure were a blessing to me today. I just know Rosie's gonna be O.K. I *feel* it somehow. And I'll be there for her, like I always been." Rita smiled again, her face transformed into that of a young woman. She went through the kitchen door, her red hair blazing like a flag.

"I guess I better get going," Violet said. "I'm starting a new job tomorrow and there's a million things I need to do, plus two more hours of driving ahead of me."

"Good luck with your new job. You know, Rosie's O.K. She's at the shelter where I work. I can't tell Rita, but I think I wanted to come in here today just to reassure her." Cheryl looked sad. "I didn't know Rita loved her so much."

"I'm glad I met you, Cheryl. Maybe we'll see each other again."

"Well, just to make sure, here's my name and address. I'll be home in October. You bring your grandma, and we'll track down those people of yours." She dug in her purse and wrote down the information on a slip of paper. "I hope you come. Everyone should know where they're from, where home is." She handed Violet the paper, their hands touching briefly.

Violet got out her wallet and left a five-dollar bill on the table. "I'll be back. Thank you, Cheryl."

"For what?"

"Oh, caring about Rita and Rosie. Everything." Violet slung her purse over her shoulder. "Tell Rita good-bye for me. Tell her . . . tell her that it might take a long time, but Rosie will make it." She smiled into Cheryl's face.

She walked out of the diner and got in her car. Turning on the ignition, Violet looked once again at the sign of the wild turkey.

"Sometimes we fly real high."

Distress

What would our mother say?
Where is our mother?
Does she know?
Does she know what is happening to us
here?
What will she do?
Will she save us? Will she come for
us?
Does she know what happens to us
here?
Is it happening to her?
To her, to her, too?

—Susan Griffin

Happy Ending

BARBARA HARMAN

The first time he yells at her she can see he is enraged, barely in control. She is not so much frightened as angry herself and, later, sad but determined to end the relationship. She sees clearly, at least this time, that he will not change. But it is only the one time. When he says, this time, that he is wrong and knows he needs to change, that he loves her and does not want to lose her, she believes him. She thinks she is lucky at last to have found someone willing to change for love of her.

The first time he tortures her it is with words. She discovers all at once that everything she has ever told him—curled against his warmth in bed after making love, crying with relief and gratitude—he has stored for future need. Her vulnerability, her stories, her shame, her fear, her insecurities and mistakes, her pain, are his weapons. He turns and twists them. They are knives to pierce her soul, the way, later, his fists will break her bones.

The first time he hits her it is an experiment. She sees it in his face—in that sharp attentiveness it sometimes wears, as if she has said something requiring his close examination, something to capture his imagination or suddenly change how he customarily regards her. He hits her again and then again. Then he smiles.

The first time he rapes her she thinks it is her fault.

At the bus stop that day they had decided to stop seeing one another—they fight all of the time they are not making love; though they agree on nothing, they can't seem either to part or to stop arguing. From their first date, a confusion of distrust and misunderstanding, each waiting for the other at a different place on campus, he has suspected her. He believes every man wants her and that it is only a matter of time before she betrays him. Later he will say he married her because she slept with him. He is not her first lover, nor, ever, her best. But the first time she comes it is with him. It so exhausts her she can't continue. He is angry until she stops having orgasms, then he is contemptuous.

He has never liked her family. Although she had few she could call friends, he has never liked them either. It has been years since that lunch with her old girlfriend from high school. She remembers the shock on her friend's face, her anger, her tears, her pleas, and, finally, her resignation. How she waited for months afterward, hoping her friend would call again, certain she would not. She thinks about the bruises on her arms and the inside of her thighs, the scars on her breasts and belly from his teeth. She remembers her sister's anger, her father's disinterest, her mother's weary despair. When she remembers these things she is ashamed. It is easier to forget everything before the life she has with him.

She is grateful he never beat her when she was pregnant. She is grateful he never hit their child. She is grateful she did not have a son. She believes she would kill a son rather than see him grow like his father. Their daughter is timid, already a target for schoolyard bullies; when he begins to yell, the child huddles against the wall, weeping and trembling. She wonders if, when, he will begin to beat the child. She hopes she will be able to prevent this but she does not know how she will. She is grateful she had no more children.

These are the rules: Don't raise your voice. Don't talk back. Don't say no to sex. Like whatever he does. Don't ask him to do anything he has not already done. Get up when he gets up. Go to bed when he goes to bed. Wait. Do what he wants to do. Never contradict him. Laugh at what he thinks is funny. Never ask for his time, his attention, his money. Have your own money, but give it to him if he wants it. Never go out alone but do not expect him to go with you. If he is angry in the car, walk home. Be his friend except when he needs an enemy. Defend his family except when he hates them. Understand everything. Eat as much as he does. Don't get fat. Like what he gives you. Know what he likes. Never complain. Never be unhappy. Tell him he makes you happy. Never want something he can't give. Do not be a burden. Be invisible except be always available. Do whatever needs to be done so that he can do what he wants. Never let him know what you can do if he can't do it; never do better what he can do. Rescue him when he wants to be rescued. Be smart but not smarter. Believe what he wants you to believe. Remember he loves you. Love him no matter what. Never leave him.

He has words that describe how she is, how he sees her. Nag. Bitch. Whore. Cunt. Stupid. She embarrasses him in front of clients by her stupidity. She humiliates him by flaunting herself and coming on to his friends. He can never relax in his own home because she is constantly nagging him to do something. She can't cook. She is unimaginative and cold in bed. She is an indifferent housekeeper. She can't manage money. She is an overindulgent mother, and their daughter is a whining brat. Lazy bitch. Stupid cunt.

He hit her once so that she saw stars. Later, as she was bathing her cut face in the bathroom, he asked her if he had done that. When she said yes he apologized. He never said he was sorry again. Her father said there had to be a man in the family.

Once he threw her against the wall, squeezed her wrists so tightly in both hands that her fingers turned white, brought his mouth an inch from her face and screamed. She doesn't remember why.

She tries to go to different hospitals, not the same one each time, ever since that time in the emergency room, after he broke her arm—the stares and whispers, the doctor's questions, his grim mouth. Somewhere she still has the brochure the social worker gave her.

He is a bald man with a receding chin and facial hair which he meticulously grooms. He showers twice daily and has annoying bodily tics, such as rubbing his fingers together without snapping them when he is angry. His neck is thick from lifting weights and his chest and arms are heavily muscled; when she puts her arms around him his muscles seem to push her away. He has powerful but beautiful forearms and long expressive fingers. He tells the same jokes over and over again, looking at her as if she should think he's cute, tucking the tip of his tongue into the corner of his mouth. He likes to tease her about things she thinks are important. He doesn't like to be touched when they have sex and his idea of foreplay is watching her while he sticks his fingers inside her and forces her legs open so he can get in. He has a long thick penis that always hurts her. He doesn't like to kiss and his tongue is cold.

They have been married for ten years and she has begun to believe that the problem is her, just as he has always said. She is confused much of the time; she finds it very difficult to think and has begun to forget things, for which he beats her. She can't conceal how she feels anymore and what she mostly feels is fear—she feels it far too much, too deeply and too often. When she thinks about him touching her, she goes numb; when they have sex, she hopes only that it will be over soon. Now when he begins to scream, when he stops screaming and begins to beat her, when he grabs her hair and pins her against the table or the wall or the floor, and forces his way into her body, she is relieved. He will not hit her again for a while. She has begun to believe he will kill her. He has begun to tell her he will.

She sleeps as much as he will allow. She is very lonely. On her worst days, she believes she is so repulsive it does not surprise her that he beats her. She sleeps all day whenever she feels this way. Every day when he leaves the house to go to work she goes back to bed. She no longer has a job or does any of the things that used to interest her, since all of them make him angry, except sleep. Her sleeping makes him angry too, but she is unable to do without sleep. When she is asleep she dreams. Once she dreams she is a tiger, sleek and powerful. She feels strong when she wakes. She dreams many times that she can fly. She flies inside a building, just under a high ceiling or, very fast, through long corridors, like a bird trapped inside trying to get out. These dreams make her feel powerful too, in an invisible way that sometimes lasts until he hits her again. This morning she dreams she sits on a toilet on a raised platform inside a room. He stands aside watching her. Suddenly, with a great tearing pain, her bowels open. She fills and then overflows the toilet bowl, the contents running down its sides and onto the floor. It is wonderful. She feels enormously relieved.

One day, shortly after this dream, she comes home to find he has left her. He has removed his clothing from the closet and taken everything from their home that he especially likes, including several gifts which, in more loving moments, he had given to her. In the long letter instructing her to see his lawyer to sign divorce papers, telling her that he has taken the money out of their bank accounts and closed their charge accounts, he says he needs to take back control of his life. This is what he has found to replace her: Someone just like she used to be.

Or, he comes home one evening, tense and looking for a fight. He yells at her and when she leaves the room to try to avoid the fight, he follows her and yells some more. She is careful for as long as she can be, but he is determined and knows what she will still refuse to endure. When she finally loses control, he smiles first and then begins to hit her. He is enjoying it so much he beats her to death. He hires a good lawyer who emphasizes his standing in the community, his productivity, his education. He is depicted as a man helplessly in love with a woman who could not be trusted, a man who finally becomes violent when he learns she is having an affair. No one comes forward to contradict this story. No one really knew his wife, an unfriendly woman, the neighbors say, an indifferent companion say his friends. Convinced his was a crime of passion, a jury convicts him of manslaughter, and a sympathetic judge, certain he presents no threat to the community at large, sentences him to the minimum term—five years in his state. He is a model prisoner. While in prison he begins to correspond with a clean Christian woman, anxious to marry and have children before it is too late. He is released for good behavior after serving two years and three months of his sentence. They marry. He doesn't hit her until she is pregnant.

Or this: He comes home in a nasty mood and picks a fight. She sees where it is going, picks up a skillet full of hot bacon grease and flings it on him. Neighbors, hearing his screams, call the police before she can kill him. She is committed to an institution for the criminally insane from which she is never released, and he is given custody of their daughter. He begins raping the child when she is eight.

The best ending to this story is that he is killed in an auto accident on the way to work one morning. He is well insured, as befits a man of his importance, and the insurance policy pays his grieving widow double indemnity of one million dollars. The mortgage on the house is paid off by a mortgage protection policy. She sees their child through an excellent college education, sells the house at a great profit and moves to a small university town, where she writes a book about her life. Although a complete fabrication, it becomes a best seller. She makes a lot of money to add to the insurance money and the proceeds from the sale of the house. She uses this money to establish a foundation to fund projects that help divorced and widowed women over forty to start new lives and careers. When people ask her if she will ever marry again, she smiles and says, "No one could ever replace my husband." Only she knows what she means by that.

This last ending is as likely as his capture by aliens who torture him for the remainder of his life (which their science extends for a very long time) in just the ways he has tortured his wife. His wife, meanwhile, has full access to all of their considerable joint assets and, after he has been missing for seven years, has him declared dead. She was of course suspected of having done away with him, but repeated investigations have never turned up any evidence to support this. She has kept up the payments on his life insurance policy and receives the full benefit when he is legally dead. The story then proceeds as above. Except, the aliens have told her what they are doing. Her new friends notice that she sometimes seems to be lost in thought, a fleeting smile on her face. When they ask her what it is that makes her look so happy, she replies, "Oh, I was just thinking of my husband."

AFTERWORD

This is my ninth book, and the seventh collection of U.S. women's short stories. Since 1972 my work has been to discover and reconstruct the history of women's work in this genre. I was forced by this book to reconsider all my previous work. And in reexamining that earlier work, I realize that I have often dealt with stories in which women are abused, are the victims of violence of one kind or another, inflicted by people, by men, who have promised to love them and to enter into mutually nurturing and nourishing relationships.

If you are a woman who wonders if you are being abused because your husband "only" lies to you, has affairs with other people, exploits your financial resources as if they were his and in his control, and betrays you emotionally, romantically, and sexually, *but he never hits you,* don't wonder anymore. Yes, you are being abused. You are being abused. Read my earlier collection, *The Other Woman: Stories of Two Women and a Man* (1984), for eighteen stories written between 1842 and 1981 about these kinds of wife abuse.

Stories about how women can and do try, and sometimes succeed, in rescuing each other from abusive situations are included in my *Women's Friendships: A Collection of Short Stories* (1991). In many of these stories written between 1846 and 1991, women create alliances that make them stronger than their abusers' threats make them afraid. I kept remembering the stories in there as I worked on this present collection. I wondered if I should reprint "A Jewel for a Friend" by J. California Cooper and "The Feeder" by Maria Bruno, both stories in which women are physically abused by their husbands, or "At Bay" by Elizabeth Stuart Phelps and "Etta Mae Johnson" by Gloria Naylor, both stories in which women are emotionally and financially abused by men they love and trust. In all of these stories friendships with women are the sources of escape or healing from abuse. Then, of course, there is the wonderful story of a triumphant survivor by Rose Terry Cooke, "How Celia Changed Her Mind," in my collection *Old Maids: Short Stories by Nineteenth Century U.S. Women Writers* (1984).

I decided not to reprint any of these stories because I have already made them available in other collections. Many people who read one of my books read them all. In the past I thought that one particular story was so important that it needed to be considered in a variety of contexts so I included it in two different collections. But I don't want regular readers to get repeats, so I won't do it anymore. In addition to that consideration, I was having a hard time trying to decide which and how many of the more than one hundred stories I had gathered on battered wives and not reprinted elsewhere were best to include in this collection. I changed the contents for this collection at least twenty-five times before I got to the present listing. There are none in here I would replace, but there are many I regret having no room for. I have stuck to my usual rule of no more than one story by each writer in any collection.

I have spent the last year and a half reading about battered women. I have read legal and social histories and sociological, psychological, and religious discussions of wife abuse; I have read multidisciplinary considerations of "family violence" and women's first-person accounts of years of torture and eventual escapes. I have read feminist theories about and analyses of men's battery of women in the context of the general subject of violence against women which treat the problem on a global scale and make the kinds of analogies that leave me feeling hopeless about any batterer ever stopping unless there is a complete social reorganization; but I also still feel hopeful about the possibility for real social change—even if not in my lifetime. The epigraphs in this book are drawn as samples from this reading. I have read treatment manuals from men's organizations founded to salvage violent men, and viewed a powerful dramatization of the history of Spruce Run, the battered women's shelter in Bangor, Maine, and spent hours talking with Marcia Niemann, director of Advocacy for The Brewster Center in Tucson, which provides shelter, counseling, and prevention and with the directors of two other shelters who wish to remain anonymous. I have talked with my cousin the lawyer, Noreen Koppelman Goldstein, about possible backlash in my personal life as a consequence of publishing this book in this way. I have exhumed and relived parts of my personal history that aren't nearly as healed or forgotten as I had hoped. I have been counseled by my cousin the therapist, Carol Tuthill Parent, about some of the old improperly healed scars. I have talked with my doctor friends Marilyn Heins and Lisa Neumann about battered women, the injuries they have seen in their medical practices, and how they have been able to respond. I have dragged my friends through the pain of talking endlessly with me about this monstrous horror that touches all our lives, spending hours on the phone, hours pacing the streets of cities all across the country from Tucson to Norman, Oklahoma, to Minneapolis, to St. Louis to Cleveland to New York to Boston to Bangor, Maine, hours sitting across tables from other survivors in our kitchens and in restaurants. I have visited shelters, sat through shifts with hot-line staffers, and participated in shelter fund raisers and discussed the difficulty of talking about this sore on our social body and the bruises on our personal bodies with development directors of shelters who tell me about the delicate line they have to observe to keep potential donors from turning away from the horror they are being enlisted to help eliminate. From all of this reading, thinking, listening, conversation, and experience, I have learned more than I had any idea was available to learn. This is the most important thing I have learned: WE MUST INTERVENE. WE MUST BE PREPARED AND WILLING TO INTERVENE ON BEHALF OF ANY WOMAN WHO IS BEING ABUSED. WE MUST INTERVENE AT ALL LEVELS: PERSONAL, SOCIAL, FINANCIAL, AND LEGAL. WE MUST INTERVENE! WE CAN MAKE IT STOP.

CREDITS AND SOURCES

Opening Epigraphs

William E. Burrows, *Vigilante!* New York: Harcourt Brace Jovanovich, 1976, pp. 37–38. Quoted by Pam McAllister, "Feminist Law-Challenging Actions." In *Fight Back! Feminist Resistance to Male Violence,* edited by Frederique Delacoste and Felice Newman. Minneapolis: Cleis Press, 1981, pp. 215–16.

Ann Landers, *St. Louis Post Dispatch.* Sunday, September 4, 1994, p. 12C.

Marcia Petchers, response to a letter to the editor in *CWRU: The Magazine of Case Western Reserve University.* August 1994, p. 6.

Diana E. H. Russell, *Rape in Marriage,* expanded and revised edition with a new introduction. Bloomington: Indiana University Press, 1990, p. 273.

Marita Golden, "Prefatory Note." In *Wild Women Don't Wear No Blues: Black Women Writers on Love Men and Sex,* edited with an introduction by Marita Golden. New York: Doubleday, 1993, p. 163.

Lenore E. Walker, "When Love Turns to Terror." In *Terrifying Love: Why Battered Women Kill and How Society Responds.* New York: Harper & Row, 1989, p. 5.

Diana Velez, introduction to *Reclaiming Medusa: Short Stories by Contemporary Puerto Rican Women,* edited and translated by Diana Velez. San Francisco: Spinsters/Aunt Lute, 1988, p. 2.

Melanie Kaye, "Scrambled Eggs 3: Women and Violence." *Sinister Wisdom* 9 (spring 1979): 76–79.

Caryn McTighe Musil, foreword to *Bridges of Power: Women's Multicultural Alliances,* edited by Lisa Albrecht and Rose M. Brewer, published in cooperation with the National Women's Studies Association. Philadelphia: New Society Publishers, 1990, p. vii.

Chapter 1

Linda Gordon, *Heroes of Their Own Lives: The Politics and History of Family Violence.* New York: Viking, 1988, p. 255.

Chapter 1 from *A New Home, Who'll Follow?* by Caroline Kirkland, 1839. Reprint edited with an introduction by Sandra Zagarell, New Brunswick, N.J.: Rutgers University Press, American Women Writers Series, 1990.

Slavery's Pleasant Homes

Cherrie Moraga, "From a Long Line of Vendidas: Chicanas and Feminism." In *Feminist Studies/Critical Studies,* edited by Teresa de Lauretis. Bloomington: Indiana University Press, 1986, p. 180.

"Slavery's Pleasant Homes" by Lydia Maria Child. From *The Liberty Bell,* 1843.

A Dorlesky-Burpy Family Story

Linda McCarriston, "Not Comedy, Not Farce." From *Eva-Mary,* Triquarterly Books: Northwestern University Press, 1991, and Another Chicago Press, 1991. Reprinted by permission of the author.

"A Dorlesky-Burpy Family Story" by Marietta Holley. From *Sweet Cicely.* New York: Funk and Wagnalls, 1887, p. 156–57. Reprinted in *Marietta Holley: Samantha Rastles the Woman Question,* edited by Jane Curry. Champaign-Urbana: University of Illinois Press, 1983, pp. 152–53.

Jack the Fisherman

James Ptacek, "Why Do Men Batter Their Wives?" In *Feminist Perspectives on Wife Abuse,* edited by Kersti Yllo and Michele Bograd. Newbury Park, Calif.: Sage Publications, 1988, pp. 142–43.

"Jack the Fisherman" by Elizabeth Stuart Phelps. First published in *Century Magazine,* June 1887. Reprinted in her collection *Fourteen to One,* 1891.

In Sabine

Ginny NiCarthy, *Getting Free: A Handbook for Women in Abusive Relationships.* Expanded second edition with a new introduction by the author. Seattle: The Seal Press, 1986, p. 293.

"In Sabine" by Kate Chopin. Written November 20–22, 1893. Published in *Bayou Folk.* Boston: Houghton, Mifflin, 1894.

Tony's Wife

Ann Jones, *Next Time, She'll Be Dead: Battering & How to Stop It.* Boston: Beacon Press, 1994, p. 133.

"Tony's Wife" by Alice Ruth Moore Dunbar-Nelson. First published in *The Goodness of St. Rocque and Other Stories.* New York: Dodd, Mead, 1899.

The Quiet Woman

Margaret Craven, fund-raising letter, December 15, 1994, for the Women's Safe House, St. Louis, Mo.

"The Quiet Woman" by Mary Heaton Vorse. From *The Atlantic Monthly,* 1907.

The Gold Vanity Set

Ginny NiCarthy, *Getting Free: A Handbook for Women in Abusive Relationships.* Expanded second edition with a new introduction by the author. Seattle: The Seal Press, 1986, p. 7.

"The Gold Vanity Set" by María Cristina Mena. First published in *The American Magazine,* November 1913. Reprinted in *North of the Rio Grande: The Mexican-American Experience in Short Fiction,* edited with an introduction by Edward Simmen. New York: Mentor, 1992.

A Jury of Her Peers

Melanie Kaye, "Scrambled Eggs 3: Women and Violence." In *Sinister Wisdom* 9 (spring 1979): 79.

"A Jury of Her Peers" by Susan Glaspell. Originally in *Every Week,* March 5, 1917. Collected in Edward O'Brien, *Best Short Stories of 1917.* Copyright 1917 by the Crowell Publishing Company. Copyright 1918 by Susan Glaspell Cook.

Sweat

Alice Walker, *The Third Life of Grange Copeland.* New York and London: Harcourt Brace Javanovich, 1970, p. 161.

Susan Jacoby, *Wild Justice: The Evolution of Revenge.* New York: Harper & Row, 1983, pp. 185–87.

"Sweat" by Zora Neale Hurston. Originally published in *Fire 1,* November 1926.

Hattie Turner versus Hattie Turner

Lenore E. Walker, *Terrifying Love: Why Battered Women Kill and How Society Responds.* New York: Harper & Row, 1989, p. 106.

"Hattie Turner versus Hattie Turner" by Fannie Hurst. First published in *Cosmopolitan,* August 1935. Reprinted in her collection *We Are Ten.* New York: Harper, 1937. Reprinted by permission of Brandeis University and Washington University.

Pre-Freudian

Michele Bograd, "Feminist Perspectives on Wife Abuse: An Introduction." In *Feminist Perspectives on Wife Abuse,* edited by Kersti Yllo and Michele Bograd. Newbury Park, Calif.: Sage Publications, 1988, p. 17.

"Pre-Freudian" by Dorothy Canfield (also known as Dorothy Canfield Fisher). Originally in *The Ladies' Home Journal,* June 1936. © 1936, Meredith Corporation. Reprinted from *Ladies Home Journal,* with the permission of Miss Canfield's estate. Included in *The Ladies Home Journal Treasury,* selected by John Mason Brown and the editors. New York: Simon and Schuster, 1956. Reprinted by permission of Vivian Scott Hixson.

The Brown House

Mitsuye Yamada, "The Club." From *Desert Run: Poems and Stories.* Copyright © 1988. Reprinted by permission of the author and of Kitchen Table: Women of Color Press, Brooklyn, N.Y.

"The Brown House" by Hisaye Yamamoto. Originally published in *Harper's Bazaar,* October 1951. From *Seventeen Syllables an Other Stories,* 1988. Reprinted by permission of the author and Kitchen Table: Women of Color Press, Brooklyn, N.Y.

That She Would Dance No More

Barbara Smith, "Notes for Yet Another Paper on Black Feminism, or Will the Real Enemy Please Stand Up?" In *Conditions: Five, The Black Women's Issue,* co-edited by Lorraine Bethel and Barbara Smith, 2, no. 2 (autumn 1979): 126

"That She Would Dance No More" by Jean Wheeler Smith (today Jean W. Smith Young). Copyright © by Jean Wheeler Smith, Originally in *Negro Digest* 16, no. 3 (January 1967). Included in *Black Fire,* edited by LeRoi Jones and Larry Neal. New York: William Morrow, 1968. Reprinted by permission of the author, Jean Wheeler Smith Young.

To Be a Man

Pat Parker, "Brother." Copyright © 1978 by Pat Parker. Reprinted by permission of Firebrand Books, Ithaca, N.Y. From *Child of Myself,* Women's Press Collective, 1974, reprinted by Shameless Hussy Press, Berkeley, Calif. Included in *Movement in Black.* Ithaca, N.Y.: Firebrand 1978, p. 46.

"To Be a Man" by Ann Allen Shockley. From *Negro Digest* 18, July 1969. Included in *Black Women's Blues: A Literary Anthology, 1934–1988,* edited by Rita B. Dandridge. New York: G. K. Hall, 1992. Reprinted by permission of the author.

After Saturday Nite Comes Sunday

Beth E. Ritchie and Valli Kanuha, "Battered Women of Color." In *Wings of Gauze: Women of Color and the Experience of Health and Illness,* edited by Barbara Bair and Susan E. Cayleff. Detroit, Mich.: Wayne State University Press, 1993, pp. 291–92.

The Day My Father Tried to Kill Us

La Dos Hermanas

bertha schneiders existential edge

Ghosts Like Them

Woman Waiting for Train at Dusk

Karen Fiser, "The Short Song of What Befalls." Copyright © 1992 by Karen Fiser. Reprinted by permission from *Words like Fate and Pain.* Cambridge, Mass.: Zoland Books, 1992.

"Woman Waiting for Train at Dusk" by Constance Pierce. From *When Things Get Back to Normal: Stories.* Normal and New York: Illinois State University and Fiction Collective, 1985. First appeared in *Alaska Quarterly Review* 1, nos. 1 & 2 (fall 1982): 30–31. Reprinted by permission of Curtis White of Fiction Collective II and of the author.

I Don't Believe This

Barbara Hart, "Beyond the 'Duty to Warn': A Therapist's 'Duty to Protect' Battered Women and Children." In *Feminist Perspectives on Wife Abuse,* edited by Kersti Yllo and Michele Bograd. Newbury Park, Calif.: Sage Publications, 1988, pp. 240–43.

"I Don't Believe This" by Merrill Joan Gerber. Copyright © 1986 by Merrill Joan Gerber. Originally in *The Atlantic,* October 1984. Reprinted in *The O. Henry Prize Story Awards, 1986,* edited by William Abrahams. Garden City, New York: Doubleday, 1986. Reprinted in Merill Joan Gerber, *Honeymoon, Stories.* Champaign-Urbana: University of Illinois Press, 1985; in *Sisters,* edited by Susan Cahill. New York: Putnam, 1989; in *Contemporary West Coast Stories,* edited by C. Michael Curtis, The Globe Pequot Press, 1993; in *Seasons of Women,* edited by Gloria Norris. New York: W. W. Norton, 1995. Reprinted by permission of the author. A production of "I Don't Believe This" was staged directly from the story by Book-It at the Seattle Fringe Festival, March 1995.

Minerva Writes Poems / Linoleum Roses

Barbara Smith, "Notes for Yet Another Paper on Black Feminism, or Will the Real Enemy Please Stand Up?" In *Conditions: Five, The Black Women's Issue,* co-edited by Lorraine Bethel and Barbara Smith, 2, no. 2 (autumn 1979): 124.

"Minerva Writes Poems" and "Linoleum Roses" by Sandra Cisneros. Copyright © by Sandra Cisneros. From *The House on Mango Street.* Houston, Texas: Arte Publico, 1984. Published by Vintage Books, a division of Random House Inc., New York, and in hardcover by Alfred A. Knopf.

Noises

Marita Golden, "Walking in My Mother's Footsteps to Love." In *Wild Women Don't Wear No Blues: Black Women Writers on Love Men and Sex,* edited with an introduction by Marita Golden. New York: Doubleday, 1993, p. 93.

B. Y. Avery, speaking in Cambridge, Mass., July 1988. Quoted in Melba Wilson, *Crossing the Boundary: Black Women Survive Incest.* Seattle: The Seal Press, 1993, p. 208.

"Noises" by Jane Bradley. From *Powerlines*. Reprinted by permission of the University of Arkansas Press. Copyright © 1989.

If It Weren't for the Honeysuckle . . .

Lenore E. Walker, "When Love Turns to Terror." In *Terrifying Love: Why Battered Women Kill and How Society Responds*. New York: Harper & Row, 1989, p. 7.

"If It Weren't for the Honeysuckle . . ." by Estela Portillo Trambley. From *Rain of Scorpions and Other Stories* 1993. Reprinted by permission of Bilingual Press/Editorial Bilingü. Arizona State University, Tempe, Ariz. Also in *Rain of Scorpions and Other Writings*, 1975, and in *Grito del Sol* 1, no. 1 (April-June 1976): 7–21. Significantly revised for new edition of *Rain of Scorpions* in 1990.

Women in the Trees

Ginny NiCarthy, *Getting Free: A Handbook for Women in Abusive Relationships*. Expanded second edition with a new introduction by the author. Seattle: The Seal Press, 1986, pp. 287–89.

"Women in the Trees" by Pat Murphy. Copyright © 1990 by Pat Murphy. Reprinted from Pat Murphy, *Points of Departure*. New York: Bantam Books, 1990. Reprinted by permission of the author.

The Man Who Loved His Wife

Demie Kurz and Evan Stark, "Not-So-Benign Neglect: The Medical Response to Battering." In *Feminist Perspectives on Wife Abuse*, edited by Kersti Yllo and Michele Bograd. Newbury Park, Calif.: Sage Publications, 1988, p. 253.

"The Man Who Loved His Wife" by Janet LaPierre. Copyright © 1990 by Janet LaPierre. Originally published in *Sisters in Crime 3* edited by Marilyn Wallace. New York: Berkeley Publishing Group, 1990. Unabridged audio presentation on *Femmes and Fatalities: Third Annual "Masters of Mystery,"* edited by Martin H. & Rosalind M. Greenberg by Dercum Audio, West Chester, Penna. Reprinted by permission of the author.

Wild Turkeys

Ginny NiCarthy, *The Ones Who Got Away: Women Who Left Abusive Partners*. Seattle: The Seal Press, 1987, p. 5.

"Wild Turkeys" by Beth Brant. From *Food & Spirits*. Ithaca, N.Y.: Firebrand Books, 1991. Copyright © 1991 by Beth Brant.

Happy Ending

Susan Griffin, "Distress." From *Unremembered Country*. Copyright © 1987 by Susan Griffin. Reprinted by permission of Copper Canyon Press, Port Townsend, Wash.

"Happy Ending" by Barbara Harman. Copyright © 1994 by Barbara Harman. Used by permission of the author.